REASON, RULE, AND REVOLT

IN ENGLISH CLASSICISM

Reason, Rule, and Revolt
in English Classicism

BY

FRANCIS GALLAWAY

OCTAGON BOOKS

A DIVISION OF FARRAR, STRAUS AND GIROUX

New York   1974

Reprinted 1965
by special arrangement with the University of Kentucky Press

Second Octagon printing 1974

OCTAGON BOOKS
A Division of Farrar, Straus & Giroux, Inc.
19 Union Square West
New York, N. Y. 10003

Library of Congress Catalog Card Number: 65-16773
ISBN 0-374-92983-1

Manufactured by Braun-Brumfield, Inc.
Ann Arbor, Michigan

Printed in the United States of America

To my wife

MARGARET DOWNER GALLAWAY

PREFACE

Despite many brilliant monographs on various aspects of English classicism, there is still no synthetic presentation of the artistic outlook of the age, no place to which the student or general reader can turn for an introduction to the æsthetic ideals of an age as complex as any in the range of English literature. The investigations of R. D. Havens, A. O. Lovejoy, L. I. Bredvold, C. A. Moore, R. S. Crane, P. S. Wood, J. W. Draper, S. H. Monk, and Lois Whitney have revealed this complexity, but the textbooks still continue the false approach which seeks in classicism the roots of the Romantic Movement and generally ignores the fact that classicism attempted to establish a coherent view of life and art, and was only dimly aware of the coming Romanticism. To be understood classicism must be studied from within, not from without. It must be studied by a student interested primarily in classicism; not by a student of Romanticism concerned only with the far-flung origins of Romantic attitudes. This error of emphasis impairs the value of the studies of William Lyon Phelps, H. A. Beers, and H. G. de Marr.

In the second place, critics of classicism have often placed unjust emphasis on minor figures, because the minor critic of the age is often most dogmatic and furnishes the neatest illustration of extreme classical points of view. The opinions of Rymer, Dennis, Gildon, and Welsted cannot be neglected, but the views of the greater men—Dryden, Swift, Pope, Addison, Steele, Richardson, Fielding, Boswell, Johnson, Burke, and Cowper—are more properly the views of the classical period, for they are the views of the creative artists who make the period worthy of investigation.

In the present study I have tried to avoid these mistakes in approach. For the past eight years I have compared the opinions of eighteenth-century critics and creative artists on every aspect of their artistic outlook. I hope that I have neglected no significant writer of the age, though it has been, of course, impossible to present every opinion in the body of this study. The notes are not exhaustive, but they are designed to give full support to the views which seem to me correct, and to present interesting parallels with the ideas of Græco-Roman and Renaissance criticism. I have not neglected recent scholarship, but my conclusions are based almost exclusively on independent investigation of primary sources.

An unbiased study of the opinions of the age reveals that the genuine man of letters was remarkably tolerant: on many points of criticism opinion was almost equally divided; on no point was there real unanimity among the men who made the age conspicuous by their literary productions. It seems, however, that the influence of Græco-Roman literature on the masterpieces of the age has been unduly stressed, for the foundations of classicism lay in the view of the world and of the mind of man produced by the mathematical and scientific consciousness of the seventeenth century. From this fundamentally rational outlook certain corollaries were deduced. This group of logical principles derived by reason from the view of an orderly universe ruled by law formed the heart of classicism. But these principles were accepted only by the upper classes, and by them accepted with numerous qualifications. I found that within this body of classical doctrine there were certain elements of disintegration which paved the highroads to the Romantic Movement despite the best efforts of the classicists to uphold the life of reason. In any analysis of a complex attitude artificial distinctions are inevitable and some overlapping unavoidable. I can only hope that such repetition and the separation of closely interwoven aspects of classicism have been reduced to the minimum compatible with clarity.

Without the persevering efforts of Miss Norma Cass, reference librarian at the University of Kentucky, to secure several hundred indispensable items, this study would have been impossible. I am particularly indebted to the Library of Congress and to the University of Michigan for the loan of half a hundred volumes each. I also wish to thank Professors L. L. Dantzler and E. F. Farquhar for reading a large portion of this study in manuscript. For invaluable aid in the preparation of the manuscript I am indebted to my wife and to my sister, Mary Harrell Taylor.

FRANCIS GALLAWAY.

Lexington, Kentucky
September, 1939

CONTENTS

CONTENTS

BOOK THREE

SEEDS OF REVOLT

BOOK ONE

REASON AND CLASSICISM

CHAPTER I

THE INTERPLAY OF LITERATURE AND SCIENCE

ENGLISH classicism is a complex interweaving of pure rationalism, the Rules of art derived from Greece and Rome, and various forms of emotional revolt which early pointed to the ultimate victory of Romanticism. Even the origins of classicism are still in dispute, though a reaction is now apparent against the earlier over-emphasis on the role played by the Ancients. Historians have come more and more to regard the revival of classical studies during the Renaissance as the result of a new critical spirit in man. In the pro-duction of this modern spirit, intellectual curiosity and the resultant study of man and of his world are essential; classical scholarship is not, for "if the manuscripts of Greece and Rome had perished every one beneath the monk's missal, the outcome would not have been essentially different."[1] Even if the humanistic literature of the Ren-aissance throughout Europe—the neo-Latin poetry and the Cicero-nian prose—were proved to be the direct result of classical imitation, it still would have to be proved that the worship of the Ancients was a dominant force in the *English* Renaissance, and that this imi-tative spirit survived—purely because of the authority of Aristotle and Horace—to produce the masterpieces of the English classical period—the work of Dryden as critic and poet, of Defoe and Swift, of Fielding and Jane Austen, even of Addison and Pope, of Gibbon and Doctor Johnson. Influence from Greece and Rome there was indeed, but for the most part the Rules produced a host of forgotten pastorals and occasional verses, and innumerable controversies over minutiæ which did not seriously affect the really creative writers of the period. The dominance of Græco-Roman influence between 1660 and 1800 is by no means axiomatic. Upon investigation it may be found that Reason was much more significant than the Authority of

3

the Ancients to the artistic outlook of the age, and that the fresh winds of an awakening spirit of criticism did more to determine the climate of the period than the hothouse atmosphere of an artificially preserved culture.

Other influences than those of the overrated Ancients were at work. Paul S. Wood has pictured classicism as a recrudescence of "native elements" and as a reaction against the extravagances of the Puritan spirit.[2] A. F. B. Clark emphasizes the influence of France. Pope himself recognized the vogue of French ideas, but the popularity of Boileau and the French critics in England coincided with the development of science and with the spread of the cult of reason, common sense, and the light of nature. Clark recognizes the significance of Descartes in the formation of French classicism, an admission which strengthens the probability that the growth of rationalism was a decisive factor.[3]

Among modern scholars Arthur Lovejoy, Louis Bredvold, and R. F. Jones are pioneers in the attempt to explain English Classicism in the light of the new interest in experiment and in logic, in the Royal Society, in Descartes, and in Newton. If not the origin, almost certainly the continued vitality of classicism after Authority was discredited and the Rules were questioned must be sought in the suitability of classical modes of literature to the views of the world and of man produced by the rational spirit in cosmology, religion, and psychology. Parallels in ideology between the English classicists and the Ancients cannot be neglected, but in default of proof positive to the contrary they cannot be regarded as the vital springs of impulse for the enduring masterpieces of the age. That the influence of the Ancients explains the forgotten imitations of the period, no one will dispute.[4]

The roots of the artistic outlook of Dryden, Pope, and Johnson must be sought in the scientific thought of Bacon as well as in the pronouncements of Ben Jonson; in the rationalism of Descartes as well as in the *Art Poetique* of Boileau; in the English Royal Society as well as in the *Discourses* of the French Academy. A new era of human thought was introduced by Bacon and Descartes, an era of rebellion against tradition, of new standards of clarity in thought and expression and of organization in the pursuit of knowledge.

Bacon helped to clear away the accumulated rubbish of tradition, pointed out the reasons for the failure of the human intellect, presented induction as the new tool for scientific advance, and envisaged in the House of Solomon a pattern for the future Royal Society. Descartes, more purely rational, was perhaps even more important for the new period in his insistence on the supremacy of reason and on the uniformity of natural law. Descartes' *Discourse on Method* was followed by similar works by Arnauld and Nicole, by Malebranche, by Pascal, and by Leibnitz. Outside of such formal discussions, expressions of the purely rational attitude were soon to be met on all sides. Voltaire found all nature nothing but mathematics, and Fontenelle thought that "a work of ethics, of politics, of criticism, perhaps of eloquence, will be finer if it is made by the hand of a geometrician."[5]

In England the *Discourse on Method* was translated by 1649. Two years earlier Henry More had already come under its influence, and became an important force in the diffusion of Cartesianism. Descartes aided the break with tradition which was initiated by Bacon; he emphasized method and clarity; he helped to spread the idea of man as a unit of reason possessed (in common with all other such units) of a sense which was at its best as a tool of thought when it was stripped of the accretions of custom and prejudice and used as an abstract instrument. The result of this abstract thinking was the prevalence of abstract systems of politics, economics, and criticism; the discussion of institutions, contracts, and forms *in vacuo*; and the development of statistics, the human arithmetic that seemed such a dismal science to the later Romantics. The supremacy of mathematics among the sciences in the seventeenth century is a sign of this rational emphasis.[6]

Because of the dualism set up by Descartes between the material world (which included man's body as a living machine) and man's "rational soul," he came to be regarded as a bulwark against pure materialism as embodied in Hobbes. In time, however, many members of the Royal Society including Cudworth, More, Sprat, and Glanvill became suspicious of unfettered rationalism and began to insist on careful investigation as a counterbalancing force. Glanvill advocated a skeptical approach free from the fallacies of the imagination and the prejudices of the affections, as well as from the burdens of Ancient authority—an excellent program for the judicious scientist, but notably hostile to the enthusiasm of Puritan religion and the emotional verve of Cavalier poetry. There was no place in Glanvill's scheme for brave romantic dreams without a basis in fact.[7]

Experimental science was the rage. Kings and noblemen, queens and great ladies—Charles II and Queen Christina, the Duke of Orleans and the Duchess of Newcastle—lent it their countenance. Scientific reviews came into existence with the publication of the *Journal des Savants* in 1665. The same year saw the first issue of the *Philosophical Transactions* of the Royal Society. Before the end of the century Pierre Bayle edited the first magazine of popular science, the *Nouvelles de la République des Lettres*, at Rotterdam (1684–1687). The study of statistics was started with Graunt's *Natural and Political Observations upon the Bills of Mortality*, and was developed in Sir William Petty's *Treatise on Taxes* and the much more important *Political Arithmetic*, finished in 1676 and published in 1690.

Hostile as Swift was to the projectors of Lagado, he bought Stella a microscope, and declared that "method is good in all things. . . . The Devil is the author of confusion." James Thomson called Bacon "the great deliverer," and addressed Newton as one of England's glories. Akenside begged Science to disperse with "resistless light"

> The scholiast's learning, sophist's cant,
> The visionary bigot's rant,
> The monk's philosophy.

The noblest field of science was, according to Akenside, the human mind where the sallies of fancy are checked, and reason

> recalls the soul
> To truth's severest test.[8]

The English Royal Society had been patterned on foreign models. Informal gatherings as early as 1645 led to incorporation by 1662. Davenant, following Bacon, had pictured a scientific academy in *Gondibert*. Cowley had published in 1661 his *Proposition for the Advancement of Learning*, and had begun to work with John Evelyn for a systematic scholarly foundation for conducting experiments.

Cowley himself studied botany, wrote a Latin poem on plants, and produced in the last years of his life a simple prose in striking contrast to his metaphysical verse. Pepys was an active member of the Royal Society. Dryden praised science in an *Epistle to Doctor Charlton* (1662), and lauded the work of the Royal Society in *Annus Mirabilis*. In 1693 the youthful Addison delivered a Latin academic oration at Oxford in defense of scientific method. Among the forerunners and founders of a new prose style not already mentioned in this connection, Sprat, Petty, Wilkins, Tillotson, and Barrow were all Academicians.[9]

This general enthusiasm could not go long unchallenged. Pure science was in time regarded as hostile to the type of humanism embodied in Pope's dictum, "The proper study of mankind is man," and to the common sense in which all men shared. These antinomies will be examined later.

II

The new respect for reason was conspicuous in religion as well as in scientific research. Even in orthodox circles religious enthusiasm was checked by religious rationalism. In opposition to the special revelation of Christianity arose Deism, a religion of essentials discoverable by all men through the light of reason. The basis of both Deism and classicism lay in the Cartesian explanation of reason as a faculty identical in all men, so that only such truths as have been known to all ages, races, and temperaments could be regarded as rational truths. As each individual partakes of the uniform light of nature his mind is capable of discovering truth without the interposition of ecclesiastical tradition, and the truth of any dogma may be tested by an appeal to the sum of these rational minds. The greater the degree of conformity, the greater likelihood of the truth. Enthusiasm, defined as a belief in private supernatural revelation, and originality, dependent on the special intuitions of genius, are without validity, for all minds that are not immeshed in system or swamped by futile pedantry are absolutely equal. Since rational beings are equal and reason everywhere is uniform, there is no significance in national tradition and no point in the study of history, which is merely the record of the progressive corruption of the pure light of nature. Rather it is useful to get back to pure common sense as it existed in the primitive epoch when man, guided by natural law, was happy in a rational Eden.[10]

The opposition to Christianity— a religion revealed at an historical epoch to a chosen people, unknown to millions of men, undiscoverable by reason alone, corrupted by a mass of accumulated dogma— is obvious. The Deist stripped religion to a body of reasonable doctrines—the existence of God, the obligation of worship, the necessity of repentance, the emphasis on a life of virtue as the best means of worship, and the doctrine of future rewards and punishments.[11] "Miracles, special providences, supernatural revelations, were discarded . . . not only as incredible in the light of science, but as unworthy of the creator of the universe and the source of all general truth."[12] The writings of Hume were less virulent than those of the earlier Deists, but more significant in their complete destruction of the orthodox arguments. In four works—*Of Superstition and Enthusiasm* (1742), *An Essay on Miracles* (1747), *Natural History of Religion* (1757), and the *Dialogues Concerning Natural Religion* (posthumous, 1779)—Hume made a break between religion and reason imperative.

Few significant men of letters were admittedly Deists, but the writings of the ethical and philosophical poets—Pope, Thomson, and Akenside—were tinged with the thought of Bolingbroke and Shaftesbury, the polite leaders of the Deist cause in the England of George I. Pope's *Universal Prayer* was a Deist hymn:

> Father of all! in ev'ry age,
>   In ev'ry clime adored,
> By saint, by savage, and by sage,
>   Jehovah, Jove, or Lord!

Religious notions, proclaimed Amory's John Buncle,

that are not characterized by the reason of things, and the moral fitness of actions, I considered as repugnant to the veracity, wisdom, and goodness of the Almighty. . . .

John Armstrong was another rationalist who emphasized the significance of virtuous action rather than of faith, and persistently refused to believe that God could be less rational than intelligent men, who would not condemn good Jews and Mohammedans for believing a religion "in which they were arbitrarily born."[13]

The opposition to enthusiasm in religion paralleled the hostility to enthusiasm in poetry. At the Restoration a reaction against the rampant enthusiasm of the Puritans was certain. Men turned from the inner light to experimentation, and from indulgence in imagination to the cultivation of reason.[14] The Anglican Church took up a moderate position between the authoritarian emphasis of Rome and the enthusiasm, respect for private judgment, and decentralization of the Dissenters. Dryden's *Religio Laici* illustrated the appeal to common sense, to universal consent, and to the spirit of moderation that was characteristic of the best Anglican churchmen. The decorum of the Anglican Church paralleled the decorum of literature. Much as Dissenters in religion were condemned for singularity, so eccentrics in art were disparaged as unnatural.[15]

Hobbes and Glanvill vindicated reason as an antidote to enthusiasm. Meric Casaubon described enthusiasm as an "extraordinary . . . fervency . . . producing strange effects, apt to be taken for supernatural." It infected the understanding. Henry More called imagination the soul's weakness which undermined the faculties of reason and understanding. Locke wrote a hostile critique of enthusiasm. Shaftesbury regarded sound sense as an instrument to test whether a spirit be of God. If a "sedate, cool, and impartial" reason is in abeyance, "every dream and frenzy" will be an inspiration. Hume was no less hostile to a swollen imagination, which, unless it were checked in time by reason, would lead to enthusiasm.[16]

If one turns to the creative artists he will recall at once Swift's scathing attacks on enthusiasm in the *Tale of a Tub* and in the *Discourse on the Mechanical Operation of the Spirit*. That good bourgeois, Richardson, disliked enthusiasm. Goldsmith agreed with Shaftesbury that it must be opposed with ridicule. Gray's feeling in religion has been described by Edmund Gosse as one of "high and dry objection to enthusiasm." Boswell dreaded it. Fanny Burney found Mrs. Rowe's *Letters from the Dead to the Living* "so very enthusiastic, that the religion she preaches rather disgusts and cloys than charms and elevates." Thomas Warton found "narrowness of mind" and "ignorance of human affairs" inseparable from enthusiasm. Pinkerton felt that enthusiasm "always comes through a crack in the skull." Richard Graves gently ridiculed his enthusiastic spiritual Quixote, and Matthew Green pointed to enthusiasm as one of the causes of the spleen. Such illustrations can easily be multiplied. It is no wonder that an age impressed with the abuse of the imagination in religion should have been hesitant about its value in the realm of art.[17]

But it must not be thought that reason and orthodoxy were necessarily antagonistic. Even when there was no question of attacking enthusiasm, the defenders of the faith employed reason and common sense against skeptic and Deist until controversial tome was piled on tome and the confusion of distinction and counterdistinction rivalled the confusion of tongues at Babel. Milton judged revelation by reason. Tillotson, the popular preacher of the Restoration, declared that "nothing ought to be received as a revelation from God which plainly contradicts the principles of natural religion." Evelyn defended the Anglican view of the communion as more in consonance than the Popish with "the common principles of science, and even common sense." Benjamin Whichcote wrote: "To act contrary to the reason of one's own mind, is to do a thing most unnatural and cruel: it is to offer violence to a man's self." He went on to declare that God was knowable by the use of reason and understanding in the observation of the fitness and proportion of the universe.[18]

Locke, Addison, and Young illustrate the interrelations of reason and faith. Locke was a rationalist to the core, and sought to prove the truths of Christianity by the same appeal to ordinary reason that sufficed in history or secular philosophy. Locke was thankful for reason as a means by which to read the "legible characters of His works and providence" in the world around him. Revelation could never be so certain as the conviction of reason, and he limited the function of the former to the few things not knowable by the earnestly enquiring mind.[19] The influence of Addison was more extensive than that of Locke. To Addison, moral practice was more important than faith, since it was more useful, more likely to perfect human nature, more universally agreed upon among all nations, more certain to lead to salvation, and more unchanging than theological dogmas. Revelation clarified a few obscurities in morals, gave right living a strong motivation, presented a more sublime notion of God than could be evolved by reason alone, and showed to its fullest extent the blackness of vice. In the *Spectator* (No. 590) Addison followed Locke to prove the existence of God with the customary arguments from being and design. It is a commonplace to note that Addison wished to uphold the golden mean in religion as in other spheres of life.[20] Young proclaimed the primacy of reason over faith. The great popularity of his *Night Thoughts* is explicable in part in that it was a rhetorical resumé of the popular arguments against both Deism and Free Thought. Christian apologetics was measured off into proper lengths and provided with points of exclamation to form the staple of his verse. Young found the usual proofs for the existence of God in universal consent, in the necessity for a first cause, and in the argument from design in which the new discoveries in astronomy and physiology were squeezed of every indication of adaptation to environment and apparent purpose. Immortality was essential to justify the toils of the virtuous man on earth, for without a future reward a man would be a fool to live a righteous life on earth. Young was thus both rational and practical, in keeping with the spirit of the age.[21]

It must not be supposed, however, that every Englishman surrendered all the religious beliefs that he could not defend rationally. No large percentage of the people has ever cared for reason, except as reason can be identified with intuitive common sense. To the vast majority of the Augustans, as to most men today, religion came by prescription. The faith of Paul and Silas was found sufficient for the masses, as the Wesleyan Revival indicated. Even educated men were at times skeptical of the omnipotence of reason. Dryden felt that "they who would prove religion by reason, do but weaken the cause they endeavor to support." In an early ode, Prior rebuked the presumption of human reason that was impotent to explain the wonders of God. Swift was hostile to rationalistic dogmatism throughout his life. It was William Law, however, who called attention in *A Serious Call to a Devout and Holy Life* to the parting of the ways between reason and revelation. It seemed to Law that Christianity was based on the miraculous. If reason could not swallow the miracles, either reason or religion must be abandoned. Like Law,

Joseph Butler and John Wesley gave up the rational defense of Christianity and attempted to revive a personal religion based on an inner spiritual experience. Evangelicism spread in England, preparing subterranean reserves of emotionalism for the Romantic. Revolution, but during most of the eighteenth century it flourished only belowstairs, while above, parson and squire reasoned amiably about ethics—or fox-hunting—and toasted Church and King in ripe October ale.[22]

It was inevitable that the application of reason to religion should have weakened genuine religious emotion. Addison, Goldsmith, and Crabbe all called attention to the lessening hold of religion, but the evidence for such a condition is largely of the negative sort discoverable even by a casual reading of the plays and novels of the period. The age seemed to feel that if religion was not practical, it was nothing—except a career for younger sons. The clergy sought advancement through literary criticism almost as often as in theological controversy. They engaged in politics during the first half of the period; in archeology during the latter. Hell was becoming unfashionable. Though the lower classes were devout, and read more theology than fiction, the clergyman who addressed the upper classes was expected to preserve good taste and good form in a discourse, lucid, reasonable—and without influence—directed to the common sense of the wealthy pewholders. The upper-class as a rule conformed outwardly to set a good example to tradesmen and servants, but a real spiritual indifference existed in drawing-room and boudoir.[23]

III

Reason and morality were more compatible than reason and deep religious feeling. In fact, the emphasis on practical morality dominates the period. A more universal moral code than that provided by Revelation was sought as a desirable concomitant to the universal validity of the "light of nature." A detailed study of the divergent ethical theories of Locke, Shaftesbury, Hutcheson, Hume, and Adam Smith is not called for in a general study of literary classicism, though it is essential to realize that all the various systems were devised in an attempt to find a basis in universal custom, in universal benevolence, or in universal principles of self-interest for a permanent and universal code of ethics which could be perceived by the uniform light of nature without the assistance of supernatural revelation.

Hobbes and Locke sought to discover laws of mind as regular in their operation as the mathematical laws of the universe. In the quest it was necessary to ignore the irrational, customary, or intuitive actions of man, in order to consider him as a consciously rational being, and to posit a uniform and lucid light of nature as the basis for the moral code. Human nature was everywhere the same, and men in all countries who were unblinded by custom were equally capable of perceiving the fitness of right action. Morality was presumed to be as absolutely true as a proposition in geometry. The justice of God himself could be judged by this immutable standard, for God commands what is good; it is not good because He commands it. In this point the orthodox Samuel Clarke and the Deist Shaftesbury agreed.[24]

The desire for a rational code of right and wrong as a key to happiness meets one on every side. Addison felt that a wise man will suspect those actions to which he is directed by anything other than reason, "whether by his age, temper, way of life, or possible pleasure or profit," for such peculiar considerations will distort the pure life of reason. Doctor Johnson hoped that Du Halde's *History of China* would show that "virtue is in every place the same," and he argued in the *Adventurer* that principles of morals were everlasting and invariable. "Hermes" Harris tried to discover a basis for happiness through an examination of those things universally esteemed by men.[25]

As anthropological investigations became more common and voyager after voyager returned from primitive lands, the ideal of a universal moral law was shattered before the growing realization that even incest and murder were righteous acts in Egypt or Brazil. Even before this conviction became inescapable various bases were sought on which a rational system of ethics might be erected. Man was impelled by self-interest to seek pleasure and to avoid pain according to Locke; or, according to Shaftesbury and Hutcheson, he was a benevolent and social creature, moved by a taste for the beauty of moral actions or by sympathy, and prone to promote the happiness

of his fellow man. Even more frequently self-interest and benevolence were combined in the same system, for an enlightened self-
interest was proved time and again to be identical with the welfare
of the social group.[26]

The attempt to maintain the supremacy of common sense in the
daily life of man, and to restrain emotion and passion as things unworthy of a rational being will be considered later.[27] It remains to
suggest how the theories of self-interest and of utility, of benevolence and of the moral sense tended to break down the universal
rule of right that they were originally designed to support. Whether
self-interest was guided by reason or by an instinctive reaction to
pleasure and pain, it involved individuals who by their past training,
and by their particular sense of values chose one thing or another,
responded to a present pleasure at the risk of future pain, or chose
present pain to gain a future pleasure. Shaftesbury's theory of
benevolence became an early form of utilitarianism in the hands of
Hutcheson, for it was found necessary to decide which was the truly
benevolent act by the "moral arithmetic" that gauged the greatest
happiness of the greatest number. Such calculation involved analysis
of personal ethical problems which must be decided by the individual, until in time a system of customary action bolstered by civil
and criminal law, by public opinion, and by hope of Heaven or fear
of Hell, would enable the individual to dispense with complicated
moral measurements. To the man who was proud of his ethical
independence, however, utilitarianism inevitably became a system
of casuistry, more and more remote from the eternal and natural
laws of right and wrong.[28]

In morals, as in so many other spheres, the destructive analysis
of Hume cleared the road, already marked out by Shaftesbury, for
the Romantic morality of sentiment. Hume rejected the theories
that

virtue is nothing but a conformity to reason, that there are eternal fitnesses
and unfitnesses of things, which are the same to every rational being that
considers them; that the immutable measures of right and wrong impose
an obligation, not only on human creatures, but also on the Deity himself;

he denied that reason could ever be the sole motive for any action
of the will; and he declared frankly that, "Reason is, and ought only

to be the slave of the passions, and can never pretend to any other office than to serve and obey them." In short, "morality is determined by sentiment"; reason can only point out the tendencies of actions; humanity leads us to favor useful actions. Hume thus linked utility and humanitarian feeling, unconsciously lent support to the sentimental theories of man's inherent goodness, and paved the way for the emergence of the man of feeling in Sterne and Mackenzie.[29]

In the conviction that man's natural reason or his natural goodness of heart could equally guide him aright in the ethical life the Deistic and the pre-Romantic systems of morality had a common root. Both convictions led to primitivism; but the first was rational, the second progressively more emotional. In the Romantic Movement sentimental ethics won the victory. This idea of human nobility arose as a reaction against the concept of original sin and the arbitrary and irrational ethics of the Mosaic code. It was fostered by men—Locke, Shaftesbury, Hume, and Smith—who were by nature classicists, though in their roles as Deists, skeptics, or rationally minded Christians they set going trains of thought destined to destroy the Horatian and Aristotelian ideals of life that were doubtless to them most congenial.

IV

The influence of science on literature was already recognized in the eighteenth century. According to Thomas Warton rationalism advanced judgment but weakened fancy. The establishment of Rules checked "the brave eccentricities of original genius." Warton lamented:

We have parted with extravagances that are above propriety, with incredibilities that are more acceptable than truth, and with fictions that are more valuable than reality.[30]

Joseph Warton also regretted that the "geometrical and systematical spirit . . . has spread itself from the sciences . . . into polite literature" diminishing sentiment and causing poets to write from the head rather than from the heart. Oliver Goldsmith agreed with the Wartons, but his mentor, Doctor Johnson, was far more favorable to a literary criticism parallel in its nature to scientific investigation. Doctor Johnson thought that the function of criticism was

> to establish principles; to improve opinion into knowledge, and to distinguish those means of pleasing which depend upon known causes and rational deductions, from the nameless and inexplicable elegancies which appeal only to the fancy. . . . Criticism reduces those regions of literature under the dominion of science, which have hitherto known only the anarchy of ignorance, the caprices of fancy, and the tyranny of prescription.[31]

The large number of Restoration writers interested in science would point to an influence of science on style. Cowley abandoned "metaphysical wit" for simple prose. Dryden developed a lucid prose as a vehicle for a criticism fundamentally rational. John Wilkins called for a "plain and natural" style in preaching. William Petty made a "direct, simple style free from metaphor" a distinguishing mark between the experimental philosophers and those who held to the old scholastic traditions. Samuel Parker wrote:

> True philosophy is too sober to descend to these wildernesses of the imagination, and too rational to be cheated by them. She scorns, when she is in chase of truth, to quarry upon trifling gaudy phantasms; her game is in things not words. . . .

All of these men were amateurs of the new science, and their interest in exact experimentation and accurate statement did for the new prose style more than the expansion of the reading public, the pamphlets of political controversy, the growth of journalism, the plain speech of the Quakers, or the growing commercial preoccupation of Englishmen. Gone were the involved sentences, the antithetical balance of sonorous clauses, the unwieldy parentheses, the luscious Latinized diction, the mass of corroborative quotations from books ancient and modern; the new style, in the words of Fontenelle, seemed to be "written by the hand of a geometer."[32]

In much the same manner in which the new science was attempting to explain what had hitherto seemed the inexplicable mysteries of the external world, the new criticism was revealing works of literary art to be, not miracles of inspiration, but cleverly contrived mechanisms that could be imitated by the Glovers and the Wilkies of the age. A passage from Mulgrave's *Essay upon Poetry* will illustrate this attitude. Mulgrave was speaking of the *Iliad and Odyssey:*

Had Bossu never writ, the world had still
Like Indians view'd this wondrous piece of skill;
As something of Divine the work admired,
Hoped not to be instructed, but inspired;
Till he, disclosing sacred mysteries,
Has shown where all the mighty magic lies,
Described the seeds, and in what order sown,
That have to such a vast proportion grown.[33]

The desire to systematize language and literature in keeping with the scientific temper of mind led many Englishmen to wish for the establishment of an English Academy, though it was not until the foundation of the French Academy by Richelieu and the organization of the Royal Society in London that the agitation became general. James Howell praised Richelieu's establishment, and Robert Hooke favored an academy to license books, purify the language, regulate decorum in style, superintend translations, and prepare a dictionary. In 1664 a committee was appointed by the Royal Society to reform the English tongue. John Evelyn was interested in the project, and Dryden supported it in the Epistle Dedicatory to *The Rival Ladies*. The effort proved abortive, however.

Four years later Sprat, in his *History of the Royal Society*, returned to the scheme for an academy to bring the language, which "has hitherto been a little too carelessly handled, . . . to its last perfection." The Royal Society had already done much, according to Sprat, in insisting on plain speech, on the avoidance of tropes and figures, and on the elimination of a "vicious abundance of phrase." The Society had shown a

constant resolution to reject all amplifications, digressions, and swellings of style; to return back to the primitive purity and shortness, when man deliver'd so many *things* almost in an equal number of *words*. They have exacted from all their members a close, naked, natural way of speaking, positive expressions, clear senses, a native easiness, bringing all things as near the mathematical plainness as they can, and preferring the language of artisans, countrymen, and merchants, before that of wits or scholars.

In the reign of Queen Anne, Addison and Swift, Prior, and Tickell revived the project of an academy. Swift sought to interest the cabinet minister, Harley, in the plan, and a list of twenty names was actually compiled, but war and peace were more vital to the Tory Ministry than nouns and verbs, and again the project was allowed to slumber. The effort of Swift seems to have been the last to progress beyond a hopeless wish, though Joseph Warton in 1756, Oliver Goldsmith in 1759, and even the iconoclast Pinkerton as late as 1785 wished scientific attention conferred on the language by an academy. Only Johnson, among the major figures, was keen enough to realize that, despite the reign of science, Englishmen lacked sufficient reverence for authority to make feasible a rational control of the manifestations of the spirit.[34]

The direct influence of rationalism and experimentation was not confined to a growing simplicity in style and a futile attempt to parallel the Royal Society with an English Academy. Much more important was the support given to the idea of Nature as a norm, to the Rule of Probability, and to the redefinition of wit. The æsthetics based on symmetry, proportion, and fulfillment of function; the supremacy of the judgment over the imagination; the emphasis on realism; the attempt to find a universal foundation for taste; and the effort to re-establish the Rules on the basis of reason are all more or less intimately connected with the basic temper of the Age of Reason. Each of these points, however, requires separate and more detailed treatment.

NOTES TO CHAPTER I

1. J. H. Randall, *The Making of the Modern Mind*, New York, 1926, p. 115.

2. P. S. Wood, "Native Elements in English Neo-classicism," *Modern Philology*, XXIV, 201 ff.

3. A. F. B. Clark, *Boileau and the French Classical Critics in England* (*1660–1830*), Paris, 1925, p. 382.

4. I refer specifically to A. O. Lovejoy's "The Parallel of Deism and Classicism," *Modern Philology*, XXIX, 281, and to the same critic's "Optimism and Romanticism," *P. M. L. A.*, XLII, 921; to L. I. Bredvold's *The Intellectual Milieu of John Dryden*, Ann Arbor, 1934, and to his "Dryden, Hobbes, and the Royal Society," *Modern Philology*, XXV, 417; to Marjorie Nicolson's "The Early Stage of Cartesianism in England," *Studies in Philology*, XXVI, 356; to R. F. Jones's "Science and English Prose Style," *P. M. L. A.*, XLV, 977; and to G. N. Clark's *The Later Stuarts*, Oxford, 1934, pp. 27–30.

5. In the pages that follow I rely largely upon J. B. Bury's *The Idea of Progress*, London, 1921; Preserved Smith's *A History of Modern Culture*, New York, 1930–1934; J. H. Randall's *The Making of the Modern Mind*; A. F. Whitehead's *Science and the Modern World*, New York, 1926; and upon the articles of Lovejoy, Bredvold, Nicolson, and Jones listed in the previous note. There are some suggestive

pages also in Alfred Cobban's *Edmund Burke and the Revolt against the Eighteenth Century*, London, 1929. My indebtedness to all of them is so pervasive that, save in the case of actual quotation, I have not made specific reference to them.

6. Preserved Smith, *op. cit.*, II, 123.

7. These ideas will be developed in Chapter IV, and in Chapter VIII, Section Three.

8. Joseph Glanvill, *The Vanity of Dogmatizing*, London, 1661 (The Facsimile Text Society, New York, 1931), pp. 62–147; Bredvold, *The Intellectual Milieu of John Dryden*, p. 89.

9. Swift, *Journal to Stella*, October 26 and November 15, 1710; Thomson, *Summer*, in Chalmers, *Works of the English Poets*, London, 1810, XII, 433; Akenside, "Hymn to Science."

10. George Williamson, "The Restoration Revolt against Enthusiasm," *Studies in Philology*, XXX, 598; R. F. Jones, "Science and English Prose Style," *loc. cit.*, p. 1002; A. C. Howell, "Sir Thomas Browne and Seventeenth-century Scientific Thought," *Studies in Philology*, XXII, 71; Addison, *Works*, VI, 607 ff.

11. Lovejoy, "Parallel of Deism and Classicism," *loc. cit.*, pp. 282–291.

12. Leslie Stephen, *A History of English Thought in the Eighteenth Century*, New York, 1927, I, 84 ff.

13. C. A. Moore, "Shaftesbury and the Ethical Poets in England, 1700–1760," *P. M. L. A.*, XXXI, 284 ff.; Amory, *Life and Opinions of John Buncle*, ed. E. A. Baker, London, 1904, pp. 7, 217; Armstrong, *Miscellanies*, London, 1770, II, 178. The whole of the Deist controversy is fully treated in the work of Leslie Stephen cited above.

14. Williamson, "The Restoration Revolt against Enthusiasm," *loc. cit.*, XXX, 597.

15. P. S. Wood, *op. cit.*, pp. 203–205; Bredvold, *Intellectual Milieu of John Dryden*, pp. 80–81.

16. Hobbes, *Leviathan*, ed. A. R. Waller, Cambridge, 1904, p. 47; Glanvill, *op. cit.*, Epistle Dedicatory; Williamson, *op. cit.*, pp. 583–584; Locke, *An Essay Concerning the Human Understanding*, London (Routledge), n. d., p. 591; Shaftesbury, *Characteristicks*, London, 1723, I, 54–55, III, 40–41; Hume, *Essays, Moral, Political, and Literary*, ed. T. H. Green and T. H. Grose, London, 1907, I, 145.

17. Richardson, *Correspondence*, ed. Mrs. Barbauld, London, 1804, VI, 13; Goldsmith, *Citizen of the World*, Letter CXI, and *Bee*, No. VII; Edmund Gosse, *Gray*, London (English men of Letters), 1902, p. 71; Boswell, *The Hypochondriack*, ed. Margery Bailey, Stanford University (California), 1928, II, 86, and note 11; Fanny Burney, *Early Diary*, ed. Annie Ellis, London, 1913, I, 186; Thomas Warton, *History of English Poetry*, p. 589; Pinkerton, *Letters of Literature*, London, 1785, p. 210; Graves, *The Spiritual Quixote*, London, 1810, I, 26–27; Matthew Green, "The Spleen."

18. Leslie Stephen, *op. cit.*, I, 78–79; E. M. W. Tillyard, *Milton*, New York, 1930, pp. 215–217; Evelyn, *Diary and Correspondence*, III, 231 ff.; W. E. Alderman, "The Significance of Shaftesbury in English Speculation," *P. M. L. A.*, XXXVIII, 184–185.

19. Locke, *Essay*, pp. 396–397; Leslie Stephen, *op. cit.*, I, 100.

20. Addison, *Spectator*, Nos. 458, 459, 590, and *Whig-Examiner*, No. 2.

21. Young, *Poetical Works*, Boston, 1854, I, 87; Paul Van Tieghem, *Le Pre-*

romantisme, Paris, 1930, II, 34; Isabel Bliss, "Young's *Night Thoughts* in Relation to Contemporary Christian Apologetics," *P. M. L. A.*, XLIX, 37 ff.

22. John Dryden, Preface to *Religio Laici*; Prior, in Chalmers, *op. cit.*, X, 130; Addison, *Freeholder*, No. 51; Wedel, "On the Philosophical Background of *Gulliver's Travels*," *Studies in Philology*, XXIII, 444; Randall, *Modern Mind*, pp. 298–304; Bredvold, *op. cit.*, p. 109.

23. Addison, *Spectator*, No. 458; Goldsmith, *Citizen of the World*, Letter XLI; Crabbe, "The Village"; Randall, *op. cit.*, p. 283; Leslie Stephen, *English Literature and Society in the Eighteenth Century*, London, 1907, pp. 45–47, 131 ff.; Amy Reed, *The Background of Gray's Elegy*, New York, 1924, p. 29; Cobban, *op. cit.*, pp. 233–234; Hume, *Essays*, I, 125.

24. Shaftesbury, *Characteristicks*, II, 267; Mandeville, *Fable of the Bees*, ed. F. B. Kaye, Oxford, 1924, I, 49; Stephen, *English Thought in the Eighteenth Century*, I, 124.

25. Addison, *Spectator*, No. 399; Johnson, *Adventurer*, No. 74, and Review of Du Halde's *History of China*; James Harris, *Three Treatises*, London, 1772, pp. 121–192; Alexander Dyce, *Memoir of Beattie* in Beattie's *Poetical Works*, Boston, n. d., p. xxiii.

26. Stephen, *op. cit.*, II, 13.

27. In Chapters III and XIII.

28. Hutcheson, *An Inquiry into the Original of our Ideas of Beauty and Virtue*, London, 1726, pp. 177, 180, 187–195; Hume, *Essays*, II, 172 ff., 196.

29. Hume, *A Treatise of Human Nature*, ed. L. A. Selby-Bigge, Oxford, 1896, pp. 413–415, 456–457, and *Essays*, II, 172, 218, 259–260.

30. Thomas Warton, *History of English Poetry*, pp. 626–627.

31. Joseph Warton, *An Essay on the Genius and Writings of Pope*, London, 1806, I, 198–199; Goldsmith, *Miscellaneous Works*, pp. 437–438; Johnson, *Rambler*, No. 92.

32. R. F. Jones, *op. cit.*; L. I. Bredvold, "Dryden, Hobbes, and the Royal Society," *loc. cit.*; G. N. Clark, *op. cit.*, pp. 347–348.

33. Mulgrave, in Spingarn, *Critical Essays of the Seventeenth Century*, Oxford, 1908, II, 295.

34. Richard Carew's *Letter to Sir Robert Cotton*, as well as the relevant passages in Sprat's *History of the Royal Society* will be found in Spingarn, *op. cit.*, II, 113, 117–118, 337. Swift's *Proposal for Correcting, Improving and Ascertaining the English Tongue* is well known. Other references will be found in Swift, *Correspondence*, ed. F. E. Ball, London, 1910, I, 268, 325, 331; Dryden, *Essays*, ed. W. P. Ker, Oxford, 1926, I, 5; Addison, *Spectator*, No. 135; Goldsmith, *Bee*, No. VII; Joseph Warton, *Essay on Pope*, I, 192; Pinkerton, *Letters of Literature*, pp. 247–248; Johnson, *Lives of the Poets*, ed. Waugh, I, 245–246, III, 211, *Idler*, No. 61, and Preface to the *Dictionary*; Edmund Freeman, "A Proposal for an English Academy in 1660," *Modern Language Review*, XIX, 291–300; Preserved Smith, *op. cit.*, II, 305.

CHAPTER II

FACETS OF THE CLASSICAL WAY OF LIFE

SCIENTIFIC rationalism was not the only force molding the outlook of the period. The optimism of the period, its attitude
towards progress and luxury, its degree of urbanization in
spirit, its aristocratic bias, and its humanitarianism all affect the content, if not always the form, of eighteenth-century literature. It will
be best to dispose of these non-æsthetic factors before examining in
detail the logical framework of the classical attitude.

To replace the Christian belief that was steadily waning among
the upper classes during the Enlightenment, Newtonian science gave
to humanity a new faith in the mind of man and in the perfection
of God as the all-wise designer of a harmonious universe. Science,
still in its infancy, as yet entertained no doubts as to the universal
validity of its conclusion; it had not yet had time to reform the
world—and fail in the reformation. In the year in which Newton
published his *Principia* the scientist had the world before him where
to choose, and Providence was still his guide. Nature was not the
field of an irrational conflict; it was the beautifully co-ordinated
handiwork of the Great Designer, a harmonious whole in which the
earth, man's dwelling place, was still the most important creation.
It was still possible for Deistic poets like Thomson to regard the
music of the spheres as hymned by angels for the ears of men who
were the highest manifestations of physical life in the universe. It
was felt that reason was autonomous, and that the conception of the
world, discovered by reason, was not merely relative, but real. To
most men it seemed that reason was a sufficient guide to happiness,
and that a progressive revelation of the immutable laws of cause and
effect would give to man a greater and greater rational control
over his physical environment.[1]

It is true that to the advanced thinkers of the age God was no longer an ever-present Providence concerned with the rescue of virgins and the discovery of hidden crimes. He had become the Great First Cause, who, in His infinite wisdom, had fashioned a universe moving beautifully by scientific law, moving so perfectly that there could be no cause for future interference on the part of the Creator, and yet moving throughout the centuries according to His purpose and design. The glad acceptance of this scientifically-controlled universe may be seen in poem after poem during the period. Dryden sang in "A Song for St. Cecilia's Day:"

> From harmony, from heav'nly harmony
>   This universal frame began;
>   From harmony to harmony
> Thro' all the compass of the notes it ran,
> The diapason closing full in man.

Pope showed his faith in reason in *An Essay on Man* (II, 19–22):

> Go, wondrous creature! mount where science guides!
> Go, measure earth, weigh air, and state the tides;
> Instruct the planets in what o:bs to run,
> Correct old Time and regulate the sun!

The minor poets composed panegyrics on the universe almost as frequently as they wrote the praises of Queen Anne and Queen Caroline. Henry Baker wrote *The Universe* in 1727; Henry Brooke, *Universal Beauty* in 1728; John Gilbert Cooper, *The Power of Harmony* in 1745; and James Harris, nephew of the Earl of Shaftesbury, *Concord*, in 1751. Thomson and Young shared in this movement. All of them found the prevailing system "the wisest and best, because fittest for mankind, to whose wants it is accommodated, and to whose faculties it is proportioned."[2]

Wisest and best: the best of all possible worlds. These phrases derived from the metaphysical conceptions of Leibnitz and Wolff in Germany and of Shaftesbury and Bolingbroke in England lent their support to the more general trust in the new science. Space will permit only the simplest explanation of the logical processes by which the rationalists convinced themselves that this was the best of all possible worlds. Among the universal systems conceivable by the mind of God, there must have been a difference in degree of perfection. God chose to bring only one of these potential systems into being. As God possessed perfect wisdom served by perfect will He was compelled by the necessity of His own being to body forth the best of them all. Infinite wisdom and power would be incompatible with error; hence the universe, perfectly designed in the beginning has functioned perfectly since without repair.[3]

Mark Akenside contemplated the universe and found

> Through all its fabric, wisdom's artful aim
> Disposing every part, and gaining still
> By means proportion'd her benignant end.
>
> .   .   .   .
>
> One order, all-involving and entire.
>
> .   .   .   .
>
> The best and fairest of unnumber'd worlds
> That lay from everlasting in the store
> Of his divine conceptions.

Edmund Law and Samuel Johnson both found that the universe revealed the goodness of God. Law pointed to science as the means of discovering new "glory and perfection" in the architect of nature; Johnson argued that God had proportioned His gifts to man's real needs. Adam Smith believed that God maintained in the universe "the greatest possible quantity of happiness." Goldsmith's story of Asem reveals the same belief. Pope hymned the new faith vigorously:

> Of systems possible, if 'tis confest
> That wisdom infinite must form the best,
> Where all must full or not coherent be,
> And all that rises, rise in due degree,
> Then, in the scale of reas'ning life, 'tis plain,
> There must be somewhere, such a rank as Man; . . .[4]

The quotation from Pope introduces two closely linked ideas—the doctrines of plenitude and of the scale of being—which came to form an integral part of the conception of the best of all possible worlds. Evil was not caused by man's perversity or by a Satanic power, but by philosophical necessity. God could not be good without desiring to impart Himself, to embody Himself forth in created beings. He could not create another perfect being (for the idea of two coexistent perfect beings is contradictory), but creation, even of imperfection, was preferable to nonentity. The idea of plenitude was derived from this assumption of the value of existence, to which each idea in the mind of God had a right, unless its creation was hindered by the laws of contradiction. If the claim to full creation were denied, the universe would be incomplete and irrational; hence it would be evil as a whole. The fulfillment of the idea of plenitude gave an unbroken series of minutely differentiated created things in the Chain of Being. Each had the limitations of its class and could not escape from it, though it might strive for perfection within the class. The limitations of each class explained evil, moral and physical. Even the general evils of the system—crowding, competition, and death—were considered by the ingenious thinkers of the eighteenth century to be better than nonexistence.[5]

The idea of the Scale of Being was first explained in detail by Bishop King in *De Origine Mali* in 1702. The idea was eagerly seized by Bolingbroke and Pope, by Thomson, Young, and Cooper. In the *Spectator*, No. 519, Addison gave clear expression to it:

Infinite goodness is of so communicative a nature, that it seems to delight in the conferring of existence upon every degree of perceptive being. The scale of being contains creatures who almost reach each step above. All matter swarms with life. Had he only made one species of animals, none of the rest would have enjoyed the happiness of existence: he has, therefore, specified in his creation every degree of life, every capacity of being.

Doctor Johnson was one of the chief dissenters to this specious optimism. In a review of Soame Jenyns' *Origin of Evil* Johnson disposed of the Chain of Being by arguing that the highest being that was not infinite must be at an infinite distance below infinity, and that each vacuity in the scale, no matter how small, could conceivably be filled. The scale failed to link man to God, and it did not permit a logical end to the process of creation. Johnson's rational attack was a fair answer to what was no more than an ingenious rationalization of the problem of evil.[6]

The thinkers who adhered to the idea of the Scale of Being placed man in the scale between beast and angel. He was the highest of physical beings:

> Far as Creation's ample range extends,
> The scale of sensual, mental powers ascends:
> Mark how it mounts, to man's imperial race.

Man's senses were admirably adapted by the Creator to his needs:

> Why has not man a microscopic eye?
> For this plain reason, man is not a fly.
> Say what the use, were finer optics given,
> T'inspect a mite, not comprehend a heaven?
> Or touch, if tremblingly alive all o'er,
> To smart and agonize at every pore?
> Or quick effluvia darting thru the brain,
> Die of a rose in aromatic pain?[7]

Pope developed another corollary of the Chain of Being.

> Respecting man, whatever wrong we call,
> May, must be right, as relative to all.

The best of all possible worlds contained evil for the particular species and for the individual, but this "partial evil" was "universal good":

> All nature is but art, unknown to thee;
> All chance, direction, which thou canst not see;
> All discord, harmony not understood;
> All partial evil, universal good:
> And spite of pride, in erring reason's spite,
> One truth is clear, WHATEVER IS, IS RIGHT.[8]

Great ingenuity was exerted to reveal the compensations for all apparent evils. Between Shaftesbury and Malthus, who justified war, vice, and pestilence as a part of God's beneficent plan to keep population within the means of subsistence, Akenside, Hughes, Addison, Hawkesworth, and Goldsmith made conspicuous attempts to convince the public of the perfection of God's world.[9]

The new Lockian psychology eliminated original sin and provided another ground for optimism. Man's mind was an unspotted tablet at birth on which experience wrote its messages of good and evil. Education was all; heredity nothing. The proper education of a single generation could conceivably transform the world. Time was to reveal that this belief was a bitter fallacy, but it took two centuries of "enlightened" educational experiment and attempted social reform to dash the high hopes of classical psychology.[10]

The older view of man's corrupt nature was retained, however, by more conservative thinkers and more realistic analysts of human nature. The great French moralists, Pascal, La Bruyère, Bayle, and Vauvenargues, painted dark pictures of the power of man's instincts. Locke himself considered man's appetites dangerous unless controlled by the prospect of rewards and punishments. Shaftesbury felt that a cultured gentleman could trust his "moral sense," but conceded that the ignorant must be kept in order by the church. Mandeville erected his ethical, and Adam Smith his economical, theory on the conviction that the selfishness of the individual would effect the good of the community. To Bolingbroke, Shaftesbury's instinctive moral sense was a "Platonic whimsy." Swift scathingly pictured humanity as a "pernicious race of little odious vermin." Churchmen like Edward Young and John Wesley, Blue Stockings like Mrs. Montagu and Hannah More, and humanists like Doctor Johnson were alike distrustful of human nature; but this skepticism scarcely lessened general optimism, for religion, law, education, common sense, and public opinion were regarded as sufficient checks on man's animal nature.[11]

Locke's view of the mind of man at birth can be reconciled with two of the opinions concerning the nature of man prominent during the century; with the realistic view that man is a compound of good and evil, for good and evil may be largely the product of education; and with the Romantic view of man's fundamental goodness and benevolence, provided all the evil is laid to the charge of an educational system and an environment that have not yet been brought to perfection. To most thinkers of the age, unblinded by sentiment, man was a rather unruly beast to be disciplined and tamed. The idea that nature was opposed to grace had been too deeply imbedded in the consciousness of humanity by centuries of Christianity to be easily cast aside, though in the eighteenth century the opposition was generally expressed as one between appetite and reason.

A rapidly increasing material prosperity and a new political security were powerful allies of the speculative optimist. As in the reign of Elizabeth, Englishmen were justly proud of England. The Revolutionary Settlement had removed any serious danger of a Catholic monarch allied to France, whose military power had, in fact, been humbled by Marlborough. The aristocratic *respublica* that was to weather the storms of the eighteenth century and defeat England's enemies in Flanders, in India, and in America was ushered in with the first Hanoverian. The colonial empire grew steadily until the momentary crisis of the American revolutionary period. Commerce was expanding and a rise in prices indicated a similarly expanding industrial economy free from depression. Prophets of evil might declaim against luxury, but their voices were voices crying in the wilderness. For the aristocracy and for the upper middle-class eighteenth-century England seemed to be a favored spot in one of the best of all possible worlds.

Save for the dark days of the American Revolution and the Jacobin baiting interlude paralleling the Terror in France, philosophical pessimists were largely ignored, and yet amidst general optimism and national prosperity individual melancholy—the dreaded Spleen—flourished apace. Some perverse minds attended more to partial evil than to general good. Whether the luxury and idleness of the upper classes, the fogs of the British Isles, the acerbity and virulence of controversy, or the evil humors for which Englishmen were noted abroad were chiefly responsible, this disease, already well known to the Elizabethans as Shakespeare bears witness, was especially prevalent in the eighteenth century and was fully described by Doctor Cheyne as *The English Malady* in 1731. This melancholia which was marked by *tædium vitæ*, inertia, irritability, and gloomy brooding often led to madness and must be carefully distinguished from the "white melancholy" of the Romantics, the pensive maid that haunted ruins and wastelands after twilight to listen to the owl or to the knell of the hours marking the sad passage of time and bringing pregnant realization of the transiency of power and beauty to the poet.[12]

To the classical spirit the Spleen was anathema, something to be fought and overcome. Congreve, Lady Winchelsea, and Addison resisted it. In *The Spleen* Matthew Green traced its origins and suggested temperance, exercise, occupation, and society as useful remedies. With Gray it was a disease; in Collins, Cowper, and Smart it led to madness. Goldsmith fought against it; Sheridan found melancholy at the elbow of his mirth; Johnson was a victim; Boswell had his melancholy fits as he testified in the *Hypochondriack* in which he gave a picture of the melancholy man as distrustful of himself, envious, hopeless, indifferent, irritable, inattentive, torn between indolence and shame, and inclined to distrust a reality so often distorted by his mental states—a picture that was important as a contrast to the "white melancholy" of the Romanticists.[13]

On the dark background of melancholia the Graveyard Poets embroidered their poetic designs. These religious poets turned away from the fair gifts of science and philosophy, the fleeting joys of this world, to thoughts of man's life beyond the grave. Before the end of the seventeenth century serious religious thought had produced the work of Thomas Flatman, of Nahum Tate, of John Norris, and of Mrs. Elizabeth Rowe, but it only began to make its impress on the major writers with the production of Young's *The Last Day* in 1713 and of Parnell's *Night Piece on Death* published posthumously in 1722. Blair's *The Grave*, Young's *Night Thoughts* and the early verses of the Wartons gave extensive vogue to the school of melancholy to which Gray's *Elegy* gave æsthetic immortality.[14]

II

Optimism was strengthened by the dawn of the idea of progress. The theory of man's gradual degeneration propounded by Donne and Godfrey Goodman early in the seventeenth century had been almost forgotten by 1700, but the cyclical theory of history was dominant during the first half of the new century.[15] Precedents for the belief in cycles were found in Greek thought, and the rise and fall of empires lent illustrative support. The eighteenth-century mind was particularly impressed by the Gothic gap or downward movement between the high periods of Rome and Renaissance. The men who held this pre-Spenglerian theory could reverence antiquity, and yet be awake to improvement everywhere in their own time. To

Shaftesbury, for instance, history was the record of man's repeated rise and fall:

. . . from woods and wilderness, to cities and culture, again into woods; one while barbarous, then civilized, and then barbarous again; after darkness and ignorance, arts and sciences, and then again darkness and ignorance as before.

Henry Brooke developed the same idea in *The Fool of Quality*, and Boswell combined a belief in cycles with a firm conviction that in his own day science was progressing and the arts of comfort were on the increase.[16]

Before the belief in steady progress could triumph over the idea of the eternal ebb and flow in human affairs many prepossessions had to be removed. Classicism was indeed bound hand and foot to the notion of an unchanging law for the world of nature and the world of man. The universality of art, the unchanging standard of taste, the eternal truths of morality had logical validity only if man was everywhere and forever essentially the same beneath surface divergences of speech, costume, and social institutions. The development of historical criticism, which paralleled the expanding idea of progress, was in time to shake the validity of the Rules and the proud pre-eminence of Greece and Rome to their foundations, but for decades the idea of progress was checked by a belief in immutable law, which justified a neglect of history, by the theological belief in man's corruption and in the end of the world, by the weight of admiration for antiquity which humbled the pride of the moderns, and by the fall of great empires in Egypt, Babylon, Macedon, and Rome. The influence of Greek thinkers strengthened the same belief, for the Greeks tended to value the immutable above the variable and impermanent; to believe that institutions were created by the wisdom of a single legislator rather than evolved by experience; to remain resigned to fate as the order fixed by the gods; or, at best, to feel with the Epicureans that there had been an advance to their own day which was to be followed by a period of ruin.[17] The Renaissance gave modern man a new confidence, despite the fact that the early humanists turned to the past for inspiration and ideals and did their best to create a new Rome in imitation of the old. Ardent Christianity

and fervid reverence for Antiquity had to cool before the notion of
steady progress could become one of the faiths by which men live.
It was in France that the Moderns first won the victory with Fontenelle, who saw mankind progressing forever; with the Abbé de Saint-
Pierre, who extended the idea of progress to include social conditions
and man's moral nature; and with Sebastian Mercier, the author
of the first Utopian novel of the future, *L'An 2440*. In France, also,
the quarrel over the supremacy of the Ancients and the Moderns
resulted in the victory of the writers who were the pride of the court
of the *roi soleil*.[18]

These theories became known in England where meanwhile the
theory of a progressive increase of religious truth had been evolved
to answer the argument of the Deists that a religion necessary to
salvation must have been revealed by a just God universally to all
men at the beginning of time. The orthodox argument implied the
gradual, but steady improvement of men's minds and moral notions.
As man gradually became able to understand and draw profit from
them, God made successive revelations of eternal truth. An analogy for man's gradual discovery of religious truth was found in
the steady development of man's control over the material world
through science. In 1699 John Edwards published his *Compleat History of all the Dispensations of Religion*, in which he supported the
idea of progress in religion by the analogy with scientific progress,
which he reviewed at some length. In 1743 William Worthington
published *An Essay on the Scheme and Conduct, Procedure and Extent of Man's Redemption* in which he not only supported gradual
revelation, but predicted the eventual elimination of sin and evil,
until, after the Millennium, the last days bring a new period of sin
to be ended by the Second Advent of Christ. In 1745 Law's reply to
Tindal's *Christianity as Old as the Creation* entitled *Considerations
on the State of the World with Regard to the Theory of Religion* not
only gave the fullest explanation and defense of the progressive
theory of religious revelation, but by a brilliant *tu quoque* showed
that the religion of nature, because of men's differing mental powers,
was as little universal as Christianity.[19]

Another support for the idea of progress, which served as a prop
for the pride of the Augustans, was the view that the race gains

experience like the individual, with the result that the moderns are in a sense the real ancients. Francis Bacon had presented the idea lucidly:

The opinion which men cherish of antiquity is altogether idle, and scarcely accords with the term. For the old age and increasing years of the world should in reality be considered as antiquity, and this is rather the character of our own times than of the less advanced age of the world in those of the ancients. . . . And as we expect a greater knowledge of human affairs, and more mature judgment from an old man than from a youth, on account of his experience, and the variety and number of things he has seen, heard and meditated upon, so we have reason to expect much greater things of our own age (if it knew but its own strength and would essay to exert it) than from antiquity. . . . Reverence for antiquity has been a retarding force in science.[20]

It was through the conspicuous advance of the physical sciences that the educated public was led to see that Aristotle and the Ancients were not infallible. From speculative and applied science the opposition to Aristotle was transferred to literature and a new basis in reason was sought for the Rules. Bacon's appeal for self-reliance and experiment was echoed not only by the Royal Society, but by Edward Young in his *Conjectures* as well. Joseph Glanvill pointed out material advances and disparaged Aristotle in *The Vanity of Dogmatizing*. Cowley called for independent investigation. Thomas Burnet defended modern learning. Dryden, Thomson, Lady Mary Wortley Montagu, and Hume all preceded Young in specific reference to the progress of science.[21]

Biology, psychology, and economics in time supported the notion of progress. The evolution of man from a less complex animal organism was hinted by Rousseau, made into a "pet" theory by Lord Monboddo, and almost fully displayed by Erasmus Darwin.[22] In psychology Hartley and Priestley traced the growth of complex ideas from simple perceptions, and defended the proposition that complexity both in men's minds and in human institutions denoted advance.[23] The classical economic theory of Adam Smith in *The Wealth of Nations* supported likewise the perfection of a complex society in which an infinity of needs fostered a diversity of production on a level far higher than that of primitive peoples. It was the conviction of the century that English civilization had progressed to a point at which men were more happy, more moral, and more creative than their forefathers had been. The sentimental primitivists were out of keeping with the dominant trend of the times.

III

Much confusion has arisen in the discussion of Augustan ideals because of the hasty conclusion that every attack on luxury was a glorification of the life of nature, every address to the sweet maid Solitude a longing for romantic isolation on the wild mountainside, every plea for simplicity a note of pure primitivism. Such was not the case. To many the simple life meant a bourgeois existence of moderate ease with friends, a garden, and one's books—an existence as unromantic as that of the professional man today. To others it meant an assertion of middle-class worth against aristocratic degeneracy; to still others a reaction—present in all advanced civilizations—against an elaborate and sophisticated code of life, in which delight in the pastoral mode, in Dresden shepherdesses and Watteau fêtes champêtres was a delicious aspect of an insincere game played in a social paradise of dainty devices.

Before sketching the compromise between complexity and simplicity that is so important for a correct understanding of the eighteenth century a few words must be devoted to the full-hearted supporters of luxury. It is not to be expected that the court poets and court dramatists of the Restoration in their newly found haven at Whitehall should long for the hardships of the simple life which they had so recently tasted in exile. Their work is notably free from primitivism, but they took their luxury as they found it and seldom sought to justify it. By the turn of the century the movement of social life, the growth of commerce, and the first beginnings of machine industry drew patriotism to the side of luxury. The Whig panegyrists headed by Addison and Thomson responded to the call, though there was much confusion, in Thomson especially, between the glorification of English trade and the lament for the passing of the virtues of the traditional English yeomanry. To this general pride in England's greatness, economics added a new support for luxury in the theory of expanding consumption necessary to parallel the in-

dustrial expansion of the period. This economic argument aligned
men like Adam Smith and David Hume on the side of luxury.[24]

In 1691 Dudley North had shown that simplicity of life enforced
by sumptuary laws could not make a nation great. Mandeville
pointed out that luxury

> Employ'd a million of the poor
> And odious pride a million more.

Chesterfield followed Mandeville at a distance. Prior, Young,
Thomson, and Glover were all advocates of an expanding commerce.
Hume defended luxury all along the line. Luxury, Boswell believed,
was the incitement "to everything great and elegant in society, to
all our commerce, and to almost all our arts"; while a "return to
nature" would produce narrowness and torpidity of mind together
with the loss of positive pleasures. Thomas Warton thought that refinement was more conducive to virtue than was simplicity. Goldsmith showed that luxury stimulated knowledge, increased happiness,
and gave livelihood to thousands; though he was later to sing his
sentimental palinode in *The Deserted Village*.[25]

The ideal life of the eighteenth century was that of the country
gentlemen. It had the sanction of Virgil, Horace, and the Epicureans,
and seemed to satisfy the Aristotelian doctrine of the Golden Mean.
In England Abraham Cowley preferred

> that sort of people whom King James was wont to call the happiest of our
> nation, the men placed in the country by their fortune above a high-constable,
> and yet beneath the trouble of a justice of peace, in a moderate plenty, with-
> out any just argument for the desire of increasing it by the care of many
> relations, and with so much knowledge and love of piety and philosophy . . .
> as may afford him matter enough never to be idle though without business;
> and never to be melancholy though without sin or vanity.

To Cowley the seat of freedom and virtue

> Is in the golden mean,
> She lives not with the poor, nor with the great.[26]

Pomfret's *The Choice* (1700) "was read for a hundred years because it perfectly expressed the universal longing for a life of moderation, composure, and thoughtfulness passed in rural surround-

ings."[27] Many of Pomfret's contemporaries not only read his verses, but expressed similar ideas. Addison wished to escape the hurry and fatigue of an ambitious career. Budgell esteemed moderation in fortune. Pope's praise of study, exercise, and ease in *Windsor Forest* was perhaps not perfectly sincere, but Defoe was doubtless expressing the views of his Dissenting reading public when he let Crusoe's father tell the future mariner that his

> was the middle state . . . which he had found by long experience was the best state in the world, the most suited to human happiness, not exposed to the miseries and hardships, the labour and sufferings, of the mechanic part of mankind, and not embarrassed with the pride, luxury, ambition, and envy of the upper part of mankind.

Hume wrote an essay in praise "Of the Middle State of Life," and Goldsmith pictured in *The Vicar of Wakefield* the happiness of a moderately well-to-do family:

> The year was spent in a moral or rural amusement, in visiting our rich neighbors, and relieving such as were poor. We had no revolutions to fear, nor fatigues to undergo; all our adventures were by the fire-side, and all our migrations from the blue bed to the brown.[28]

Cowper's choice also was the domestic life "in rural leisure pass'd" with his friends, his books, and his pen where one could hold fast to the golden mean. There had been no change from Cowley at the dawn of the period to Cowper at its dusk.[29]

Attacks on luxury imply neither admiration for the Noble Savage nor conviction of the happiness of the poor. It was *excessive* luxury that annoyed the moralists, who were for the most part unromantic members of the middle class. The most spirited attack was John Brown's *Estimate of the Manners and Principles of the Times,* but Brown was primarily concerned with the growing effeminacy and political corruption which threatened the fall of empire. To Brown and his followers Juvenal furnished the requisite quotations from the classics and, even before Gibbon's *Decline and Fall,* Rome was the stock example. In 1788 Lord Kames gave a brief, but spirited picture of the historical progression:

> In all times luxury has been the ruin of every state where it prevailed.

Nations originally are poor and virtuous. They advance to industry, commerce, and perhaps to conquest and empire. But this state is never permanent: great opulence opens a wide door to indolence, sensuality, corruption, prostitution, perdition.

The point-of-view represented by Lord Kames had echoed down the century. It is found in Addison, Dennis, Swift, Fielding, Dyer, Thomson, Akenside, Goldsmith, Richard Price, and Cowper. Cowper's fear of excessive luxury is sounded in *Table Talk:*

> But that effeminacy, folly, lust,
> Enervate and enfeeble, and needs must,
> And that a nation shamefully debas'd
> Will be despis'd and trampled on at last,
> Unless sweet penitence her pow'rs renew,
> Is truth, if history herself be true.[30]

Other objections to luxury were found in its injury to health. Addison pointed out that hale constitutions are found only

among the meaner sort of people, or in the wild gentry, who have been educated among the woods and mountains: whereas many great families are insensibly fallen off from the athletic constitution of their progenitors, and are dwindled away into a pale, sickly, spindle-legged generation of valetudinarians.

Joseph Warton, Samuel Johnson, Richard Price, James Beattie, and Lord Monboddo, that early disciple of physical culture, agreed with Addison in upholding temperate living and exercise as a regimen necessary to bodily health.

To Fielding it seemed that the crimes of the poor were stimulated by the lavish living of the rich. Brooke, Beattie, Addison, Wesley, and Hannah More dreaded the evil effect of luxury on purity of morals. The *Lounger* (No. 100) feared the loss of aristocratic prestige in the levelling of all distinction not based on money. Addison and Goldsmith, among men of letters, kept a watchful eye on the balance of trade, which might be upset by a flood of foreign luxury. None of these objections, however, imply any wish to sacrifice material comfort or to turn away from gains in culture to pursue the naïve simplicities of South Sea Islanders or the primitive austerities of medieval anchorites.[32]

IV

The pronouncements of Boswell and Johnson concerning the joys of London life are so well known that it has been too easily assumed that they were quite typical of the age, and that the normal Englishman of the eighteenth century was an urban individual enthusiastic for the wax lights of the playhouse, for the mob at fashionable routs and masquerades, and for the sights of the ill-lit London streets. Only during the Restoration period when court poet and court dramatist hovered, mothlike, round the brilliant flame of Charles II would such a generalization approach accuracy. In that brief day of genius and disgrace Dryden and Pepys throve in the smoke of London; Etherege, Farquhar, Vanbrugh, and Congreve wrote for the sophisticated habitués of the court circle; while Rochester and Sedley, Roscommon and Dorset appealed to the wits and to the fair, frail ladies of the royal entourage. With the accession of the Hanoverians and the passing of patronage from the court to the landed nobility and its subsequent decline before subscription and public sale, the centers of intellectual life tended to shift from coffee house to manor house, so that suburban and rural estates like Twickenham and Prior Park took over much of the celebrity of Will's.

In Edinburgh and London, it is true, brilliant writers met and matched their wits during the second half of the eighteenth century. At any other period the northern Athens would have been pre-eminent with its brilliant lawyers, critics, historians, and poets— Lords Dalrymple and Hailes, Blair and Kames, Robertson and Hume, Allan Ramsay and Robert Burns. But in the last golden glow of classicism it was the Club of Johnson's London which rivalled in its assemblage of genius, learning, and wit any other group in the development of world culture. Where can one match Johnson and Boswell, Goldsmith and Burke, Fox and Sheridan, Gibbon and Joshua Reynolds? In London, too, Mrs. Montagu held her salon in the famous Chinese room, Mrs. Thrale hung her walls with the portraits of her celebrated guests, and Doctor Burney brought his brilliant daughter Fanny into touch with the great and with the foolish of her day. Sterne paid his visits, Walpole was close at hand at Strawberry Hill, and John Wilkes varied exile with a term as Lord Mayor of London.

Never since have there been such coherent groups, but it is more correct to regard Augustan literature as broadly social than as strictly urban. The man of letters wrote for the social group and expressed, as a rule, not his own feelings, but the will of the class to which he belonged. Often he sought, like Addison and Pope, the co-operation of his friends, or, like Richardson, read his works to a chaste harem who helped to make them a true expression of group feeling. Satire and comedy, *vers de société* and didactic verse could be written only with definite reference to a social group and a social point of view, and these were the dominant literary forms until the emergence of the novel in the middle of the century. The solitary artist breathes forth his soul in lyric strains, or imposes his ego on characters of play and novel in a markedly subjective manner. The literature of the classical period was notably objective. Even memoirs and diaries were seldom confessional; their wit plays like lightning over the social horizon as they describe the amours of Lady Lovemore or the idiosyncrasies of Sir Peculiar Fashion. In the mind of the artist common sense controlled individual sensitivity until well past the middle of the eighteenth century.

It is true that Boswell and Johnson found Fleet Street more entrancing than Greenwich Park; that Johnson, Reynolds, and Gibbon thought that "when a man is tired of London, he is tired of life." It is true that Richardson thought that London smoke was healthy (though he moved into the suburbs), and that the poets who falsified rural pleasures were "madmen"; that Hume regarded the town as the true scene for a man of letters; that Chesterfield found London "le seul sejour d'un honnête homme"; and that Walpole declared, "Were I a physician, I would prescribe nothing but *recipe ccclxv drachm, Londin*." It is also true that many poets who started to sing the charms of nature were engulfed like Pope, Armstrong, Dyer, Thomson, Akenside, Ramsay, and Beattie by the moral and didactic spirit of the age, though not always by the spell of London.[83]

All of this is true, but it is less than half the picture. Gay in *Trivia*,

Swift in "A City Shower" and "A Morning Walk," and Johnson in *London* seemed to be fully aware of the ugliness of the city. Many of the authors already cited hymned the joys of retirement as often as they praised the thrill to be gained by the bustle and glare of London. They loved intellectual and moral pleasures among their books and gardens more than the cynical wit and amorous play of Drury Lane and Covent Garden. Gay, Hill, Granville, Steele, Walsh, Hughes, Mrs. Rowe, Somerville, Broome, Thomson, Dyer, Savage, Boyce, Shenstone, Gray, Armstrong, and the two Wartons all expressed their love for rural ease, though few of them were even mildly romantic.[34]

Among the major writers of the eighteenth century there was more dislike for London than affection for it. The famous passage of Milton, perhaps the most popular poet of the period, must have been present to many minds:

> As one who long in populous city pent,
> Where houses thick, and sewers annoy the air,
> Forth issuing on a summer's morn, to breathe
> Among the pleasant villages and farms,
> Adjoin'd from each thing met, conceives delight:
> The smell of grain, or tended grass, or kine,
> Or dairy; each rural sight, each rural sound.

Cowley wrote: "Happy are they . . . who have not only quitted the metropolis, but can abstain from ever seeing the next market town of their country." Evelyn lamented the exorbitant growth of London. Sir William Temple considered that the narrative of the Garden of Eden showed that God esteemed life in a garden the happiest for man, and he himself passed five years without going to town. The *Guardian*, No. 22, agreed with Temple as to God's intentions in regard to man. Pope did much to develop more natural gardens, and was scornful of those who preferred operas to them. Both in *Joseph Andrews* and in *Love in Several Masques* Fielding pictured the joys of retirement, though for much of his own life he was bound to London. Frances Brooke, Thomas Gray, Mrs. Montagu, Henry Brooke, Adam Smith, and, of course, William Cowper were hostile to the city. A passage from Cowper will reveal the moral abhorrence that was typical of the middle-class attitude that tinged so much of eighteenth-century literature with its special ethical bias. The lines are an apostrophe to London:

> Oh, thou, resort and mart of all the earth,
> Chequer'd with all complexions of mankind,
> And spotted with all crimes; in whom I see
> Much that I love, and more that I admire,
> And all that I abhor; thou freckled fair,
> That pleasest and yet shock'st me, I can laugh
> And I can weep, can hope, and yet despond,
> Feel wrath and pity, when I think of thee!
> Ten righteous would have sav'd a city once,
> And thou hast many righteous.—Well for thee!
> That salt preserves thee; more corrupted else,
> And therefore more obnoxious, at this hour,
> Than Sodom in her day had pow'r to be,
> For whom God heard his Abr'am plead in vain.

In view of this extensive love for a manor-house existence passed in civilized ease equally distant from the smoke and fog of London, and from the sublime horrors of the Peak, it is perhaps unwise to read a completely Romantic implication into Cowper's famous line:

God made the country, and man made the town.[35]

V

The literature of the Augustans is essentially aristocratic. The pious tracts, the chap-books and romances, the political pamphlets and pasquinades read by the butcher, baker, and candlestick-maker have failed to descend to Prince Posterity. They did not form a genuine part of the classical literature of the period, for their readers cared little or nothing for rules and forms, for probability and the Unities. Classical art was not for the masses, but for the courtier, the clergyman, the scholar, and the wealthy and well-educated merchant or banker, who, in the true sense of the word, comprised the aristocracy of the period.

From Lely to Reynolds the canvases of English painters reveal

the refined features of noble lord and noble dame. Architecture then
as always was dependent upon wealth. In literature court patronage
and subscription compelled the artist to appeal directly to the upper-
classes until almost the end of the period. Since the day of the
aristocratic Elizabethan critics—Sidney, Puttenham, and Harington—criticism had largely ignored Italian tales, popular drama,
and folk poetry. Even when the Restoration had passed into the
Age of Anne only Defoe sought a wide popular audience. Defoe,
himself, as well as Locke, Addison, Steele, Prior, Gay, and Congreve, enjoyed government employ or received a government
pension, and most of them looked to patrons or wealthy subscribers
for aid.[36]

During the course of the eighteenth century the basis of appeal
was gradually widened by the growth of the reading public, but
literature was still addressed to the man of taste. The Blue Stockings who surrounded Richardson and Johnson might be the jest of
a Chesterfield or a Walpole, but they were often well educated,
familiar with the classics (at least in translation), and lovers of true
elegance. Even Richardson, risen recently from his printing office,
would have been horrified at Lady Mary Wortley Montagu's
sneering remark that *Pamela* was the delight of chambermaids,
for at the end of the rainbow for Pamela and Harriet Byron there
was the golden promise of reception into the bosom of the aristocracy. Though Addison and Steele sought to fashion a public
opinion to mediate between the courtly libertine and the Puritan
shopkeeper, the readers of the *Tatler* and the *Spectator* were largely
of the fashionable and scholarly classes. It was for them that the
subjects of the papers were chosen, and it was at them that the
authors directed their delicate irony and satire.[37]

The aristocratic spirit of eighteenth-century literature was an
inheritance of the gentlemanly criticism of the Renaissance in Italy,
France, and England. The views of the French Pleiade were representative of continental opinion. The bias of Du Bellay was distinctly
scholarly for he thought that the poet must flee "inept admirers"
and "the ignorant people—the people who are the enemies of all rare
and antique learning—, and . . . content himself with few readers,
following the example of him who did not demand for an audience

any one besides Plato himself." Boileau reveals the continuance of the tradition:

> Travaillez pour la gloire, et qu'un sordide gain
> Ne soit jamais l'objet d'un illustre écrivain.
> Je sais qu'un noble esprit peut, sans honte et sans crime,
> Tirer de son travail un tribut légitime;
> Mais je ne puis souffrir ces auteurs renommés
> Qui dégôutés de gloire et d'argent affamés
> Mettre leur Appolon aux gages d'un libraire,
> Et font d'un art divin un métier mercenaire.

In England Ascham censured poets for seeking to please "the humour of a rude multitude." Gabriel Harvey praised Spenser's lost *Dreams* for being "a degree or two . . . above the reach and compass of a common scholar's capacity." Webbe paraphrased from Horace: "The common people's judgment of poets is seldom true, and therefore not to be sought after." The whole tenor of Sidney's *Apologie* was aristocratic, and even Jonson, the satirist of vulgar humors, scorned the verdict of the multitude.[38]

Dennis echoed Milton in prizing the verdict of the few. Shaftesbury started with the light of nature, but developed "the notion of moral excellence as dependent upon a refined taste for beauty, proportion, and grace in the moral life . . ., a notion whicn leads him into an aristocratic exclusiveness that paved the way for the fashionable cultivation of sensibility throughout the century." Pope spoke of

> The many-headed monster of the pit;
> A senseless, worthless, and unhonoured crowd.

Chesterfield took pride in manners, taste, and learning, though not in mere birth. Reynolds felt that the painter who lusted after fame would come to have vulgar views and his taste would soon be corrupted, for "the vulgar will always be pleased with what is natural, in the confined and misunderstood sense of the word."[39]

In politics the eighteenth-century regime was aristocratic also. The tyranny of the Stuarts was overthrown not by a mass democracy wielding the weapons of universal suffrage, but by an aristocracy of large landowners and wealthy merchants who felt that government was designed to protect property, and that the intelligent

minority with most at stake was best fitted to decide the destinies
of the people at large. Through heavy property qualifications for
suffrage, through a tradition of large electoral expenditures, and
through the maintenance of pocket boroughs, the aristocratic
democracy of Locke and Burke, of Walpole, Bute, and North kept
itself free from the rule of the mob, that showed itself in the
Middlesex elections and in the Gordon riots as a many-headed
beast to be crushed or flattered, but not enfranchised. The liberty
so often proclaimed by poet and patriot was not to become license;
it was a liberty carefully poised by the system of checks and balances
esteemed so highly by Locke and Montesquieu. At the root of the
political philosophy of the century, as at the root of the conception
of the man of taste, there was a widespread distrust of the capacity
of the common man.[40]

VI

So much has been made of Romanticism as a humanitarian movement that it is well to bear in mind that at least one scholar has
declared that it is doubtful whether the nineteenth century "in laying down noble and generous ideals for the human race to follow
went beyond the humanitarianism of the eighteenth century. Indeed, many feel today that the great leaders of the Enlightenment
marked the farthest advance that men have yet made in the realm
of social progress."[41] The Goddess of Reason, worshipped long before the French Revolution, had much to do with this humanitarian
spirit, for reason pointed out the irrational tangles of the law; it
undermined the supernatural, and taught men that heaven must be
introduced on earth and not sought in an after-world that would
compensate with its streets of gold and its rivers of honey for the
evils of this life; and it pointed out the way to an improvement of
conditions with its theories of the influence of education and environment in a social system where laws of cause and effect were inevitably
operative.[42]

Yet there were distinct differences between the humanitarianism
of the Enlightenment and that of the Romantic Movement. In so
far as pity was founded on emotional sensitivity to pain or evil, in

so far as prisons were reformed because criminals were victims of society, in so far as men believed that all poverty and vice could be rapidly eliminated as the world returned rapidly backward to primitive simplicity; in so far as men believed that humanitarianism necessitated a radical upheaval of the social structure it is possible to detect seeds of Romanticism; though even here it is dangerous to regard attitudes which were held by so many of the significant figures of the eighteenth century as completely Romantic. Normally the age was opposed to *indiscriminate* benevolence; it believed that the poor would be present always in any social system short of Utopia; and it distinctly preferred to better the condition of the suffering classes without turning the world upside down in the process. The chief limitation of classical humanitarianism was, in fact, its failure to face fundamental social and ethical problems.

In the humanitarian movement the influence of Thomson's *Seasons* was important. The followers of Shaftesbury shed "dew-drops of tenderness" for the unfortunate and came to consider the relief of misery as "the most exquisite of all sensations." Even "Estimate" Brown, that early Spengler, prophetic of evil, pointed to the humane spirit as one of the few alleviating features of the age, and Doctor Johnson agreed that "almost all the goodness" of the period consisted in charity.[43]

Scores of writers protested against cruelty to animals. Hospitals, orphanages, and refuges for prostitutes were founded. The London Foundling Hospital (1739) united the support of Handel, who contributed the score of his *Messiah*, of Fielding, of George II, and of a group of high born ladies. By 1786 an institute for repentant prostitutes had cared for 2400 women. Addison, Fielding, and Johnson supported this branch of humanitarianism.[44] Some attempts were made at old-age insurance and model villages for laborers. Kindness to servants was practised by Johnson and Chesterfield in reality and by the Grandisons and Allworthys in fiction.[45] Oglethorpe, a pioneer in the relief of debtors, was followed by Fielding, Richardson, Thomson, Henry Brooke, Cowper, and Doctor Johnson.[46] In a wider sense prison reform was in the air. Thomson paid tribute to an early attempt. Goldsmith and Fielding excoriated existing conditions. John Wilkes gave them his personal attention. In 1777 John Howard published his epoch-making *The State of the Prisons*. Torture was abandoned, but little or nothing was done to lessen capital offenses, and, as every reader of Dickens knows, penology and the law were still crying abuses a century later.[47]

Opposition to the slave trade was slower to develop because of widespread participation in the enormous profits. Humane men like Locke and Berkeley, Oglethorpe and Whitefield supported it. One of the first denunciations was contained in Mrs. Behn's *Oroonoko* and in Southerne's popular dramatization of that story. Defoe attacked slavery in 1702, but later recanted, in part. Thomson, Hume, Adam Smith, Smollett, Sterne, and Mackenzie were conspicuous opponents of the slave trade. Johnson even justified slave rebellions. In 1788 Cowper devoted a group of poems to the Negro question. The same decade witnessed other protests from minor poets, and finally the Romantics came to swell the chorus with such poems as Blake's "Little Black Boy," Burns's "The Slave's Lament," and Hunt's "The Negro Boy." Here again Romanticism was building on foundations laid by classicism.[48]

These evidences are not intended to be exhaustive, but merely representative of the feelings of the major writers of a period so often accused of cynical indifference to social evils. That more such evils were not eliminated is explainable in part by the belief of men like Addison and Fielding that humanitarianism was only a virtue when it operated by rules of reason and duty, in part by certain preconceptions of the age—the whatever-is-is-right philosophy of Pope and Shaftesbury, the belief that severity in the long run was more humane than leniency in that it would be a more effectual deterrent of crime, and the feeling that economic laws were natural laws and the effects of their operation unavoidable. Perhaps these eighteenth-century thinkers were right. Certainly most social workers today have learned the importance of rational control in the exercise of charity. Certainly the sentimental theories of criminology have not ended crime, nor the torrents of Romantic tears eliminated social injustice. After a century of class legislation and industrial "reform" the life of the proletariat is still no bed of roses.[49]

NOTES TO CHAPTER II

1. Herbert Read, *Reason and Romanticism*, London, 1926, pp. 6–7.

2. C. A. Moore, "Shaftesbury and the Ethical Poets," *P. M. L. A.*, XXXI, 293–297.

3. Bury, *Idea of Progress*, p. 75, and Lovejoy, "Optimism and Romanticism," *P. M. L. A.*, XLII, 921–939.

4. Akenside, *Pleasures of the Imagination*. Book II, lines 123–126, 322, 332–337; Pope, *Essay on Man*, lines 43–48; Johnson, *Idler*, No. 37; Stephen, *English Thought in the Eighteenth Century*, II, 65, 71; R. S. Crane, "Anglican Apologetics and the Idea of Progress," *Modern Philology*, XXI, 365 ff.

5. Lovejoy, "Optimism and Romanticism," *loc. cit.*, 921–939; *The Chain of Being*, Cambridge (Mass.), 1936.

6. Burton, *Anatomy of Melancholy*, ed. A. R. Shilleto, London, 1903, II, 196; Sir Thomas Browne, *Works*, ed. Simon Wilkin, London, 1915, II, 371; Locke, *Essay Concerning the Human Understanding*, p. 362; Thomson, in Chalmers, *op. cit.*, XII, 424; Young, *Poetical Works*, I, 6, 154; Beattie, *Dissertations*, I, 84–85; Cooper, *Letters Concerning Taste*, p. 132; Lovejoy, *Optimism and Romanticism*, pp. 921–939; Lois Whitney, *Primitivism and the Idea of Progress*, Baltimore, 1934, pp. 142–145.

7. Pope, *Essay on Man*, Book I, lines 207–209, 193–200. *Cf.*, Locke, *Essay*, p. 214.

8. Pope, *Essay on Man*, Book I, lines 51–52 and the concluding passage of the book. Lovejoy, *op. cit.*, pp. 921 ff.

9. Shaftesbury, *Life, Unpublished Letters, and Philosophical Regimen*, pp. 188, 15–17, 31–32, and *Characteristics*, II, 20, 360; Akenside, *Pleasures of the Imagination*, Book II, lines 705–711, and "For the Winter Solstice" (as originally written); Hughes, *Spectator*, No. 237; Amory, *John Buncle*, p. 4; Addison, *Spectator*, Nos. 69, 115, 120, 121; Hutcheson's views are quoted with complete approval by Joseph Warton, *Essay on Pope*, II, 88; Hawkesworth, *Adventurer*, No. 76; Goldsmith, *Essay III*.

10. Locke, *Some Thoughts Concerning Education*, New York (Harvard Classics), 1910, pp. 9, 47, 195; Bury, *The Idea of Progress*, pp. 165–166.

11. T. O. Wedel, "The Philosophical Background of *Gulliver's Travels*," *loc. cit.*, pp. 438–439, 442; Hobbes, *Leviathan*, Chapter 13; Locke, *Essay*, p. 34; Moore, "Shaftesbury and the Ethical Poets," *loc cit.*, pp. 303–304; Paul Elmer More, *Shelburne Essays*. Sixth Series, New York, 1909, p. 219; Swift, *Gulliver's Travels, A Tale of a Tub, Battle of the Books*, ed. W. A. Eddy, New York (Oxford Standard Edition), 1933, pp. 153–154; Stephen, *English Thought in the Eighteenth Century*, II, 420, 432; Young, *Night Thoughts*, Night VII, lines 1150–1155, 1169–1176, 1179–1180; Johnson, *Rambler*, Nos. 172, 175, and *Idler*, No. 52; Hoxie Fairchild, *The Noble Savage*, New York, 1928, p. 332; Hannah More, *Letters*, p. 140; Reginald Blunt, *Mrs. Montagu, "Queen of the Blues," her Letters and Friendships from 1762–1800*, New York, n. d., II, 252; Richardson, *Correspondence*, VI, 43; Hume, *Essays*, I, 118; Mandeville, *Fable of the Bees*, I, 24.

12. Marjorie Bailey, Introduction to Boswell's *Hypochondriack*, I, 83 ff.; J. W. Draper, *The Funeral Elegy and the Rise of English Romanticism*, New York, 1929, *passim*; Amy Reed, *The Background of Gray's Elegy*, pp. 19–20 *et passim*.

13. Congreve, *Complete Works*, ed. Summers, London, 1923, III, 206; Lady Winchelsea, in *Minor Poets of the Eighteenth Century*, ed. Hugh l'Anson Fausset, London (Everyman's Library), 1930, p. 101; Addison, *Spectator*, No. 26; Pope, *Works*, VI, 181, IX, 275, 330; Gay, *Poetical Works*, ed. G. C. Forbes, Oxford, 1926, pp. 199, 205, 208; Tickell, in Addison, *Works*, I, xiv; Pope's *Eloisa to Abelard*, and *The Elegy to the Memory of an Unfortunate Lady* both show the author's appreciation of the emotional value of gloom and melancholy; Green, *The Spleen*, in *Minor Poets*, ed. Fausset, pp. 209 ff.; Gray, *Letters*, ed. D. C. Tovey, London, 1909, I, 4, 6, 8, 30, 102–103, III, 282; Gosse, *Gray*, pp. 13, 21; Goldsmith, *Works*, ed. J. W. M. Gibbs, London, 1885, I, 425, 448; Walter Sichel, *Sheridan*, New York, 1909, I, 5; Boswell, *Letters*, pp. 12, 14, *Hypochondriack*, No. XXXIX, and *Life of Johnson*, III, 475, *et passim*.

14. Harko de Marr, *History of Modern English Romanticism*, pp. 203 ff.; Draper, *The Funeral Elegy and the Rise of English Romanticism*, *passim*; Amy Reed, *op. cit.*, pp. 61 ff.

15. The early controversy concerning the decay of nature is succinctly treated by R. F. Jones, *The Background of the Battle of the Books*, Washington University Studies, Vol. VII, Humanistic Series, No. 2, St. Louis, 1920.

16. Shaftesbury, *Life, Letters, and Philosophical Regimen*, p. 70; Henry Brooke, *The Fool of Quality*, p. 145; Boswell, *Hypochondriack*, I, 251, II, 52, 148–149.

17. Bury, *op. cit.*, pp. 10–19; A. O. Lovejoy, "Schiller and the Genesis of Romanticism," *Modern Language Notes*, XXXV, 6; F. E. Guyer, "C'est nous qui sommes les anciens," *Modern Language Notes*, XXXVI, 258. *Cf.*, Lucretius, *De Rerum Natura*, Book V.

18. Bury, *op. cit.*, pp. 22–24, 30–31, 66, 109, 140–141, 193 ff.

19. R. S. Crane, "Anglican Apologetics and the Idea of Progress," *Modern Philology*, XXI, 273 ff., 349 ff.; Stephen, *English Thought in the Eighteenth Century*, I, 407.

20. Guyer, *op. cit.*, p. 259; Bury, *op. cit.*, p. 58.

21. Glanvill, *Vanity of Dogmatizing*, pp. 148 ff.; Cowley, *Essays*, p. 27; Dryden, *Essays*, I, 163; Lady Mary Wortley Montagu, *Letters and Works*, ed. W. M. Thomas, London, 886, II, 178; Hume, *Essays*, II, 7; Young, *Conjectures on Original Composition* in *English Critical Essays*, XVI–XVIIIth Centuries, ed. E. D. Jones, Oxford (World Classics), 1922, p. 346; R. F. Jones, *op. cit.*, pp. 142–144; R. D. Havens, "Primitivism and the Idea of Progress in Thomson," *Studies in Philology*, XXIX, 41–51.

22. A. O. Lovejoy, "Monboddo and Rousseau," *Modern Philology*, XXX, 279; C. B. Tinker, *Nature's Simple Plan*, Princeton, 1922, p. 13; Lois Whitney, *Primitivism and Progress*, p. 162.

23. Lois Whitney, *op. cit.*, pp. 179–182.

24. A. O. Lovejoy, Foreword to Lois Whitney, *op. cit.*, p. xviii.

25. Mandeville, *Fable of the Bees*, I, 25, and 108, note 1; Prior, in Chalmers, *op. cit.*, X, 163; Young, *Poetical Works*, II, 321; Thomson, in Chalmers, *op. cit.*, XII, 436; Hume, *Essays*, I, 290–304; Goldsmith, *New Essays*, ed. R. S. Crane, Chicago, 1927, p. 28, and *Citizen of the World*, Letters III, XI, LXXXII; Chesterfield, *Works*, V, 132, 136, 216; R. D. Havens, *The Influence of Milton on English Poetry*, Cambridge (Mass.), 1922, p. 383; R. D. Havens, "Primitivism and the Idea of Progress in Thomson," *loc. cit.*, pp. 41 ff.; Thomas Warton, *History of*

English Poetry, p. 285; Boswell, *Hypochondriack*, I, 158–160; Pinkerton, *Letters of Literature*, pp. 316–320.

26. Amy Reed, *op. cit.*, pp. 38–41; Cowley, *Essays*, pp. 121, 124, 137, 139, 179, 199.

27. G. G. Williams, "The Beginning of Nature Poetry in the Eighteenth Century," *Studies in Philology*, XXVII, 597.

28. Addison, *Spectator*, No. 27; Budgell, *Spectator*, No. 283; Pope, *Works*, I, 354; Defoe, *Robinson Crusoe*, ed. H. C. Hutchins, New York, 1930, p. 2; Hume, *Essays*, II, 376; Moore, *World*, Nos. 16, 174; Goldsmith, *Vicar of Wakefield*, Chapters II, IV; Thomas Warton, in Chalmers, *op. cit.*, XVIII, 97, 98, 100, 108.

29. Cowper, *The Task*, Book III, lines 290–292, Book IV, lines 1–193, and *Poetical Works*, ed. H. S. Milford, Oxford, 1913, p. 314.

30. Lord Kames, quoted by Lois Whitney, *Primitivism and Progress*, pp. 277–278; Addison, *Works*, I, 526–527; Mandeville, *Fable of the Bees*, II, 409; Swift, *Gulliver's Travels*, p. 239; Fielding, *Historical Register for the Year 1763*, Act II, scene 1; Dyer, *Ruins of Rome*; Thomson, *Liberty*, Book III, lines 350–390; Akenside, "Ode IX. To Curio"; John Brown, *An Estimate of the Manners and Principles of the Times*, Dublin, 1757, pp. 20–25, 93; Warton, *Idler*, No. 96; Goldsmith, *Citizen of the World*, Letter CXVII, *New Essays*, p. 81 ff., and *Miscellaneous Works*, p. 581; Cowper, *Table Talk*, lines 394–399; Stephen, *English Thought in the Eighteenth Century*, II, 257.

31. Addison, *Tatler*, No. 148, and *Guardian*, No. 102; Joseph Warton, "The Enthusiast"; Johnson, *Rambler*, No. 33; Richard Price, quoted by Lois Whitney, *Primitivism and Progress*, p. 49; Beattie, The Minstrel, Book I, viii–ix; Lovejoy, "Monboddo and Rousseau," *loc. cit.*, p. 281.

32. Fielding, *The Covent-Garden Journal*, ed. Jensen, New Haven, 1915, I, 19; Henry Brooke, *The Fool of Quality*, p. 144; Beattie, *The Minstrel*, Book I, x–xi, Book II, xvi; Evelyn, *Diary*, pp. 565, 587; Addison, *Tatler*, No. 123; Stephen, *English Literature and Society in the Eighteenth Century*, p. 142; Addison, *Works*, I, 526–527; Goldsmith, *Bee*, No. 5.

33. Boswell, *Life of Johnson*, I, 533–534, III, 5, 202, 202 note I, 287, IV, 390, *Hypochondriack*, II, 16–17, and *Letters*, pp. 21, 276, 449; Johnson, *Rambler*, Nos. 135, 138, and *Idler*, No. 71; Richardson, *Correspondence*, I, 84, II, 246; Hume, *Letters*, I, 3; Chesterfield, *Works*, V, 434; Walpole, *Letters*, I, 381–382, III, 339; Amy Reed, *op. cit.*, p. 161.

34. G. G. Williams, "The Beginning of Nature Poetry in the Eighteenth Century," *loc. cit.*, pp. 587–594.

35. Milton, *Paradise Lost*, Book IX, lines 445 ff.; Cowley, *Essays*, p. 204; Evelyn, *Diary*, p. 575; Temple, "Upon the Gardens of Epicurus"; Pope, *Works*, VI, 383, IX, 307, 440; Fielding, *Joseph Andrews*, Book III, Chapter IV, and *Love in Several Masques*, Act I, scene ii; W. L. Cross, *The History of Henry Fielding*, New Haven, 1918, I, 94; Frances Brooke, *Lady Julia Mandeville*, ed. E. P. Poole, London, 1930, p. 75; Gray, *Letters*, III, 52; Blunt, *Mrs. Montagu*, I, 105; Adam Smith, *The Wealth of Nations*, ed. C. J. Bullock, New York (Harvard Classics), 1909, p. 321; Cowper, *The Task*, Book I, lines 678–749, Book III, lines 835 ff.

36. R. D. Havens, *The Influence of Milton on English Poetry*, p. 129; Gregory Smith, ed. *Elizabethan Critical Essays*, Oxford, 1904, I, xx; Randall, *Making of the Modern Mind*, p. 165; Paul Hamelius, *Die Kritik in der englischen Literatur des 17. und 18. Jahrhundert*, Leipzig, 1897, pp. 38–39, 50.

37. Lady Mary Wortley Montagu, *Letters and Works*, II, 209.

38. J. E. Spingarn, *A History of Literary Criticism in the Renaissance*, New York, 1925, pp. 191, 215, 218; Gregory Smith, *op. cit.*, I, 31, 114–115, 298; Jonson, in Spingarn, *Critical Essays of the Seventeenth Century*, I, 18. Boileau, *Oeuvres*, ed. M. Amar, Paris, n. d., pp. 160–161, 217.

39. Dennis, in Durham, ed., *Critical Essays of the Eighteenth Century*, 1700–1725, New Haven, 1915, p. 128; D. S. Sarma, "Two Minor Critics of the Age of Pope," *Modern Language Review*, XIV, 387; Lois Whitney, *Primitivism and Progress*, p. 38; Pope, *Works*, III, 367; Chesterfield, *Works*, V, 336; Armstrong, *Miscellanies*, II, 210, 224, 274; Reynolds, *Discourses*, ed. Helen Zimmern, London, 1887, p. 73.

40. For political echoes in the literary work of the period see Fielding, *Champion*, May 8, 1740; Gibbon, *Autobiography*, ed. Lord Sheffield, with an introduction by J. R. Bury, Oxford (World's Classics), 1923, pp. 216–217, 258, 277; Goldsmith, *Citizen of the World*, Letter L, and *Vicar of Wakefield*, Chapter XIX.

41. Randall, *Making of the Modern Mind*, p. 365.

42. Preserved Smith, *History of Modern Culture*, II, 578; S. F. Damon, *William Blake. His Philosophy and Symbols*, New York, 1924, pp. 15–16.

43. Moore, "Shaftesbury and the Ethical Poets," *loc. cit.*, pp. 290–291; Cooper, *Letters Concerning Taste*, pp. 111, 117; John Brown, *Estimate*, pp. 13–16; Johnson, *Idler*, No. 4; Walpole, *Letters*, IV, 346 ff., 354.

44. *Spectator*, Nos. 190, 266, 274, 277, 286; *Rambler*, Nos. 107, 170, 171; Richardson, *Correspondence*, V, 97, VI, 108; Hannah More, *Letters*, p. 14; Turberville, ed. *Johnson's England*, I, 330.

45. Addison, *Spectator*, No. 549, and *Guardian*, No. 105; *Guardian*, Nos. 26, 79, 83, 126; Fielding, *Covent-Garden Journal*, Nos. 39, 45; Cross, *History of Henry Fielding*, II, 271–273; Jensen, Introduction to the *Covent-Garden Journal*, I, 24; Armstrong, *Miscellanies*, II, 213; Blunt, *Mrs. Montagu*, I, 9, 164, II, 35–36; *Mirror*, No. 26; Cowper, *Charity*, lines 217–218.

46. Fielding, *Pasquin*, Act IV, scene i, and *Champion*, Feb. 16, 1740; Richardson, *Correspondence*, VI, 27–28; Johnson, *Adventurer*, No. 62, and *Idler*, No. 38; Henry Brooke, *Fool of Quality*, p. 171 ff.; Cowper, *Charity*, lines 282–289.

47. Thomson, in Chalmers, *op. cit.*, XII, 448; Cross, *op. cit.*, II, 37; Sichel, *op. cit.*, I, 120; O. A. Sherrard, *A Life of John Wilkes*, New York, 1930, p. 254; Goldsmith, *Citizen of the World*, Letter LXXX.

48. Moore, "Whig Panegyric Verse, 1700–1760," *P. M. L. A.*, XLI, 389–396; Havens, *Influence of Milton in English Poetry*, pp. 401, and 268, with note 5; Gray, *Letters*, I, 8, with note 3; Thomson, in Chalmers, *op. cit.*, XII, 429; Smith, *Wealth of Nations*, p. 85; Hume, *Essays*, I, 385; Lewis Melville, *The Life and Letters of Tobias Smollett*, New York, 1927, p. 304; Sterne, *Tristram Shandy*, Book IX, chapter 6; Mackenzie, *Julia de Roubigné*, pp. 208–212; Cowper, *Poems*, pp. 371 ff., 415; John Scott, *Critical Essays*, p. 278.

49. Addison, *Spectator*, No. 177; Fielding, *Covent-Garden Journal*, Nos. 44–45; Turberville, ed. *Johnson's England*, I, 330; Shaftesbury, *Life, Letters, and Philosophical Regimen*, p. 90; Mandeville, *Fable of the Bees*, I, 274, 311; Cobban, *Edmund Burke*, pp. 191–193.

CHAPTER III

COMMON SENSE

COMMON sense is an element of natural intelligence which each man possesses in equal measure with all other men. "Good sense," proclaimed Descartes, "is the most widespread thing in the world." Since every man has by nature an equal measure of this common sense it would seem that no differences could arise in the opinions of men. In the self-evident axioms of mathematics no difference does arise, but in complicated problems men use their powers of reasoning differently so that erroneous opinions result from incorrect methods of thought; or else reason falls under the dominion of passion, of fancy, or of pedantic logic so that the conclusions to which men come are not the conclusions of common sense at all.[1]

In England Hobbes connected common sense with nature and with the knowledge of consequences based upon the calculation of probabilities—a connection of the highest importance for classical art for it shows the rule of probability in epic or dramatic fable to be based on common sense. According to Hobbes, "all men by nature reason alike, and well, when they have good principles." Men err looking for "somewhat beyond nature, and thus miss the truths nature presses upon them. . . ." Meanwhile theologians like Cudworth and Whichcote were contending that the essence of truth was discernible by common sense, which to them was a rational faculty already verging on intuition or instinct.[2]

From the basic identification of common sense with the individual's share of the light of nature significant derivative meanings arose in which group consciousness was implied. Common sense was the viewpoint of enlightened men, the concurrence of competent judges in contrast to the eccentricities of the individual who fol-

lowed whim and singularity. In this aspect common sense was the
essential basis of satire and comedy, expressions of group censure
against individual absurdity. Common sense became an aristocratic
perquisite, for the lower classes were prejudiced and consequently
incapable of using effectively the common sense which they possessed.[3]

Even more significant was the shift of emphasis from rationalism
to intuition. As early as 1675 Rochester identified sense, which he
called the light of nature, with instinct as opposed to reason. Samuel
Johnson himself made a similar identification, and by the end of
the eighteenth century common sense had become "a natural faculty
of the heart by which eternal law can be recognized." Using the
word in this sense Godwin wrote to Thelwall:

To quote authorities is a cold business, it excites no responsive sentiments
and produces no heart-felt conviction. . . . Appeal to that eternal law which
the heart of every man of common sense recognizes immediately.

In *The Philosophy of Rhetoric* Campbell explains clearly the
relation of common sense to intuition. What the mind perceives
"immediately on a bare attention to the ideas under review" is perceived intuitively. Mathematical axioms, most perceptions of size
or shape, and ideas of pain and pleasure, of beauty and harmony
are so perceived. Common sense accepts "certain principles in which
we must acquiesce, and beyond which we cannot go, principles
clearly discernible by their own light," which can derive no additional evidence from logic. To reject these principles implies insanity. Statements such as, "Whatever has a beginning has a cause,"
and "The course of nature will be the same tomorrow as today,"
are not capable of logical proof, but without them knowledge
would be impossible. It is common sense working intuitively which
recognizes them as axiomatic.[4]

II

It was this almost intuitive perception of the fitness of things
which controlled the life of the rational man in The Age of Reason.
To Steele a gentleman was simply a reasonable creature. To Gold-

smith politeness seemed to be founded on good sense and good nature. To Chesterfield, who was one of the supporters of the periodical *Common Sense* in 1737, common sense was to the intellect what conscience was to the heart. He was convinced "that no man commits either a crime or a folly, but against the manifest and sensible representations of the one or the other." Even virtue was defended as conformity to common sense. Young wrote that

> All vice is dull,
> A knave's a fool;
> And virtue is the child of sense;

and asked in the later *Epistle to Mr. Pope*, "What is virtue but superior sense?"[5]

Since the virtuous gentleman was supposedly ruled by common sense it was only to be expected that common sense should hover over play and essay as the invisible standard of appeal by which the laughter of the social group could be directed by the Congreves and the Addisons against nonconformers with the social code. Common sense was the guide of the comic spirit, as George Meredith was to point out more than a century later. By its light the cries of the London streets and the petticoats and high heels of the London ladies were ridiculed. By its light the nation, tired of Puritan individuality, sought to banish eccentricity and to restore order and sobriety of judgment. By its light the seventeenth-century characters of Overbury, Earle, and Butler, and the eighteenth-century journeys of Oriental travelers were composed; for the "characters" were types designed to picture the golden mean of common sense or to warn against any divergence from it, and the Persian and Chinese visitants were not so much evocations of the romantic Orient as technical devices for bringing criticism, free from prepossession and prejudice, to bear on the accumulated absurdities of complex Western European civilization.[6]

So it was in Goldsmith's *Citizen of the World*, for Lien Chi Altangi was an Oriental only in name, planned by his creator as an embodiment of common sense, "entirely a stranger" to English manners and customs. In the light of his common sense, signs and wigs, virtuosi collectors and lawyers engrossed in precedents, the preoccupation with remote astronomical calamities, and the indiscriminate charity of the Man in Black were successively rebuked. The use of the Oriental traveler in satire, as well as the employment of Oriental apologue or allegory, can be regarded as pre-Romantic only in the rare cases in which an effort was made to develop the exoticism of the East. Such was not often the case in the work of Addison, Hawkesworth, or Johnson. The true attitude of the age is revealed in the advice of Pope and Warburton to Richardson upon the appearance of *Pamela*. These representative classicists wished Richardson to employ Pamela as a sort of Indian who could bring her unbiased judgment to bear on everything she saw in high life just "as simple nature dictated"—an association of ideas which shows that the age was interested in the Oriental only as he partook of the common light of nature and was free from the prepossessions of custom.[7]

III

In the literature of the neo-classical period the school of common sense played an important role. Fundamentally, its proponents wished to apply the common light of reason to the criticism of art without any interference from accumulated rules or deductions from sanctified models. In its purest form such a school believed that Malherbe's servant and Molière's cook could be used as standards by which to judge the potential effects of new literary compositions. Boileau, who recounted these anecdotes of his predecessors, did not think that such a test was universally practicable, but he did believe that the public—in whom common sense was not obscured by learning—was an incorruptible judge, and, like D'Aubignac and Corneille, he relied on common sense for the support of the rules.[8]

In England the school of common sense was born with *The Rehearsal* (1671), an attack on heroics from the standpoint of reason, which remained popular for a hundred years. Thomas Rymer was the real leader of the English group. He thought that the reasonable nature of a dramatic plot could be detected by common sense: "Rarely have I known the *women-judges* mistake in these points, when . . . left to their own heads, they decided with their own sense." *The Tatler* represented a debate between a young woman "who had that natural sense which makes her a better judge than a thousand critics," and Sir Timothy Tittle, one of those men who "without entering into the sense and soul of an author has a few general rules, which, like mechanical instruments, he applies to the works of every writer, and as they quadrate with them, pronounces the author perfect or defective." There is no doubt that the young lady had the support of *The Tatler*. *The Guardian* carried on the battle by presenting a foot-soldier who was genuinely moved at a tragedy as "the politest man in a British audience, from the force of nature, untainted with the singularities of an ill-applied education."[9]

By the light of common sense opera was found absurd. Steele and Addison, Dennis and Fielding, Johnson and Chesterfield regarded it as childish, anachronistic, improbable, and illegitimate in its confusing blend of art forms.[10] Common sense was at its worst in the critique of Italian opera but in seeking a rational basis for the Rules in the acquiescence of reasonable men everywhere, in founding realistic art on the identification of truth with normal probability, in checking the extravagances of metaphysical wit, and in the quest for a universal standard of taste resting on universal good sense the age made effective use of common sense.[11] The basis of the Rules in common sense is admirably illustrated in the *Discourses* of Joshua Reynolds. Questions of taste can be settled

by an appeal to common sense deciding upon the common feelings of mankind. This sense, and these feelings, appear to me of equal authority, and equally conclusive. Now this appeal implies a general uniformity and agreement in the minds of men. It would be else an idle and vain endeavor to establish rules of art; it would be pursuing a phantom, to attempt to move affections with which we were entirely unacquainted.

A man acquainted with different works of divers countries and ages has more materials, and more means of knowing what is analogous to the mind of man. . . . What has pleased, and continues to please, is likely to please again: hence are derived the rules of art.[12]

On the same foundation Blair erected his *Principles of Rhetoric*. Into common sense all qualities could be resolved, if one can accept the opinion of André Chenier:

C'est le bon sens, la raison qui fait tout,
Vertu, génie, esprit, talent et goût.
Qu'est ce vertu? raison mise en pratique;
Talent? raison produite avec éclat;
Esprit? raison qui finement s'exprime;
Le goût n'est rien qu'un bon sens delicat;
Et le génie est la raison sublime.[18]

IV

The role of common sense will be clarified by observing its opposites. The seventeenth century had prized wit and conceit which implied an ingenuity or quickness of fancy too often remote from the workings of the normal mind. Augustan common sense was a reaction against this fantasticality which had run to seed in Cowley, Cleveland, and Benlowes. The Age of Pope recaptured what Doctor Johnson was to call "the grandeur of generality" and disparaged invention to the degree that Pope could plausibly define wit as

What oft was thought but ne'er so well expressed.

The acolytes of common sense were propriety, clarity, regularity, and force. Sensibility and imagination were disparaged. Fancy was exalted only by "madmen or fools."[14]

Common sense was often opposed to imagination and fancy. Bacon had assigned poetry to the sphere of the imagination, but he considered poetry itself trivial and lamented that men's affections were not "pliant and obedient to reason," and their characters not firm enough to forego the consolations of poetic fiction. Naked proposition and proof would replace imaginative rhetoric in Bacon's ideal state, where scientific investigation, not art, would occupy men's minds.[15] Seventeenth-century France chimed in. Chapelain considered that good sense was of more service to the poet than learning. The rules were the codification of sense. The opinions of Aristotle and the conclusions of reason were demonstrably the same. The age was marked by the prevalence of sense over fancy, and the dominance of reason in the kingdom of taste. This opinion propounded by D'Aubignac, Corneille, Molière, La Fontaine,

Racine, Boileau, and Saint-Évremond became current in England after the Royal Society had prepared the ground.[16]

Boileau was popular in translation, but the exiled Saint-Évremond provided a personal link with French criticism for many Restoration writers. He esteemed reason more than rule, solidity of sense more than invention. As an opponent of the classics and of the fantasies of the metaphysical tradition he was a powerful ally of Davenant, Hobbes, Sprat, Dryden, and Mulgrave in founding the school of sense. It was Mulgrave who declared that "without judgment, fancy is but mad." It was Locke who identified the law of nature and the law of reason, and feared the guidance of the imagination. A man's

fancy and passion must needs run him into strange courses if reason, which is the only star and compass, be not that he steers by. The imagination is always restless and suggests variety of thoughts, and the will, reason being laid aside, is ready for every extravagant project.

Pope esteemed sense more vital than taste. Warburton thought wit injurious to common sense,

for wit consisting in choosing out, and setting together such ideas from whose assemblage pleasant pictures may be drawn on the fancy, the judgment, through an habitual search of wit, loses, by degrees, its faculty of seeing the true relation of things; in which consists the exercise of common sense.[17]

In *A Tale of a Tub* Swift scornfully explained the power of imagination over men's minds. When fancy and imagination subdue reason and the senses, common sense is kicked out of doors and a man consoles himself for the pettiness of reality by the magnificence of fiction. As Swift scornfully notes, "happiness . . . is a perpetual possession of being well deceived," since few men are strong enough to toss away artificial light and varnish and tinsel, and to look in the glass of nature. Doctor Johnson was equally aware of the alluring snares of the imagination. Let a man but begin to "conceive himself what he is not" and

. . . in time, some particular train of ideas fixes the attention; all other intellectual gratifications are rejected; the mind, in weariness or leisure, recurs constantly to the favorite conception, and feasts on the luscious falsehood, whenever she is offended with the bitterness of truth. By degrees the reign of fancy is confirmed; she grows first imperious, and in time despotic. Then fictions begin to operate as realities, false opinions fasten upon the mind, and life passes in dreams of rapture or anguish.[18]

If classicism can be shown to be a coherent code based on common sense buttressed by the scientific view of nature as the norm, the attitude of Bacon, Locke, Pope, Swift, and Johnson must be regarded as the logical position for the classicist to hold. However, the wave of opposition to a completely rational foundation for the arts soon started its sweep towards the shores of Romanticism. Some of this opposition is seen in the developing love for the strange superstition of Norseman and Celt, in a revival of interest in Spenser's irrational knights and ladies, in a recrudescence of man's will to escape by dreaming from the too severely logical world of Newtonian mathematics and the too neatly rational life of the golden mean. There were always rebels against reason, for, as Swift knew, sanity and moderation have always had less general appeal than sentimentality and humbug. In the Prologue to *Tyrannick Love* (1669) Dryden proclaimed the right of men to be well deceived by Heroic Tragedy. Before he was in his grave the old gospel of Longinus, as interpreted by his disciple Boileau, revealed the function of poetry to be the creation of ecstasy. The marvellous, not the convincing, cast the most effective spell. Pope was at times restive under the yoke of sense. He was intrigued by the fancy of Provençal poetry and of Persian tales, and confessed to "an inclination to tell a fairy tale, the more wild and exotic the better," or to try his hand at a *vision*, which is "confined to no rules of probability."[19]

Passing on to the mid-eighteenth century one finds Lord Lyttelton representing Boileau in one of the *Dialogues of the Dead* censuring "common-place morals in very smooth verse, without any absurdity, but without a single new thought, or one enlivening spark of imagination." Edward Young placed poetry "beyond prose reason": poets who think otherwise are infidels to their divinity. The two Wartons extolled imagination and Richard Hurd lamented the scientific revolution in human thought in a famous passage:

What we have gotten by this revolution, it will be said, is a great deal of good sense. What we have lost is a world of fine fabling; the illusion of which is so grateful to the charmed spirit; that, in spite of philosophy and fashion, Faery Spenser still ranks highest among the poets.[20]

Thus the proponents of sense and of imagination battled each other. Other battles had to be fought as well. Common sense as a guide to the practical conduct of life was opposed to the learning of the schools. The man of sense placed emphasis on observation, experience, and the wisdom gained from contacts in society. He expected the poet to be a man living among men, not a scholastic pedant in the cloistered walls of the university, nor a hermit on the lone hillside. *The Tatler* and *The Spectator* ridiculed pedantry. Addison proclaimed his intention of writing against "editors, commentators, interpreters, scholiasts, and critics; in short, all men of deep learning without common sense." It seemed to Addison that the "worst kind of pedants among learned men are such as are naturally endued with a very small share of common sense, and have read a great number of books without taste or distinction." It was probably Steele who, in *Tatler*, No. 30, found a good mien and good manners more useful than the mere lumber of learning, which could not bring happiness without good sense. Learning itself, he declared, was not knowledge: knowledge was the application of common sense in the use of learning. John Hughes thought that "a plain unlettered man is always more agreeable company, than a fool in several languages." Pope warned the readers of the *Essay on Criticism* that good sense could be defaced by false learning, and with the arrogance of ignorance attacked men more learned than he in the text and notes of the *Dunciad*. It was in the *Memoirs of Martinus Scriblerus*, however, that Pope, Swift, Arbuthnot, and Gay immortalized the pedants, Cornelius and Martinus, father and son, most brilliantly. In a later period Doctor Johnson proclaimed with his accustomed pontifical air: "To enter the school of wisdom is not the peculiar privilege of geometricians; the most sublime and important precepts require no uncommon opportunities, no laborious preparation." Looking back on the work of Pope, Johnson declared that its fundamental intellectual principle was good sense. It should be apparent from the preceding pages of this study that this opposition of common sense to learning was quite in keeping with the conception of a universal light of nature.[21]

Common sense was also opposed to the flimsy fabrics of pure logic. Metaphysics had no charms for the school of sense. Hobbes opposed natural reason to metaphysical speculation, which Bolingbroke thought a subject fit only for a madman. The inhabitants of the flying island in *Gulliver's Travels* reveal the attitude of Swift, which had not changed since his school days in Dublin. Pope printed in the *Dunciad* a satiric picture of the scholar who takes the *a priori* road to truth:

> Let others creep by timid steps, and slow,
> On plain experience lay foundations low,
> By common sense to common knowledge bred,
> And last, to Nature's cause, thro' Nature led. . . .
> We nobly take the high Priori road,
> And reason downward, till we doubt of God; . . .

Lord Chesterfield gave his son some good advice in contrasting common sense to pedantry and to logic:

Read and hear, for your amusement, ingenious systems, nice questions subtilely agitated, with all the refinements that warm imaginations suggest; but consider them only as exercitations for the mind, and return always to settle with common sense.

The Connoisseur declared that common sense, not metaphysical subtlety, was the best sense. Fielding, Gray, Boswell, and Thomas Warton all distrusted metaphysics, while Cowper apostrophized common sense to come to his aid:

> Defend me, therefore, common sense, say I,
> From reveries so airy, from the toil
> Of dropping buckets into empty wells,
> And growing old in drawing nothing up!

For Cowper the "empty wells" were the deep speculations of hyper-rational metaphysicians.[22]

Such was the common-sense ideal; founded on a belief in universal reason open to all men it aimed to fashion life and art in its own image, to oppose its clear and steady light to the fireflies of fancy and to the sudden bursts of illumination of the poetic imagination, and to show how empty were the structures of the logician and how dusty the cogitations of mere scholars. In art the victory of common sense was never complete, for feeling and imagination always had their proponents. In its application to the daily lives of men limitations were imposed on Queen Common Sense, as Fielding called her, by certain persistent thought currents of the period —the doctrine of the ruling passion, the admiration for animal instinct, the theory that man was a mechanism controlled by pleasure and pain, the survival of philosophic pyrrhonism, and the elevation of imagination and belief by Hume to the dominant place in man's life.

▼

Paul Van Tieghem considers the reaction against the Enlightenment to be a common feature of all pre-Romanticisms.[28] The innate tendency of man to dream and to hope "against experience," as well as his attempt to sentimentalize and emotionalize a world he cannot stomach led to the triumph of Romanticism, but certain qualifications on common sense were so fully developed during the eighteenth century that they must be considered a part of classicism itself.

In much the same fashion in which Ben Jonson had pictured man's personality as dominated by one of the various humors which colored his whole outlook on life, so, in the Age of Anne, writers like Pope spoke of the "ruling passion" to which all of a man's actions were subservient. Through devious channels a man followed the darling passion of his heart, whether it were love of fame, love of riches, or love of power. To this one aim every action of a man tended; common sense, common decency, even life itself might well be sacrificed if the ruling passion could be appeased. By this ruling passion men were driven like derelicts before the wind, powerless to alter their courses. Passion, not common sense, was the gale that blew them on. This view, popularized by Pope in his *Moral Essays*, was not original with him. Montaigne, Spinoza, La Rochefoucauld, Pascal, Fontenelle, and Bayle had all insisted that reason was often the tool of passion. In addition to this concurrence of opinion based on the observation of human nature, the theory of the ruling passion had the support not only of the Jonsonian comedy of humors as continued in the work of Shadwell, but also of the traditional interpretation of personality in the seventeenth-century type "characters" of Overbury, Earle, and Butler, which in turn can be traced easily to Theophrastus and the *Ethics* of his master, Aristotle.[24]

Admiration for the instinct of animals likewise revealed suspicion of reason on the part of many classicists. In his illuminating *Critical Study of Gulliver's Travels*, W. A. Eddy has traced this praise of animals from Plutarch's version of Ulysses and the Beasts to the Houyhnhnms of Swift—the most famous example of the antithesis between man and beast in the eighteenth century. From Burton to Cowper the thought found expression in English literature. Burton found beasts more contented with nature:

> When shall you see a lion hide gold in the ground, or a bull contend for a better pasture? When a boar is thirsty, he drinks what will serve him, and no more; and when his belly is full, he ceasest to eat, but men are immoderate in both; as in lust, they covet carnal copulation at set times, men always, ruinating thereby the health of their bodies.

Sir Thomas Browne thought that reason might well go "to school to the wisdom of bees, ants, and spiders." Rochester extolled beasts in *A Satyr Against Mankind*, since they attain their end "by surest means," while man with all his boast of reason errs "fifty times for one." Addison praised instinct in a series of *Guardian* essays on the ant. Mandeville found animals superior to rational man, and presented the story of the merchant and the lion to enforce his belief in the beast's comparative freedom from cruelty. Prior found it difficult to distinguish animal instinct from human reason. Frances Brooke drew the moral clearly:

> When I see the dumb creation . . . pursuing steadily the purposes of their being, their own private happiness, and the good of their peculiar species, I am astonished at the folly and degeneracy of man, who acts in general so directly contrary to both.

Henry Brooke in *Universal Beauty* pointed to the moral lessons that might be learned from the instinctive goodness of beasts:

> Those rules from insects, birds, and beasts discern
> Which from the Maker you disdain to learn!

The social friendship, and the firm ally,
The filial sanctitude, and nuptial tie,
Patience in want, and faith to persevere,
Th'endearing sentiment, and tender care,
Courage o'er private interest to prevail,
And die all Decii for the public weal.

Cowper closes a long succession of skeptics as to man's superiority with a quatrain from "The Doves":

Reas'ning at every step he treads,
    Man yet mistakes his way,
While meaner things, whom instinct leads,
    Are rarely known to stray.[25]

Equally opposed to the complete supremacy of common sense in the lives of men was the psychological theory which represented the human will as moving, more or less instinctively, in response to stimuli of pleasure or of pain. Only in the case of comparatively dull stimuli could reason choose to suffer present ill to gain a future bliss. Desire compelled the will, and the rational choice of right by a free agent became a negligible consideration for the early mechanist who believed that man could be made a social creature only by the clever maneuvers of church and state to align Hell and Tyburn on the side of the possible pain liable to result from antisocial actions. In England Hobbes first promulgated this egoistic theory of morals, which Locke developed and tried to reconcile with orthodoxy by showing that the prospect of eternal rewards or punishments must determine the choice of any man "against whatever pleasure this life can show." Bernard Mandeville, by defining a rational act as one in which emotion played no part, and a virtuous act as one in which a man acted "contrary to the impulse of nature . . . out of a rational ambition of being good" completely denied the force of reason and virtue in controlling a man's actions. In Mandeville's cynical scheme flattery was employed as a pleasant inducement by scheming politicians to keep the masses content and submissive to their plans. Restraint was compensated by pride in public approbation, and forgiveness and humility were subtly represented as more Godlike than revenge. Public esteem gave its pleasant rewards to those who were willing to acquiesce in the social scheme dictated by the group who could control public opinion. Thus, in the work of Hobbes, Locke, and Mandeville the rule of reason was distinctly limited. In the formation of this mechanistic school Gassendi and La Rochefoucauld were influential, and it was in France that the doctrine reached its fullest development with La Mettrie's *L'Homme Machine* (1748), with Condillac's *Traité des Sensations* (1754), and with d'Holbach's *Système de la Nature* (1700).[26]

General skepticism of the capacity of human reason as developed by Sextus Empiricus proved useful to churchmen who wished to exalt faith. Knowledge, the pyrrhonist argued, depends on sense perception. Since the very foundation of knowledge was unsure, how could the elaborate intellectual structures erected on such foundations be certain? So Vivès, Sebond, Boucher, and Belin argued in France; so Montaigne argued in the *Apology of Raymond Sebond*, the *locus classicus* of Renaissance skepticism. Montaigne questioned the value of mental attainments for happiness, and withdrew from intellectual disputes in which no conclusion was possible. In *De la Sagesse* (1601) Charron, only less influential in England than Montaigne, carried on the destructive analysis of human certitudes. In England Sir Thomas Browne and John Dryden paved the way for Mandeville and Swift, who, poles asunder on ethical and religious attitudes, were yet alike in their hostility to intellectual dogmatism.[27]

And then came Hume, the complete pyrrhonist, who in his resolution of human reason into probable beliefs held on a basis of imagination and emotion, put an end to the reign of reason in philosophy, though among laymen, like Johnson, and among second-rate thinkers, like Beattie and Reid, reason still lingered on, ghostlike, to the end of the century. Hume pointed out that

all probable reasoning is nothing but a species of sensation. 'Tis not solely in poetry and music, we must follow our taste and sentiment, but likewise in philosophy. When I am convinc'd of any principle, 'tis only an idea which strikes more strongly upon me. When I give the preference to one set of arguments above another, I do nothing but decide from my feeling concerning the superiority of their influence.

It is custom, operating upon the imagination, that leads men to draw "logical inferences," for reason is simply "a wonderful and unintelligible instinct" and belief is "more properly an act of the sensitive, than of the cogitative part of our nature." Hume was influenced by the egocentric theories of Hobbes and Mandeville to posit self-interest as the original, or natural, motive for the establishment of justice and morality, but he thought that sympathy, inherent in man's nature, explained his usual approbation of moral acts. Having reduced human reason to basic instincts, and common sense to a variety of belief founded in imagination, Hume was compelled to regard morality as a sentiment, guided by "some internal sense or feeling . . . which distinguishes moral good and evil, and which embraces the one and rejects the other." Thus the greatest of the eighteenth-century rationalists reduced reason to impotence and lent support to the rising wave of feeling and imagination. The wheel of rationalism had come full circle—the attempt had been made to impose an ideal of common sense rooted in Cartesian ideology on the lives and artistic productions of men, but the attempt had never succeeded even in the mid-season of classicism. In the conduct of life feeling was opposed to reason; in art, imagination to common sense. In speculative thought the ruling passion, the pleasure-pain motivation of action, and the respect for animal instinct were all opposed to the purely rational attitude. With Hume time brought in his revenges.[28]

NOTES TO CHAPTER III

1. Descartes, *Discours de la Méthode*, in Vial et Denise, *op. cit.*, p. 303; Randall, *Making of the Modern Mind*, p. 222; Lois Whitney, *Primitivism and the Idea of Progress*, pp. 8–9.

2. Hobbes, *Leviathan*, pp. 25–29, 82, 197; Swift, *Correspondence*, III, 209; Pope, *Works*, IX, 360; Whitney, *Primitivism and the Idea of Progress*, pp. 12, 18–19. *Cf.* a quotation from Claude Buffier's *Traité des Premières Vérités*, in E. N. S. Thompson, "The *Discourses* of Sir Joshua Reynolds," *P. M. L. A.*, XXXII, 339, and Steele, *Spectator*, No. 259.

3. This meaning is apparent in many of the usages quoted later in this chapter. It is suggested by Crofts in his article on "Enthusiasm" in *Eighteenth Century Literature. An Oxford Miscellany*, Oxford, 1909, and by Spingarn in the Introduction to *Critical Essays of the Seventeenth Century*.

4. Rochester "Satyr Against Mankind," lines 10–13; Johnson, *Lives of the Poets*, V, 195; George Campbell, *Philosophy of Rhetoric*, Baltimore and Boston, n. d., pp.

57–66; Hoxie Fairchild, *The Romantic Quest*, New York, 1931, p. 31; Stephen, *English Thought*, II, 334.

5. Steele, *The Lying Lover*. Preface; Goldsmith, *Citizen of the World*, Letter XXXIX; Chesterfield, *Works*, V, 173; Young, *Poetical Works*, II, 173, 350.

6. *Spectator*, Nos. 6, 75, 251; *World*, No. 88; Matthew Green, *The Spleen*, line 354; Wood, "Native Elements in English Neo-classicism," *Modern Philology*, XXIV, 201.

7. Goldsmith, *Citizen of the World*, Letters I, II, III, XXXIV, XLI, XCVIII, XCII, XVI, XXVII; Richardson, *Correspondence*, I, 134; W. F. Gallaway, "The Sentimentalism of Goldsmith," *P. M. L. A.*, XLVIII, 1167.

8. Boileau, *Réflexions Critiques sur Longin*, Préface à Epitre X, *L'Art Poétique*, in *Œuvres*, pp. 430, 402, 170, 189; Spingarn, *Literary Criticism of the Renaissance*, pp. 247–248; Spingarn, *Critical Essays of the Seventeenth Century*, I, lxix.

9. Rymer, *Tragedies of the Last Age*, in Spingarn, *Critical Essays of the Seventeenth Century*, II, 183; Goethe to Friederike Oeser, April 8, 1769; Addison, *Spectator*, No. 74; *Guardian*, No. 19; *Tatler*, No. 165. *Cf.* Pinkerton, *Letters of Literature*, pp. 94–95, and D. S. Sarma, "Two Minor Critics of the Age of Pope," *Modern Language Review*, XIV, 386.

10. *Tatler*, No. 4; Steele, *The Funeral*, Act II, scene I, *The Tender Husband*, Epilogue, and *The Conscious Lovers*, Act II, scene II; Addison, *Spectator*, Nos. 5, 13, 18, 28; Dennis, *Taste in Poetry*, in Durham, *op. cit.*, p. 140; Gildon, *Art of Poetry*, in Durham, p. 32; Fielding, *Author's Farce*, Act. III, scene I; Johnson, *Lives of the Poets*, III, 184; Chesterfield, *Works*, V, 295; Hannah More, *Letters*, p. 24.

11. Spingarn, *Critical Essays of the Seventeenth Century*, I, lxv, lxix ff., lxxvii ff.

12. Reynolds, *Discourses*, pp. 115–117.

13. Blair, *Lectures on Rhetoric*, I, 4, 43; Chenier is quoted by Sainte-Beuve, *Causeries de Lundi*, Paris (7ème édition), n. d.

14. Irving Babbitt, *Rousseau and Romanticism*, Boston, 1919, pp. 9–12; Spingarn, *Literary Criticism of the Renaissance*, pp. 239–241; George Williamson, "The Restoration Revolt Against Enthusiasm," *Studies in Philology*, XXX, 588.

15. Murray W. Bundy, "Bacon's True Opinion of Poetry," *Studies in Philology*, XXVII, 244–259; George Williamson, *op. cit.*, p. 573.

16. Deimier, *Académie de l'Art Poétique*, in Vial et Denise, *op. cit.*, p. 70; René Bray, *La Formation de la Doctrine Classique en France*, Paris, 1927, pp. 118–121; G. B. Dutton, "The French Aristotelian Formalists and Thomas Rymer," *P. M. L. A.*, XXIX, 177.

17. John Locke, *Of Civil Government*, London (Everyman's Library), n. d.; Pope, *Works*, III, 175; Warburton, "Notes on an Essay on Criticism," in Pope, *Works*, II, 103; Atterbury to Pope, in Pope, *Works*, IX, 22.

18. Swift, *Gulliver's Travels*, etc., pp. 494–495; Johnson, *Rasselas*, Chapter XLIV; *Rambler*, No. 8. For other passages in which common sense is opposed to imagination see Chesterfield, *Letters*, II, 274; Goldsmith, *Citizen of the World*, Letter XXXIII; Pinkerton, *Letters of Literature*, p. 189.

19. Montaigne, "Of Cato the Elder"; Longinus, *On the Sublime*, I, 3–4; Pope, *Works*, IX, 431, I, 203, note 1.

20. Lyttleton, *Dialogues of the Dead*, quoted A. F. B. Clark, *Boileau and the French Classical Critics in England*, p. 47; Young, *Conjectures on Original Com-*

position in E. D. Jones, *English Critical Essays, XVI–XVIIIth Centuries*, Oxford, 1922, p. 326; Thomas Warton, *History of English Poetry*, pp. 626–627; Joseph Warton, *Essay on Pope*, Dedication to Edward Young; Hurd, *Letters on Chivalry and Romance*, p. 154. For other such passages see W. L. Phelps, *The Beginnings of the English Romantic Movement*, New York, 1893, pp. 107, 145.

21. Addison, *Tatler*, Nos. 105, 158, and *Freeholder*, No. 33; *Tatler*, Nos. 58, 197; Hughes, in Durham, *op. cit.*, p. 79; Pope, *Essay on Criticism*, lines 25–26; Johnson, *Rambler*, No. 54, and *Lives of the Poets*, V, 195.

22. Hobbes, *Leviathan*, pp. 495–497; Cowley, *Essays*, p. 146; Bolingbroke, quoted by Stephen, *English Thought*, I, 178; Gray, *Letters*, I, 3; Swift, *Gulliver's Travels*, p. 186 ff.; Pope, *Works*, IV, 214, X, 310; Chesterfield, *Letters*, I, 273, 406, 409, II, 194; *Connoisseur*, No. 107; Fielding, *Covent-Garden Journal*, Nos. 8, 70; Armstrong, *Miscellanies*, II, 190; Boswell, *Hypochondriack*, II, 126; Thomas Warton, *History of English Poetry*, p. 923; Cowper, *The Task*, Book III, lines 187–190.

23. Van Tieghem, *Le Preromantisme*, II, 308.

24. Prior, in Chalmers, *op. cit.*, X, 135; F. B. Kaye, Preface to Mandeville's *Fable of the Bees*, I, lxxviii ff.; Dryden, *Essays*, I, 215; Roscommon, in Spingarn, *Critical Essays of the Seventeenth Century*, II, 300; Steele, *The Lying Lover*, Act II, scene II; Prior, in Chalmers, *op. cit.*, X, 221; Pope, *Moral Essays*, Epistle I, *passim*; Chesterfield, *Letters*, I, 154; Johnson, *Lives of the Poets*, V, 157–158.

25. Burton, *Anatomy of Melancholy*, I, 52; Sir Thomas Browne, *Works*, II, 340; Boileau, *Œuvres*, pp. 67–75; Addison, *Guardian*, Nos. 153, 156, 157, 158; Mandeville, *Fable of the Bees*, I, 176, II, 187; Prior, in Chalmers, *op. cit.*, X, 209; Young, *Poetical Works*, I, 170; Frances Brooke, *Lady Julia Mandeville*, p. 102; Henry Brooke, *Fool of Quality*, p. 259, and *Universal Beauty*; Cowper, *Poems*, p. 303. In *Boileau and the French Classical Critics in England*, pp. 123 and 220, Clark calls attention to two passages in the same tenor from Robert Gould and Lord Hervey, and in her study of *Primitivism and the Idea of Progress* Lois Whitney notes a passage in *The London Magazine* for 1779. A complete study of this aspect of eighteenth-century thought is desirable.

26. Locke, *Essay*, pp. 29, 34, 160, 180–181, 198, 279–281; F. B. Kaye, Preface to Mandeville's *Fable of the Bees*, I, xlvii, lxxviii ff.; Preserved Smith, *History of Modern Culture*, II, 183–188. *Cf.* Glanvill, *Vanity of Dogmatizing*, pp. 121–124 and Henry Brooke, *Fool of Quality*, p. 394.

27. Bredvold, *The Intellectual Milieu of John Dryden*, pp. 16–46; Dedieu, "L'Apologetique Traditionelle dans les 'Pensées,' ", *Revue d'Histoire Litteraire de la France*, XXXVII, 8–9.

28. Hume, *Treatise*, pp. 103, 179, 183, 470, 499–500, and *Essays*, II, 265, 172 ff.; Hoxie Fairchild, *The Noble Savage*, p. 28; Wyndham Lewis, *Time and Western Man*, New York, 1928, pp. 365–367.

CHAPTER IV

THE FUNCTION OF THE POET

I

THE VERY form and pressure of the times compelled the artist of the seventeenth and eighteenth centuries to emphasize the usefulness of his art. When ignorant armies clash by night their camps afford no support for the mere entertainer. In epochs of tense political and religious controversy the artist must justify himself by proving his worth. To the serious attacks of the Puritans on art, and to the controversial disputes of the Commonwealth, succeeded the practical spirit of the Enlightenment with its delight in instruction and in social reform. Neither the ascendency of religion nor of science allowed much room for art for art's sake.

Renaissance criticism was on the defensive. Poetry had been universally esteemed in all ages: it could not be worthless. It was an art of imitation; it was an allegorical account of truth; it could teach as well as delight; it was more universally true than history which presented the particular rather than the probable; it was more influential than bare logic for it taught by example: hence, it could mold men to morality by instruction in life. Such were the arguments of Sidney and his fellows in Elizabethan England which set the tone for the practical emphasis of the two centuries that followed.[1]

The advice of Horace to blend utility with sweetness was quoted *ad nauseam*. Poetry must please and instruct, teach delightfully, present truths in sugar-coated pills. It is the opinion of Jonson, of Dryden, of Boileau. Swift made his literary cake "with a layer of *utile* and a layer of *dulce* . . . in compliance with a lesson of great age and authority." Farquhar thought that the mixture of the useful and the true was the only refuge of the dramatist from prosecution. Cibber, Dennis, and Addison agreed. The purpose of *The World* was "to entertain and instruct the public." Cowper thought art for art's sake no better than "a nurse's lullaby at night," and in his letters he stressed the ethical function of art again and again. When Wordsworth declared, "Every poet is a teacher; I desire either to be considered as a teacher or as nothing," he was in line with a long classical tradition.[2]

Frequently instruction was given priority. Poetry written solely for pleasure was compared to fiddling and legerdemain. Poetry should be regarded as a body of ethical doctrine. Its noble end must be the instruction of the understanding. Illustrations are innumerable. Atterbury wrote to Pope that poetry without a moral could give "no true delight to a reasonable mind." Dennis objected to *The Rape of the Lock* because it was an empty trifle in comparison with the serious *Lutrin*. Edward Young gave expression to his views in an *Epistle to Mr. Pope:*

> Serious should be a writer's final views;
> Who write for pure amusement, ne'er amuse. . . .
> Nothing but what is solid or refin'd
> Should dare ask public audience of mankind.

Samuel Richardson took an active part in the campaign started by *The Gentleman's Magazine* in 1739 in favor of works useful for young girls. He thought that love poets should have been strangled in their cradles, for it was abominable to abuse God-given gifts to inflame the imagination. Fielding quoted Horace and Richardson in emphasizing the subordination of wit and humor to instruction. He preferred the Greek historians to Homer, and thought that romance corrupted and confounded true history. Smollett insisted on the usefulness of the realistic novel. Goldsmith would have liked to be an eighteenth-century Horatio Alger writing novels in which the hero "might be praised for having resisted allurements when young," and shown later as Lord Mayor with a wife "of great sense, fortune, and beauty." In *The Industrious Apprentice* Hogarth, in a measure, fulfilled Goldsmith's ideal. Mrs. Montagu thought the "noblest end of fable, moral instruction." Doctor Johnson may well close the account with his remarks on Addison:

He has dissipated the prejudice that had long connected gaiety with vice, and easiness of manners with laxity of principles. He has restored virtue to its dignity, and taught innocence not to be ashamed. This is an elevation of literary character, *above all Greek, above all Roman fame.* No greater felicity can genius attain than that of having purified intellectual pleasure, separated mirth from indecency, and wit from licentiousness; of having taught a succession of writers to bring elegance and gaiety to the aid of goodness.[3]

The chief objection to the supremacy of instruction came from those who argued that literature must please *in order to* instruct. In antiquity Aristotle and Longinus; in the Italian Renaissance Castelvetro; in France Ronsard and Malherbe resisted the identification. of poetry with verse used to adorn the truths of agriculture and astronomy. Corneille, Molière, La Fontaine, Racine, La Bruyère, and Boileau recognized the significance of pleasure as an indispensable means, if not an end, in art. In England Rymer proclaimed that the "end of all poetry is to please," and that some sorts of poetry please without profiting. Dryden, at least for a moment in 1668, believed that "Delight is the chief, if not the only, end of poesy. . . . Poesy only instructs as it delights." Dryden admitted that even the exact imitation of nature must be sacrificed if it interfered with delight. Sir William Temple thought that Spenser neglected artistic principles to overemphasize instruction. Lady Mary Wortley Montagu wished gallantry, not dull morals, in memoirs, and David Hume failed to see why bawdy works "executed with decency and ingenuity" should be banned from the Advocates' Library in Edinburgh. Neither Lady Mary nor Hume *published* such views as they expressed in private correspondence, and very few went so far in the defense of pleasant vice. John Brown and Bishop Hurd argued that instruction was secondary to pleasure, and Henry Fielding found sufficient justification for comedy in the relief of spleen by means of laughter. Goldsmith hoped that his *Life of Nash* might be justified by the innocent pleasure it gave, "however it may fail to open the heart, or improve the understanding." On another occasion Goldsmith told Reynolds that if *She Stoops to Conquer* had made him laugh that was all he asked. Even Johnson, at least once, defined the great end of comedy as "making an audience merry."[4]

In the latter half of the century such views were expressed more freely. Lord Kames was willing for fiction to be regarded as the resource of solitude and solace of an idle hour. In his *Essay on Genius* Gerard linked poetry with pleasure. Beattie declared that the fine arts were ornamental, valuable only as they pleased. In the *Letters of Literature* Pinkerton found poetry useful in that it amused. In the notes to his edition of the *Poetics* in 1789 Twining ridiculed the absurd idea that "Homer wrote his *Iliad* on purpose to teach mankind the mischiefs of discord among chiefs and his *Odyssey* to prove to them the advantages of staying at home and taking care of their wives." Sheridan laughed at Sneer's comedy, *The Reformed House-Breaker*, "Where, by the mere force of humor, house-breaking is put into so ridiculous a light, that if the piece has its proper run, I have no doubt but that bolts and bars will be entirely useless by the end of the season." In the Prologue to *The Rivals* the speaker points to the Muse of Comedy:

> Should you expect to hear this lady preach?
> Is grey experience suited to her youth?
> Do solemn sentiments become that mouth?
> Bid her be grave, those lips should rebel prove
> To every theme that slanders mirth or love. . . .
> Can our light scenes add strength to holy laws!
> Such puny patronage but hurts the cause:
> Fair virtue scorns our feeble aid to ask;
> And moral truth disdains the trickster's mask.

Finally, beyond the end of the century, Mrs. Barbauld, a product of the age of classicism, presented her British Novelists as a source of delight. The novel

is always ready to enliven the gloom of solitude, to soothe the languor of debility and disease, to win the attention from pain or vexatious occurrences, to take man from himself, (at many seasons the worst company he can be in,) and, while the moving picture of life passes before him, to make him forget the subject of his own complaints. It is pleasant to the mind to sport in the boundless regions of possibility; to find relief from the sameness of everyday occurrences by expatiating amidst brighter skies and fairer fields; to exhibit love that is always happy, valour that is always successful; to feed the appetite for wonder by a quick succession of marvellous events; and to distribute, like a ruling providence, rewards and punishments just where they ought to fall.

Here is the escape theory of literature fully developed, but unfortunately Mrs. Barbauld goes on with ethical emphasis to point out in the novel many elements both of utility and of danger.[5]

II

These swallows did not indicate a general freeing of artistic consciousness from the wintry chill of moral responsibility. The great majority of critics demanded that literature serve some useful end. What precise function could the creative artist serve? To this question various answers were given: the poet could condemn vice and praise virtue, he could make of his work a school of manners, he could discipline the affections, he could draw forth refined feelings, he could interpret life and furnish vicarious experience, or he could give direct instruction.

The majority of critics from the Renaissance to the Romantic Revolution believed that art should strengthen the moral fiber of the race. In the Elizabethan period Webbe, Puttenham, Chapman, and Harington supported such a view; in the seventeenth century Hobbes, Milton, and Dryden; in the eighteenth Cibber, Welsted, Steele, Chesterfield, Richardson, and Fielding. The most direct method was the praise of virtue and the presentation of the ideal. Milton held a conception of a pulpit-stage as a means to virtue. The magistrate should conduct public spectacles to

civilize, adorn, and make discreet our minds by the learned and affable meeting of frequent Academies, and the procurement of wise and artful recitations sweetened with eloquent and graceful enticements to the love and practice of justice, temperance, and fortitude, instructing and bettering the nation at all opportunities, that the call of wisdom and virtue may be heard everywhere. . . . Whether this may not be, not only in pulpits, but after another persuasive method, at set and solemn panegyrics, in theatres, porches, or what other place or way may win most upon the people to receive at once both recreation and instruction, let them in authority consult.

Richardson explained the moral purpose of his books in the Preface to *Clarissa:*

What will be found to be more particularly aimed at in the following work is—to warn the inconsiderate and thoughtless of the one sex, against the

base arts and designs of specious contrivers of the other—to caution parents
against the undue exercise of their natural authority over their children,
against preferring a man of pleasure to a man of probity upon that dangerous
but too-commonly-received notion, *that a reformed rake makes the best
husband*—but above all, to investigate the highest and most important doctrines not only of morality, but of Christianity, by showing them thrown
into action in the conduct of *worthy* characters; while the *unworthy*, who set
those doctrines at defiance, are condignly, and as may be said, consequentially
punished.

Lest Richardson be regarded as a peculiarly persistent moralist it will
be well to remember Fielding's statement that *Tom Jones* was
designed "to recommend goodness and innocence" and "to laugh
mankind out of their favorite follies and vices." This was no hypo-
critically pious declaration; the bulk of Fielding's mature work
bears witness to its truth.[6]

The function of the artist was less distinctly ethical, but equally
social when he aimed to bring the straying sheep into the social fold,
to see that he conformed to good taste and to good manners, and that
he served a useful role in the structure of society. Literature could be
a school of manners as well as a school of virtue. Shadwell believed
that comedy should present, not great crimes, but the "affected
vanities and artificial fopperies" that might be mended. *The Tatler*
could not agree with the Reformers of Manners in their severity towards the stage, for a "good play acted before a well-bred audience,
must raise very proper incitements to good behavior, and be the most
quick and prevailing method of giving young people a turn of sense
and breeding." Lord Chesterfield defended the stage in his speech
before Parliament on the Play-house Bill (1737) by declaring that
the proper business of the stage "is to expose those vices and follies,
which the laws cannot lay hold of." Welsted thought that poetry
polished manners. Theobald reiterated Shadwell's view that comedy
should expose humor and caprice. George Campbell in his *Philosophy of Rhetoric* distinguished two ends of art—morals and manners;
epic, tragedy, and high satire exposed vice; the mock epic, comedy,
and low satire eradicated folly.[7]

Poetry was frequently represented as refining the heart. Humane
feelings of pity were to be developed through the arts in order to
lessen man's inhumanity to man. Tragedies, Addison believed, elimi-

nate mean and little thoughts, and "cherish and cultivate that humanity that is the ornament of our nature. They soften insolence, soothe affliction, and subdue the mind to the dispensations of providence." Steele believed that drama should draw forth generous feelings by the representation of generous actions on the stage of sentimental comedy. Edward Moore's *The Foundling* was likewise designed "to touch the strings that humanize the mind":

> He forms a model of a virtuous sort,
> And gives you more of moral than of sport;
> He rather aims to draw the melting sigh,
> Or steal the pitying tear from beauty's eye,
> To touch the strings that humanize our kind,
> Man's sweetest strain, the music of the mind.

Pope had introduced Addison's *Cato* to the public by developing this same view of the artistic function:

> To wake the soul by tender strokes of art,
> To raise the genius, and to mend the heart;
> To make mankind in conscious virtue bold,
> Live o'er each scene, and be what they behold:
> For this the Tragic Muse first trod the stage.

Akenside called attention to the humanitarian influence of poetry. Smollett fully displayed the role of art in rousing human passions. In the novel

the reader gratifies his curiosity in pursuing the adventures of a person in whose favour he is prepossessed; he espouses his cause, he sympathizes with him in distress; his indignation is heated against the authors of his calamity; the human passions are inflamed; the contrast between dejected virtue and insulting vice appears with greater aggravation; and every impression having a double force on the imagination, the memory retains the circumstance, and the heart improves by the example.

Hugh Blair went still further towards the romantic ideal of sensibility in arguing that a cultivated literary taste increased sensibility "to all the tender and humane passions," by giving them frequent exercise; but to such a view as Blair's there was strong opposition from those who felt that it was unwise to rouse too much sensibility.[8]

Emotion could be stilled; emotion could be aroused; emotion could be wisely guided by the prudence gained through vicarious experience of the pitfalls of life; Clarissas could learn to stay at home, Wildgooses be hindered from attempting to convert the world, unsuspecting young Primroses warned against exchanging horse-flesh for blue spectacles. In the eighteenth century the idea rapidly spread that novels and plays might present transcripts of life so full and truthful that from acquaintance with them useful experience could be gained. Steele and Lillo developed bourgeois drama on the theory that knowledge of middle-class life would be profitable to many more readers than the usual stage histories of the unfortunate crowned heads. Johnson believed that the purpose of fiction was not

to show mankind, but to provide that they may be seen hereafter with less hazard; to teach the means of avoiding the snares that are laid by treachery for innocence . . . ; to give the power of counteracting fraud . . . ; to initiate youth by mock encounters in the art of necessary defence, and to increase prudence without impairing virtue.[9]

Virtue, sensibility, and experience are aspects of a well-developed personality. The Augustan Age did not, however, envisage many modern theories of the cultural function of art. Little notice was taken of art as a training for enjoyment in life, for the creation of a personality capable of savoring with a palate finer than that of the Philistine all the dishes at life's feast. From Spenser to Wordsworth the artist was concerned with fashioning a virtuous gentleman in gentle discipline. It remained for the Romanticists to teach a man to "burst Joy's grapes against his palate fine." It was left to moderns like Anatole France to point out the wisdom of detachment, the delight that can be found in smiling at men who congregate into absurdities, if one is not too concerned with moral considerations. It remained for the æsthetic critics of the last century to expound the faith that beauty is its own excuse for being. It was left for Freud to suggest the psychic releases and the sublimations possible in art. The Augustan view was limited. Many functons of art were seen, if at all, through a glass darkly, for the classical view of art was conditioned by a social consciousness that demanded from the artist service for the common good. The ideal had its disadvantage: its great merit was in keeping art in touch with the normal and in compelling it to give an unparalleled picture of the contemporary scene.

The function of art was reasonably clear. How could the artist fulfill that function? How could he expect to make men virtuous and keep them so? In the first place he could show that virtue was rewarded, that the idle apprentice would come to the gallows and the industrious lad marry his master's daughter, that Clarissa would be guided by angels to heaven and that Mrs. Sinclair would die of gangrene in terror of hell. This concept of poetic justice will be treated fully elsewhere. The employment of poetic justice was not the only way to instill virtue, for even though the artist could not conscientiously display virtue triumphant in this world he could paint contrasting pictures of vice and virtue so powerfully that the reader must inevitably hate wickedness and love virtue. Milton believed that the artist could render pleasing the paths of virtue; Doctor Johnson thought that vice should always be displayed as disgusting. Doctor Beattie, too, thought that the artist could promote the love of virtue by "displaying the deformity of moral evil" and "the charms of moral goodness." Closely allied with this belief that goodness would inspire emulation if skillfully presented even in misfortune, was the theory that the praise of great and good men in panegyric verse and the preservation of worthy actions in immortal poesy would lead youth to strive for a similar recompense from fame. As Samuel Johnson phrased it, "To encourage merit with praise is the great business of literature." Thus panegyric, which might seem to be an unworthy form of occasional verse, was justified by the canons of ethical criticism.[10]

Poetry might further the cause of virtue by holding up an ideal: the epic might have its perfect hero, the novel its Clarissa, "an exemplar to her sex." It might, as has been already indicated, serve by presenting an accurate picture of the world, or by the development of proper feeling. The poet might give advice directly. "Moral sentences" designed skillfully by the artist to stick in the memory might be spoken with apothegmatic force by the proponents of virtue in play or poem. In the drama the last lines of the play might present the moral of the whole in a well-turned couplet, as Congreve advised; or, as was the practice of Fielding, the novelist might give a running commentary on the action to indicate the moral significance of his characters. In these ways direct instruction could be blended with amusement, but advice could be given even more openly in periodical essay, literary criticism, and moral treatise.[11]

Finally, the useful end of art could be fulfilled by Aristotelian purgation. The words of Aristotle concerning catharsis were on many lips, but their exact significance seemed uncertain. The chief point of divergence was on the question as to whether or not all passsion was to be purged by means of pity and terror, or whether only pity and terror were to be purged by a homeopathic treatment. In England Milton, Dennis, Trapp, and Tyrwhitt developed the homeopathic interpretation of purgation. Dennis considered terror and pity the only emotions proper to tragedy;

for as the humors in some distempered body are raised in order to the evacuating that which is redundant or peccant in them, so tragedy excites compassion and terror to the same end; for the play being over, an audience becomes serene again, and is less apt to be moved at the common incidents of life, after it has seen the deplorable calamities of heroes and sovereign princes.

In his *Praelectiones Poeticae*, Trapp, the Oxford Professor of Poetry, developed this idea with acknowledgments to Milton's Preface to *Samson Agonistes*, but the significance of the theory was not fully grasped until Tyrwhitt published his edition of the *Poetics* in 1794. In the meanwhile some interesting remarks had been made by Harris, Boswell, and John Brown. Harris had suggested the possibility of conquering emotion through familiarity with tragic events much as soldiers and physicians customarily did; Boswell thought that passion could be checked by seeing the ravages of excessive passion; John Brown, in 1764, attempted an historical interpretation in *The Rise and Progress of Poetry*, in which he pictured drama as the creation of a primitive and warlike civilization desirous of destroying pity and fear in the young warrior by familiarity with suffering in tragedy, and eliminating cowardice by ridicule in comedy. Despite such intuitive flashes it must be confessed that there was considerable confusion as to Aristotle's meaning, and much less discussion of the purgation theory than might be expected from a period of classical criticism.[12]

Enough has been said of the attitude of the age towards art to make it apparent that the pure esthete would have found little encouragement. There was no school of art for art's sake during the period to bring such a theory to the tribunal of popular opinion, for the existence of such a viewpoint was rendered impossible by the survival of Puritan moral emphasis, by the practical spirit of the Enlightenment, by the respect for the group as opposed to the individual, and by the finer spirit of ancient culture. Had not Aristotle linked rhetoric closely with ethics and politics because all were concerned with human happiness and virtue? Had not Strabo maintained that Homer had the same ends in view as the historian or narrator of fact? Had not Cicero declared that eloquence and beauty of style were empty sounds, unless there were substance and knowledge in the work; had he not emphasized the view that style is born from the substance of thought? Art for art's sake was repugnant to the mind of antiquity at its best, and dilettantism was left to the late Alexandrian school. High ethical purpose marked the significant work of the Romans, and the purely didactic was by no means neglected. To all intents the Latin genius agreed with the ideal of the eighteenth century: the proper study of mankind is man.[13]

III

Purity was generally connected with utility in art. Standards of good breeding change, but most classicists were morally impeccable in their creative work; and in criticism even more uniform in their demand that nothing be written that might bring a blush to a virtuous cheek. On this aspect of English literature Goldsmith dilated:

'The dullest writer talks of virtue, and liberty, and benevolence, with esteem; tells his true story, filled with good and wholesome advice: warns against slavery, bribery, or the bite of a mad dog; and dresses up his little useful magazine of knowledge and entertainment at least with a good intention. The dunces of France, on the other hand, who have less encouragement, are more vicious. Tender hearts, languishing eyes, Leonora in love at thirteen, ecstatic transports, stolen blisses, are the frivolous subjects of their frivolous memoirs.[14]

In the very heyday of Restoration license the forces of morality were reforming their ranks. Before Collier wrote *The Short View,*

Evelyn, Flecknoe, Shadwell, Wright, Vanbrugh, Dilke, and Black-more had objected to the licentiousness of the stage. Common sense, as has been shown, supported morality as well as good taste. The most characteristic form of "neo-classical" literature, the periodical essay, was not a product of classical imitation, but of the bourgeois journalism evolved in the late seventeeth century, although not per-fected until *The Tatler* appeared. The same ethical spirit accounted for the popularity of the Oriental allegory, and played some part in the esteem awarded Spenser and Milton. Dryden dominated Restora-tion literature and though he was compelled in the last years of his life to repent his *practice*, he had preached with growing emphasis through the years the moral responsibility of the artist.[15]

By 1700 moral reform was fashionable. As early as 1674 a *Pro-posal for a National Reformation of Manners* had appeared, and Societies for the Reformation of Manners were organized. Collier's attack was a culmination, not an isolated phenomenon; but after Col-lier action became imperative. Legal proceedings against Congreve and D'Urfey were threatened in 1698; in 1701 the cast of *The Provok'd Wife* was arrested, and the casts of *Sir Courtly Nice* and *The Humour of the Age* followed them into court, though no severe action could be taken, because the plays had been regularly licensed. In 1699 Nahum Tate proposed new schemes for the regulation of plays. In 1696, 1697, and 1699 the court made efforts to improve the methods of licensing, to prevent the presentation of unlicensed plays, and to hinder the addition of bawdy songs and epilogues to plays previously licensed. Direct action was unsuccessful, but a general improvement was brought about by the cumulative efforts of the Societies for the Reformation of Manners, by continued direct attacks on immoral plays, and by the influence of Addison and Steele.[16]

Addison and Steele were consistently pure. Steele represented in-decency as deficiency of wit and extolled the power of poetry in recommending virtue. Dennis cried out against the pernicious effects of *All for Love*. Broome thought that "the wittiest poetry in the world loses all value if it raises an unchaste thought in a virtuous heart." Swift declared that he had never written without a moral view. Fielding was a champion of virtue, despite Richardson's horror at the dubious morality of *Tom Jones*. Edward Young proclaimed that "he that does most good is the best author." Thomson praised the Greeks for displaying

Each moral beauty to the ravish'd eye.

Joseph Warton preferred the *Odyssey* to the *Iliad* because of its superior morality, and imitated the mouthings of Collier in a glance back at Restoration drama in which adultery had been a jest, obscenity wit, and debauchery amiable. With the passing years the moral emphasis grew. The evidence is overwhelming from Defoe to Boswell, from Walpole to the pious emulators of Daddy Richardson, who regarded himself as a mentor, a guide for youth, a champion of virtue.[17]

IV

The vogue of purely didactic poetry has little direct connection with the moral emphasis just considered, though behind both phenomena looms the dictum of Horace. Many didactic poems were technical treatises giving instruction on subjects so various as poetry, gardens, health, angling, hunting, dancing, cosmetics, coquetry, whist, conversation, war, and child-raising with little or no ethical implication. Raymond D. Havens has discovered more than seventy such technical treatises between 1680 and 1820, though his list does not include general philosophical and religious poems. Most of these poems are buried in oblivion; six or seven are familiar to the student: perhaps only Pope's *Essay on Man* and *Essay on Criticism* mean much to the general reader. Before 1800, however, Phillips' *Cider*, Dyer's *Fleece*, Akenside's *Pleasures of the Imagination*, Armstrong's *Art of Preserving Health*, and Grainger's *Sugar-Cane* were almost as familiar to readers as the *Georgics* of Virgil or the *Ars Poetica* of Horace. Then Young's *Night Thoughts* was the rage; who would voluntarily read it now? Who would now lament the loss of Doctor Burney's verse treatise on astronomy?[18]

In the Renaissance didactic poetry was supported by the allegorical interpretation of the ancients, one result of the defensive warfare waged to rescue poetry from the charges of the Puritan and the priest. The Ancients used fable to draw men to wisdom, concealing beneath the pleasing surface deep mysteries and divine philosophy.

In this view Lodge, Webbe, Nash, Puttenham, and Harington were agreed. After the Restoration the allegorical theory lost ground. As late as 1769 Robert Wood felt obliged to combat the notion that the Homeric poems contained abstruse learning skillfully concealed in allegory, but the major critics of the eighteenth century disdained to battle shadows. Fable and parable continued popular, as is witnessed by the success of Gay and Addison, but, in general, it seems that the purely didactic technical treatise was distinguished from the more subtly instructive epic, tragedy, and novel.[19]

The attempt to include all poetry in the province of didacticism failed, but didactic poetry itself was not affected by the decline of the allegorical school of criticism. Support for such an employment of verse was found in the examples of Horace, Virgil, and Lucretius—precedents stronger than the authority of Aristotle, who declared that Herodotus in verse would still be history, not poetry. Despite the classical models there was little direct didacticism in verse until the Restoration. In the *Proposition for the Advancement of Learning* (1661) Cowley, who was to become the author of a Latin poem on botany, regretted the want of "good poets . . . who have purposely treated of solid and learned, that is, of natural matters." Dryden, and after him Addison, considered the *Georgics* more perfect than the *Æneid*. Goldsmith feared that the use of blank verse would injure the popularity of England's deservedly famous didactic poetry. Arthur Murphy supported didacticism wholeheartedly. He thought that *The Essay on Man* would "always stand at the top of the sublime character: a noble work, indeed, where we find the thorny reasonings of philosophy blooming and shooting forth into all the flowers of poetry." Much of Cowper's poetry was as didactic as Pope's or Dryden's. The poems of 1782 were completely so, while *The Task* contains in the first three books satire and advice which deepen in the last three into an argument against the infidel in the manner of *Night Thoughts*.[20]

The didactic poets did not have it all their own way. Gray declared "a metaphysical poem a contradiction in terms," and soon let his *De Principiis Cogitandi* drop. Hobbes, Locke, and Bolingbroke had already objected to the mixture of ornament and truth. Johnson scorned both Dyer's *Fleece* and Grainger's *Sugar-Cane:* "What could he make of a sugar-cane? One might as well write the 'Parsley-Bed, a Poem'; or 'The Cabbage-garden, a Poem!' " But it was this same Doctor Johnson who praised Phillips' *Cider*, and preferred the *Essay on Criticism* to *The Rape of the Lock.* In the Preface to his *Odes* (1746) and in the *Essay on Pope* Joseph Warton battled in behalf of the imagination which he felt to be seriously threatened by the vogue of moralizing in verse.[21]

Critical opinion was divided somewhat equally on the advisability of employing the adornments of verse in the handling of technical subjects, but in the more significant, because more widely spread, emphasis on morality and utility the age spoke almost in unison. There were a few scattered pleas for pure delight in art; there was rather more disagreement as to the exact nature of utility and the means to its attainment, but such divergences indicate that the function of literature was being seriously studied as a vital problem, and not merely accepted on the authority of Horace or justified by the example of the *Georgics.* Though the lines of Horace were interpreted in various ways, the dictum *miscere utile dulci* was one of the ties that bound imitative classicist, rationalist, and moderate pre-Romanticist in a similar view of the artist and of his responsibilities.

NOTES TO CHAPTER IV

1. Horace, *Ars Poetica*, lines 334–335, 343–344; George Saintsbury, *A History of Criticism and Literary Taste in Europe*, New York, 1908, II, 8–9; Spingarn, *Literary Criticism of the Renaissance*, pp. 3–14, 49–56, 314–315; Gregory Smith, *Elizabethan Critical Essays*, I, xxi–xxv; Sidney, *Apology for Poetry, ibid.*, I, 162–169, 183–192; James Routh, "The Purpose of Art as Conceived in English Literary Criticism of the Sixteenth and Seventeenth Century," *Englische Studien*, XLVIII, 124.

2. Swift, *Gulliver's Travels*, p. 460; Farquhar, *Discourse upon Comedy*, in Durham, *Critical Essays of the Eighteenth Century*, p. 274; Dennis, *Grounds of Criticism in Poetry, ibid.*, pp. 146–147; Colley Cibber, *An Apology for the Life of Colley Cibber*, London (Everyman's Library), n. d., pp. 138–39; Addison, *Spectator*, Nos. 10, 369; Cowper, *Conversation*, line 242; Cowper, Letters to Newton, February 18, 1781, December 3, 1785, and to Lady Hesketh, January 16, 1786; Barry Cerf, "Wordsworth's Gospel of Nature," *P. M. L. A.*, XXXVII, 631.

3. Spingarn, *Literary Criticism of the Renaissance*, p. 48; Bray, *Formation de la Doctrine Classique en France*, pp. 67, 73, 83; Marvin T. Herrick, *The Poetics of Aristotle in England*, New Haven (Cornell Studies in English), 1930, pp. 74–75, 55; Pope, *Works*, IX, 16; A. F. B. Clark, *Boileau and the French Classical Critics*

in England, p. 11; Edward Young, *Poetical Works*, II, 348, 51; Paul Dottin, *Samuel Richardson, 1689–1761*, Paris, 1931, p. 50; Fielding, *Covent-Garden Journal*, No. 10, and *Author's Preface to a Voyage to Lisbon*; Edward Young, *Conjectures on Original Composition*, in E. D. Jones, *op. cit.*, p. 316; E. A. Baker, *The History of the English Novel*, London, 1930, IV, 201; Goldsmith, *Bee*, No. VI, *Works*, ed. Gibbs, V, 61, *Citizen of the World*, Letter LXXV; Goldsmith, *New Essays*, ed. Crane, p. 63; Mrs. Montagu, *Essay on Shakespeare*, p. xvi, 5 ff.; Johnson, *Lives of the Poets*, III, 149–150. *Cf.* Boswell, *Life of Johnson*, III, 361–362, 432, note 3; IV, 439, note 1; I, 361–362; Cowper, Letters to Mrs. Cowper, Oct. 19, 1791, to Unwin, Aug. 25, 1781, Jan. 17, 1782, and to Newton, Aug. 16, 1789; Alison, *Essays on Taste*, p. 249; Marr, *History of Modern English Romanticism*, I, 25.

4. Spingarn, *Critical Essays of the Seventeenth Century*, I, lxxiv–lxxv; Bray, *Formation de la Doctrine Classique*, pp. 23, 67; Racan, *Vie de Malherbe*, in Vial et Denise, *op. cit.*, pp. 68–69. *Cf.* Vial et Denise, pp. 40, 121; Rymer, *Tragedies of the Past Age*, in Spingarn, *op. cit.*, II, 206; Dryden, *Essays*, I, 121; Wolseley, Preface to Rochester's *Valentinian*, in Spingarn, *op. cit.*, III, 15–25; Sir William Temple, *Of Poetry*; Lady Mary Wortley Montagu, *Letters*, I, 31; Hume, *Letters*, I, 212; Fielding, Preface to *Joseph Andrews*; John Brown, *Essays on the Characteristics*, London, 1751, p. 18; Hurd's views are cited by Herrick, *The Poetics of Aristotle in England*, p. 122; Goldsmith, *Miscellaneous Works*, p. 512; Boswell, *Life of Johnson*, II, 268, and note 1.

5. Lord Kames, *Elements of Criticism*, Boston, 1796, I, 87; Alexander Gerard, *An Essay on Genius*, London, 1774, p. 314; Beattie, *Dissertations*, I, 182; Pinkerton, *Letters of Literature*, p. 399; Clark, *Boileau and the French Classical Critics in England*, p. 261; Sheridan, *The Critic*, Act I, scene I, and the Prologue to *The Rivals*; Mrs. Barbauld, *On the Origin and Progress of Novel Writing*, in *British Novelists*, I, 46–55.

6. Webbe, *Discourse of English Poetry*, in Gregory Smith, *op. cit.*, I, 234–235; Puttenham, *Arte of English Poesie*, *ibid.*, II, 24–34; Harington, *Brief Apologie of Poetry*, II, 197; Chapman, *Achilles' Shield*, *ibid.*, II, 306, *Dedication to the Revenge of Bussy D'Ambois*; Milton, *Reason of Church Government*, in Spingarn, *Critical Essays of the Seventeenth Century*, I, 198; Hobbes, in Spingarn, *op. cit.*, II, 54; Dryden, *Observations on Rymer's Remarks*, in Johnson, *Lives of the Poets*, II, 273; Dryden, *Essays*, I, 141–143; *Welsted*, in Durham, *Critical Essays of the Eighteenth Century*, pp. 382–383; Colley Cibber, Epilogue to Fielding's *Modern Husband*; Fielding, Dedication of *Tom Jones* to Lord Lyttleton.

7. Shadwell, *Preface to the Humorists*, in Spingarn, *op. cit.*, II, 154; *Tatler*, Nos. 3, 8; Welsted, in Durham, *op. cit.*, pp. 382–383; Chesterfield, *Works*, V, xii; Theobald, *Preface to Shakespeare*, in Nicoll Smith, *op. cit.*, p. 84; Campbell, *Philosophy of Rhetoric*, p. 39, and note.

8. Addison, *Spectator*, No. 39; Steele, *Tatler*, No. 8; Henry Brooke, Prologue to Edward Moore's *The Foundling*; Pope, Prologue to Addison's *Cato*; Akenside, *Ode XVIII*; Smollett, Preface to *Roderick Random*; Blair, *Rhetoric*, I, 15; Campbell, *Philosophy of Rhetoric*, p. 16.

9. Steele, *Tatler*, May 16, 1710; Lillo, Preface to *George Barnwell*; Johnson, *Rambler*, No. 4.

10. Milton, *Reason of Church Government*, quoted by Tillyard, *Milton*, p. 98; Johnson, *Rambler*, No. 4; Beattie, *Dissertations*, I, 182; Johnson, *Rambler*, No. 136;

Steele, *Tatler*, No. 24, 1709; Welsted, *State of Poetry*, in Durham, *op. cit.*, pp. 382–383.

11. Richardson, *Writings*, V, x–xi; Blair, *Rhetoric*, III, 303; Congreve, *Complete Works*, III, 174.

12. Aristotle, *Poetics*, VI, 2; Spingarn, *Literary Criticism of the Renaissance*, pp. 76–81; Dennis, *Impartial Critic*, in Spingarn, *Critical Essays of the Seventeenth Century*, III, 184–185; Herrick, *The Poetics of Aristotle in England*, pp. 110, 140; Harris, *Three Treatises*, p. 86; Boswell, *Hypochondriack*, I, 115; John Brown, *The History of the Rise and Progress of Poetry*, Newcastle, 1764, p. 34.

13. Aristotle, *Poetics*, I, ii, 7; Cicero, *De Inventione*, I, 1; Cicero, *De Oratore*, I, 12; II, 24; Strabo, *Geography*, I, ii, 9; *Cf.* Plutarch, *De Audiendis Poetis*, and Butcher, *Aristotle's Theory of Poetry and Fine Art*, Chapter V.

14. Goldsmith, *Citizen of the World*, Letter LXXV; Bernbaum, *Drama of Sensibility*, p. 80, note 2.

15. Evelyn, *Diary and Correspondence*, III, 78, 152; Spingarn, *Critical Essays of the Seventeenth Century*, I, lxxxii–lxxxiii; J. W. Draper, "The Rise of English Neo-Classicism," *Revue Anglo-Américaine*, Juin, 1933; Paul Hamelius, *Die Kritik in der englischen Literatur*, p. 86; Dryden, *Essays*, I, 191, 123, II, 263, 274; Ker, Introduction to Dryden's *Essays*, I, lxiii.

16. Joseph Wood Krutch, "Governmental Attempts to Regulate the Stage after the Jeremy Collier Controversy," *P. M. L. A.*, XXXVIII, 153–174; Leslie Stephen, *English Literature and Society in the Eighteenth Century*, p. 62.

17. Steele, Epilogue to the *Funeral*; Steele, Preface to the *Lying Lover*; *Spectator*, No. 51; *Tatler*, Nov. 24, 1709; Steele, *Epistolary Correspondence*, ed. John Nichols, London, 1809, II, 561–562; Pope, *Works*, VIII, 128; Swift, *Correspondence*, IV, 328–329; Fielding, *Covent-Garden Journal*, No. 10, *Champion*, Dec. 22, 1739; Dedication of *Tom Jones* to Lord Lyttleton; Richardson, *Correspondence*, II, 4; Thomson, *Liberty*, Book II, lines 340–343; Joseph Warton, *Adventurer*, Nos. 75, 105; Goldsmith, *Works*, ed. Gibbs, IV, 251; Boswell, *Life of Johnson*, II, 268, note, II, 421, III, 46, IV, 71; Boswell, *Hypochondriack*, II, 67, 73; Johnson, *Lives of the Poets*, I, 114; Bailey, *Dr. Johnson and His Circle*, p. 27; Cowper, Letter to Unwin, Jan. 17, 1782; Cowper, *Table-Talk*, lines 598–599, *Task*, Book II, lines 313–315, *Retirement*, line 806; Blair, *Rhetoric*, III, 68–69; Clara Reeve, *Progress of Romance*, II, 321.

18. R. D. Havens, *Influence of Milton*, p. 360 ff. and Appendix IV where authors, titles, and dates are given. For Dr. Burney's poem see *The Early Diary of Fanny Burney*, ed. Ellis, I, lxx.

19. Lodge, *Defense of Poetry*, in Gregory Smith, *op. cit.*, I, 65; Webbe, *Discourse of English Poetry*, *ibid.*, I, 238; Nash, *Anatomie of Absurditie*, *ibid.*, I, 328; Puttenham, *Arte of English Poesie*, *ibid.*, II, 40; Sir William Temple, *Upon Ancient and Modern Learning*, in Spingarn, *Critical Essays of the Seventeenth Century*; Blair, *Rhetoric*, I, 375; Lois Whitney, "English Primitivistic Theories of Epic Origins," *Modern Philology*, XXI, 364–365.

20. Aristotle, *Poetics*, I, ii; Spingarn, *Critical Essays*, II, 331; Gregory Smith, *Elizabethan Critical Essays*, I, 196; Spingarn, *Literary Criticism of the Renaissance*, pp. 41–45; Sidney, *Apology*, in Gregory Smith, *op. cit.*, I, 159; Cowley, *Essays*, p. 40; Dryden, *Essays*, I, 16; Addison, *Works*, I, 155, 161; Dyce, *Memoir of Akenside*, in Akenside, *Poetical Works*, Boston, 1864, p. 84; Cooper, *Letters Concerning Taste*, p. 64; Goldsmith, *Miscellaneous Works*, p. 439; Arthur Murphy, *An*

Essay on the Life and Genius of Henry Fielding, Esq., in *Works of Henry Fielding*, ed. Murphy, London, 1806, I, 31–32; John Scott, *Critical Essays*, p. 361, note.

21. Gray, *Letters*, I, 88; Hobbes, in Spingarn, *Critical Essays*, II, 56; Locke, *Essay*, p. 411; Bolingbroke is quoted by Elwin in Pope, *Works*, II, 336; Boswell, *Life of Johnson*, II, 519–520; Johnson, *Lives of the Poets*, II, 96, V, 206, VI, 74; R. D. Havens, "Changing Taste in the Eighteenth Century. A Study of Dryden's and Dodsley's Miscellanies," *P. M. L. A.*, LXIV, 534; W. L. Phelps, *The Beginnings of the English Romantic Movement*, p. 90.

CHAPTER V

THE ENDOWMENT OF THE POET

W HAT should be the character of the man who is to inculcate virtue and give salutary warnings to youth? In the first place he must be a good man, for not every well-meaning rake could, like Sir Richard Steele, hide his identity behind some kindly Isaac Bickerstaff. The insistence on the moral rectitude of the artist goes back to Strabo and Quintilian in antiquity who thought that the training of the orator or poet necessitated the development of all the virtues of the soul. Ben Jonson echoed the Ancients: a good poet must be a good man, for the poet "is the interpreter and arbiter of nature, a teacher of things divine no less than human, a master in manners; and can alone, or with a few effect the business of mankind." The passage from Milton's *Apology for Smectymnuus* is famous: "He who would not be frustrate of his hope to write well hereafter in laudable things, ought himself to be a true poem." To this *The Tatler* assented. Shaftesbury declared that those who in Greece and Rome wrote best were "either in private life *approv'd good men*, or noted such by their actions in the public." George Campbell insisted that the orator must have an excellent moral character to gain the confidence of the hearer. To such a qualification for the poetic character there seems to have been no express opposition.[1]

More stress was laid on learning. To imitate everything the poet must know everything—philosophy, science, and the arts, as well as human nature. Ben Jonson wished the poet to possess exact knowledge "of all virtues and their contraries." Milton at Cambridge, at Horton, and in Italy set about securing through "industrious and select reading, and steady observation, insight into all seemly and generous arts and affairs." In 1674 Dryden wrote:

Mere poets and mere musicians are as sottish as mere drunkards are, who live in a continual mist, without seeing or judging anything clearly. A man should be learned in several sciences, and should have a reasonable, philosophical, and in some measure a mathematical head, to be a complete and excellent poet; and besides this should have experience in all sorts of humours and manners of men; should be thoroughly skilled in conversation, and should have a great knowledge of mankind in general.

John Dennis agreed. *The Tatler* emphasized knowledge of the human heart. Johnson was as insistent as Dryden on the learned endowments of the poet:

He must estimate the happiness and misery of every condition; observe the power of all the passions in all their combinations, and trace the changes of the human mind, as they are modified by various institutions and accidental influences of climate or custom, from the sprightliness of infancy to the despondence of decrepitude. . . . He must know many languages and many sciences; and, that his style may be worthy of his thought, must by incessant practice familiarize to himself every delicacy of speech and grace of harmony.[2]

The poet must also be a man of common sense and experience, familiar with the ways of the world, not a lone huntsman of exotic beauties through realms of fancy. Boileau's advice was remembered:

Que les vers ne soient votre éternal emploi.
Cultivez vos amis, soyez homme de foi:
C'est peu d'être agréable et charmant dans un livre;
Il faut savoir encore et converser et vivre.

Joseph Warton quoted Boileau with approval. Johnson wrote that "the student must learn by commerce with mankind to reduce his speculations to practice, and accommodate his knowledge to the purposes of life." Little is said directly on the social qualifications of the poet, but the opposition to pedantry, the constant emphasis on the study of mankind, the innumerable assemblies at Will's, at the Club, at Twickenham, Prior Park, and elsewhere suggest the actual attainment of Boileau's ideal in eighteenth-century England.[3]

II

Such were the general endowments of the poet. On such questions there was no dissent except in so far as disagreement is implied in the extended debate over the relative importance of nature and art in the make-up of the poetic character. Could an unlearned genius divinely blessed create masterpieces of art? Could a diligent student of the arts without a special genius successfully emulate by patient practice the great works of antiquity? Few were prepared to give a clear affirmative to either question, but it is possible to group eighteenth-century writers into one of two categories according to the emphasis on nature or genius on the one hand, art or technique on the other. Neither group sensibly predominates during the century. Both can be regarded as classical, for both found support in Greece and Rome, and in the expressed opinions of the masters of English "classical" literature.

Certain attempts were made, it is true, to reconcile nature and art. Sir Thomas Browne declared that "art is the perfection of nature. . . . All things are artificial; for nature is the art of God." Gildon declared that "art entirely includes nature," for it is "nature reduc'd to form." Adam Ferguson argued that art was the best part of nature. Burke echoed Ferguson in declaring that "art is man's nature," and Johnson failed to see how the two terms could be properly opposed. In an effort to avoid laying a stress upon either nature or art Longinus was the most important support. Among the five sources of the sublime, weightiness of thought, and emotion, Longinus thought, were largely the result of nature; the proper use of figures, nobility of phrase, and elevation were partially the effect of art. After a century of conflict Hugh Blair was compelled to confess that the controversy was still undecided, and that its due share must be allowed to each factor—to genius and to art.[4]

Horace had perhaps been the first to phrase the question as to whether nature or art was of more benefit and to refuse his answer on the ground that nature and art must work together. Elsewhere in the *Ars Poetica,* however, he, like Aristotle before him and Quintilian after him, reprehended the long-haired esthete who trusted to genius alone. Aristotle had defined art as a system based on the examination of method, and opposed art to natural ability. Quintilian felt that even when the artist acted by instinct there must always be "some principle of art underlying the promptings of nature." Art consummates what nature begins; the perfect orator owes most to art. This emphasis on art was characteristic of the classical critics.[5]

In France the Pleiade, in England Ben Jonson continued this emphasis. Jonson reminded the admirers of Shakespeare that a poet is made as well as born, and thought it "only the disease of the unskilful to think rude things greater than polish'd, or scatter'd more numerous than compos'd." The French seventeenth century continued to stress art, knowledge, and patient workmanship while rendering lip service to spontaneous genius.[6] In England the Restoration distrusted genius and inspiration as cousins german of enthusiasm. Davenant wrote that poets "are but as children to philosophers (though of some giant race), whose first thoughts, wild, and roaming far off, must be brought home, watch'd, and interrogated." Rochester stressed careful workmanship. Sir William Temple accepted a similar point of view:

'Tho invention be the mother of poetry, yet this child is like all others born naked, and must be nourished with care, clothed with exactness and elegance, educated with industry, instructed with art, improved by application, corrected with severity, and accomplished with labour and with time before it arrives at any great perfection or growth.

Shaftesbury contrasted the evident pride of the ancients in conscientious effort with the modern boast of dependence on genius alone. Pope's couplet is well known:

> True ease in writing comes from art, not chance,
> As those move easiest who have learned to dance.

John Brown found the work of Homer so vast, so complex, and yet so perfect that he was compelled to regard it as the work of careful artistry rather than the product of pure genius. Even Goldsmith, conspicuous for his own genius, felt that art must be present in the poet if the passions are to be turned to use.[7]

As the concept of genius, shortly to be traced, gained ground there was a conscious attempt on the part of wiser heads to stem the torrent. Doctor Johnson, as early as 1751, wrote that,

The mental disease of the present generation is impatience of study, contempt of the great masters of ancient wisdom, and a disposition to rely wholly

upon unassisted genius and natural sagacity. The wits of these happy days
. . . solve difficulties by sudden irradiations of intelligence, and comprehend
long processes of argument by immediate intuition.

George Colman held the same position. According to Reynolds application would be of aid even to invention, and in all aspects of art
industry was safer than dependence upon genius.[8]

Such insistence upon art and learning was not universal. At every
period from Renaissance to Romanticism proponents of genius and
nature struck back at the laborious and careful craftsman. The victory
finally went to the cult of genius which sought support for its
doctrines in a revival of primitive art and in a worship of the work
of Homer, Shakespeare, and Ossian as examples of spontaneous
creation. By most classicists *genius,* which had formerly implied the
possession of supernatural gifts, was used principally to suggest exceptional native gifts, entirely human, but incapable of definition and
unobtainable by learning or art. Gradually the emphasis on the control of these innate powers and on submission to judgment gave way
to an uncritical acceptance of the work of the natural poet, Stephen
Duck the thresher, Mary Collier the poetical washerwoman, Henry
Jones the bricklayer, James Woodhouse the shoemaker, and Ann
Yearsley the Bristol milkwoman. Such a cult of the uneducated is
distinctly opposed to the whole mental fabric of classicism, but it is
impossible to say at any point in the gradual evolution of the concept of genius, here classicism ends, there romanticism begins.[9]

In antiquity Aristotle had considered poetry as the production
of a sympathetic nature ($\epsilon \dot{v} \phi v \epsilon s$) or of an inspired $\mu a \nu \iota \kappa \acute{o} s$ who is
out of himself ($\dot{\epsilon} \kappa \sigma \tau \acute{a} \tau \iota \kappa o s$) and able to fill emotionally the role he
wishes to portray. According to Horace, Democritus excluded sane
poets from Helicon. Longinus insisted on the need for a genuine
emotion to inspire the poet's words as it were with a certain madness
and divine afflatus. Most of the scholarly critics of the English
Renaissance refer without elaboration to the importance of genius.
After the Restoration, when rationalism and the rules were being
urged on the poet as indispensable, one finds that Edward Phillips
can still insist on a "poetic energy" like that of Shakespeare and
Spenser, not "obtainable by any study or industry," but necessary to
give life to a correct work. Mulgrave declared correctness futile

Without a genius too, for that's the soul,—
A heat that glows in every word that's writ,
That's something of divine, and more than wit.

Sir William Temple found it desirable to defend the Ancients by emphasizing the role of natural invention, in order to lessen the significance of accumulated experience in art, which was urged by his opponents as one of the grounds for the supremacy of the Moderns. Dryden recognized the danger to natural ability latent in the emphasis on correctness in his day, and compared Congreve to Shakespeare in the possession of natural genius, the gift of heaven.[10]

Addison's comparison of the two types of genius has been often cited, but it is too important to omit. It must be remembered, however, that Addison considered these differing geniuses as of equal rank, though he admitted the relative scarcity of "the prodigies of mankind" who

by the strength of natural parts, and without any assistance of art or learning, have produced works that were the delight of their own times, and the wonder of posterity. There appears something nobly wild and extravagant in these great natural geniuses, that is infinitely more beautiful than all the turn and polishing of what the French call a *bel esprit;* by which they would express a genius refined by conversation, reflection, and the reading of the most polite authors.

Addison pointed to Pindar as a genius of this first class. Of the second type—not to be confused with the mere *bel esprit*—who "formed themselves by rules, and submitted the greatness of their natural talents to the corrections and restraints of art" Plato, Virgil, and Milton were representative. Elsewhere Addison adds Shakespeare and Homer to Pindar as prodigies of mankind. It is well, in connection with this analysis of genius, to bear in mind Addison's Scales of True Value in which natural parts gained a hundred times in weight when weighed in conjunction with learning, though learning in itself weighed less than natural parts.[11]

Swift and Pope could on occasion see the value of intuition, and Pope, a man without formal university training, was regarded by Spence and others as a striking example of the force of nature or of genius—a self-trained man who rivaled university graduates in ability. Gildon admitted the natural witchery of Shakespeare. Colley

Cibber thought that art and good sense could only preserve the poet from absurdity; "nature must do the rest." In 1730 Edward Young appealed to Pope to

> Let nature art, and judgment wit, exceed.

Young was in time to develop a theory of genius linked with originality, imagination, emotional revery, and egocentric individuality that suited admirably his melancholy disdain for the world, his love of solitude suitable to imaginative excursions among the stars, and his pride in lonely uniqueness. Genius was

> the power of accomplishing great things without the means generally reputed necessary to that end. A genius differs from a good understanding, as a magician from a good architect: that raises his structure by means invisible; this by the skilful use of common tools.

Genius produces "unprescribed beauties, and unexampled excellence." Genius is the "God within," an inner light of art that "can set us right in composition, without the rules of the learned." Learning gives pleasure, genius rapture; "that informs, this inspires, and is itself inspired; for genius is from heaven, learning from man." With lines such as these from the *Conjectures on Original Composition* in 1759 and the earlier picture of the poet in *Night Thoughts* the concept of romantic genius was ushered into the world.[12]

In the meanwhile Hume, Chesterfield, Akenside, Spence, Hawkesworth, Cooper, and Amory all showed their awareness that the poet was born, not made; though Chesterfield and Amory felt that native powers should be controlled by judgment. In 1757 Samuel Rogers gave the palm to Shakespeare's genius over Jonson's art. *The Critical Review* rebutted the view of Armstrong that genius was merely a "perfect polish of soul, which receives and reflects the images that fall upon it, without warping or distortion." In the year of Young's *Conjectures* (1759) Gerard published his *Essay on Taste* outlining a conception of genius in which the power of invention was of major importance. Invention depended on "an extensive comprehensiveness of imagination, on a readiness of associating the remotest ideas that are any way related." Gerard's closely reasoned exposition was less influential than Young's impassioned appeal for self-reliance, but he made a significant connection between genius and the sensibility that was spreading as a counteragent to rationalism and common sense.[18]

In 1774 Gerard returned to the subject of genius and gave what may be regarded as the central conception of the term during the century. Again he built with the blocks of associational psychology. Having identified genius with invention he pointed out the prime role of imagination in calling up concepts necessary to the completion of the artist's design. An infallible instinct directs the associating principle in the choice of proper ideas and connects each new idea with the design of the whole. In the ideal genius activity of mind, regularity, and enthusiasm play roles subordinate to comprehensiveness of imagination. Judgment is necessary to eliminate false ideas and to direct the exuberant imagination to the exact imitation of nature. In this faculty Gerard found Shakespeare deficient. Gerard closed this essentially sane discussion of genius by pointing out that artistic and scientific genius differ in kind; the one directed to beauty, the other to truth; the one concerned with ideas of pleasure and pain, the other indifferent to them; the first seeking striking associations of resemblance, the latter associations of causation and coexistence. The mind at birth is directed into the one channel or the other by an inborn preference for one type of association over the other. Education, habit, and accident fail to explain the path that genius takes.[14]

Between Gerard's *Essay on Taste* and his *Essay on Genius* of 1774 the most important work was William Duff's *Essay on Genius* (1767) which exalted genius as a faculty able "to explore unbeaten paths, and make new discoveries" both in art and science. Duff thought that an equipoise of imagination and judgment in genius was the ideal, for unchecked imagination produces the "reveries of a lunatic"; but that if either must predominate it should be imagination, for a "vigorous, extensive, and *plastic* imagination is needed to *invent* incidents or characters, to create new and uncommon scenery, and to describe every object it contemplates, in the most striking manner, and with the most picturesque circumstances." Unaided genius will not always succeed for a too volatile fancy may be prejudicial to distinct and vivid conception; it may conceive ideas too great to express; it may lose sight of the just and natural; or it may seek too high the new and wonderful and tumble from its height.[15]

Among the major writers of the last quarter of the eighteenth

century William Cowper was most insistent on natural simplicity
and the felicities of spontaneous genius. In a letter to Newton, written on December 10, 1785, he justified his translation of Homer:
"No writer more pathetic than Homer, because none more natural;
and because none less natural than Pope in his version of Homer,
therefore than he none less pathetic." *Table Talk* pictured the first
Eden of poetry:

> In Eden, ere yet innocence of heart
> Had faded, poetry was not an art;
> Language, above all teaching, or, if taught,
> Only by gratitude and glowing thought,
> Elegant as simplicity, and warm
> As ecstasy, unmanacled by form. . . .

Cowper was scarcely dead before Blake advanced the complete romantic conception of "the spontaneous, impulsive elements of genius
in opposition to all restraints of convention or the guidance of
reason."[16]

Many of the writers quoted in defense of nature as opposed to
art were typical men of the century. It is, of course, possible to
regard all of them, and indeed the whole age, as permeated with
pre-Romanticism, but it would be wiser, in view of the fact that
both attitudes towards art persist with almost equal strength throughout the century, to cease applying the epithets *classical* and *romantic*
to expressions of opinion in which nature or art is exalted unless it
is quite evident that the concept held by the individual is in keeping with his whole attitude towards life, and that in the one case that
attitude is dominated by reason, judgment, and form, and in the
other by emotion, imagination, and neglect of form. It is the new
role given to emotion in the concepts of genius as developed by
several writers and critics of the latter half of the century that makes
them particularly significant. In such definitions of genius the cult
of sensibility is married to the cult of genius.

John Armstrong first stated with perfect clarity the significance
of sensibility in the constitution of the man of genius. In the second
volume of his *Miscellanies*, 1758, he declared that there was a
standard of beauty both in the natural and the moral world which
the exquisitely constituted mind perceives most clearly. "It is chiefly

this sensibility that constitutes genius." Armstrong insisted that the poet needed a sound head but he gave the chief honor to sensibility. In assessing the share that taste played in genius Gerard proclaimed "sensibility and delicacy of taste" to be "an essential part" of genius. "By means of this, every form strikes a man of true genius so forcibly, as perfectly to enrapture and engage him, and he selects the circumstances proper for characterising it, and impresses them upon others, with the same vivacity, that he apprehends them himself." Arthur Murphy declared that the imagination of the genius must, in particular, be very quick and susceptible, or, as a fine poet has expressed it, it must be *feelingly alive all o'er*. In *Table Talk* Cowper defined the poetic character. The poet

> Acts with a force, and kindles with a zeal,
> Whate'er the theme, that others never feel;
> If human woes her soft attention claim,
> A tender sympathy pervades the frame,
> She pours a sensibility divine
> Along the nerves of ev'ry feeling line.

It will be recalled that to Wordsworth, too, the poet, though a man like other men, was of keener sensibility than they.[17]

To support the contention that nature was more powerful than art in the production of works of genius it was necessary to find illustrations. They were plentiful, it seems. Burke, Young, Burns, and the Biblical prophets were cited, but it was especially to Homer and to Shakespeare that the critics turned for a triumphant vindication of the supremacy of nature. Jonson had in vain insisted on the role of art in Shakespeare's masterpieces. Ever since Milton's day Shakespeare had warbled his native woodnotes wild through the criticism of Dryden, Rowe, Dennis, Constable, and Armstrong. Pope's opinion is notable:

If ever any author deserved the name of an *original* it was Shakespeare. Homer himself drew not his art so immediately from the fountains of nature. . . . The poetry of Shakespeare was inspiration indeed: he is not so much an imitator, as an instrument, of nature; and 'tis not so just to say that he speaks from her, as that she speaks thro' him. . . . He seems to have known the world by intuition, to have look'd thro' human nature at a glance, and to be the only author that gives ground for a very new opinion, that the philosopher, and even the man of the world, may be *born*, as well as the poet.[18]

In 1767 Richard Farmer in his *Essay* on the learning of Shakespeare rather decisively settled the controversy as to whether the bard of Avon owed most to natural genius or to art by minimizing his knowledge of the classical tongues and casting considerable doubt on his knowledge of modern languages. To Walpole, Malone, Johnson, and Morgann among others the arguments of Farmer seemed convincing.[19]

In Morgann's *Essay on the Dramatic Character of Falstaff* Shakespeare idolatry was carried to a degree of artistic sacrilege. Shakespeare was made the norm by which nature, whose laws give way before him, may be judged. If the events of years must be

comprised within the hour;—with what a magic hand does he prepare and scatter his spells! The understanding must, in the first place, be subdued; and lo! how the rooted prejudices of the child spring up to confound the man! The weird sisters rise, and order is extinguished. The laws of nature give way, and leave nothing in our minds but wildness and horror. No pause is allowed us for reflection: horrid sentiment, furious guilt and compunction, air-drawn daggers, murders, ghosts, and enchantment, shake and *possess us wholly*. We never once awake to the truth of things, or recognize the laws of existence, for he creates a more compendious *nature* . . . of effects only, to which neither the relations of place, or continuity of time, are always essential.[20]

The example of Shakespeare would perhaps have been sufficient to have turned the tide of criticism to the side of genius. The proponents of genius, however, found another ally in Homer, who, in the opinion of Robert Wood, was forced to be original in the absence of any model other than the works of nature herself. To Richard Hurd it seemed that Homer had written before composition became an art and that as a writer of "vehement and impassioned genius" he had been content with his "first thoughts." Adam Ferguson believed that Homer wrote by a "supernatural instinct, not by reflection." To Hugh Blair Homer was the great example of the "masterly genius," who "untaught" will compose "in such a manner as shall be agreeable to the most material rules of criticism."[21]

Homer was a link between the critics who looked for a native endowment in the poet superior to acquired experience of life or knowledge of rules, and those who argued that a primitive stage of culture was more favorable to the arts than the sophisticated, intellectualized world of Versailles and London. In Scotland, particularly, the cult of the primitive was riveted to the cult of genius early in the eighteenth century. Primitive man was more passionate, nobler; primitive poetry more spontaneous, impetuous, warm, and rapid. So early as 1731 John Husbands contended that poetry was the natural language of man, and that the primitive Hebrew, Norse, and Welsh poets had produced sublimity with no guide but nature. Husbands apparently remained obscure, but in 1735 Thomas Blackwell argued in his *Inquiry into the Life and Writings of Homer* that the Greek poet had the advantage of his successors in that the early Greeks were natural, without rules to check rapture and enthusiasm; they were sincere and spontaneous, distinguished not by acquired knowledge and abilities, but by natural simplicity. A spontaneous utterance, pure and strong, reflected this state of manners. These views of Blackwell were echoed by Joseph Warton in 1753. The publication of the first Ossianic poems in 1760 lent new impetus to the movement. Gray was so "extasié" with the "infinite beauty" of the Erse fragments that his subsequent disbelief in their authenticity merely increased his admiration for Macpherson. He came to feel that imagination "reigns in all nascent societies of men, where the necessities of life force every one to think and act for himself," and in *The Progress of Poesy* and *The Bard* he gave poetic expression to his theories. More Ossianic poetry appeared between 1760 and 1763. In the latter year Bishop Percy published the *Five Fragments of Runic Poetry from the Icelandic;* in 1764 appeared Evans's *Specimens of the Poetry of the Antient Welsh Bards;* in the following year came the famous *Reliques* of Percy. Percy's own attitude towards the primitive was decidedly hesitant, but Blair, in his *Critical Dissertation* on the poems of Ossian (1763), and Duff, in his *Essay on Genius* (1767), accepted wholeheartedly the primitivistic views theoretically promulgated by Blackwell and practically exemplified by Ossian and the ballads. Duff found that the superiority of primitive poetry lay in the freshness of view, in the spontaneity and openness of feeling, in the absence of Rules and the freedom from learning, and in the leisure and tranquillity of an unhurried mode of life. Later enthusiasts like Thomas Warton and Hugh Blair did little more than expand the views of Duff.[22]

III

The belief in the supernatural inspiration of the artist is closely involved with the conception of nature as superior to art in poetic composition. During the Renaissance the artist referred to his inspiration on every occasion. The French Pleiade resurrected the idea of divine madness from Plato. In England, Lodge insisted that poetry "comes from above, from a heavenly seat of a glorious God"; "E. K." called poetry "no art, but a divine gift and heavenly instinct . . . poured into the wit by a certain celestial inspiration"; Sidney thought that the poet could outdo nature, because God set him

beyond and over all the works of that second nature, which in nothing he shows so much as in poetry, when with the force of a divine breath he brings things forth far surpassing her [nature's] doings.

Puttenham spoke of the Platonic *furor poeticus;* Meres quoted Ovid's *est deus in nobis;* and even the learned Jonson cited Seneca, Aristotle, Plato, and Lipsius in support of the view that there was something beyond mortality in poetic genius.[23]

Henry Reynolds' *Mythomystes* (1633) was the product of a mind saturated with the neo-Platonic tradition that the poet must be incited by a divine breath, "separated as it were from the body," entranced and elevated in mind, until he partakes of heavenly love, is "ecstatic, and as it were quite ravished and exalted above the earth and all earthly amusements." Milton referred to his

> celestial Patroness, who deigns
> Her nightly visitation unimplored,
> And dictates to me slumbering, or inspires
> Easy my unpremeditated verse. . . .

After 1660 classicists like Boileau, Roscommon, and Prior are still found repeating, though with less conviction, the same formulas. Listen to Roscommon:

So when a *Muse propitiously invites,*
Improve her favours and *indulge* her flights;
But when you find that vigorous heat *abate,*
Leave off, and for *another summons* wait.[24]

As the scientific preoccupations of the century developed, little
was said of inspiration and even less of its supernatural aspects. Hume
supported the view that inspiration was simply a contagion that
"runs along the earth; is caught from one breast to another; and
burns brightest, where the materials are best prepared, and most
happily disposed." A general state of refinement and advancing culture furnishes inspiration or incitement to the individual who tends
to create images and find associations readily. Duff identified "divine
inspiration" with an ardor of fancy worked up to transport, a condition of the mind resulting from vigor and intensity of sensation
sufficient to hurry the mind out of itself. Gerard, however, gave the
fullest explanation of inspiration produced by natural causes. According to Gerard a keen sensibility and enthusiasm make it possible
for the poet to be moved at will by the passions he wishes to excite
in others. As his fiery and spirited genius pursues its course it becomes more impetuous until the mind is enraptured with the subject, and exalted into an ecstasy. In this manner the fire of genius,
like a divine impulse, raises the mind above itself, and by the natural
influence of imagination actuates it as if it were supernaturally inspired. This

enthusiastic ardour elevates and enlivens the fancy, gives vigour and activity
to the associating power, enables it to proceed with alacrity in searching out
the necessary ideas; and at the same time, by engrossing us wholly in the
present subject, preserves us from attending to foreign ideas, which would
confound our thought, and retard our progress.[25]

Save during the Restoration period there was little direct opposition to the doctrine of inspiration, except as it implied the necessity
of waiting for moments favorable to composition. The rationalist
Davenant regarded the claim of inspiration as a pious pretense.
Dryden disliked the possible connection between it and the inner
light of the fanatics. Temple rejected the possibility. Shaftesbury
considered that those who asserted that they were inspired were
probably self-deceived. Sir Joshua Reynolds regarded the idea of

inspiration as "not only groundless but pernicious." Despite the hostility of scientist and rationalist the idea of inspiration was too familiarly associated with the personality of the poet in ancient and Renaissance criticism to be dismissed lightly, and only the extreme rationalist shook himself entirely free. Most classicists were content to use the term conventionally, or to give to it an interpretation based, as was Gerard's, on the psychology of association.[26]

The pure rationalist should be able to work at any hour and at any season. The poet who must await inspiration or who conceived sensibility to be the principal factor in genius had to await the "lucky moments of animated imagination" before he could create. The story goes that Milton could compose only between the autumnal and the spring equinox. Akenside awaited "favorable seasons." Goldsmith, Gray, and Cowper were notoriously temperamental. Boswell was affected by the weather and the seasons. Doctor Johnson contended that Burke and Reynolds were not temperamental, and indeed Reynolds expressed his disgust for temperament in his *Discourses*. Though Doctor Johnson was not always consistent, he seems to have generally regarded the belief that there were times and seasons especially suitable for creative work as an unsubstantiated supposition.[27]

On the whole the evidence here is slight, but it is sufficiently clear that opinions concerning inspiration and temperament, like those concerning genius, do not fall along classical and Romantic lines. It remains to be seen whether judgment or imagination was considered most essential to the endowment of the poet. Here the answer is much clearer, for praise of the *unfettered* imagination is rare before Thomas Warton proclaimed the greatness of Spenser in 1754.

IV

The imaginative faculty has been variously understood. The minute distinctions that have been made between imagination and fancy, and imagination and memory, as well as the subtle investigations of the exact function performed by the imagination in the mental make-up of mankind, fall under the purview of the historian of classical psychology. For the historian of critical opinion two aspects of the imagination are important—the imagination as a free creative faculty molding a picture of the world which does not correspond with reality, and the imagination as an associative power opposed to judgment, which is a power of distinction.

What must be regarded as the logical classical preference for the judgment over the imagination was already apparent in Renaissance classicists like Gabriel Harvey and Ben Jonson. Spenser's mentor, Harvey, breathed a fervent prayer for the man who should let "a fantastical imagination" usurp "the chair of scrupulous and rigorous judgment." Ben Jonson admitted that the imagination could produce many things pleasant at birth, but thought that the very ease with which the images were produced rendered them "justly suspected" until they had been reviewed by the judgment. Shakespeare, so it seemed to his contemporary friend and rival, gave too free a rein to the imagination: he had "an excellent *fancy*, brave notions, and gentle expressions, wherein he flow'd with that facility that sometime it was necessary he should be stop'd: *sufflaminandus erat.* . . ."[28]

After the Restóration it was inevitable that judgment should be even more stressed by the wits and scientists hostile to enthusiasm, lacking in emotional fervor, and in love with the study of fact. Dryden found the imagination wild and lawless unless checked by rime which gave "leisure for the judgment to come in," and Mulgrave proclaimed fancy to be mad without judgment. Rymer, however, was the principal spokesman for the School of Sense:

Say others, *poetry* and *reason*, how came these to be cater-cousins? Poetry is the *child* of *fancy*, and is never to be school'd and disciplin'd by reason; poetry, say they, is *blind* inspiration, is pure *enthusiasm*, is *rapture* and *rage* all over.

But fancy, I think, in poetry, is like *faith* in *religion:* it makes far discoveries, and soars above reason, but never clashes or runs against it. *Fancy* leaps and frisks, and away she's gone, while *reason* rattles the chains and follows after. *Reason* must consent and ratify what-ever by *fancy* is attempted in its absence, or else 'tis all *null* and void in law. However, in the contrivance and *economy* of a play, reason is always principally to be consulted. Those who object against reason are the fanatics in poetry. . . .[29]

After 1700 *The Tatler* lamented that so many men were governed by imagination, and posited good judgment as requisite for a fine gentleman. Dennis, also, thought judgment rarer than imagination, but more valuable. Shaftesbury, like *The Tatler*, esteemed imagination dangerous to strength of mind and to control over one's ideas of pleasures. Addison was not far from agreement with Shaftesbury, though he attempted to distinguish sound imagination from vagaries contrary to reason. *The Guardian* wished imagination and reason to go hand in hand, so that the latter could control the former. Aaron Hill compared the imagination unchecked by judgment to a rudderless ship. Hughes bemoaned the fact that torrents of imagination overbore judgment in Spenser. Gildon, who associated imagination with nature or genius, and judgment with art, thought that nothing entirely beautiful could be produced without judgment as a fire to purify and refine the crude ore of the imagination. Edward Young compared imagination to a beautiful mistress who should be properly subservient to her master judgment. Fielding, Chesterfield, and Akenside agreed with Young, while Warburton went even further to identify judgment with genius.[30]

Though imagination played so important a role in Hume's theory of knowledge that it is possible to regard his *Treatise* and *Enquiry* as sounding the passing bell of classical rationalism, his comparison between judgment and imagination as forces operative in daily life showed no predilection for the latter. The passage presented succinctly the views of the opposing schools:

The *imagination* of man is naturally sublime, delighted with whatever is remote and extraordinary, and running, without control, into the most distant parts of space and time in order to avoid the subjects, which custom has rendered too familiar to it. A *correct judgment* observes a contrary method, and avoiding all distant and high enquiries, confines itself to common life, and to such subjects as fall under daily practice and experience; leaving the more sublime topics to the embellishment of poets and orators, or to the arts of priests and politicians.[31]

In 1767 William Duff defined the role of judgment in art. Unchecked imagination was extravagant and would produce "false and fallacious systems" and "irregular and illegitimate" performances. Judgment makes the "productions of genius regular and just, as well as elegant and ingenious."

The proper office of judgment in composition is to compose the ideas which imagination collects; to observe their agreement or disagreement, their relations and resemblances; to point out such as are of a homogeneous nature; to mark and reject such as are discordant; and finally, to determine the truth and utility of the inventions or discoveries which are produced by the power of the imagination.

Judgment is "cool, attentive, and considerate"; imagination "volatile and rambling": judgment does not find beauties; but it hinders faults contrary to the rules of art. Little purpose would be served by quoting further to illustrate a position which should be sufficiently clear. Judgment had its proponents down to the end of the century—John Brown, Hawkesworth, Richardson, Langhorne, Herbert Croft (author of the life of Young in Johnson's *Lives of the Poets*), Boswell, Blair, Beattie, and Pinkerton carried on the warfare against the freedom of the imagination. In 1805 John Foster summed up the case for classicism in his brilliant—and neglected—essay *On the Application of the Epithet Romantic*. Foster found that the ascendency of imagination over judgment was the chief characteristic of the works of romance that gave rise to the epithet *romantic*. Imagination, unchecked by judgment, permitted inconsistencies, improbabilities, and impossibilities, as wild as the dreams of childhood or of insanity. The dominance of imagination in youth or in inexperienced maturity led to the belief that one had uncommon talents, and this in turn led to the avoidance of common dress and the common forms of speech. Imagination would form schemes impractical in execution, and lead to the expectation of results out of all proportion to the means of attainment if judgment was not present.[32]

Not every one was able to agree with Foster as to the dangers of imagination. Even men who preferred reason and judgment in actual life were sometimes willing to allow imagination a special role in poetry. Bacon and Hobbes were willing to go thus far. Sidney glorified the imagination as a faculty which enabled the poet to create a more beautiful, more moral world than that in which he lived. During the Restoration period wholehearted praise of the imagination *as opposed to judgment* is lacking. It was in 1709 that Rowe struck a decisive blow in behalf of imagination in his *Preface to Shakespeare:* "But certainly the greatness of this author's genius does no where so much appear, as where he gives his imagination an entire loose, and raises his fancy to a flight above mankind and the limits of the visible world." To Addison it seemed that imagination could preserve writings that had no other claim to regard, and that the fantastic Caliban was a greater mark of genius than the realistic Hotspur or Cæsar.[33] As the writer of the papers on *The Pleasures of the Imagination* Addison has been regarded as laying "the foundation of the whole romantic æsthetics in England."[34] To praise of Shakespeare's imagination was soon added praise of Spenser's, and in 1715 one finds Pope expressing a general preference for imagination over judgment, because the latter rather prevents faults than creates beauties.[35]

For forty years little more was heard of the restrictions of judgment until in 1754 Thomas Wartòn's *Observations on the Faerie Queene* sounded a trumpet call to renewed action. Spenser should not be judged by the Rules, for his poetry was "the careless exuberance of a warm imagination and a strong sensibility." He

engages the affections . . . of the heart, rather than the cold approbation of the head. If there be any poem, whose graces please, because they are situated beyond the reach of art, and where the force and faculties of creative imagination delight, because they are unassisted and unrestrained by those of deliberate judgment, it is this.

In the same year John Gilbert Cooper condemned Addison and Pope on the ground that "unconstrained fire of imagination . . . constitutes the true poet." About this time Richardson and his circle began to read Spenser and Ariosto with enthusiasm. Joseph Warton's *Essay on Pope* proclaimed "a creative and glowing imagination" the only stamp of a poet. Only Spenser, Shakespeare, and Milton could qualify. Gray expressed a preference for remote subjects that

leave an unbounded liberty to pure imagination and fiction (our favorite provinces), where no critic can molest or antiquary gainsay us.

In 1762 Richard Hurd defended "the golden dreams of Ariosto" and "the celestial visions of Tasso" against the charge of improbability, and enunciated the doctrine of imaginative possibility as a substitute for logical probability in a manner that would have rejoiced John Dryden. This substitution left little room for the operation of judgment.[36]

After the Wartons and Hurd little remained to be done. The gospel of the imagination had been proclaimed. Minor disciples could spread the glad tidings. This was the function of Webb, of Evans, of Mrs. Montagu, and of other amateurs of criticism. The depreciation of judgment aided the dawning conception of literary evolution to undermine the standard of taste, and to permit a new awareness of the fascination of strange Oriental beauties. After 1760 few Atterburys could be found to damn the fantasies of Arabia as intolerable. Magic was considered delightful to the imagination, and the imagination was now the sole judge of poetry. The less familiar superstitions of Wales and Iceland were discovered to have a weird interest which had faded from the too-often-rationalized myths of Greece and Rome. Baldur and Merlin were evoked in place of Neptune and Minerva in this new era of the arts. But the extension of the bounds of taste is another story.[37]

NOTES TO CHAPTER V

1. Strabo, *Geography*, I. 2. 5; Quintilian, *Institutes*, 1, Preface, 9, and 11. 15. 1; Saintsbury, *History of Criticism*, II, 45–47; Spingarn, *Literary Criticism of the Renaissance*, p. 53; Jonson, Epistle Dedicatory to *Volpone*; Milton, in Spingarn, *Critical Essays of the Seventeenth Century*, I, 202; *Tatler*, No. 47; Shaftesbury, *Characteristicks*, I, 208, 338; Campbell, *Philosophy of Rhetoric*, p. 132.

2. Spingarn, *Literary Criticism of the Renaissance*, pp. 22, 43; Du Bellay, *Deffense et Illustration*, in Vial et Denise, *op. cit.*, p. 8; Jonson, *Timber*, in Spingarn, *Critical Essays*, I, 28; Milton, *Reason of Church Government*, *ibid.*, I, 199; Dryden, Postscript to Notes and Observations on the *Empress of Morocco*, quoted by Bredvold, *Intellectual Milieu of Dryden*, p. 9; Dryden, *Essays*, II, 36; Dennis, *Taste in Poetry*, in Durham, *op. cit.*, p. 134; *Tatler*, No. 47; Johnson, *Rasselas*, Chap. X, and *Lives of the Poets*, I, 180.

3. Boileau, *Œuvres*, p. 217; Joseph Warton, *Essay on Pope*, I, 242; Johnson, *Rambler*, No. 137.

4. Sir Thomas Browne, *Works*, II, 342; Gildon, *Art of Poetry*, in Durham, *op. cit.*, p. 22; Adam Ferguson, quoted by Whitney, *Primitivism and Progress*, p. 152; Stephen, *English Thought*, II, 220; Johnson, *Lives of the Poets*, V, 232; Longinus, II, 2 and VIII, 1; Blair, *Rhetoric*, I, 7, 11, 189.

5. Horace, *Ars Poetica*, lines 295–298, 408–411; Aristotle, *Rhetoric*, 1. 1. 2; Quintilian, *Institutes*, 11. xvii. 8; 11. xix. 1–2; IX. iv. 3–5; IX. iv. 120; Cicero, *De Oratore*, I. 23.

6. Bray, *Formation de la Doctrine Classique*, pp. 38, 87–92; Vial et Denise, *op. cit.*, pp. 4, 69; Harvey, *Four Letters*, in Gregory Smith, *Elizabethan Critical Essays*,

II, 236; Jonson, "To the Memory of my Beloved Master William Shakespeare," and Preface to *The Alchemist;* Boileau, *Œuvres,* pp. 193, 210.

7. Davenant, Preface to *Gondibert,* in Spingarn, *Critical Essays,* II, 27–28; Rochester, "An Allusion to Horace," *ibid.,* II, 285; Sir William Temple, "Of Poetry," *ibid.,* III, 80; Shaftesbury, *Characteristicks,* I, 233, III, 258–259; Pope, *Essay on Criticism,* lines 362–363, and *Works,* I, 4, 8; Gildon, *Art of Poetry,* in Durham, *op. cit.,* p. 23; John Brown, *Rise and Progress of Poetry,* p. 104; Goldsmith, *Works,* ed. Gibbs, IV, 340.

8. Johnson, *Rambler,* No. 154. For other allusions to genius in Johnson see Boswell's *Life,* II, 500, note 2, *Idler,* No. 39, *Rambler,* No. 25, *Preface to Shakespeare,* in Nicoll Smith, *op. cit.,* p. 138, and *Lives of the Poets,* I, 8, V, 195, 200–201. Colman, "The Genius," quoted by Paul Kaufman, "Heralds of Original Genius," in *Essays in Memory of Barrett Wendell,* Cambridge (Mass.), 1926, p. 206; Reynolds, *Discourses,* pp. 21, 78–81; Aiken, *Miscellaneous Pieces in Prose,* pp. 32–33; Fanny Burney, *Cecilia,* I, 13–15, III, 119; Pinkerton, *Letters of Literature,* pp. 72–75.

9. Paul Kaufman, *op. cit.,* pp. 193–197; Tinker, *Nature's Simple Plan,* pp. 92–100.

10. Aristotle, *Poetics,* XVII, 1–4; Horace, *Ars Poetica,* line 296; Longinus, VII, 4. Ascham, *Scholemaster,* in Gregory Smith, *op. cit.,* I, 40; Sidney, *ibid.,* I, 195; Chapman, *ibid.,* II, 298; Daniel, *ibid.,* II, 359–366; Reynolds, *Mythomystes,* in Spingarn, *Critical Essays,* I, 142–143; G. M. Miller, *The Historical Point of View in English Literary Criticism from 1570–1770,* Heidelberg (Anglistische Forschungen, Heft 35), 1913, p. 52; Hamelius, *Die Kritik,* pp. 18, 59–60; Phillips, *Theatrum Poetarum,* in Spingarn, *op. cit.,* II, 271; Mulgrave, *Essay upon Poetry, ibid.,* II, 286, 289–290; Sir William Temple, "On Ancient and Modern Learning," *ibid.,* III, 47–48; 80; Dryden, *Essays,* II, 138, and "To my Dear Friend, Mr. Congreve, on his Comedy Called 'The Double-Dealer.'"

11. Addison, *Spectator,* Nos. 160, 463, 592, and *Tatler,* No. 152.

12. Swift, *Correspondence,* IV, 403, V, 31, 375; Cibber, *Apology,* p. 52; Welsted, *State of Poetry,* in Durham, *op. cit.,* p. 373; Young, *Poetical Works,* II, 355, and *Conjectures,* in Edmund D. Jones, *op. cit.,* pp. 326–330; Harry H. Clark, "A Study of Melancholy in Edward Young," *Modern Language Notes,* XXXIX, 199–202; Sherburn, *Early Career of Pope,* p. 40; Gildon, quoted by C. C. Green, *op. cit.,* pp. 80–81.

13. Hume, *Treatise,* p. 24; and *Essays,* I, 197; Chesterfield, *Letters* I, 99, 132, 156; Akenside, *Pleasures of the Imagination,* Book I, 34–41 and General Argument to the 1757 text; Richardson, *Correspondence,* II, 324–326; Hawkesworth, *Adventurer,* No. 2; John Gilbert Cooper, *Letters Concerning Taste,* p. 95; Amory, *John Buncle,* p. 2; Goldsmith, *Works,* ed. Gibbs, IV, 418, 421–422, 429 and *Bee,* No. VII; Armstrong, *Miscellanies,* II, 134–135; Edward Niles Hooker, "The Reviewers and the New Criticism, 1754–1770," *Philological Quarterly,* XIII, 193; Gerard, *Essay on Taste,* pp. 173–178. *Cf.* Hume, *Treatise,* pp. 348–410.

14. Gerard, *Essay on Genius, passim.*

15. Mrs. Montagu, *Essay on Shakespeare,* pp. x–xi, 18; Eric Partridge, "The 1762 Efflorescence of Poetics," *Studies in Philology,* XXV, 31; Richard Farmer, *An Essay on the Learning of Shakespeare,* in Nicoll Smith, *op. cit.,* pp. 168–169, 199; Beattie, *Poetical Works,* p. 3; Duff, *Essay on Genius,* pp. 4, 6, 22–24, 58–59, 165–166.

16. William Cowper, *Table Talk*, lines 584–592. *Cf.* Cowper, *Task*, Book V, 122, 124. For other expressions of admiration for nature as opposed to art see Thomas Warton, *History of English Poetry*, pp. 34, 330; *Lounger*, Nos. 42, 97 (on Burns, the "heaven-taught ploughman"); Mrs. Radcliffe, *Romance of the Forest*, p. 294; Paul Kaufman, *Heralds of Original Genius*, pp. 211–212.

17. Armstrong, *Miscellanies*, II, 134–135, 169, 195; Gerard, *Essay on Taste*, p. 178; Arthur Murphy, *Essay on Fielding*, pp. 33–34; Cowper, *Table Talk*, lines 480–487, 493, 495; 497–499; Beattie, *Dissertations*, I, 188.

18. Reginald Blunt, *op. cit.*, II, 250; Joseph Warton, *Essay on Pope*, II, 144; John Brown, *Rise and Progress of Poetry*, p. 74; Van Tieghem, *Le Préromantisme*, I, 61; *Lounger*, No. 97; Dryden, *Dramatic Works*, ed. Montague Summers, London, 1931, II, 154; Rowe, *Preface to Shakespeare*, in Nicoll Smith, *op. cit.*, p. 4; Dennis, *On the Genius and Writings of Shakespeare*, *ibid.*, p. 24; Constable, *An Essay Towards a New English Dictionary*, quoted by Marr, *Modern English Romanticism*, p. 193; *Adventurer*, No. 90; Armstrong, *Miscellanies*, II, 198; Pope, *Preface to Shakespeare*, in Nicoll Smith, *op. cit.*, pp. 48–49; Theobald, *Preface to Shakespeare*, *ibid.*, p. 76.

19. Richard Farmer, in Nicoll Smith, *op. cit.*, pp. 162 ff.; R. W. Babcock, "The Attitude toward Shakespeare's Learning in the Late Eighteenth Century," *Philological Quarterly*, IX, 116–122.

20. Maurice Morgann, *Essay on the Dramatic Character of Falstaff*, in Nicoll Smith, *op. cit.*, pp. 249–251.

21. Robert Wood, *Essay on Homer*, pp. 33, 170–172; Hurd, *Works*, I, 369; Adam Ferguson, *Essay on the History of Civil Society*, quoted by Whitney, *English Primitivistic Theories of Epic Origins*, p. 363; Blair, *Rhetoric*, I, 44–45.

22. Lois Whitney, *English Primitivistic Theories of Epic Origins*, pp. 356–361; R. S. Crane, "An Early Eighteenth-Century Enthusiast for Primitive Poetry: John Husbands," *Modern Language Notes*, XXXVII, 27–36; Lois Whitney, "Thomas Blackwell, a Disciple of Shaftesbury," *Philological Quarterly*, V, 200–202; Joseph Warton, *Adventurer*, No. 80; Gray, *Letters*, II, 145 ff., 154, 286, III, 9; Tinker, *Nature's Simple Plan*, pp. 62–64, 72; Van Tieghem, *Le Préromantisme*, I, 137; Blair, *Critical Dissertation on the Poems of Ossian*, p. 90; Duff, *Essay on Genius*, pp. 262–277; Mrs. Montagu, *Essay on Shakespeare*, p. 129; Thomas Warton, *History of English Poetry*, p. 310; *Mirror*, No. 13; Pinkerton, *Letters of Literature*, pp. 1–6; Kaufman, *Heralds of Original Genius*, p. 210; Blair, *Rhetoric*, I, 72, 133, 146, 336–337, 377, III, 117, 245. In his *Philosophy of Rhetoric*, 1776, p. 210, Campbell tried in vain to oppose the torrent.

23. Spingarn, *Literary Criticism of the Renaissance*, pp. 158, 194–197; Hamelius, *Die Kritik*, p. 11; Lodge, *Defense of Poetry*, in Gregory Smith, *op. cit.*, I, 71; "E. K.," Argument of October in *Shepherd's Calendar*, *ibid.*, I, 396; Sidney, *Apology*, *ibid.*, II, 157; Puttenham, *Arte of English Poesie*, *ibid.*, II, 3; Meres, *Palladis Tamia*, *ibid.*, II, 313; Chapman, Preface to the Reader, in Spingarn, *Critical Essays*, I, 67; Jonson, *Timber*, *ibid.*, I, 52.

24. Henry Reynolds, *Mythomystes*, in Spingarn, *Critical Essay*, I, 150–151; Milton, *Paradise Lost*, Book IX, 21–24; Boileau, *Œuvres*, p. 188; Roscommon, *Essay on Translated Verse*, in Spingarn, *op. cit.*, II, 306; Prior, "Another Epistle to the Same" [Fleetwood Shepherd], in Chalmers, *op. cit.*, X, 133.

25. Hume, *Essays*, I, 177; Duff, *Essay on Genius*, p. 171; Gerard, *Essay on*

Genius, pp. 68–69; J. G. Robertson, *Studies in the Genesis of Romantic Theory in the Eighteenth Century*, Cambridge, 1923, pp. 81–82.

26. Davenant, Preface to *Gondibert*, in Spingarn, *Critical Essays*, II, 25; Shaftesbury, *Characteristicks*, I, 5–7; Reynolds, *Discourses*, p. 101; Bredvold, *Intellectual Milieu of John Dryden*, p. 9; Sir William Temple, "Of Poetry," in Spingarn, *op. cit.*, III, 74–75; Williamson, The Restoration Revolt Against Enthusiasm, *Studies in Philology*, XXX, 571.

27. Stern, *Milton und seine Zeit*, Leipzig, 1877–79, IV, 50; Akenside, *Pleasures of the Imagination*, Book I (1757), 294–296; Gosse, *Gray*, pp. 53, 129, 173; Gray, *Letters*, I, 103, II, 31; Cowper, Letters to William Bull, June 3, 1783, and to Unwin, Sept. 29, 1783; Boswell, *Hypochondriack*, II, 33, note 4, and *Life of Johnson*, I, 385, III, 219; Johnson, *Idler*, No. 11, *Lives of the Poets*, II, 219.

28. Gabriel Harvey, *Four Letters*, in Gregory Smith, *op. cit.*, II, 238; Jonson, *Timber*, in Spingarn, *Critical Essays*, I, 19, 32.

29. Dryden, *Essays*, I, 8, 106–107; Mulgrave, *An Essay upon Poetry*, in Spingarn, *op. cit.*, II, 287; Rymer, *Tragedies of the Last Age*, *ibid.*, II, 185.

30. *Tatler*, Nos. 21, 27, 66; Dennis, *Taste in Poetry*, in Durham, *op. cit.*, p. 118; Shaftesbury, *Characteristicks*, I, 312; Addison, *Spectator*, Nos. 12, 37; *Guardian*, No. 127; Aaron Hill, in Richardson, *Correspondence*, I, 27; Marr, *History of Modern English Romanticism*, pp. 23, 25; Gildon, *Art of Poetry*, in Durham, *op. cit.*, p. 25; Edward Young, *Poetical Works*, II, 159, 161; Fielding, *Champion*, March 15, 1740, and *Tom Jones*, Book IX; Chapter I, Book XIII, Chapter I, Book XIV, Chapter I; Chesterfield, *Works*, V, 90–91; Akenside, *Poetical Works*, pp. 191–195; Warburton, Commentary on *An Essay on Criticism*, in Pope, *Works*, II, 86.

31. Hume, *Essays*, II, 133, and *Treatise*, pp. 265–268.

32. Duff, *Essay on Genius*, pp. 7–10; John Brown, *Essays on the Characteristicks*, pp. 12–14; Hawkesworth, *Adventurer*, No. 2; Richardson, *Writings*, XIV, 22–23; A. D. McKillop, "The Romanticism of William Collins," *Studies in Philosophy*, XX, 4–5; Johnson, *Lives of the Poets*, VI, 125; Boswell, *Hypochondriack*, I, 181, and *Letters*, p. 50; Blair, *Rhetoric*, I, 371, II, 28, III, 84; Pinkerton, *Letters of Literature*, p. 298; Foster, "On the Application of the Epithet Romantic," in *Essays in a Series of Letters*, pp. 178–209; Beattie, *Dissertations*, I, 206.

33. Sidney, *Apology*, in Gregory Smith, *op. cit.*, I, 152–157; Bacon, *Advancement of Learning*, in Spingarn, *Critical Essays*, I, 4–5. Cf. Spingarn, *op. cit.*, I, x–xi. Hobbes, *Leviathan*, pp. 41–44; Rowe, *Preface to Shakespeare*, in Nicoll Smith, *op. cit.*, p. 14; Addison, *Spectator*, Nos. 419, 421, 512, 279, 333, *Tatler*, No. 111.

34. Robertson, *Studies in the Genesis of Romantic Theory*, p. 241.

35. John Hughes, *Essay on Allegorical Poetry*, and *Remarks on the Faerie Queene*, in Durham, *op. cit.*, pp. 87, 105; Pope, *Works*, VIII, 27, and *Preface to the Iliad*, in Durham, *op. cit.*, p. 341.

36. Thomas Warton, *Observations*, I, 15–16, II, 3, 56. Warton felt that the *critic* needed more judgment than imagination. Cf. *ibid.*, II, 263. Cooper, *Letters Concerning Taste*, pp. 28–29; Richardson, *Correspondence*, II, 74, 93, 245; Joseph Warton, *Essay on Pope*, I, ii, vii, 115; Gray, *Letters*, I, 360; Hurd, *Letters on Chivalry and Romance*, pp. 134–136; for Dryden see Chapter VIII.

37. E. N. Hooker, "The Reviewers and the New Criticism, 1754–1770," *Philological Quarterly*, XIII, 196; Evans, *Some Specimens of the Poetry of the Ancient Welsh Bards*, quoted by Phelps, *The Beginnings of the English Romantic Movement*, p. 145; Mrs. Montagu, in Blunt, *op. cit.*, II, 269; Pinkerton, *Letters of Literature*, p. 487.

CHAPTER VI

THE OBLIGATIONS OF THE POET

I

THE CLASSICAL poet was well aware of his ethical responsibility. His function as a moral guide committed him to a serious consideration of man's happiness, and a faithful representation of man's life. The proper study of mankind is man; not the stars in the heavens nor the flowers in the fields. Science had done much to mold the spirit of the age, but science in turn became suspect when it seemed indifferent to man's well-being. To the Augustan humanist Addison's work seemed more useful than Newton's. As a consequence of this belief the age attacked the virtuosi, ridiculed metaphysics, and insisted that reason be employed in ethics and psychology for the furtherance of man in society. The Enlightenment was a humanist interlude between a medieval world in which man minimized this life to magnify the life hereafter, and a modern world in which man has lost his dignity before the sweep of scientific forces. The new astronomy did not at first reveal all its terrors, but rather aided the "proper study of mankind" by lessening man's concern with final causes, original sin, and futurity and by lending support to the view that nature operated by reasonably simple laws; while the new psychology of sensation supported man's self-esteem by picturing his senses as the measure of all things, and made the discovery of a true science of the human mind imperative. The rallying cry of the age is Pope's oft-quoted line:

The proper study of mankind is man.

Voltaire sounded a similar note: "O mankind, God gave thee intelligence for the wise conduct of thy life, not as a means to penetrate into the essence of the things which He has created." Johnson, the last of the titans of the humanist tradition, acclaimed Socrates for drawing "the wits of Greece . . . from the vain pursuit of natural philosophy to moral inquiries," and turning their thoughts "from stars and tides, and matter and motion, upon the various modes of virtue and relation of life."[1]

Before Bacon and Descartes, the Academy of Sciences and the Royal Society had developed the experimental method of investigation and altered the temper of man's mind; the psychology of sensation and of association, utilitarian ethics, and the statistical method in "political arithmetic" could scarcely have been envisaged. To these forerunners the eighteenth century owed an incalculable debt, but their successors, the mathematical-astronomical scientists and virtuosi of a later period, were often compelled to see their instruments of thought turned against themselves in behalf of those branches of philosophy which the Earl of Shaftesbury defined as "the study of happiness." From Locke to Hume, English philosophers laid stress on knowledge that was supposed to have a direct bearing on man's well being. In the *Thoughts Concerning Education*, 1693, Locke insisted that it was of much more use for a man

to judge right of men, and manage his affairs wisely . . . , than . . . to have his head fill'd with the abstruse speculations of natural philosophy and metaphysicks.

Francis Hutcheson declared "the just knowledge of human nature" the most important part of philosophy. David Hume asked the readers of his *Enquiry:*

Shall we esteem it worthy the labour of a philosopher to give us a true system of the planets, and adjust the position and order of those remote bodies; while we affect to overlook those, who, with so much success, delineate the parts of the mind, in which we are so intimately concerned?[2]

The periodical essayists endeavored to popularize the humanist attitude by insisting on self-knowledge, on the significance of man in the Scale of Being, on the emptiness of the Newtonian discoveries, and on the desirability of studying human institutions on the Continental Tour. Sir William Temple doubted that natural science had ever made any real contribution to man's happiness. The Dean of St. Patrick's wrote ironically of the Brobdingnagians:

The learning of this people is very defective, consisting only in morality, history, poetry, and mathematics, wherein they must be allowed to excel. But the last of these is wholly applied to what may be useful in life, to the improvement of agriculture, and all mechanical arts; so that among us it would be little esteemed.

Akenside, Young, Green, Fielding, Whitehead, Harris, Blair, and Pinkerton considered a knowledge of man more important than an acquaintance with the world in which he moved. It was Pinkerton who preferred Addison to Sir Isaac Newton:

There is more real glory in having written two pages that have actually taught mankind how to be virtuous and happy, than in composing whole systems of speculations; more illustrious fame arising from one of Mr. Addison's papers in the *Spectator*, than from the whole works of Sir Isaac Newton, even though he had demonstrated an acute and stupendous theory of deity itself.[3]

Attack on the scientist offered more scope for variety than the reiteration of the famous words of Pope—the useless collections of the virtuosi could be detailed by an Addison (*Spectator*, No. 216); the foolish experiments of scientists presented on the stage by a Shadwell, whose Sir Nicholas contented himself with the speculative study of swimming but never swam; the meetings of the Royal Society parodied by a Swift; the investigations of fossils, shells, and butterflies compared to a lady's passion for old china by a Gay; or the members of the Royal Society pictured as the favorites of the Goddess of Nonsense by a Fielding. *The Tatler* and *Spectator*, Pope and Shaftesbury, Goldsmith and Smollett, Kames and Gibbon, Welsted and Whitaker, poets and novelists great and small, assailed the scientist whenever he ventured from the study of mankind, but no one did so more eloquently than Robert Burton at the beginning of the Age of Reason:

For what matter is it for us to know how high the *Pleiades* are, how far distant *Perseus* and *Cassiopea* from us, how deep the sea, etc.? We are neither wiser . . . nor modester, nor better, nor richer, nor stronger, for their knowledge of it.[4]

It is clear that many of the leading writers of the period regarded the painstaking investigation of nature as a waste of time and talent.

Content to take at second hand the orderly conception of the universe, they preferred to apply the experimental methods of science to the study of psychology and the embryonic social sciences, or to deflate the bubbles of vanity with the pin pricks of wit and to undermine the approaches of dullness with the petards of common sense. If they seem to us today too often to have been seeds in a dry pod while Newton roared in the pines, it is nevertheless true that they fought against the luxury of idle dreaming, kept contact with reality, and stirred successive younger generations towards a goal of moderation in life more frequently attainable than the lofty ideals of the later Romanticists. With the realistic emphasis of the age of classicism the contemporary world has less reason to quarrel than with its neglect of natural science.

II

Fidelity to truth was the second obligation of the poet. During the Renaissance and Restoration periods in England the question of realism seems to have been raised only in connection with the rule of probability—the theme of the next chapter—but at the beginning of the eighteenth century Addison gave expression with perfect clarity to the ideal of classical realism in *Spectator*, No. 523: "No thought is beautiful which is not just; and no thought can be just which is not founded in truth, or at least in that which passes for such." *The Guardian* was even more explicit:

> Poetry being imitation, and that imitation being best which deceives the most easily, it follows that we must take up the customs which are most familiar or universally known, since no man can be deceived or delighted with the imitation of what he is ignorant of.

Shaftesbury called truth "the most powerful thing in the world, since even fiction itself must be governed by it, and can only please by its resemblance." Hume thought that tragedy should be founded in fact to secure easier reception for extraordinary events. Joseph Warton, Oliver Goldsmith, Fanny Burney, Samuel Johnson, John Scott, and John Pinkerton echoed the same opinions in the latter half of the century.[5]

In the realm of pure fantasy there was nothing that could move the poet who, according to Shaftesbury, must be moved, "or at least seem to be so, upon some probable grounds," if he is to move the reader. Could Busiris or Pharimond be of any concern to the reader? Could the Delias and Neæras with their frisking lambs arouse any passionate conviction, Doctor Johnson asked. Mythology and heroic tragedy were effete. The mood of the age was prepared for middle-class drama and fiction.[6]

The ordinary concerns of humanity are more gripping than the evocations of the unfettered imagination. The closer the relationship the more powerful is the appeal. Like Goldsmith's Primroses we are interested in the petty concerns of our neighbors, in Tom Jones and Evelina more than in *le grand Cyrus* or Alexander. Steele and Lillo presented the earliest critical apologia for the new realism of literature. Steele wrote in *The Tatler:*

> I was thinking it would be of great use (if anybody could hit it) to lay before the world such adventures as befall persons not exalted above the common level. This, methought, would better prevail upon the ordinary race of men, who are so prepossessed with outward appearances that they mistake fortune for nature, and believe nothing can relate to them that does not happen to such as live and look like themselves.

Aaron Hill repeated Steele's argument in 1721:

> To ills remote from our domestic fears,
> We lend our wonder, but withhold our tears.

Lillo agreed with Steele and Hill in the Preface to *George Barnwell* (1731):

> Plays founded on moral tales in private life may be of admirable use, by carrying conviction to the mind with such irresistible force as to engage all the faculties and powers of the soul in the cause of virtue, by stifling vice in its first principles.[7]

III

The objections to the sentimental portrayal of life in the romances and in novels of sensibility make clearer the realistic basis of English classicism. Romances, it was believed, tended to undermine chastity by an overemphasis on passion, and to destroy the com-

monly accepted code of morality by the elevation of right feeling
in the place of right conduct; they gave an exaggerated view of
life which prevented the performance of useful duties or led to
grievous disappointment; they produced absurdity in conduct, if not
actual immorality; they failed to give the instruction that it was
reasonable to expect from more accurate pictures of life; and they
offended good taste and common sense with a tissue of improbabilities and nonsense.

Lady Lurewell in Farquhar's *Trip to the Jubilee* (1699) blamed
credulous innocence and the moving power of romances for her early
fall from virtue. In *The Spectator* Budgell warned feminine readers
against romances which were likely to inflame the passions. Chesterfield, often accused of a lack of ethical feeling, attempted to do his
bit in the defense of innocence by picturing in *The World* a young
girl led to ruin by glowing sensibility and romantic notions of "divine honour, spotless virtue, and refined sentiment," which blinded
her to the wiles of her seducer. One recalls Ascham's description
of his books of bold bawdry when one hears Goldsmith finding use
for every variety of book except romances, which he considered "no
better than instruments of debauchery," since they exalted love as
the ruling passion. Beattie, too, thought that romances "tend to
corrupt the heart, and stimulate the passions," but it remained for
Cowper to pen the most vigorous attack:

> Ye writers of what none with safety reads,
> Footing it in the dance that fancy leads:
> Ye novelists, who mar what ye would mend,
> Sniv'ling and driv'ling folly without end,
> Whose corresponding misses fill the ream
> With sentimental frippery and dream
> Caught in a delicate soft silken net
> By some lewd earl or rake-hell baronet:
> Ye pimps, who, under virtue's fair pretense,
> Steal to the closet of young innocence,
> And teach her, inexperienc'd yet and green
> To scribble as you scribbled at fifteen;
> Who, kindling a combustion of desire,
> With some cold moral think to quench the fire;
> Though all your engineering proves in vain,
> The dribbling stream ne'er puts it out again.[8]

An even more sweeping accusation was brought against the romance for producing a general confusion of moral values. A corre-
spondent in *The Connoisseur* was bitterly ironic:

> But the age is more particularly indebted, for its present universal purity
> of manners, to those excellent rules for the conduct of life contained in
> our modern novels. From these moral works might be compiled an entire new
> system of Ethics, far superior to the exploded notions of musty academies,
> and adapted to the practice of present times.

Goldsmith was very skeptical of "the exquisite raptures of sentimental bliss" free from all taint of sensuality. Those who attempted
to picture pleasure remote from sense deluded themselves and could
delight only fools, while there was a real danger that the reader
would be lulled into a false sense of security and fail to realize that,
like the Platonic lover of a former century, he was treading on a
coating of very thin ice. *The Mirror* thought that the young reader
of sentimental novels would imitate the conduct of the unwary
heroine as "natural and allowable in common life," or would learn
to sacrifice prudence and propriety as "the invention of cold and
selfish minds" to romantic sentiment and sensibility. *The Lounger*
carried on the attack against novels which produced a "mistaken and
pernicious system of morality" contrasting duty, justice, prudence,
and economy on the one hand with love, generosity, benevolence,
and compassion (the expansive sentiments) on the other. In a case of
conflict the novelist exercised great ingenuity to award the decision
to the "least obvious, and therefore generally the least reasonable"
emotion, to visionary ideals rather than to practical duties.[9]

In sentimental comedy good intentions and a feeling heart were
more important than action. Steady devotion on the part of the
loyal wife or faithful maiden would in time redeem the erring husband and bring back the absent lover. The generous friend or the
elderly idealist would be justified in the trust he reposed in the sensibility of the wayward characters whose deviations from moral rectitude were less significant than their essential goodness. It was a
consoling moral code in which repentant tears could wipe out the
memory of sin, but it seemed to the classicist much easier to be
generous on the stage than in real life which the sentimentalist consistently falsified. Goldsmith's attack is famous:

In these plays almost all the characters are good, and exceedingly generous; they are lavish enough of their tin money on the stage; and though they want humour, have abundance of sentiment and feeling. If they happen to have faults or foibles, the spectator is taught, not only to pardon, but to applaud them, in consideration of the goodness of their hearts; so that folly, instead of being ridiculed is commended, and the comedy aims at touching our passions without the power of being truly pathetic.

Goldsmith was aided by Whitehead and by Foote, and when his own *Deserted Village* laid him open to attack he was rebuked by Crabbe in *The Village*. A generation after Goldsmith, Coleridge included a brilliant destructive analysis of sentimental drama in *Biographia Literaria*.[10]

A less serious result of romance reading than a topsy-turvy moral code—or an illegitimate child—but surely a more frequent one, was the development of great expectations which made the fulfilment of normal duties unpleasant and the attainment of normal happiness unlikely while the brain of the young lad or young maiden was stuffed with the dreams of unrealizable bliss. Doctor Johnson's Imperia, for instance, read romances and became so proud that no lover who did not speak of vows, altars, and sacrifices could hope to please her. Johnson, indeed, seemed to dread the powers of the imagination more than most of his contemporaries, as all readers of *Rasselas* knew, and considered that "it would be undoubtedly best, if we could see and hear everything as it is, that nothing might be too anxiously dreaded, or too ardently pursued." In the sphere of art only the most careful realism could answer Johnson's demand, yet he did not stand alone. Richardson's Charlotte Grandison argued that

mild, sedate convenience is better than a stark staring mad passion. The wall-climbers, the hedge and ditch-leapers, the river forders, the window-droppers, always find reason to think so. Who ever hears of darts, flames, Cupids, Venuses, Adonises, and such like nonsense in matrimony? Passion is transitory; but discretion, which never boils over, gives durable happiness.

Goldsmith's Lady Betty Tempest had learned from plays and romances that "a plain man of common sense was no better than a fool; such she refused, and sighed only for the gay, giddy, inconstant, and thoughtless." In verse and prose Beattie pursued the same theme:

> Eyes dazzled long by fiction's gaudy rays
> In modest truth no light nor beauty find.

Readers of romance, Beattie wrote in his *Dissertations,*

form a thousand schemes of conduct, few of which can be reduced to practice; and look down with contempt on those plodding mortals, who, having only good sense to guide them, and disclaiming all extravagant hopes, aim at nothing beyond the common pursuits of life.

Clara Reeve's Hortensius agreed with Beattie, and John Foster included an indictment of the false expectations sown by romance in his arraignment of the romantic attitude.[11]

Such absurd dreams were certain to lead to disappointment. For few indeed of the romantic young maidens could there be a Prince Charming, for few young men could the quest of the Blue Flower be successful. Foster had concluded his attack on the romantic attitude with the hint that foiled expectations led to melancholy. To Prior, a survivor of the light-hearted coterie of Restoration gallants, romance reading seemed a certain pathway to a false idea of love's fidelities. In much the same spirit Lady Mary Wortley Montagu rebutted Pope's sentimental lament for the country lovers struck by lightning with a realistic picture of the probable future of their romance that might have given hints to Rupert Brooke for his devastating picture of the old age of Helen and Menelaus. Goldsmith's "True History for the Ladies" in the *British Magazine* for July, 1760, illustrated the swift disillusionment that follows upon romantic passion. Even more vigorously he sought to save his own nephew from the perpetual disappointments which the romanticist must face. Goldsmith was writing to his brother concerning the boy's education:

Above all things, let him never touch a romance or novel; these paint beauty in colours more charming than nature, and describe happiness that man never tastes. How delusive, how destructive, are those pictures of consummate bliss! They teach the young mind to sigh after beauty and happiness which never existed; to despise the little good which fortune has mixed in their cup, by expecting more than she gave; and, in general, take the word of a man who has seen the world, and has studied human nature more by experience than precept—take my word for it, I say, that books teach us very little of the world.[12]

Quixoticism in attitude and absurdity in conduct would be frequently apparent in the devotee of romances, according to the practical moralists of the day. Steele's Biddy Tipkin, like the later Lydia Languish of Sheridan, refused to abridge her amour by marriage, for she loved "disguise, serenade, and adventure," and knew that no knight ever "entered tilt or tournament after wedlock." *The Tatler* represented a lady "far gone in poetry and romance" who erected a black marble tomb with Cupids at the corners for a lamented lover. Addison's Leonora, in much the same state of mind, became a decided eccentric and hung cages of turtle doves in her woods. It was Addison, too, who toyed with the idea of picturing a young Don Quixote who took all his notions of life from the stage and "directed himself in every circumstance of his life and conversation by the maxims and examples of the fine gentlemen in English comedies." Cornelia Lizzard of the *Guardian* series was another romantic young lady who longed to live "in a wood among choirs of birds, with zephyrs, echoes, and rivulets to make up the concert." George Colman continued these attacks on romantic absurdities of conduct in *Polly Honeycombe*, Arthur Murphy in *The Apprentice*, Charlotte Lennox in *The Female Quixote*, Richard Graves with Miss Townsend and Lady Sherwood in *The Spiritual Quixote*, and Richard Brinsley Sheridan in *The Rivals*. Maria Edgeworth and Jane Austen as well as Barrett and Peacock fought on the side of sanity and realism even when Romanticism was triumphing.[13]

The novel aroused less criticism than the romance. Fielding distinguished the "history" or novel from the romance as a valuable instrument of instruction in the Preface to *Joseph Andrews*. Goldsmith insisted that more real improvement could be gained from "relations which are levelled to the general surface of life, which tell—not how men learned to conquer, but how they endeavoured to live—not how they gained the shout of the admiring crowd, but how they acquired the esteem of their friends and acquaintances." Hugh Blair preferred novels to romances for much the same reason: in novels "relations have been professed to be given of the behaviour of persons in particular interesting situations, such as may actually occur in life; by means of which, what is laudable or defective in character and in conduct, may be pointed out, and placed in a useful light." Doctor Johnson described the modern novel as a food for mature minds in contrast to the romance with its appeal the childish intellect. It is the realistic or satiric eighteenth-century novel, not the Gothic romances, which are remembered today.[14]

This emphasis on the realistic presentation of the life of man combined with the ethical insistence in an age controlled in large measure by the common sense of the group explains the dominance of certain literary forms and "kinds" during the century. Satire, with irony as its most brilliant weapon, and didacticism, with the "character" as an ever-ready tool, were dominant. The prose comedy, the social essay, and the realistic novel were the most successful vehicles for this satiric and didactic spirit. Within these forms the whip of satire could be flicked across the back of laggards in the process of social regimentation; or undesirable social types could be embodied in characters who acted out their absurdities before the eyes of audience or reading public. The polished verse satire of Pope owed much to Horace and to Juvenal, but it was in the novel, the essay, and the comedy that the age was best portrayed, and there the writer of the eighteenth century was most original. Unfettered by the burden of great classical models or by the precepts of Aristotle, the leading writers of the period could portray their age each in his own way. Remove the artificial epics, the Horatian satires, the second-hand Georgics, the *Catos* fashioned by French Aristotelian formalists, and there would indeed be a gap, but the Age of "Classicism" would still have most of its Dryden and its Swift, the best of its Addison and Steele, much of its Pope, its Restoration social comedy, and its enduring contributions to fiction in the work of Defoe, Richardson, Fielding, Smollett, Goldsmith, Edgeworth, and Austen. It would still possess the common-sense humanism of Doctor Johnson, and the wit and wisdom of its great letter writers. None of these works could be produced by the egocentric and often maudlin emotionalism of the ideal Romanticist, though he likewise has his glories in lyric and autobiographical confession, in the impassioned sympathy of social protest, and in the cry of the wounded heart. None of these works was fashioned on an ancient framework in strict accord with classical

Rules; they were developed by the mind of the Enlightenment to give adequate expression to the social conscience of the period in a profoundly ethical and realistic art that was definitely English in spirit.

NOTES TO CHAPTER VI

1. Bury, *The Idea of Progress*, pp. 160–161; Randall, *Making of the Modern Mind*, pp. 132, 212–213; Johnson, *Rambler*, No. 24; Pope, *Essay on Man*, Book II, line 2; Cobban, *Edmund Burke*, p. 22.

2. Shaftesbury, *Characteristicks*, II, 438; Locke, *Thoughts Concerning Education*, p. 81; Hutcheson, *Inquiry*, p. lx; Hume, *Essays*, I, 87; II, 10; Bury, *op. cit.*, p. 159.

3. *Spectator*, Nos. 10, 408, 519; *World*, No. 141; *Idler*, No. 97; Temple, "Upon the Gardens of Epicurus"; Swift, *Gulliver*, p. 158; Akenside, *Pleasures of the Imagination*, Book III (1744), lines 7–11; Young, *Poetical Works*, II, 36–37; Green, *The Spleen*, lines 774–775; Fielding, *Tom Jones*, Book VIII, Chap. I; Whitehead, "The Enthusiast"; Harris, *Three Treatises*, p. 229; Blair, *Rhetoric*, I, 11; Pinkerton, *Letters of Literature*, pp. 328, 345, 350.

4. Claude Lloyd, "Shadwell and the Virtuosi," *P. M. L. A.*, XLIV, 489, *et passim*; C. S. Duncan, "The Scientist as a Comic Type," *Modern Philology*, XIV, 97–98; Gay, *Poetical Works*, p. 180; Fielding, *Author's Farce*, Act III, scene I; Burton, *Anatomy of Melancholy*, I, 421; Swift, *Gulliver*, pp. 119, 127, 192, 209 ff., 235; Fielding, *Covent-Garden Journal*, I, 277, and *Pasquin*, Act V, scene I; Cross, *Fielding*, pp. 390–392; Akenside, *Pleasures of the Imagination*, Book III, lines 163–170; Johnson, *Preface to the Preceptor*, *Rambler*, Nos. 82, 83, 161, *Adventurer*, No. 119, *Lives of the Poets*, III, 41, and *Rasselas*, Chap. XLVI; Smollett, *Peregrine Pickle*, Chap. XCV; *Tatler*, No. 236; *World*, No. 83; Welsted, in Durham, *op. cit.*, p. 381; Goldsmith, *Citizen of the World*, Letter LXIII; Shaftesbury, *Philosophical Regimen*, pp. 121–122, 267, 402–403, and *Characteristicks*, III, 156; Pope, *Works*, IV, 35–36; Sherburn, *The Early Career of Alexander Pope*, p. 81; Gibbon, *Autobiography*, p. 74; Kames, *Elements*, I, 17; Boileau, *Œuvres*, pp. 148–149.

5. *Guardian*, No. 30; Shaftesbury, *Characteristicks*, I, 4; Hume, *Treatise*, pp. 121–122; Joseph Warton, *Essay on Pope*, I, 249; Goldsmith, *Works*, ed. Gibbs, IV, 290; Fanny Burney, *Early Diary*, I, 9; Johnson, *Lives of the Poets*, I, 13–14; John Scott, *Critical Essays*, pp. 59, 113; Pinkerton, *Letters of Literature*, p. 44.

6. Shaftesbury, *Characteristicks*, I, 4; Johnson, *Lives of the Poets*, IV, 122, VI, 149; Goldsmith, *Works*, IV, 390; Richardson, *Correspondence*, IV, 209, 220.

7. Mrs. Montagu, *Essays on Shakespeare*, pp. 35–36; *Mirror*, No. 63; Aaron Hill, Preface to *The Fatal Extravagance*; Steele, *Tatler*, No. 172; Lillo, Preface to *George Barnwell*.

8. Farquhar, *A Trip to the Jubilee*, Act III, scene V; Budgell, *Spectator*, No. 365; Chesterfield, *World*, No. 25; Goldsmith, *Citizen of the World*, Letter LXXXIII, and *Miscellaneous Works*, p. 512; Beattie, *Dissertations*, II, 320; Cowper, *Progress of Error*, lines 307–322; W. F. Gallaway, "The Sentimentalism of Goldsmith," *P. M. L. A.*, XLVIII, 1167 ff.

9. *Connoisseur*, No. 17; Goldsmith, *Citizen of the World*, Letter VI; *Mirror*, Nos. 54, 101; *Lounger*, No. 20; Blunt, *op. cit.*, II, 125; Mrs. Montagu, *Essay on Shakespeare*, pp. 287, 294.

10. Bernbaum, *Drama of Sensibility*, pp. 80, 106–107, 243–244; Goldsmith, *Essay XXII*; Coleridge, *Biographia Literaria*, pp. 336 ff.

11. Johnson, *Rambler*, No. 115, and *Idler*, No. 50; Richardson, *Writings*, XVII, 161, XIX, 15–16; Goldsmith, *Citizen of the World*, Letter XXVIII; Beattie, *The Minstrel*, Book II, xl, and *Dissertations*, I, 237; Clara Reeve, *Progress of Romance*, II, 78; Foster, "On the Application of the Epithet Romantic," *loc. cit.*, p. 205; Hume, *Essays*, II, 388; Dottin, *Samuel Richardson*, p. 69.

12. Foster, *op. cit.*, p. 205; Prior, in Chalmers, *op. cit.*, X, 153; Pope, *Works*, IX, 409; Lady Mary Wortley Montagu, *Letters*, II, 289; Goldsmith, *Works*, I, 449; IV, 483–486.

13. Steele, *Tatler*, No. 85, and *The Tender Husband*, Act IV, scene II; Addison, *Spectator*, Nos. 37, 446; *Guardian*, Nos. 5, 31, 150; Graves, *Spiritual Quixote*, I, 116, 240–241, II, 329; Edgeworth, *Belinda*, I, 38, 159, 310; II, 156; Austen, *Northanger Abbey*, Chap. XXV; W. H. Rogers, "The Reaction Against Melodramatic Sentimentality in the English Novel, 1796–1830," *P. M. L. A.*, XLIX, 98.

14. Goldsmith, *Miscellaneous Works*, p. 515; Blair, *Rhetoric*, III, 101–102; Congreve, Preface to *Incognita*; Shaftesbury, *Characteristicks*, I, 344–350; Fielding, *Joseph Andrews*, Book III, Chap. I; Johnson, *Rambler*, Nos. 4, 151.

CHAPTER VII

REALITY AND NATURE

I

THE REALITY that played so important a part in the classical outlook on art was distinctly different from the realism or naturalism of recent decades. The contemporary realist makes a minute study of the individual; the eighteenth-century realist sought to present a type. Contemporary naturalism involves a detailed study of a distinctive heredity and environment as it affects an individual who is often abnormal, because of the greater ease of observation in the exceptional case; classical naturalism meant a study of the normal (and *therefore* natural) workings of the unchanging laws of nature on a person regarded as typical of his age and class. The views are poles asunder. A minutely observed Elmer Gantry would be regarded by the classical critic as false or monstrous because he was not typical of the clerical group, or would be dismissed as uninteresting—much as a lyrical confession would be uninteresting—because no large number of readers could believe in his actions or sympathize with his peculiar problems. The classicist considered that the artist falsified the average truths of life by the exactness of differentiating detail, and preferred to seek truth to human nature in a moral realm apart from space and time. To this ideal he sacrificed the unusual, the complex, and the abnormal.

This classical realism was intimately connected with the methods of the physical sciences. As Lewis Mumford has pointed out in *Technics and Civilizations:*

The method of the physical sciences rested fundamentally upon a few simple principles. First: the elimination of qualities, and the reduction of the complex to the simple by paying attention only to those aspects of events which could be weighed, measured, or counted, and to the particular kind of space-time sequence that could be controlled and repeated. . . . Second: concentration upon the outer world, and the elimination or neutralization of the observer as respects the *data* with which he works. Third: isolation: limitation of the field: specialization of interest and subdivision of labor. In short, what the physical sciences call the world is not the total object of common human experience: it is just those aspects of this experience that lend themselves to accurate factual observation and to generalized statements.

This scientific basis for classicism was supported by the general concept of Nature as envisaged by the legalistic and philosophic mentality of Rome, and by the concept of pure common sense as developed by Descartes. Nature was the realm of law, of rule, of the probable event. As Spinoza described it:

Nothing comes to pass in nature in contravention to her universal laws, nay, everything agrees with them and follows from them, for . . . whatever comes to pass comes to pass according to laws and rules which involve eternal necessity and truth, although they may not all be known to us, and therefore she keeps a fixed and immutable order.

It seemed to Spinoza that the emotional life of man was a matter of the mathematical calculation of probabilities. John Dennis drew the application between this view of Nature and the æsthetic outlook of a reasonable man:

There is nothing in nature that is great and beautiful without rule and order; and the more rule and order and harmony we find in the objects that strike our senses, the more worthy and noble we esteem them. . . . Now nature, taken in a stricter sense, is nothing but that rule and order and harmony which we find in the visible world, so reason is the very same throughout the invisible creation. For reason is order and the result of order.

From this view of human nature the law of artistic probability was born, and as its corollaries the laws of decorum and universality, already envisaged by the critics of Greece and Rome. What calculations of reality could conceivably be made if the soldiers of the poet's imagination could not be relied upon to be soldierly and the kings to be kingly? How could the probability so essential to belief be obtained unless the characters of fiction acted as one was accustomed to see their counterparts in real life act? How could the arts fulfil their moral function if the actions of the fictitious personages were lacking in verisimilitude, if the audience or readers remained incredulous and failed to apply the poetic justice of the imaginary

world to their own lives? With thoughts like these in mind Pope
penned his famous lines:

> First follow nature, and your judgment frame
> By her just standard, which is still the same:
> Unerring nature, still divinely bright,
> One clear, unchanged, and universal light,
> Life, force, and beauty, must to all impart,
> At once the source, the end, and test of art.

Dryden, Shaftesbury, Richardson, Goldsmith, Johnson, and Blair
were among the prominent preachers of the doctrine superbly
phrased by Pope. And there were countless others.[1]

The just appreciation of the significance of Nature to the classical
critic gives a key to much of the artistic activity of the period of
classicism. Unfortunately the interpretation of the term *Nature* was
by no means uniform between 1660 and 1800. The usual connection
of Nature was with the rational, the normal, and the general, as
opposed to exceptional divergences from common conduct, to the
monstrous *lusus naturae*, and to specific historic fact. In spheres to
which inductive science was not applicable resort was made to the
deductive rationalism of Descartes, which pictured Nature as controlled by laws perceptible by ordinary reason. "Hence," as Randall
explains it, "what was natural was easily identified with what was
rational, and conversely, whatever, particularly in human society,
seemed to an intelligent man reasonable, was regarded as natural
and somehow rooted in the nature of things."[2] To follow Nature
was to follow common sense. Only what appealed to common sense
could please; hence the basis for admiration of the Greeks and
Romans who had pleased so long. The rules were a codification of
ancient practice; hence the rules were the keys to rational pleasure;
they were, as Pope proclaimed, "nature methodised." The rational
classicist found no contradiction in the terms common sense, Nature,
universality, the rules, or correctness. They were terms intimately
interlinked, for all of them were based on the operations of law in
the external world and in the mind of man.[3]

Not always, however, was the term Nature, when applied to art,
identified with an inevitable chain of causes and effects in which the
actions of the characters are sufficiently normal to permit the ob-

server, who can judge of probability only by his knowledge of individuals of the same general type, to predict the course of the action without disconcerting surprise. This was the dominant view, and was most fully in conformity with the scientific bias of the age. Less frequently, to follow Nature meant to imitate the Platonic ideal in an endeavor to create a beauty more perfect than the actually existing copies of the ideas in this world of shadows could show; it might mean, with Aristotelian moral emphasis, the imitation of life as it ought to be; it might imply merely the reflection of the surface reality of life; or it might mean the adoption of devices appropriate to a specific artistic form; or, and that all too frequently, it might mean almost nothing at all, be, in fact, a counter term like *democracy* or *liberty* used to justify whatever to the artist seemed desirable in his art.[4] In the interest of clarity it seems best to examine probability, decorum, and universality—the three applications of Nature as a norm for art—in turn, and to develop the less important definitions as attempts on the part of artists like Dryden to justify artistic devices which apparently conflicted with Nature as commonly conceived.

II

The law of probability is as old as Aristotle, who had written in the *Poetics* that, "A poet's object is not to tell what actually happened, but what could and would happen either probably or inevitably." Poetry, like philosophy or science, must deal, not with "sports," but with general truths or laws. Only by following this rule could poetry assume its true dignity, and be regarded justly as more scientific and serious than history, the mere record of what has actually happened. During the Renaissance it was especially necessary to insist on the rule of probability, in view of the manifold impossibilities of medieval romance which continually obscured the sense of reality. Typical critics like Castelvetro and Sidney developed the distinction of Aristotle between the probability and necessity that reigned in the poetic world and the truth to fact of history, as a means of defense against attacks upon the utility of poetry.[5]

In 1623 Chapelain laid down the logical basis for the rule of probability:

Where belief is lacking, attention or interest is lacking also; but where there is no interest, there can be no emotion and consequently no purgation or amendment of men's manners, which is the end of poetry. Belief, therefore, is absolutely necessary in poetry.

This was the typical justification of the rule, and sufficed, together with the influence of Aristotle, to give theoretic support to the growing psychological realism of literature, until the scientific revolution of the late seventeenth century revealed the orderly structure of Nature in which, according to the earlier view, uniformity actually reigned, or, according to the later, reigned in appearance because of the working of the law of averages in dealing with large numbers. Once this idea of Nature became popular it was clear that to follow Nature implied an obligation to preserve probability. From Hobbes to Blair probability was the watchword of the classicist. Thomas Rymer believed that the probabilities of the drama would heighten man's faith in Providence:

Something must stick by observing that constant order, that harmony and beauty of Providence, that necessary relation and chain, whereby the causes and the effects, the virtues and rewards, the vices and the punishments are proportion'd and link'd together, how deep and dark soever are laid the springs and however intricate and involv'd are the operations.

Edward Phillips attacked "romantic actions" as violations of probability. Blackmore defined unity of action as a series of events based on a probable chain of causes and effects. Congreve and Addison, Dennis, Hume, and Fielding were all offended by violations of probability, while from Rowe to Johnson critics of Shakespeare lamented his violations of so essential a rule.[6]

This widely accepted law of probability was used to attack many abuses in art. With the rallying cry of probability the unities of time and place were both defended and attacked. If the stage were undeniably a single spot what could be more improbable than permitting it to represent Rome at one moment, Athens at the next? Such was the view of the strict neo-Aristotelians, who insisted on complete illusion in the drama. What could be more improbable than the presentation of events which would normally require weeks or months within the cycle of a single sun, the critics of the Unities replied. The rimed drama was declared improbable; the aside, the soliloquy, set speeches, and the chorus met no better fate. Dryden found sudden conversions a violation of probability. Battles and deaths on the stage were for the same reason abandoned in France, and rested uneasily on the critical conscience in England. The violations of probability in opera rendered that art form repugnant to common sense. Classical myths could no longer be believed, and must be replaced by Christian story if probability was to be preserved. But it was above all the "romantic" that was looked on askance by the adherents of probability.[7]

The use of historical events in tragedy complicated the problem for those who insisted on the higher truth of poetry. After all, the justification of the rule of probability to a large extent lay in the conviction imparted by the art in which it was observed. History was full of improbable events, which imparted conviction because they were known to have taken place. Alteration would improve the artistic chain of cause and effect, but would alienate the belief of the audience. The artist could escape the horns of the dilemma only by avoiding historical events that were too well known and resorting to the periphery of historical knowledge. In the dim regions of legend, in the remote courts of Persia, Morocco, and Peru the artist could find material that would enhance his work with the dignity of great events, lend to it the glamor of the exotic, and yet permit him to preserve logical probability by refashioning little-known events to suit his tragic purpose. It was difficult to abandon the historical basis entirely, for the employment of names of persons and places even vaguely familiar gave a solidity to the fabric of tragedy which predisposed the audience to belief before the commencement of the drama. In practice the result of the attempt to reconcile poetic and historic truth, belief and wonder, was the Heroic Tragedy of the Restoration, and its weak-kneed descendant, the poetic drama of the Aaron Hills and Edward Youngs of the eighteenth century.[8]

The more important classical artists strove for a reasonable freedom within the rule of probability. Here Dryden is typical, for his vital artistic instincts made him restive under restraint, while his rational bent led him to justify his manipulations of the Rules. In the epic belief must be reconciled with wonder by the use of epic "machinery" to "give a colour of probability to things otherwise

incredible." The intervention of the gods—improbable in actuality—
must be admitted into the sphere of art to allow a cause sufficiently
powerful to render certain actions credible. Blackmore, Addison,
and Blair agreed with Dryden that epic "machinery" enhanced
artistic probability. Dryden clearly accepts the distinction between
Nature as reality and Nature as probability in the world of imagination:

In truth the world of fable, which is the world of the poet, has in it nothing of reality. . . . But this system having been once supposed, all that one
creates within the extent of the same system will not pass for false among
the wise, above all if the fiction preserves verisimilitude, and conceals some
moral truth.[9]

In the matter of the Dramatic Unities Dryden again was liberal.
Refusing to admit that the audience ever fully believes in the reality
of the stage performance, he advanced the theory of artistic illusion
resting on the system of probabilities *within* the play in contradis-
tinction to the complete conviction demanded by the strict neo-
Aristotelians. This artistic illusion—Coleridge's willing suspension of
disbelief—is enhanced by the power of the great artist who can impart
conviction through emotional intensity. Probability, the most important term in the definition of Nature fundamental to classical art,
can be assessed only in the moment of artistic communion between
artist and audience. The test of probability is delight. The cold
analysis of art, the separation of faults from beauties, the examination
of correctness in the light of a common sense based on external reality
can have no critical validity for the imaginative sphere of art.[10]

For Dryden the comedy of humors raised another problem, for
a humor, as Congreve phrased it, was a "singular and unavoidable
manner of doing or saying anything, peculiar and natural to one
man only, by which his speech and actions are distinguish'd from
those of other men." How could the actions "peculiar to one man
only" be judged probable or improbable? If the natural is the general and the expected, comedy must be unnatural. Dennis stated
the issue clearly: "Everything which is ridiculous must be both
particular and surprising; for nothing which is general and expected
can excite a sensible man to laughter." Despite the efforts of Shadwell, Temple, and Dryden to compromise between the general and

the particular, it became increasingly clear that the actions of a peculiar humorist could not be predicted; could not, indeed, be subject to the rule of probability from whose operations the comedy of humors must be exempt.[11] It became necessary to redefine the natural as the imitation of the unusual as well as of the normal. This was Dryden's course:

> By humour is meant some extravagant habit, passion, or affection, particular . . . to some one person, by the oddness of which, he is immediately distinguished from the rest of men; which being lively and naturally represented, most frequently begets that malicious pleasure in the audience which is testified by laughter; as all things which are deviations from common customs are ever the aptest to produce it: though by the way this laughter is only accidental, as the person represented is fantastic or bizarre; but pleasure is essential to it, as the imitation of what is natural.

This passage shows clearly that Dryden was positing the imitation of Nature as an explanation of the pleasure caused by comedy, though, at the same time, he was admitting that the divergence between the character on the stage and a norm existing in the mind of the audience was the cause of laughter. To follow Nature in tragedy meant to adhere to probability, decorum, and generality; in comedy the same term meant to reflect accurately what may be called a surface reality—the reality of the actions of particular men.[12]

It was in the defense of the Heroic Poem and the Heroic Play that Dryden was forced to stretch his conception of the natural far beyond the limits of probability. In *Of Heroic Plays* (1672) and in *The Author's Apology for Heroic Poetry* (1677) much scope was allowed to fancy. Dryden even argued for the use of ghosts and magic. " 'Tis enough that, for aught we know, they may be in Nature; and whatever is, or may be, is not properly unnatural." Dryden has come far from any conception of Nature as a chain of causes and effects; far even from the conception of Nature as "Whatever is," for the admission of the "may be" into the realm of the natural threw open the bulwarks of classicism to all the monstrosities of the Romantic imagination. And yet it would be false to describe Dryden's attitude at this moment as Romantic, for he was desperately attempting to rationalize a theory of the epic—an art form popular both in antiquity and in the seventeenth century.[13]

In *The Author's Apology for Heroic Poetry* Dryden presented a specious defense of the unnatural, as adherents to the conception of Nature as probability must logically consider it. He argued that whatever pleases all ages must be natural, that beings quite out of Nature may be "founded on the conjunction of two natures," and that whatever is founded on popular belief is an imitation of other men's fancies, and consequently an imitation of Nature. A quotation from the Preface to *Tyrannick Love* (1670) will further illustrate the extreme liberality of Dryden's position:

As for what I have said of Astral or Aerial spirits, it is no invention of mine, but taken from those who have written on that subject. Whether there are such Beings or not, it concerns not me: 'tis sufficient for my purpose that many have believ'd the affirmative: and that those Heroic Representations, which are of the same Nature with the Epic, are not limited, but with the extremest bounds of what is credible.[14]

In a last effort to escape logical classicism Dryden linked Nature and pleasure. As early as 1668 in the *Defense of an Essay of Dramatic Poetry* he had shown his willingness to sacrifice bare imitation to gain delight. A bare imitation would not affect the soul and excite the passions, nor would it move admiration, which is the delight of serious plays. Bare imitation may be sacrificed, but if pleasure ensues, the artist has still imitated Nature, for "nothing can move our nature, but by some natural reason, which works upon passions." Delight became the sole test of the naturalness of art.[15]

If pleasure is the test of the natural it is difficult to impose a check on the imagination. Dryden was willing to follow his liberal definition of the natural to its conclusion. In 1691, in speaking of his *King Arthur*, he approved the true taste of the Duchess of Monmouth, who had expressed admiration for "the parts of the airy and earthy spirits, and that fairy kind of writing, which depends only upon the force of the imagination. . . ." Dryden had not always been so favorable to fancy, for in 1671 he had linked judgment with the natural, and fancy with the unnatural, monstrous, and chimerical. In 1672, however, he had granted judgment a predominant role in comedy, and admitted that fancy could do much in serious plays (the Heroic Tragedy, of course) "which depend not much on observation." A few more years were to pass before Dryden was willing to defend epic and opera by sacrificing all legitimate meaning in the term *Nature* and admitting the validity of the fancies that exist in the minds of the people or the monsters that could be fashioned by ingenious combinations of the natural. Hippocentaurs and hippogriffs, witches and warlocks, fairies and fabulous monsters were admitted into the high places of the worship of Nature by critical ratiocination.[16]

Virgil and Homer were, of course, justified in their "Romanticism" by this critical juggling—a result that must have been eminently satisfactory to Dryden's contemporaries. Even Ovid, whose fictions, Dryden had declared, were often against the order of Nature, even the absurdities of medieval romance—the Green Knight who rides off with his severed head, and the magic and the charms—could no longer be consistently attacked if *Nature* was such a Protean term. Indeed, Dryden, in his endeavor to adapt his critical credo to his multifarious creative activities, had completely wrecked the critical machinery based on the imitation of Nature, and furnished a precedent to others who, after him, found the rule of probability barring their freedom of action.[17]

III

The rule of probability applied to character produced the law of decorum. The "manners" of the characters must above all be probable. "Manners" were supposed to differ according to humor or disposition, age, sex, climate, quality, or condition; and must be so clearly portrayed that without hesitancy the spectator could judge of the naturalness of the action which the manners produce. In each specific character the manners must be suitable, resembling, and constant—suitable to the disposition, age, and sex chosen; resembling the traditional conception of the character; and constant to the conception first revealed in the exposition. Manners are best shown and probability best preserved if in each character a ruling passion is shown and the complexity and subtlety of life reduced to order. By observing the manners the spectator may judge whether or not the dramatist has followed Nature.[18]

Though the term has disappeared, decorum is still the test of plausibility in fiction. In the classical period certain special factors rendered the rule of decorum easy of acceptance. The social system was more rigidly regimented than it is today, and the manners and dress of different social classes had much less in common. Much of decorum in this sense has faded before the democratic ideal. Except on state occasions kings dress like other men, and work in modern offices: they are not so uniformly kingly. In the second place the rule of decorum was supported by the medical theory of humors, and by its successor, the doctrine of the ruling passion. Human personality was much less complex, much more predictable. In the third place decorum of character was the natural product of the demand for tidiness and order, for abstraction, and for geometrical demonstration. If the actions of a character could not be predicated by his class, temperament, age or condition, there was an end to social control, to ethics as a science, to the rule of probability, and to the imitation of Nature itself.

Horace supported the Aristotelian notion of decorum in the *Ars Poetica:*

> intererit multum, divusne loquatur an heros,
> maturusne senex an adhuc florente iuventa
> fervidus, et matrona potens an sedula nutrix,
> mercatorne vagus cultorne virentis agelli,
> Colchus an Assyrius, Thebis nutritus an Argis.

The Renaissance critics in Italy and the French Aristotelians, Rapin, Dacier, and Chapelain, urged it on every occasion.[19]

In England the rule of decorum was seldom driven so relentlessly as in France. The Restoration period, during which Hobbes, Dryden, and Rymer upheld the rule, saw the practice at its peak, but long before Johnson's exoneration of Shakespeare in 1765 any particular respect for decorum had been merged in the more flexible regard for probability, or accepted silently as a corollary of universality that it would be unwise to stress. The early English adherents of decorum were conservatives overly impressed with the sanctity of the social order and with the majesty of kings. Flecknoe condemned Beaumont and Fletcher for treating kings irreverently. Dryden felt that a lawful king should not be given a vicious character on the stage. It was

Rymer, however, who, by attacking *Othello* in the light of a too exacting social code and a too narrow conception of a soldier's character, brought complete discredit upon the rule he so ardently enforced. Rymer denied that a soldier could be in love or jealous, and damned Othello. He insisted that a soldier must be "open-hearted, frank, plain-dealing," and damned Iago. He believed that Othello might pass for a drayman or a drunken tinker, but refused to admit that a Venetian general could rant and rail as Othello did when jealous. It was a violation of decorum, according to Dryden, for a man to wound a woman; for Rymer it was unwomanly for a woman to use a sword. No woman, indeed, must kill a man, no servant a master, no subject a king. "Poetry will allow no provocation or injury where it allows no revenge" by the code of the duel. No wonder that the world has remembered Thomas Rymer and followed the law of decorum down the years with volleys of laughter.[20]

After 1700 Dennis and Pope alone seem to have made much of decorum of character. Steele felt that many dramatists violated decorum by making "all men as witty as themselves, and making all persons of the play speak the sentiments of the author without any manner of respect to the age, fortune, or quality of him that is on the stage." In the spirit of Steele, Mrs. Montagu censured the French for converting every one into a French gallant, and John Brown objected that Virgil's shepherds were too much like fine gentlemen. Goldsmith seemed to feel that the observation of Nature would lead to decorum both of national type and of personal character, but Henry Fielding in 1749 was already paving the way for Johnson's denunciation when he expressly denied that Lady Bellaston represented the general conduct of ladies of fashion, Thwackum of clergymen, or Ensign Northerton of soldiers. Johnson gave decorum of character its *coup de grâce* in the *Preface to Shakespeare,* where he dismissed it as one of the petty cavils of petty minds. To Johnson social position was an accident; a man's share in common humanity the essential. All passions are conceivable in all men; buffoons may sit in senates, and drunkards sit on thrones. This position we have now learned to accept, but how Doctor Johnson reconciled his scorn for decorum with his respect for probability and his preference for universality he neglected to disclose.[21]

IV

The classical preference for the general over the specific was in keeping with the scientific and ethical emphasis. The connection of universality with common sense, the "light of nature," should be apparent from earlier chapters. Since Nature was controlled by uniform scientific law, the natural must be the uniform or universal. Only the general could impart conviction, when tested by the normal experience of the reading public. Only from the universal could moral lessons of general applicability be gained. Only the universal could be beautiful, for irregularity and disproportion through their infrequency were strange and repelling to an age that loved established and familiar things.

The classical point of view was fully expounded by Bishop Hurd in a note on Horace's *Ars Poetica:*

> *Truth,* in poetry, means such an expression as conforms to the general nature of things, *falsehood,* that which, however suitable to the particular instance in view, doth yet not correspond to such *general nature.* To attain to this truth of expression in dramatic poetry two things are prescribed: 1. A diligent study of the Socratic philosophy; and 2. A Masterly knowledge and comprehension of human life. The *first,* because it is the peculiar distinction of this school *ad veritatem vitae proprius accedere. . . .* And the *latter,* as rendering the imitation more universally striking. This will be understood by reflecting that *truth* may be followed too closely in works of imitation, as is evident in two respects. For, 1. the artist, when he should give a Copy of nature, may confine himself too scrupulously to the exhibition of *particulars,* and so fail of representing the *general* idea of the *kind.* Or, 2. in applying himself to give the *general* idea, he may collect it from an enlarged view of *real* life, whereas it were still better taken from the nobler conception of it as subsisting only in the *mind. . . .*
>
> We see then that in deviating from particular and partial, the poet more faithfully imitates universal truth. . . . For, by abstracting from existences all that peculiarly respects and discriminates the *individual,* the poet's conception, as it were neglecting the intermediate particular objects, catches, as far as may be, and reflects the divine archetypal idea, and so becomes itself the copy of image of truth.[22]

Irving Babbitt has affirmed correctly that "a core of normal experience" in the individual is postulated by all classicists, who write of themselves as though they were norms, rules, and laws rather than strictly individuals. Intimacy and emphasis upon one's peculiarities might interfere with universality of appeal. Local color and faithful impressionism could find no place in a period during which young artists were directed by the President of the Royal Academy to divest themselves of the prejudices of age and country, to disregard the local and the temporary, and to address themselves to every country and to every age.[23]

All readers of Oswald Spengler are familiar with his contrast between the timelessness and generality of the antique as compared with the time consciousness and individuality of the modern world. In the Newtonian universe in which "processes rolled on their way in cyclical fashion, completing themselves, like the orbits of the planets, in recurrent definite intervals; . . . there was no real change," and the Augustan Englishman attempted to fashion an equally permanent system of ethics based on an unchanging human nature, a general religion timelessly true for all peoples, and political constitutions which did not evolve, but *were*.[24]

Spengler distinguished the timeless Greek myth, eternally true like a proposition in mathematics, from the plot of modern drama which is "character-tragedy," true only for a single individual in a specific series of situations. The Greek character was subject to a fate beyond his control; the modern character is responsible for his own destiny: the Greek ideal is the type, the πρόσωπον, the mark or persona of *the* king; the modern the presentation of *a* king, a Macbeth or Lear conditioned by space-time.[25] In classical historiography the past was vague and legendary, a memory in the process of becoming myth, not a womb pregnant with the growing forces of the present hour, of which a knowledge is essential to whoever would understand the present. The individual once dead became himself a figure in a myth; Alexander was merged with Dionysus. In Greek art realistic portraiture was unknown. Even when the artist abandoned his Joves and Venuses, he gave to the individual physiognomy of hero and legislator the nobility and generality of an imaginative ideal, until in the Roman imperial period portraiture was at last developed, probably from Etruscan models. Only in such a *Weltan-*

schauung could a Cato write a history of Rome in which consuls and prætors performed their roles upon the stage, but in which no individual name was ever mentioned.[26]

No philosophical historian of the eighteenth century analyzed the ancient mind with the ingenuity of a Spengler, but the dramatic masks, the comic types without a trace of realism in their complete abstraction from particular features, the ideal nudes of the sculptor, the lofty dignity of generalized heads on Greek and Roman coins, the absence of historic consciousness, and the stress laid by Aristotle on the ought-to-be, and by Plato on the ideal—all these things were known and, although the preference for generality was easily deducible from probability and decorum, they all helped to strengthen the eighteenth-century artist in his convictions.[27]

After the early appeal of Sidney for general truth in poetry, Davenant, one of the apostles of the worship of reason, was apparently the first to elaborate the theory of universality in the *Preface to Gondibert* (1650):

> For wise poets think it more worthy to seek out truth in the passions than to record the truth of actions, and practise to describe mankind . . . not particular persons as they are lifted or levell'd by the force of fate, it being nobler to contemplate the general history of nature than a selected diary of fortune; . . .

Rymer attacked fancy as liable to lead to the creation of tragic characters, singular, monstrous, and pleasing to the writer alone, while reason, "common to all people . . . can never carry him from what is natural." Dennis most nearly perceived the mythlike (allegorical) nature of classical tragedy in a justification of his revision of *Coriolanus* in a letter to Steele:

> The "Coriolanus," as I have altered it, having a just moral, and by consequence at the bottom a general and allegorical action, and universal and allegorical characters, and for that very reason a fable, is therefore a true tragedy . . . whereas "All for Love" having no moral, and consequently no general and allegorical action, nor general and allegorical characters, can for that reason have no fable, and therefore can be no tragedy.

Mulgrave, Dryden, and Congreve insisted that satire must not stoop to show a single fop, but rather

in one piece expose,
Whole belles-assemblees of coquettes and beaux.

Shaftesbury declared that the genius formed his ideas "from the *many* objects of nature, and not from a particular one." Swift suited his writings, not to "particular occasions and circumstances of time, of place, or of person," but to "universal nature and mankind in general." Fielding justified the novel as adherence to general truth, and insisted that he himself described "not men, but manners; not an individual, but a species." Doctor Johnson defended universality vehemently. His two pronouncements on the subject are famous:

Nothing can please many, and please long, but just representations of general nature. Particular manners can be known to few, and therefore few only can judge how nearly they are copied. The irregular combinations of fanciful invention may delight awhile, by that novelty of which the common satiety of life sends us in quest; but the pleasures of wonder are soon exhausted and the mind can only repose on the stability of truth.

The business of a poet . . . is to examine, not the individual, but the species; to remark general properties and large appearances; he does not number the streaks of the tulip, or describe the different shades in the verdure of the forest. He is to exhibit in his portraits of nature such prominent and striking features as recall the original to every mind, and must neglect the minuter discriminations, which one may have remarked and another have neglected. . . .[28]

Nature as a norm was subjected to occasional attack. There was a period of transition between acquiescence in Johnsonian grandeur and the attitude of extreme Romanticists like Novalis: "The more personal, localized, immediate, specific a poem is, the nearer it comes to the central core of poesy." In this epoch of transition some critics came to suspect that the "abstract schematism" of the general resulted in monotony, poverty, and sterility. *The Lounger* tried to compromise between the general and the specific. The problem was to express the general by means of the specific, to attain concreteness and color without the loss of universality. The individual must become a symbol. Fielding succeeded with his Tom Jones, Boswell with his Doctor Johnson; but the age as a whole either failed to perceive the necessity, or failed to comprehend the means of success.[29]

Metaphysical, scientific, and purely æsthetic ideas apparently contributed to the overthrow of the normal as an artistic ideal. The monadology of Leibnitz represented the universe as composed of distinct monads. No monad was like any other. No blade of grass like any other. The specific, the individual, the characteristic were in conformity with the nature of things. Aided by the metaphysics of Leibnitz, English thinkers like Bishop King and Lord Bolingbroke developed the idea of the Scale of Being[30] to a point at which it became necessary to conceive of God as a "Cosmic Artist . . . cramming his canvas with diversified detail . . .; as caring more for fullness and variety of content than for simplicity and perfection of form; and as seeking this richness of coloring and abundance of contrast even at the cost of disharmony, irregularity, and what to us appears confusion." At the same time the natural sciences were slowly gaining the victory over mathematics, and as nature was minutely investigated by the grubbing pedants, so completely scorned by most of the men of letters, it was found that regularity dissolved into complexity, and that uniformity must be replaced by an average approximation to which no specific individual conformed. In the field of æsthetics the ideas of sublimity and of the picturesque ushered in a new appreciation for the uncontrolled and irregular in nature. The Italian school of landscape painters, headed by Salvator Rosa, fathered this new ideal of beauty.[31]

Vague hints of rebellion against the reign of universality can be found in Dryden, Addison, Gildon, and Fielding, but it was Joseph Warton who ended the period of preliminary spadework and began in earnest to undermine the citadel of classicism. In the famous *Essay on Pope* (1756) he found Pope's descriptive poetry deficient in concrete detail. "Particular and picturesque," not "general and indiscriminate" epithets strike the imagination, and in fact distinguish poetry from history and render the former "a more close and faithful representation of nature than the latter." A more complete reversal of the views of Aristotle and Sidney could scarcely be imagined.[32]

After 1756 expressions of preference for the specific were frequent. Lord Kames declared imagery "the life of poetry" and insisted that images rest on particular objects. Doctor Blair decided that "all distinct ideas are formed upon particulars," and that "no description that rests upon generals can be good." Both Kames and Blair as academic lecturers and compilers of texts must have had an incalculable influence on youth. William Duff postulated "a particular and picturesque representation of nature" as the mark of a genuine poet. Gerard and Campbell agreed. By 1783 James Beattie was able to write:

> That poetical description ought to be distinct and lively, and such as might both assist the fancy, and direct the hand of the painter, is an acknowledged truth of criticism. The best poets are the most picturesque. Homer is in this respect so admirable, that he has been justly called the prince of painters, as well as of poets. And one cause of the insipidity of the Henriade is, that its scenery and images are described in too general terms, and want those distinguishing peculiarities that captivate the fancy, and interest the passions.

The battle against universality had been won.[33]

The significance of the victory can scarcely be overestimated. The love of the universal, static, uncomplicated, and uniform constituted the heart of classicism. Such qualities were easy deductions from the rule of reason; love for them grew together with Deism, with universally valid ethics, and universal rights of men in the hearts of a generation which disliked the complex, the irregular, and the awareness of difference. The loss of this citadel rendered possible the multiplication of genres and of stanzaic forms, the appreciation of the nuance, of the grotesque, and of local color. It made possible the study of distinct national cultures in legend and folklore, and gave the impetus to the nationalism that defeated Napoleon and produced the first World War. It permitted personal expression in art. It secured the recognition of the Dutch school in painting. It had much to do with the growing distaste for universal formulas in politics. It allowed the forc᾽ of sensibility to be brought to bear against standardization. It made the way easy for the acceptance of originality and of the original genius. It opened wide the door for Romanticism.[34]

NOTES TO CHAPTER VII

1. Spinoza is quoted and discussed by Randall, *Modern Mind*, pp. 245–247; Dennis, Epistle Dedicatory to the *Advancement and Reformation of Modern Poetry*, quoted by Clark, *Boileau and the French Classical Critics in England*, p. 380. *Cf.* Spingarn, *Critical Essays of the Seventeenth Century*, I, lxviii; Pope, *Essay on Criticism*, I, lines 68–73; Dryden, *Essays*, I, 36, 123, 233; II, 161; Shaftesbury, *Characteristicks*, I, 354; Richardson, *Correspondence*, III, 204; Goldsmith, *Bee*,

No. 5; Johnson, *Lives of the Poets*, III, 178; Blair, *Rhetoric*, II, 437; Mumford, *Techniques and Civilizations*, pp. 46–47; Bredvold, "Platonism in Neo-Classic Esthetics," pp. 98–99.

2. Spingarn, *Critical Essays of the Seventeenth Century*, I, lxviii; Randall, *Modern Mind*, pp. 273–276.

3. Spingarn, *op. cit.*, I, lxvii ff.; Randall, *op. cit.*, pp. 276–278; Pope, *Essay on Criticism*, I, line 89.

4. In his introduction to Dryden's *Essays*, pp. xxiv–xxv, Ker expresses the opinion that Nature often meant whatever the artist found right at the moment.

5. Aristotle, *Poetics*, IX, 1–5; Spingarn, *Literary Criticism of the Renaissance*, pp. 38, 45; Sidney, *Apology for Poetry*, *passim*.

6. Chapelain is quoted by Bray, *Formation de la doctrine classique*, p. 207; Preserved Smith, *Modern Culture*, II, 125; Vial et Denise, *op. cit.*, pp. 106–107; Davenant, Preface to *Gondibert*, in Spingarn, *Critical Essays*, II, 18; Hobbes, Answer to Davenant's Preface, *ibid.*, II, 61–62; Blair, *Rhetoric*, III, 304–305; Rymer, *Tragedies of the Last Age*, in Spingarn, *op. cit.*, II, 206; Phillips, Preface to *Theatrum Poetarum*, *ibid.*, II, 268; Blackmore, Preface to *Prince Arthur*, *ibid.*, III, 237; Congreve, *Complete Works*, I, 103; Addison, *Works*, I, 146; Herrick, *Poetics of Aristotle in England*, p. 85; Hume, *Essays*, I, 240; Fielding, *Tom Jones*, Book VIII, Chap. I; Rowe, Preface to *Shakespeare*, in Nicoll Smith, *op. cit.*, p. 12; Samuel Johnson, *General Observations on the Plays of Shakespeare*.

7. For typical arguments on the Unities see Whetstone, Preface to *Promos and Cassandra*, in Gregory Smith, *Elizabethan Critical Essays*, I, 59–60, and Racine, Preface de *Berenice*, in Vial et Denise, *op. cit.*, p. 164. The arguments on both sides are presented by Dryden in *An Essay of Dramatic Poesy*. Dryden also discusses rime, violent action on the stage, and sudden conversion. The hostility to opera had been treated already. *Cf.*, however, Rymer, *A Short View of Tragedy*, in Spingarn, *Critical Essays*, II, 214. Dennis objected to the chorus, but the chorus had no real vitality in England at any time. Cf. *The Impartial Critic*, in Spingarn, *op. cit.*, III, 148. The Christian Epic will be discussed in Chap. XII.

8. Bray, *Formation de la doctrine classique*, pp. 194, 199, 203; R. C. Williams, "Two Studies in Epic Theory," *Modern Philology*, XXII, 133 ff.; Phillips, Preface to *Theatrum Poetarum*, in Spingarn, *Critical Essays*, II, 267–268; Boileau, *Œuvres*, p. 202; Dryden, Preface to *Don Sebastian*; Fielding, *Tom Jones*, Book VIII, Chap. I; Kames, *Elements*, II, 294–298, 301; Blair, *Rhetoric*, III, 304–305.

9. Dryden, *Essays*, II, 209; Blackmore, Preface to *Prince Arthur*, in Spingarn, *Critical Essays*, III, 238; Addison, *Spectator*, No. 35; Blair, *Rhetoric*, III, 236–238; Bouhours, quoted by Spingarn, *op. cit.*, III, 338.

10. Sir Robert Howard, Preface to *The Great Favorite*, in Spingarn, *Critical Essays*, II, 109; Dryden, *Essays*, I, 91–93, 128–129, 184–186, 247.

11. Congreve, *Concerning Humour in Comedy*, in Spingarn, *Critical Essays*, III, 248; Dennis, *The Impartial Critic*, *ibid.*, III, 150; Shadwell, Preface to the *Humorists*, *ibid.*, II, 157; Temple, *Of Poetry*, *ibid.*, III, 103; Dryden, *Dramatic Works*, ed. Summers, III, 279.

12. Dryden, *Essays*, I, 84–86, 136. For the naturalness of rime see the *Essays*, I, 100–101, 112–114.

13. Dryden, *Essays*, I, 153–154. In 1650 Hobbes had admitted that the artist might transcend truth provided he did not soar beyond "the conceived possibility of nature."

Answer to Davenant's *Preface,* in Spingarn, *Critical Essays,* II, 61–62. *Cf.* Wolseley, Preface to Rochester's *Valentinian, ibid.,* III, 18.

14. Dryden, *Dramatic Works,* ed. Summers, II, 332; Dryden, *Essays,* I, 270.

15. Dryden, *Essays,* I, 112–114, 212, and *Dramatic Works,* ed. Summers, VI, 23.

16. Dryden, *Essays,* I, 136, 146–147, 177, and *Dramatic Works,* VI, 242.

17. Dryden, *Essays,* II, 194.

18. Aristotle, *Poetics,* XV, 1–6, and *Rhetoric,* III, vii, 6–7; Dryden, *Essays,* I, 208–210, 213–218.

19. Aristotle, *loc. cit.;* Cicero, *De Inventione,* I, 21; Horace, *Ars Poetica,* 114–118, 156–157, 227–230; Dutton, "The French Aristotelian Formalists and Thomas Rymer," *P. M. L. A.,* XXIX, 162; Spingarn, *Literary Criticism of the Renaissance,* pp. 87–89; Williams, *Two Studies of Epic Theory,* pp. 133, 143; Babbitt, *Rousseau and Romanticism,* pp. 22–23, 105; Chapelain, in Vial et Denise, *op. cit.,* p. 110; Bray, *Formation de la doctrine classique,* p. 221.

20. Flecknoe, *Short Discourse of the English Stage,* in Spingarn, *Critical Essays,* II, 94; Dryden, *Essays,* I, 9, 166, 218, 236, 247, 265; Hobbes, Answer to Davenant's *Preface,* in Spingarn, *op. cit.,* II, 64; Rymer, *Short View of Tragedy, ibid.,* II, 169; Rymer, *Tragedies of the Last Age, ibid.,* II, 194–199; Johnson, *Preface to Shakespeare,* in Nicoll Smith, *op. cit.,* p. 118.

21. John Dennis, *On the Genius and Writings of Shakespeare,* in Nicoll Smith, *op. cit.,* pp. 26, 41; Pope, *Works,* I, 48, and Preface to the *Iliad, passim;* Steele, *Tatler,* No. 193; Mrs. Montagu, *Essay on Shakespeare,* pp. 28–29; John Brown, *Rise and Progress of Poetry,* p. 256; Goldsmith, *Works,* ed. Gibbs, V, 62; Fielding, *Tom Jones,* Book XIV, Chap. I; Johnson, *Preface to Shakespeare,* in Nicoll Smith, *op. cit.,* p. 118.

22. Hurd, *Works,* I, 255–257.

23. Irving Babbit, *Rousseau and Romanticism,* pp. 17, 173; Denis Saurat, *Milton, Man and Thinker,* New York, 1925, p. 56; Randall, *Modern Mind,* pp. 276–278; Sir Joshua Reynolds, *Discourses,* p. 34.

24. Randall, *Modern Mind,* pp. 275–276.

25. Oswald Spengler, *The Decline of the West,* New York, 1926, I, pp. 143–146, 317–320.

26. Spengler, *op cit.,* I, 10–11, 13–14, 314–317; Grenier, *Le Genie romain dans la religion, la pensée, et l'art,* pp. 45, 181, 209–210, 410.

27. Grenier, *op. cit.,* pp. 209–210; Aristotle, *Poetics,* V, 2, 6.

28. Davenant, Preface to *Gondibert,* in Spingarn, *Critical Essays,* II, 3–4; Rymer, *Tragedies of the Last Age, ibid.,* II, 192; Steele, *Correspondence,* II, 563. *Cf.* Dennis, in Spingarn, *op. cit.,* III, 187, and in Durham, *op. cit.,* p. 251. Mulgrave, *Essay upon Poetry,* in Spingarn, *op. cit.,* II, 293; Dryden, Epilogue to Etherege's *Man of Mode;* Congreve, Epilogue to *The Way of the World;* Shaftesbury, *Characteristicks,* I, 145; Swift, *Gulliver,* etc., p. 578; Fielding, Preface to *Joseph Andrews;* Johnson, *Rambler,* No. 36, *Lives of the Poets,* I, 29–30, 57, and *Rasselas,* Chap. X; Johnson, *Preface to Shakespeare,* in Nicoll Smith, *op. cit.,* p. 121; Lillo, Preface to *George Barnwell;* Richardson, *Writings,* V, xi; Hoole, *Life of John Scott,* in Scott, *Critical Essays,* p. liii; Thomas Warton, *History of English Poetry,* p. 782; Pinkerton, *Letters of Literature,* pp. 217–218; *Mirror,* No. 31.

29. A. O. Lovejoy, "Schiller and the Genesis of Romanticism," *Modern Language*

Notes, XXXV, 1–2; Novalis, *Fragmenten*, in *Deutsche Literatur. Romantik*, III, 229; Hamelius, *Die Kritik*, pp. 33–34; *Lounger*, No. 49.

30. Arthur Lovejoy, *The Great Chain of Being*, Cambridge (Mass.), 1936, *passim*.

31. Arthur O. Lovejoy, "Optimism and Romanticism," *P. M. L. A.*, XLII, 941–943; Frank P. Chambers, *A History of Taste*, New York, 1932, pp. 112, 115.

32. Saint-Évremond, in Vial et Denise, *op. cit.*, p. 304; Dryden, *Essays*, II, 139; Gildon, *Vindication of Cowley and Waller*, in Durham, *op. cit.*, pp. 5–6; Clark, *Boileau and the French Classical Critics in England*, p. 381; Addison, *Remarks on Italy*, in *Works*, I, 395; Fielding, *Champion*, Dec. 15, 1739; Joseph Warton, *Essay on Pope*, I, 12–13, 19, 26, 28, 42, 47.

33. Lord Kames, *Elements*, I, 191; Blair, *Critical Dissertation*, p. 148 and *Rhetoric*, III, 175, 179; Harris, *Three Treatises*, pp. 90–91; Duff, *Essay on Genius*, pp. 158–159; Gerard, *Essay on Genius*, pp. 340–342; Campbell, *Philosophy of Rhetoric*, pp. 360–362, Beattie, *Dissertations*, II, 406, note.

34. Here I am much indebted to Lovejoy's article, "Optimism and Romanticism," *P. M. L. A.*, XLII, 941 ff.

CHAPTER VIII

POETIC JUSTICE AND IDEAL NATURE

I

IN THE best of all possible worlds virtue must somehow receive its reward. That such was actually the case the thinkers of the Enlightenment, whether Deist or Christian, had little doubt. Right living would lead to happiness, here or hereafter, in one form or another, through material prosperity or through inward contentment at the practice of righteousness. The insistence on poetic justice, on the revelation through the medium of art of a world governed by a moral power which would somehow bring good out of evil, was intimately linked with this sublime faith that, despite occasional mysterious moves on the part of Deity, optimism was justified by fact, and that only the atheist could conceive of the final triumph of wickedness. It is true that the rewards of virtue were variously explained, but the reward would be unfailing; the wages of wickedness might be delayed, but they were unescapable. The artist, limited by form, could not always display the immaterial rewards of virtue to advantage, but that inability made it all the more desirable that he distribute such rewards as lay within his power. An analysis of the attitude of the age towards the good life must precede a study of poetic justice.

In a famous passage of *Comus* Milton had pictured the magic power of chastity and represented virtue as ultimately triumphant against all attack. Addison assured the virtuous man that no "real evil" could come into his lot, and found in history many instances of virtuous men finding "extraordinary escapes out of dangers . . . which have seemed inevitable." The adventures of Mrs. Heartfree in Fielding's *Jonathan Wild* were a triumphant justification of her conviction "that Providence will sooner or later procure the felicity of the virtuous and the innocent." Shielded by the hand of a benevolent God, she was as safe from the attacks of libertines as a Daniel in his den of lions from the beasts. Richardson's Lovelace was abashed by Clarissa's goodness (temporarily, at least), and the worthy and talented Dorothy Dix of the eighteenth century assured his readers that nine of ten fallen women have fallen because they failed to flash the sword of conscious virtue before the eyes of their assailants. In *The Vicar of Wakefield* the reader could learn that "none but the guilty can be long and completely miserable," and the concluding chapters of the book presented a picture of virtue riding out the storms of mischance so extravagant that it is difficult to believe that Goldsmith took the denouement of his novel seriously. Richard Graves's Miss Townsend set out alone for London, but was shielded by Providence from any greater evil than fright. Clarissa and Lovelace were reproduced in the Adeline and Marquis de Sengalt of Mrs. Radcliffe. The Marquis, apparently unaware of the fact that innocence was clad in Miltonic steel, attempted to embrace Adeline, but she

liberated herself . . ., and with a look, on which was empressed the firm dignity of virtue . . . awed him to forbearance. Conscious of a superiority, which he was ashamed to acknowledge, and endeavouring to despise the influence which he could not resist, he stood for a moment the slave of virtue, though the votary of vice.

There were few discordant notes in the harmony of praise of virtue.[1]

At times it was judged wise to ally prudence with virtue. Shaftesbury thought that caution was desirable. *The Guardian* warned the virtuous man against an undue softness of heart and an unwise surrender to pity, love, and friendship. Addison declared himself "heartily concerned" to see "a virtuous man without a competent knowledge of the world." Fielding's Tom Jones and Booth illustrate the need for prudence as a companion to goodness of heart. Mrs. Sheridan's *Sidney Biddulph* heaped distress on virtue and innocence to prove that "the best dispositions are not always sufficient to ward off the evils of life." Goldsmith insisted on the value of prudence in a letter to his brother Harry:

I had learned from books to be disinterested and generous, before I was taught from experience the necessity of being prudent. I had contracted the habits and notions of a philosopher, while I was exposing myself to the insidious approaches of cunning; and often by being, even with my narrow finances, charitable to excess I forgot the rules of justice, and placed myself in the very situation of the wretch who thanked me for my bounty.

Goldsmith's Man in Black, Good-Natured Man, and Primrose family illustrate this text. Boswell devoted an essay to prudence, and near the end of the century Paley defined virtue itself as prudence in the light of a reward in heaven—a conclusion eminently satisfactory to an age desirous of uniting the prudence of the counting-house with the optimistic regard for virtue in a world of fine moral feeling.[2]

Many writers pictured the success of virtue, however, without any qualification. Though Clarissa and Adeline could not redeem their bold assailants, most heroines were more fortunate in leading erring lovers and husbands to the peaceful blessedness of the hearthstone. Edward Revet's Fickle was converted in 1671. D'Urfey's Olivia (*The Virtuous Wife*, 1679) reclaimed her husband, and his Angelica (*The Campaigners*, 1698) won her lover by gentleness and virtue to an embrace over their, alas! illegitimate child. Colley Cibber's Loveless was roused by Amanda's goodness from his "deepest lethargy in vice" and on his knees gave thanks "to her whose conquering virtue had at last subdued him"; while Cibber's Sir Charles was won by Lady Easy's gentleness and forbearance. Vanbrugh borrowed Cibber's Amanda, and wrote a scene in which her virtue caused her would-be seducer to exclaim:

Sure there's divinity about her; and sh'as dispens'd some portion on't to me. For what but now was the wild flame of love, or (to dissect that specious term) the vile, the gross desires of flesh and blood, is in a moment turn'd to adoration. The coarser appetite of nature's gone, and 'tis, methinks, the food of angels I require.

Farquhar's Sir Harry Wildair was another libertine converted by the virtue of a woman. Steele's Jenny Distaff reformed a rake by appealing to his innate goodness: "Assume yourself, my lord, and do not attempt to violate a temple sacred to innocence, honour, and religion." Hughes pictured a third Amanda who changed a wicked lord's scheme of seduction into an offer of marriage. *The Guardian* also had its young girl who won a dowry and her poor but honest lover by softening the cynical heart of a gallant by means of tears and virtuous protestations. The stage was indeed well prepared for the entrance of Pamela, the paragon of servant maids, whose calculating reluctance to oblige her Mr. B—— seemed to her creator to justify his reformation and her reward. It was not in Pamela, however, but in Clarissa that the power of virtue was best displayed. Lovelace and his aides in the attempt to rape the glorious maiden found their guilt looked into confusion. Lovelace himself is made to describe the appearance of Clarissa

confiding in her own innocence; and with a majesty in her person and manner, that is natural to her; but which then shone out in all its glory!—Every tongue silent, every eye awed, every heart quaking, mine, in a particular manner sunk, throbless . . . :—a shameful recreant. . . . Such the glorious power of innocence exerted at that awful moment.[3]

The conversion of the libertine often brought with it a material reward in the form of marital bliss, wealth, or high station in life. Revet's virtuous and honest Lovewell defeated the calculating schemes of Letetia's father, and the curtain fell on the comforting assurance:

> For by this precedent you plainly see,
> Fate still reserves rewards for honesty.

By obedience to his father and chaste respect for Indiana, Bevel won his bride in Steele's *Conscious Lovers*. The popularity of Mouhy's *Paysanne Parvenue* in England, where it was translated as *The Fortunate Country Maid*, and again as *The Virtuous Villager*, or *The Virgin's Victory*, attested the early alliance of sentimentality with the optimistic philosophy of the Enlightenment. Fielding argued in *The Champion* that virtue was the only sure road to honor, pleasure, and wealth; and, despite his dislike for Richardson's conception of the virtuous maiden, he rescued Mrs. Heartfree, rewarded Fanny by a chain of improbabilities paralleled only in *The Vicar of Wakefield*, and brought his Amelia through darkness into the light of a happy day. In Fielding's world, even more consistently than in Richardson's, poetic justice was preserved. Thomson, Hawkesworth, and Goldsmith all revealed the rewards of virtue. Even Hume, at times a scoffer, admitted that *in general* virtue brought prosperity, vice misery.[4]

The rewards of virtue were not always material. Admiration, beauty of countenance, and pleasure in the performance of a social duty must at times suffice in place of a lovely bride or a titled husband. Not every Dick Whittington could become Lord Mayor of London, but righteousness would shine forth even in the den of iniquity, and "people even of bad hearts would admire and love people of good ones." So Richardson thought, while Doctor Blair could describe the effect of goodness:

Bad as the world is, nothing has so great and universal a command over the minds of men as virtue. No kind of language is so generally understood, and so powerfully felt, as the native language of worthy and virtuous feelings.

It was Richardson again who felt that beauty was the gift of virtue. "No one can be either *sweet* or *pretty*, that is not modest, that is not virtuous." Hawkesworth hinted at the coming æsthetics of association when he declared in *The Adventurer* that beauty depended on sensibility and expression of character. Only through virtue can one obtain beauty: "those who wish to be lovely, must learn to be good." Henry Brooke insisted in most detail on this reward of virtue:

> 'Tis goodness forms the beauty of the face,
> The line of virtue is the line of grace.
> Beauty is internal grace,
> Pregnant in the form and face;
> The sentiment that's heard and seen
> In act and manners, voice and mien.
> It is the soul's celestial ray
> Breaking through the veil of clay.

Shaftesbury and his school identified public and private interest, and proclaimed "virtue . . . the advantage . . . of every creature." The social virtues, love, generosity, and pity, alone could give a color of delight to sensual pleasures which, separated from benevolence, would soon be recognized as "low, mean, and sordid."[5]

Many classicists were too clear-sighted to believe that honesty paid its dividends in coin of the realm, but they merely withdrew the defense of virtue to a more impregnable line. Virtue was its own reward: the consciousness of moral integrity, the inner content of a day well spent could not be impugned, for it was necessary to accept the contention of the virtuous man concerning his inner joy. There were a few skeptics, but the weight of expressed opinion was against such doubters. If the wicked knew better, they prudently concealed their opinions.[6]

From Prior to Cowper the inner content of righteousness was hymned by England's poets and explained by her popular moralists. *The Tatler* represented the vicious life as wayward and uneasy; life "under the regulation of virtue, a reasonable and uniform habit of enjoyment." *The Spectator* pictured virtue as producing its inward heaven and vice its inward hell as Doctor Scott had argued in *The Christian Life.* Gay wrote fables to show that virtue produced content which riches could not buy. Fielding represented virtue as a joy in itself on which all other joys depended. To Thomson virtue gave

> Sacred, substantial, never-fading bliss.

Cowper was certain that

> Peace follows virtue as its sure reward;
> And pleasure brings as surely in her train
> Remorse, and sorrow, and vindictive pain;

a doctrine which *The Lounger* set in a clear light by means of a contrast between two young women:

> Yet with all her afflictions, and all her sorrows, who would not rather be the suffering and virtuous Aurelia, than the gay and thoughtless Cleora? The one may enjoy the dissipation of the world, and the good-liking of its votaries; but the other must possess that approbation from her own mind, which infinitely surpasses all the external enjoyment which the world is able to bestow.[7]

Richardson's *Clarissa* represented a final reward of virtue, not on earth, but in heaven. It was felt by some that no earthly reward could suffice for the sufferings of virtue; by others that the reward of virtue in this life encouraged atheism by removing the need of future rewards in heaven. Among literary men Edward Young and James Beattie were the most outspoken in their contention that selfishness succeeds on earth, and that heaven must be posited to overbalance earthly "disappointment, penury, and pain." In imaginative literature this last defense of virtue's rewards was seldom resorted to.[8]

II

Virtue was the rock on which happiness was founded. Learning, genius, and noble actions were disparaged by poets and moralists who praised the mute inglorious Miltons and the Cromwells guiltless of their country's blood in a sustained effort to console the mediocre and to instill resignation in the poor. From their comfortable London residences and rural estates, sentimentalists could extol the merit of resisting the lures of ambition and of following true happiness instead of false. Incidentally they could bolster the social status quo against the mobs of Wilkes and Gordon and, at the end of the century, repel the tides of Jacobinism flowing in from France. Hutcheson had demonstrated that achievement must be evaluated by its ratio to ability. The "honest trader, the kind friend, the faithful prudent adviser, the charitable and hospitable neighbor, the tender husband and affectionate parent, the sedate yet cheerful companion, the generous assistant of merit, the cautious allayer of contention and debate, the promoter of love and good understanding among acquaintances" who does all within his power must be judged "as amiable as those whose external splendor dazzles an injudicious world into an opinion that they are the only heroes in virtue." The few skeptics as to the reality of pure benevolence and the worth of simple goodness, like Mandeville and Hume, discovered that their unpleasant cynicism was drowned by the chorus of praise for virtue in which Addison and Steele, Richardson and Sterne, Gray and Cowper lifted their voices.[9]

The profoundly ethical feeling of the age wedded morality to art and blessed their principal offspring, poetic justice. Cowley prized good humor and honesty above eloquence and knowledge. Dryden found "true greatness" in "private virtue." Richardson stated dogmatically that "goodness . . . was greatness," and created Clarissa and Grandison to enforce his point. Gray spoke of himself as

> Beneath the good how far—but far above the great.

Goldsmith thought that

the modest virgin, the prudent wife, or the careful matron, are much more serviceable in life than petticoated philosophers, blustering heroines, or virago queens. She who makes her husband and her children happy, who reclaims the one from vice, and trains up the other to virtue, is a much greater character than ladies described in a romance, whose whole occupation is to murder mankind with shafts from the quiver of their eyes.

Cowper's famous comparison of Voltaire and a lowly English cottager is the extreme expression of the cult of simple goodness:

> Yon cottager, who weaves at her own door,
> Pillow and bobbins all her little store;
> Content, though mean; and cheerful, if not gay;
> Shuffling her threads about the live-long day,
> Just earns a scanty pittance; and at night
> Lies down secure, her heart and pocket light:
> She, for her humble sphere by nature fit,
> Has little understanding, and no wit,
> Receives no praise; but though her lot be such,
> (Toilsome and indigent) she renders much;
> Just knows, and knows no more, her Bible true—
> A truth the brilliant Frenchman never knew;
>
> .   .   .   .
>
> Oh, happy peasant! oh, unhappy bard!
> His the mere tinsel, her's the rich reward; . . .[10]

Greatness was eyed askance. Every one remembers Fielding's ⌐lashing attack on the greatness of Sir Robert Walpole, *alias* Jonathan Wild, in that series of panels contrasting so completely with the miraculous career of the innocent Mrs. Heartfree. Before Fielding's masterly irony saw the light of day Steele had branded as "romantic madness" the belief that great actions could be performed only in a great station, and had expressed a greater admiration for Cicero the husband and father than for Cicero the consul. Edward Young thought

> A life well spent, not the victorious sword,
> Awards the crown, and styles the greater lord.

The Spectator knew that "there are greater men who lie concealed among the species than those who come out, and draw upon themselves the eyes and admiration of mankind," and that in the eyes of angels

a contemplation on God's works; a voluntary act of justice to our own detriment, a generous concern for the good of mankind; tears that are shed in silence for the misery of others; a private desire or resentment broken and subdued; in short, an unfeigned exercise of humility, or any other virtue . . . denominate men great and reputable.

Pope was in the spirit of the times when he wrote

> Oh keep me innocent, make others great.

Parnell agreed with his friend Pope. Soame Jenyns thought that "one good-natured act" deserved more praise

> Than armies overthrown, and thousands slain;

while Johnson objected, in the vein of Fielding, to the glorification of wickedness in Cæsar, Alexander, and Peter the Great. The times were ripe for Gray's great *Elegy*.[11]

When knowledge and genius were not allied with goodness of heart they too were disparaged. Addison ranked knowledge *second* to virtue, while Steele thought that the "unhappy affectation of being wise rather than honest, witty than good natured, is the source of most of the ill habits of life." The Duke of Buckingham felt that

> One moral, or a mere well-natur'd deed
> Can all desert in sciences exceed.

Swift represented the Lilliputians, in the Utopian sixth chapter, as convinced that honesty, experience, and good intentions were more important than genius in the conduct of public affairs. To Edward Young it seemed that Addison's compositions were but "a noble preface" to a virtuous death, his goodness more important than his greatness. Armstrong and Boswell preferred the virtues of the heart to the fineness of the understanding, while Mrs. Radcliffe argued that

a bad heart and a *truly* philosophic head have never yet been united in the same individual. Vicious inclinations not only corrupt the heart, but the understanding, and thus lead to false reasoning. Virtue is only on the side of truth.

Even the learned Gibbon felt that the virtues of the heart made amends for the badness of the head.[12]

Many of the works cited in the preceding sections suggest the extent to which the rule of poetic justice was actually followed in the literature of the classical period. Popular in practice, it was well defended in theory. Rigid poetic justice is no part of Aristotle's doctrine, though he showed his sense of an audience's reaction in banning from tragedy the disasters of the worthy and the successes of the wicked. The proper tragic catharsis is possible only in the case of a moderately good man suffering a reversal of fortune caused by a flaw in his own character. Since he is weak rather than criminal he arouses our pity; since we, too, are weak we feel terror at the thought of a similar destiny.[13]

Aristotle's discussion of the proper theme for a tragedy seems to justify the demand of the audience for a resolution of a dramatic action in conformity with its feelings. In any case rebellion against injustice is clearly conceded and thus considerable support is given to those critics who refused to elevate the concept of poetic justice to the position of a law, but admitted that it would be generally necessary to please the audience. It was the moralist Plato, however, rather than Aristotle, who insisted that the artist must reveal the inevitable punishment of guilt and the assured reward of virtue.[14]

It is principally on Plato's conception of the artist's responsibility for public morals that the doctrine of poetic justice was supported in England. Both Bacon and Sidney exalted the morality of poetry above that of history. Having mentioned those who praised history "as though therein a man should see virtue exalted and vice punished," Sidney countered by contending that the commendation of virtue "is peculiar to poetry, and far from history. For indeed poetry ever setteth virtue so out in her best colours, making fortune her well-waiting hand-maid, that one must needs be enamoured of her." Thomas Rymer referred to Sophocles and Euripides as illustrious upholders of poetic justice in what was perhaps the most complete presentation of the ethical justification of the rule:

These were for teaching by *examples,* in a graver way than that of Socrates, yet extremely *pleasant* and *delightful.* And finding in history the same *end* happen to the *righteous* and to the *unjust, virtue* often opprest, and wickedness on the throne, they saw these particular *yesterday-truths* were imperfect and unproper to illustrate the *universal* and *eternal truths* by them intended. Finding also that this *unequal* distribution of rewards and punishments did perplex the *wisest,* and by the *Atheist* was made a scandal to the *Divine Providence,* they concluded that a *poet* must of necessity see *justice* exactly administered, if he intended to please.

Dryden could add nothing to Rymer, save to rescue comedy as of less serious ethical moment than tragedy from the rule. In the mid-eighteenth century criticasters of the stature of Hawkesworth were still echoing Sidney, Rymer, and Dryden.[15]

In England Addison, in France Corneille, are typical of those critics who refused to admit that poetic justice was obligatory, but were willing to concede that it was generally pleasing to an audience. Like Sidney, Bacon, and Rymer, Addison contrasted the ideal world of poetry with the world of fact as recorded in history, where events of a mixed nature happen alike to the worthless and to the deserving, and confessed: "I love to amuse myself with the accounts I meet with in fabulous histories and fictions: for in this kind of writings we have always the pleasure of seeing vice punished and virtue rewarded." Addison argued that the whole course of man in this life and the next would always show virtue rewarded, so that, in a sense, the artist who planned a catastrophe suitable to a man's deserts was adhering to truth. On Addison's hint Richardson did reveal *the whole course of man,* and rewarded his Clarissa in heaven. Johnson, like Addison, found in pleasure the main support for poetic justice:

A play in which the wicked prosper, and the virtuous miscarry, may doubtless be good, because it is a just representation of the common events of human life: but since all reasonable beings naturally love justice, I cannot easily be persuaded, that the observation of justice makes a play worse; or that, if other excellencies are equal, the audience will not always rise better pleased from the final triumph of persecuted virtue.[16]

It is notable that all of the critics just quoted distinguished the ideal world in which poetic justice was preserved from the real world in which the virtuous and the vicious suffered indifferently. The support of the principle of poetic justice almost necessitated the interpretation of the term Nature as ideal Nature, if the artist was to reconcile his moral obligations with the obligation to follow Nature. There was no contradiction, however, between the belief that virtue was actually rewarded, and the opinions expressed by Sidney and his followers as to the record of history, for history could record only the outward rewards, and many of the most significant rewards of virtue are *inward* ones. Tragedy, like history, cannot adequately represent the "Paradise within," and, again like history, it must bring its record to a close at death. The awards it provides are a *substitute* only, not a satisfactory reflection of the complete justice of God in the moral universe.

With some such train of thought the critics of the classical period must have justified the neglect of probability in the actual world, for the majority of English classicists from Ben Jonson to James Beattie urged the necessity of a just distribution of rewards and punishments. In the English Renaissance Jonson sided with Bacon and Sidney. The influential French critics of the seventeenth century supported poetic justice almost to a man. Rymer's amazement at the lack of justice in *Othello* is well known. Dennis altered *Coriolanus* to vindicate poetic justice, and defended his position in his essay *On the Genius and Writings of Shakespeare*. Among the dramatists Congreve, Farquhar, Colley Cibber, and Fielding supported poetic justice. It was the old rake Cibber who remonstrated with Richardson on the fate of Clarissa, and swore that "he should no longer believe Providence, or eternal Wisdom, or Goodness governed the world, if merit, innocence, and beauty were to be so destroyed." Richardson did not feel that the distribution of material rewards was essential, and justified his recalcitrance by the examples of Shakespeare, Otway, and Rowe, but in practice he generally conformed, as the denouements of *Pamela* and *Grandison* and the fates of Mrs. Sinclair, Tomlinson, Lovelace, Dorcas, Betty Barnes, and of James and Arabella Harlowe in *Clarissa* bear witness. Fielding, Goldsmith, and Henry Brooke were often compelled to employ series of extraordinary chances to bring justice about, but each seemed willing to sacrifice *probability* to ensure the rewards of virtue. In the *Dissertations* of Beattie (1783) and in *The Progress of Romance* of Clara Reeve (1785) the doctrine of poetic justice is followed as relentlessly as it had been a century earlier by that arch-moralist Thomas Rymer.[17]

The opposition to poetic justice argued that it was unnecessary as a support for morality, that it did not reflect reality, that it did not permit a true catharsis, and that it was contrary to both Greek and English precedents. In its presentation of the misfortunes of the pure in heart sentimental drama added a new element of protest.

Critics like Corneille reasoned that even triumphant vice would be hateful if truly described, and virtue be lovely even in tears. *The Spectator* found finer moral instruction in the *violation* of justice than in its fulfilment, for the man who witnesses the misfortunes of virtue will have his heart softened with compassion and will learn not to judge virtue by success. Richardson felt that poetic justice was contrary to the dispensation taught by Revelation and would check the passage of men's thoughts to the equitable distribution of rewards and punishments beyond the grave. *The Mirror* believed that man's feeling that virtue *should* be rewarded would be rendered stronger by opposition, and that hatred of vice would be deepened by the sight of its insolent triumph.[18]

Addison's attacks on poetic justice marked the beginning of revolt against the practice. Though he bolstered his argument with the Aristotelian views on catharsis and with the citation of repeated violation in English drama, Addison's principal objection clearly lay in the contradiction to fact: good and evil happen alike to all men this side the grave. Edward Young suggested that it was not contrary "to the common method of Providence to permit the best to suffer most." Richardson agreed with Young, as did Boswell, who supported a certain Mr. Belsham's dislike for poetic justice because it was contrary to fact as well as unnecessary to the support of virtue. At the end of the century Hugh Blair simply echoed Addison when he wrote that the tragic poet "may, indeed, nay, he must, represent the virtuous as sometimes unfortunate, because this is often the case in real life."[19]

It was Addison's colleague, Steele, who called attention to the ethical effect of Athenian drama, and argued in Aristotelian vein that emotion could not be justified by the practice of the modern stage:

Among the moderns . . . there has arose a chimerical method of disposing the fortune of the persons represented, according to what they call poetic justice; and letting none be unhappy but those who deserve it. In such cases, an intelligent spectator, if he is concerned, knows he ought not to be so; and can learn nothing from such a tenderness, but that he is a weak creature, whose passions cannot follow the dictates of his understanding.[20]

Among the precedents cited against poetic justice by such prominent men as Addison, Young, and Richardson were *Othello*, *The Orphan*, *All for Love*, *Oroonoko*, and *Venice Preserved*.[21]

These theoretical attacks were strengthened by a series of tragic tales in *The Tatler* and *The Spectator* in which the innocent suffer unmerited misfortune. A virtuous wife falls dead at the shock of seeing her husband's lifeless body on the shore. A bridegroom shoots his wife with an "unloaded" pistol and commits suicide. Two lovers perish in a theatre fire. An innocent girl is betrayed by a fake marriage. These tales by Steele pointed the way to the drama of sensibility in which the heartstrings of the spectators were wrung at the sight of characters, too virtuous to deserve serious misfortune, doomed by fatal circumstances to perish miserably. The consistent sentimentalist was compelled by his faith to neglect poetic justice; for him man was good, and the responsibility for his downfall must be laid to tragic mischance or the vicious social system. Steele himself did not write the sentimental tragedies for which his essays provided embryonic sketches, but with Lillo's *George Barnwell* (1731) and the later *Fatal Curiosity* (1736) the genre came into its own. The practice of Lillo and his lesser confrères was no more able than the arguments of Addison and Richardson to put an end to the dominance of poetic justice which was supported not only by the majority of moralists, but deeply rooted in the taste of a reading public that wished its heroes and heroines to struggle through difficulties to a happy ending at the altar—and so to bed.[22]

IV

The Platonic tradition in European thought accounts for the interpretation of the Natural as the perfection of the individual species which is never reached except in the realm of "Ideas" or in the poetic world where the artist unhindered by accidents can work with the creative freedom of a God. The theory of the Platonic ideal flourished in the Renaissance rather than during the central period of classicism, but it was significant in that it permitted the artist to neglect observation—necessary even in the quest for the normal or average—and to imitate the supreme forms of antique art as the perfect embodiment of the Natural. In Italy Dolce, Scaliger, and Bellori urged the necessity of surpassing reality by eliminating the defects in objects, and by showing in a single body what nature was not accustomed to show in a thousand. The poet, like a God, created this superior nature, more vivid, more beautiful, and more worthy of imitation than the world of accidents.[23]

While admitting the freedom of the poetic imagination to create things that "never were in nature," Sidney was led primarily by moral preoccupations to emphasize the power of the artist to transcend reality:

The poet, disdaining to be tied to any such subjection, lifted up with the vigor of his own invention, doth grow in effect another nature, in making things either better than Nature bringeth forth, or, quite anew, forms such as never were in Nature, as the *heroes, demigods, cyclops, chimeras, furies,* and such like: so as he goeth hand in hand with Nature, not inclosed within the narrow warrant of her gifts, but freely ranging only within the zodiac of his own wit.

Nature never set forth the earth in so rich tapestry as divers poets have done, neither with pleasant rivers, fruitful trees, sweetly smelling flowers, nor whatsoever else may make the too-much-loved earth more lovely. Her world is brazen, the poets only deliver a golden. [The poet conceives perfect friendship, a perfect prince, a perfect man.] Which delivering forth also is not wholly imaginative, as we are wont to say by them that build castles in the air: but so far substantially it worketh, not only to make a *Cyrus,* which had been but a particular excellency, as Nature might have done, but to bestow a *Cyrus* upon the world, to make many Cyrus's, if they will learn aright why and how that Maker made him.

Bacon, too, found the use of poetry in giving

some shadow of satisfaction to the mind of man in those points wherein the Nature of things doth deny it, the world being in proportion inferior to the soul; by reason whereof there is agreeable to the spirit of man a more ample greatness, a more exact goodness, and a more absolute variety than can be found in the Nature of things.

As has been noted in the previous section, Bacon united the concept of ideal Nature with the preservation of poetic justice.[24]

Apparently it was the necessity of poetic justice which led Dryden to toy with the concept of an ideal Nature. He was well aware that "virtue is generally unhappy in this world, and vice fortunate," but he felt that the moral responsibility of the artist demanded, in tragedy at least, a more satisfactory picture of God's universe, not so much the imitation of Nature defined as reality, as the externalization of an ideal. In *The Parallel of Poetry and Painting* (1695) Dryden showed that there was a stage beyond which he was unwilling to go in the quest of the perfect "idea." In that essay he quoted at length from Bellori, who had argued for a world of art created by the fancy more beautiful and more accurate than Nature (defined as reality), only to make an exception of portraits in painting and of characters in drama, which, according to Dryden, "are never to be made perfect" except as perfection consists in their likeness to the deficient faulty nature which is their original. Perfection (ideal Nature) cannot be reconciled with this faulty nature, for in drama each character must show a tragic flaw in order to allow for the play of motive in the chain of causes and effects, and in order to justify the tragic ending, which would be unacceptable and unpleasant in the case of innocent characters. On the other hand Dryden was willing to admit that the universe in which these reproductions of faulty nature moved must be ideal in order to reveal the poetic justice which by very definition does not exist in reality. In so far, too, as the exigencies of tragic action permit, both perfection and probability should be sought by choosing the characters from the highest forms among mankind this side of perfection. It was only in the epic, where the issue was successful, that Dryden was able to reconcile poetic justice with the perfect hero, and to obviate the necessity for a picture of faulty nature; only in this one art form did he find himself able to accept Bellori's idea of an ideal Nature in the Platonic sense.[25]

In *The Spectator*, No. 418, Addison desired the artist to mend and perfect Nature, "where he describes a reality," and to add "greater beauties than are put together in nature, where he describes a fiction." Jonathan Richardson, the painter, thought that Nature must be "raised and improved." Thomson spoke of Italian art

> In elegant design
> Improving Nature.

Gerard wished Nature to be presented as it ought to be. Sir Joshua Reynolds disparaged the minute fidelity of Dutch painting in praising an "ideal beauty, superior to what is found in individual nature." Unfortunately Sir Joshua's mind flickered back and forth between the conception of beauty as the average and the concept of corrected Nature. At times he clearly identified the two, for the artist through observation became aware of the beauty of the normal and could then refashion Nature into conformity with this inner conception with the Ancients for a guide, for the Ancients "have left models of that perfect form behind them, which an artist would prefer as supremely beautiful, who had spent his whole life in that single contemplation." At times Reynolds clearly preferred the ideal, and wished facts that conflicted with it to be ignored. What though Alexander was of small stature? The ideal hero must have a magnificent physique:

So far . . . is servile imitation from being necessary, that whatever is familiar, or in any way reminds us of what we see and hear everyday, perhaps does not belong to the higher provinces of art, either in poetry or painting. . . . Another and a higher order of beings is supposed; and to those beings everything which is introduced into the work must correspond.

Such a quotation as this shows that Reynolds was far indeed from the imitation of Nature as reality, or even as an abstracted system of probabilities operating among average human beings. Portions of his statement it would be difficult to reconcile with what Christopher Hussey suggests as his identification of the ideal form with the common average form. The emphasis, for Sir Joshua, was rather on the beauty that surpasses that of the forms to be seen in this mundane sphere.[26]

NOTES TO CHAPTER VIII

1. Milton, *Comus*, lines 420–427, 589–594; Addison, *Guardian*, No. 117; Fielding, *Jonathan Wild*, Book IV, Chap. XI; Richardson, *Writings*, VIII, 178, 264, 299, 310; Goldsmith, *Vicar of Wakefield*, Chap. XXIII *et seq.*; Graves *Spiritual Quixote*, I, 126; Mrs. Radcliffe, *Romance of the Forest*, p. 193; John Scott, *Critical Essays*, p. 81.

2. Shaftesbury, *Characteristicks*, I, 94; Addison, *Spectator*, No. 245; *Guardian*, No. 31; Cross, *Fielding*, II, 220, 318; Mrs. Barbauld, *op. cit.*, I, 44; Goldsmith, *Works*, I, 439, 449–450; *Citizen of the World*, Letters VI, VIII, XXVII, *Vicar of Wakefield*, Chaps. I, II, III, IX, and *New Essays*, pp. 99–100; Boswell, *Hypochondriack*, No. XLIV; Stephen, *English Thought*, II, 123–124.

3. C. M. Scheurer, "An Early Sentimental Comedy," *Anglia*, XXXVII, 126–128; Kathleen Lynch, "Thomas D'Urfey's Contribution to Sentimental Comedy," *Philological Quarterly*, IX, 249–256; Cibber, *Love's Last Shift*, Act IV, scene II, and *The Careless Husband*, Act V, scene IV; Vanbrugh, *The Relapse*, Act IV, scene IV; Farquhar, *A Trip to the Jubilee*, Act V, scene III; Steele, *Tatler*, June 25, 1709; Hughes, *Spectator*, No. 375; Richardson, *Writings*, X, 204–205.

4. C. M. Scheurer, *op. cit.*, 126–128; Clara Reeve, *Progress of Romance*, I, 130; Fielding, *The Champion*, Jan. 24, 1740; Thomson, in Chalmers, *op. cit.*, XII, 437; Hawkesworth, *Adventurer*, Nos. 7–8; Goldsmith, *Citizen of the World*, Letter LXII, and *The Bee*, No. VI; Pope, *Imitations of Horace*, III, line 337; Hume, *Letters*, I, 139, and *Essays*, II, 380.

5. Richardson, *Correspondence*, III, 179; Blair, *Rhetoric*, III, 6–7; Hawkesworth, *Adventurer*, No. 82; Richardson, *Writings*, VI, 170; Brooke, *Fool of Quality*, pp. 135–136; Shaftesbury, *Characteristicks*, II, 81, 99, 101, 107, 173; Hutcheson, *Inquiry*, pp. 242–244.

6. Vanbrugh, *Provok'd Wife*, Act I, scene I; Farquhar, *Twin-Rivals*, Act I, scene II.

7. Prior, in Chalmers, *op. cit.*, X, 137; *Tatler*, No. 49; Steele, *Spectator*, No. 520; Addison, *Spectator*, No. 447; Gay, *Poetical Works*, pp. 289–291; Fielding, *The Champion*, March 4, 1740; Thomson, in Chalmers, *op. cit.*, XII, 447, 463; Cowper, *Progress of Error*, lines 42–44; *Lounger*, Nos. 18, 46.

8. Isabel Bliss, "Young's *Night Thoughts* in Relation to Contemporary Christian Apologetics," *P. M. L. A.*, XLIX, 60–65; Beattie, *Minstrel*, Book I, xxvii; Blunt, *op. cit.*, II, 34; *Adventurer*, No. 79.

9. Hutcheson, *Inquiry*, pp. 194–195; Mandeville, *Fable of the Bees*, I, 36; Hume, *Treatise*, p. 604; Sprat, in Spingarn, *Critical Essays of the Seventeenth Century*, II, 138–139.

10. Sprat, *loc. cit.*, II, 138–139; Dryden, *Dedication of Aureng-zebe*; Richardson, *Writings*, V, 257; XV, 249; XVI, 175; XX, 325; Sterne, *Tristram Shandy*, Book III, Chap. 34; Gray, *Progress of Poesy*, concluding line; Goldsmith, *Citizen of the World*, Letter LXII; Cowper, *Truth*, lines 317–328, 331–332.

11. Steele, *Tatler*, No. 159, *Spectator*, No. 248; Young, "The Last Day," *Poetical Works*, II, 15; *Spectator*, No. 610; Pope, *Works*, IX, 44; Parnell, "Health," in Fausset, *Minor Poets of the Eighteenth Century*, p. 144; Jenyns, *An Essay on Virtue*; Johnson, *Adventurer*, No. 99.

12. Addison, *Guardian*, No. 111; Steele, *Spectator*, No. 6; Buckingham is quoted

by George Sherburn, *The Early Career of Alexander Pope*, Oxford, 1934, p. 220; Swift, *Gulliver*, p. 66; Aikin, *Miscellaneous Pieces in Prose*, p. 38; Young, *Conjectures*, in *English Critical Essays, XVI–XVIII centuries*, ed. Jones, p. 360; Pinkerton, *Letters of Literature*, p. 69; Steele, *Spectator*, No. 544; Young, *Poetical Works*, I, 139; Armstrong, *Miscellanies*, II, 194; Boswell, *Letters*, p. 90; Mrs. Radcliffe, *Romance of the Forest*, p. 319; Gibbon, *Autobiography*, p. 194.

13. Aristotle, *Poetics*, XIII, 3–6.

14. Corneille, *Premier Discours*, in Vial et Denise, *op. cit.*, p. 124; Plato, *Laws*, II, 660E; Spingarn, *Critical Essays*, I, lxxiii.

15. Sidney, *Apology*, in Gregory Smith, *op. cit.*, I, 169–170; Bacon, *Advancement of Learning*, in Spingarn, *Critical Essays*, I, 6; Rymer, *Tragedies of the Last Age*, *ibid.*, II, 188; Dryden, *Essays*, I, 50, 141–143; and Preface to *Don Sebastian*; Hawkesworth, *Adventurer*, No. 16.

16. Addison, *Tatler*, No. 117; Johnson, *General Observations on the Plays of Shakespeare: King Lear*, and *Preface to Shakespeare*, in Nicoll Smith, *op. cit.*, p. 123.

17. Ben Jonson, Dedicatory Epistle of *Volpone*; Bray, *Formation de la doctrine classique*, pp. 80–81; Dutton, "French Aristotelian Formalists," pp. 159–161; D'Aubignac, *Pratique du Théâtre*, in Vial et Denise, *op. cit.*, p. 104; Racine, Préface de *Phèdre*, *ibid.*, p. 186; Rymer, *A Short View of Tragedy*, in Spingarn, *Critical Essays*, II, 252; Dennis, in Nicoll Smith, *op. cit.*, pp. 27–29; H. A. Evans, "A Shakespeare Controversy of the Eighteenth Century," *Anglia*, XXVIII, 467; Congreve, *The Mourning Bride*, Act V, scene III; Farquhar, *Preface to the Twin-Rivals*, and *Discourse upon Comedy*, in Durham, *op. cit.*, p. 285; Cibber, Epilogue to Fielding's *Modern Husband*; Richardson, *Correspondence*, II, 128; Cross, *History of Henry Fielding*, II, 129, 345; Richardson, *Writings*, XII, 24; Beattie, *Dissertations*, II, 315; Clara Reeve, *Progress of Romance*, II, 94.

18. Corneille, *Épitre de Médée*, in Vial et Denise, *op. cit.*, p. 122; *Spectator*, No. 548; Richardson, *Writings*, XIII, 310–319; *Mirror*, No. 77; *Lounger*, No. 28.

19. Addison, *Spectator*, No. 40; Richardson, *Correspondence*, II, 4–5; IV, 225; Blair, *Rhetoric*, III, 302; Boswell, *Life of Johnson*, I, 450 and note 2.

20. Steele, *Tatler*, No. 82; Addison, *Spectator*, No. 40.

21. Addison, *Spectator*, No. 40; Richardson, *Writings*, XII, 24, and *Correspondence*, II, 4–5.

22. *Tatler*, Nos. 82, 94; *Spectator*, No. 322; Ernest Bernbaum, *The Drama of Sensibility*, Cambridge (Mass.), 1925, pp. 97, 112–113.

23. W. G. Howard, "*Ut Pictura Poesis*," *P. M. L. A.*, XXIV, 59; Spingarn, *Literary Criticism of the Renaissance*, pp. 133–134.

24. Sidney, *Apology*, in Gregory Smith, *op. cit.*, I, 156–157, 159; Bacon, *Advancement of Learning*, in Spingarn, *Critical Essays*, I, 6.

25. Dryden, *Essays*, I, 261, 141–143, 218; II, 125, 127.

26. E. N. S. Thompson, "The Discourses of Sir Joshua Reynolds," *P. M. L. A.*, XXXII, 351; Thomson, *Liberty*, Book IV, 232–233; Gerard, *Essay on Taste*, p. 125; Reynolds, *Discourses*, pp. 26, 29–30, 43, 53, 219, and *Idler*, No. 79; Christopher Hussey, *The Picturesque Studies in a Point of View*, London, 1927, p. 61. Towards the end of the century Clara Reeve, *Progress of Romance*, I, 141; William Cowper, *Tirocinium*, lines 21–24; and Archibald Alison, *Essays on Taste*, pp. 374, 453–454, show sympathy with Nature improved.

CHAPTER IX

STYLE AND POETIC FORM

I

SIMPLICITY and correctness were the principal aims of the classical stylist. Simplicity was a well-established classical precedent, but it was likewise intimately related to the scientific and rational spirit of the age and received its first strong impetus from the Restoration wits who followed the proceedings of the Royal Society attentively. The plea for simplicity was raised by critics from Horace and Quintilian to Goldsmith and Cowper. In Renaissance England Nash, Drayton, Sidney, and Shakespeare laughed at euphuism, but Bacon was the most influential in unmasking rhetoric as the first abuse of learning:

Men began to hunt more after words than matter, and more after the choiceness of the phrase, and the round and clean composition of the sentence, and the sweet falling of the clauses, and the varying and illustration of their works with tropes and figures, than after the weight of matter, worth of subject, soundness of argument, life of invention, or depth of judgment.

Sprat, the historian of the Royal Society, followed Bacon in linking scientific truth with lucid exposition. Glanvill praised Sprat for his "proper and familiar" style free from quotation, parenthesis, and avoidable metaphor; and began to remodel his own prose in accord with the new ideal. Cowley, too, praised Sprat, and fashioned a prose style in striking contrast to the extravagance of his metaphysical verses. Wycherley and Steele, Ramsay and Kames, Goldsmith and Cowper, Joseph and Thomas Warton, Aaron Hill and John Armstrong were joined by a host of others great and small in defense of some sort of simplicity.[1]

Minor divergences in definition occur, but, in general, simplicity implied clarity; in diction, the avoidance of Latin coinages and of difficult words in favor of a colloquial ease which should have precision as its ally; in thought, the elimination both of the "conceit" and of "false wit"; in presentation, the abandonment of elaborate artifice. At times simplicity implied the elimination of convention in the literary "kinds" (Swift), the avoidance of irregularity of fancy (Addison), or even the perfect matching of style and subject (John Brown).[2]

The redefinition of wit was one of the most prominent phases of the campaign for simplicity. Davenant was one of the first to attack the intellectual conceits of the "metaphysicals." Temple regarded wit as a mere sauce to conceal insipidity, and compared the poetry of the metaphysical school to a building that was nothing but ornament or to a cloth that was nothing but trimming. Pope found "a certain majesty in simplicity, which is far above all the quaintness of wit." Like Temple, Pope felt that over-ornamentation hinted at lack of skill; and Addison had the same suspicion of meretricious ornaments and false wit. Chesterfield abhorred Petrarch and declared that *concetti*, quaintness, and false thoughts were signs of a corrupt taste, though he admired Waller and admitted that he preferred elegance to plain diction. Goldsmith's admiration for Shakespeare was qualified by a dislike for his "forced humour, far-fetched conceit, and unnatural hyperbole."[3]

With such prominent classicists hostile to conceit and wit it was inevitable that the word *wit* should be re-explained in terms of the new demand for simplicity. At first wit was associated with ingenuity of fancy, celerity of imagination, or the ability to unite apparently dissimilar ideas. As early as 1659, however, Davenant defined wit as the representation of Nature, though he wished it to be presented "not in an affected, yet in an unusual dress." Dryden wavered between the old definition and the new, but in the Preface to *Albion and Albanius* (1685) he defined wit, after Aristotle, as "a propriety of thought and words." Mulgrave wrote in 1682 that

> 'tis the top of wit
> T' express agreeably a thing that's fit,

but it remained for Locke to develop the distinction between wit and judgment in his *Essay*, and to compel an age of reason to sacrifice ingenuity to clarity. According to Locke judgment and clearness of reason consist in the ability to distinguish nicely between the ideas presented by the memory. A person of wit may often lack clarity of judgment, for wit lies

most in the assemblage of ideas, and putting those together with quickness and variety wherein can be found any resemblance or congruity, thereby to make up pleasant pictures and agreeable visions in the fancy; judgment, on the contrary, lies quite on the other side, in separating carefully one from another ideas wherein can be found the least difference.

Pope used *wit* with divergent meanings but in the famous couplet:

> True wit is nature to advantage dressed,
> What oft was thought, but ne'er so well expressed,

he revealed his own opinion and summed up the dominant attitude of the eighteenth century to the age of Donne, Cowley, and Cleveland.[4] The older definition lingered, it must be confessed, in the work of Welsted, Theobald, Thomson, Kames, Duff, and Campbell, but wit was no longer represented as one of the higher attributes of the artist.[5]

The demand for simplicity was justified in various ways. In the service of truth the gorgeous rhetoric of Browne and Milton must give way to the directness of the scientific analyst.[6] The followers of Nature argued in a similar vein that an elaborate style was a useless veil for her beauties.[7] Proponents of the geometrical conception of beauty demanded simplicity as the Grecian ideal against the barbarous ornamentation of Gothic;[8] or, without ado, merely cited the example of the Ancients.[9] A final justification was given by Longinus and his disciple Boileau, who developed the theory that sublimity depended in large measure on greatness of conception combined with powerful simplicity of expression.[10] The illustration of Longinus, "God said, let there be light, and there was light," was a measuring rod for sublimity of style. At first distinct, the justifications from the classics in general soon coalesced with the argument drawn from Longinus in particular to form a strong secondary line of defense for a cult of simplicity founded primarily on truth, Nature, and proportion—all aspects of the same idea in a harmonious and orderly universe.

The rational spirit nurtured by science was the prime cause for the movement towards simplicity. Second in importance was the new æsthetics of the sublime. Numerous other factors contributed: the growth of the reading public, which necessitated an ever simpler structure and diction as literature penetrated to the more poorly trained classes of the population; the development of political journalism, effective only if it could with striking directness reach the voting population as a whole; the growing commercial life of the English nation; the collapse of the tradition of Ciceronian rhetoric under the successive attacks of Bacon, Glanvill, Rapin, Bouhours, and Eachard; the direct influence of France, where the adherents of simplicity had won an earlier victory; and the influence of the Bible working directly as well as through the new pulpit style of Barrow and Tillotson and through the direct force of Dissenters like Bunyan, Fox, and William Penn. Style would doubtless have been reformed in time without the exhortations of Bacon, Sprat, and Glanvill, without the new respect for accuracy engendered by scientific investigation, without the general belief in an orderly universe, even without the corresponding æsthetic delight in regularity and proportion, but the struggle would have been a much more difficult one. Worship of the Ancients would have been powerless to effect the change alone, for in England the classicist chose as he fancied from among their wares, and men like Fuller, Browne, Burton, Andrews, and Milton were turned in the direction of wit and conceit, of swelling clause and diction sweet with soft vowels and gently falling final syllables by the same Ancients who helped to guide their successors towards an almost diametrically opposite stylistic goal.[11]

II

It was in the specific matter of diction that the exponents of simplicity fought most systematically to enforce an ideal of precision, decorum, elegance, and conformity to normal usage. Despite the failure to establish an English academy for the control of language there was a growing tendency to eliminate technical terms, archaic and foreign words, provincialisms and neologisms in a "correct" style that would reflect the "conversation of people of fashion, that

speak well and without affectation," and of the small group of
acceptable writers that included at first Waller and Denham in
verse, and Temple and Tillotson in prose. To these names those
of Pope, Swift, and Addison were later added.[12]

Under the pressure of the more and more rigid standard of
elegance and ease the exuberant colloquialism of men like Nash
suffered a neglect in England as great as that which fell upon the
studied euphuism of Lyly and Greene, while in France the efforts
of the Pleiade to justify the utmost freedom of word-choice as an
essential step in developing in French the richness of the classical
tongues was shattered by the incisive comments of Malherbe on
the diction of Desportes. Dialect and archaic words, neologisms
and Latinisms, compound words and technical expressions were all
marked with strokes of Malherbe's blue pencil as violations of the
ordinary usage which should be the master. Balzac, Ogier, Vaugelas,
and Vavasseur performed in France the function of Sprat, Glanvill,
Waller, Denham, and Dryden in England. The views of Malherbe
and the somewhat later English purists never drowned out entirely
the rebellious murmurs of the small opposition which disliked limitations on genius, but they came to be so generally accepted that
they may truly be regarded as forming a classical ideal of diction.[13]

Decorum and conformity to the normal usage of polite society
were the most conspicuous features of this ideal. In some of its
aspects decorum of diction was related to the concept of decorum
of character, itself a logical outgrowth of the popular view of nature.
If the presentation of a character was to preserve probability his
actions and opinions must not only conform to his dignity, his sex,
his age, and his temperament, but the language he employs as well
must vary in conformity with the type. Had not Quintilian said
that the first principle of art was to observe decorum?[14] Was it
not a conclusion of pure reason that the language of kings must be
kingly and the language of the populace vulgar? This was not a
principle of classicism alone, but a universally valid principle of art,
which Wordsworth adopted for his Goody Blake as Masefield did
for his Saul Kane.

Only rarely was decorum of diction associated with delicacy and
moral purity, but to each degree of elevation and to each division

among the literary "kinds" was attributed a particular style.[15] Underlying this aspect of decorum was the traditional threefold distinction of style into the ornate, the medium, and the plain. There was no necessary contradiction between the lofty style of tragedy or epic, and the ideal of simplicity, for simplicity could be interpreted to mean clarity, precision, and purity—qualities quite compatible with the special color of epic diction as well as with poetic diction in general. In practice, however, the attempts of Spenser and Milton to fashion a vehicle of suitable dignity for their high heroic themes did result in some loss of simplicity, no matter how the term be interpreted, as all but their blindest admirers must admit. It was, indeed, the rule of decorum which assisted the genius of Milton, the poet, to set up that Miltonic diction which so powerfully rivalled the more direct diction of Dryden during the eighteenth century.[16]

Aristotle, Cicero, and Quintilian afforded classical precedents for decorum of style. In late eighteenth-century England Lord Kames was still insisting in his *Elements of Rhetoric* that the youth of England bear it in mind:

Heroic actions or sentiments require elevated language; tender sentiments ought to be expressed in words soft and flowing; and plain language void of ornament, is adapted to subjects grave and didactic.

Pope explained to Lord Oxford that he had followed the medium style in the translation of the *Odyssey*, though he had striven in the *Iliad* for a "venerable antique cast" by the "use of some Grecisms and old words after the manner of Milton." There would be little point, perhaps, in attempting to distinguish the decorum of diction according to "kinds" from the decorum of diction as regulated by choice of subject. Each subject and each "kind" had its appropriate degree of elevation which must be preserved lest the use of vulgar or trivial words destroy the unity of a noble style, or the employment of pedantic compounds and grandiloquent Latinisms mar the unimposing directness of a style purely expository. Violations of this decorum resulted in the mock-heroic and burlesque styles respectively, both highly popular for satiric and comic effects, but unpermissible otherwise.[17]

III

The most important distinction in diction from Renaissance to Romanticism—and beyond—was that between the language of poetry and the language of prose. Poetic diction won almost universal support. Aristotle and Quintilian, Dante and Tasso, Ronsard and Pelletier all permitted the poet to lengthen and shorten words, and to employ rare words or unusual inversions to gain distinction in style. The use of distinct words for poetry and prose was advocated so that the high spirit of poesy might not be sullied by the breath of vulgarity. The justification of poetic diction on the ground that the poet, who worked within the restrictions of meter, must be given a license not needed by the writer of prose was equally frequent. A few illustrations must serve to dispose of an aspect of classicism concerning which there was so little controversy. Addison considered Italian superior to English in its multiplicity of poetic words "that never enter into common discourse." Such common words and phrases "take off from the solemnity of the expression" and give it too great a turn of familiarity, but the English poet, who does not have at his command an adequate collection of words reserved for poetic usage must employ "metaphors and figures, or, by the pompousness of the whole phrase . . . wear off any littleness that appears in the particular parts that compose it." In *The Spectator* Addison showed his willingness to grant a considerable degree of license to the poet who must steer between the opposite shoals of meanness and stiffness, and could only avoid the former danger by metaphors, the idioms of other tongues, archaic words, and by the occasional use of lengthened or shortened forms of words. Like Addison, Gray thought

The language of the age is never the language of poetry; except among the French, whose verse, where the thought or image does not support it, differs in nothing from prose. Our poetry, on the contrary, has a language peculiar to itself; to which almost every one, that has written, has added something by enriching it with foreign idioms and derivations: nay sometimes words of their own composition or invention. Shakespeare and Milton have been great creators this way; and no one more licentious than Pope or Dryden, who perpetually borrow expressions from the former.

Joseph Warton believed that a didactic poem "ought to be enlivened by pomp of numbers, and majesty of words, and by every figure that can lift a language above the vulgar and current expressions." Doctor Johnson tried to reconcile simplicity with poetic diction. On the former point he wrote:

Language suffers violence by harsh or by daring figures, by transposition, by unusual acceptations of words, and by any license which would be avoided by a writer of prose. Where any artifice appears in the construction of the verse, that verse is no longer easy. Any epithet which can be ejected without diminution of the sense, any curious iteration of the same word, and all unusual . . . structure of the speech destroy the grace of easy poetry.

But he declared that poetical diction should be

refined from the grossness of domestic use, and free from the harshness of terms appropriated to particular arts. Words too familiar, or too remote, defeat the purpose of the poet. From those sounds which we hear on small or on coarse occasions, we do not easily receive strong impressions, or delightful images; and words to which we are nearly strangers . . . draw attention on themselves which they should transmit to things.[18]

I V

A correct style is elegant and discriminating in choice of words, in conformity with gentlemanly usage, and free from grammatical error. Grammatical correctness falls outside the sphere of poetic artistry, but the attitude of the age to vulgarisms and technical terms as well as to archaic, provincial, foreign, and newly coined words must be considered briefly.

In 1778 Doctor Johnson found elegance of style universally diffused in England. Not even a merchant's clerk would be guilty of such "sad stuff" as Martin's *Account of Scotland*, written in 1702. Later in the same year the lexicographer complacently noted that "everybody composes pretty well. There are no such inharmonious periods as there were a hundred years ago." This uniform elegance consisted in the ability to veil the impurity of things with the purity of words, to employ only the words current in the best social circles, and to avoid any suspicion of pedantry and provincialism. It was in large measure the gift of woman to literature, for it was born with

Lyly and Sidney in the circle of the Countess of Pembroke, in the France of the Hôtel de Rambouillet and of the fastidious satellites of the salons—Balzac, Vaugelas, Huet, and les Scudéry. To the influence of women something was added by the study of the Augustan purists Virgil and Cicero, and by the study of other classics in the delicately expurgated editions *pour les jeunes filles*. The study of rhetoric contributed also, for Blair, Kames, and Campbell did not labor in vain. For the pure in heart the makers of anthologies labored from Steele to Goldsmith and beyond to supply a constant succession of elegant excerpts from the poets—selections which did not contain a single word that might put a chaste cheek to the blush. A final influence was that of Boileau, who did not tire of reiterating the need for scrupulous purity:

> Et . . . même aux discours de la rusticité
> Donner de l'élégance et de la dignité;
> Quoi que vous écriviez, évitez la bassesse:
>
> .   .   .   .
>
> Du moindre sens impur la liberté l'outrage,
> Si la pudeur des mots n'en adoucit l'image.[19]

In England Addison and Steele, rather than Swift and Pope, popularized a simple elegance. Purity was demanded even more insistently by the Richardson, Johnson, and Burney circles, and by the chaste Bluestockings, who fluttered on the confines of literary London. In the light of an elegant standard Bunyan and Defoe were weighed and found wanting. Even Spenser, that greater teacher than Aquinas, did not escape censure. Johnson found Shakespeare a sinner. Addison demanded "pomp of numbers and dignity of words" particularly from the didactic poet. Swift wished the elimination of what he called Alsatia phrases. Beattie branded as inelegant words used by illiterate persons or those used on very familiar occasions, as well as vulgar proverbs, slang and colloquial usages, technical terms, provincial expressions, and common forms of compliment which were impermanent or unduly familiar. Beattie's list has much to commend it to the purists and compilers of rhetorical handbooks at the present day.[20]

In the case of technical terms the proponents of elegance won a clear-cut victory. The French Pleaide had recommended to the poet the study of mechanical arts as a source for exact yet varied imagery, but their liberal attitude awoke few echoes in post-Elizabethan England. Dryden followed the Pleaide in *Annus Mirabilis,* but before he died he modified his position and followed Virgil—in the translation of the *Æneid*—in the avoidance of technical terms,

because he writ not to mariners, soldiers, astronomers, gardeners, peasants, etc., but to all in general, and in particular to men and ladies of the first quality, who have been better bred than to be too nicely knowing in the terms.

Hobbes and Dennis came to hold the same attitude. Despite Dryden's disclaimer in the *Dedication of the Æneas* just quoted, Pope thought that Dryden had erred in the use of sea terms both because such terms were unsuitable to the character of Æneas and to "the majesty and dignity of style which epic poetry requires." Addison found technical language objectionable because the poet should make things intelligible in easy language for the ordinary reader, and because "the knowledge of a poet should rather seem born with him, or inspired, than drawn from books and systems." Gray tried to reform the practice of both Mason and Beattie. Late in the century Campbell felt that "in strict propriety technical words should not be considered as belonging to the language, because not in current use, nor understood by the generality of readers," while Doctor Johnson urged that "all appropriated terms of art should be sunk in general expressions."[21]

The correct poet must eschew pedantry and affectation. Dialect, obsolete, and foreign words were neither elegant nor perspicuous, according to Cicero and Quintilian, though they might be used occasionally for dignity or novelty. Renaissance critics, and especially the Pleaide, wished archaic words enclosed like jewels in the fabric of a poem. In England Spenser followed Ronsard and Du Bellay in practice, and was defended by "E. K.," who pointed out the gain in grace and authority as well as the retention of the spirit and sound English wording of the old authors.[22]

Around Spenser an early struggle for correctness was fought. Sidney denied that Theocritus and Virgil gave Spenser sufficient precedents for his diction. Puttenham believed that the poet must follow the usage of "men civil and graciously behavioured and bred," and not that of Chaucer, Gower, and Lydgate. Nash quoted from Aulus Gellius: *"loquere verbis praesentibus."* Edmund Bolton found the affectation of archaic words a "foul oversight." Jonson, basing his objection to obsolete words on the principle of perspicacity, branded Spenser as having "writ no language." Davenant and Dryden thought that Spenser had overdone archaism. Prior agreed. Armstrong was especially hard on archaic words, but they met with little better treatment at the hands of Goldsmith or Johnson. A quotation from Robert Lloyd must be allowed to conclude this rapid survey of the opposition to archaism:

> *Whilom, what time, eftsoons,* and *erst*
> (So prose is oftentimes beverst)
> Sprinkled with quaint fantastic phrase,
> Uncouth to ears of modern days,
> Make up the metre, which they call
> Blank, classic blank, their all in all.[23]

The Spenserian, Miltonic, and mediæval revivals of the second half of the eighteenth century were to restore archaism to popularity, but until the appearance of conscious mediævalism scant sympathy was shown for the charms of the antique. To this the "improvements" of Chaucer and Donne, and even the elegant versions of the ballads by Percy bear witness. Dryden admitted, on the authority of Horace, that

obsolete words may . . . be laudably revived, when either they are more sounding, or more significant, than those in practice; and when their obscurity is taken away, by joining other words to them, which clear the sense.

The obscure Henry Felton was quite liberal towards archaisms in his *Dissertation on Forming a Just Style,* published in 1713. Gray thought that words of archaic flavor might legitimately be employed if time had not rendered them unintelligible, and Doctor Johnson, despite a general distaste for them, included in his *Dictionary* some obsolete words with "force or beauty" sufficient to deserve revival. In the case of Hurd's approval one stands on the brink of conscious mediævalism.[24]

In the controversy as to the enrichment of a language by foreign

borrowing the French Pleaide was again important in establishing
a liberal attitude which a stricter classicism was compelled to destroy
in its effort to preserve the pure well of English undefiled. In England Elyot had already been the leader of a movement for the
enrichment of the English vocabulary by foreign borrowing, but he
found few influential followers, though Richard Carew and George
Chapman were Elizabethan liberals. After 1660 Glanvill branded
pure, unmixed English as a "dream of chimeras," for English had
been a mixed tongue for centuries. Pope seemed to be favorable to
borrowing, but Welsted expressed the attitude of extreme caution
which was characteristic of the period:

> Nor does anything . . . require greater skill or delicacy, than to improve
> a language by introducing foreign treasures into it; the words, so introduc'd,
> ought to be such, as, in a manner, naturalize themselves; that is, they ought
> to fit into the idiom, and suit with the genius of the tongue, they are brought
> into, so luckily, as almost to seem, originally, of its own growth; otherwise
> the attempt will end in nothing but an uncouth, unnatural jargon, like the
> phrase and stile of *Milton*, which is a second Babel, or confusion of all
> languages.

Scattered expressions of approval during the course of the century
were insignificant in comparison with the extent of the opposition.[25]
  This opposition was already fully formulated during the Elizabethan period. In his *Rhetoric* of 1553 Wilson showed a general
reluctance to admit foreign terms. Cheke wished to preserve the
purity of Saxon English and translated a portion of the Gospel of
Matthew to illustrate the feasibility of avoiding Latinisms. He preferred archaisms and Teutonic compounds to foreign importations.
Ascham, as usual, followed his master, Cheke. "E. K." blamed the
disuse of older English words for the poverty which seemed to
justify foreign borrowing. Spenser's vocabulary was essentially English, though he admitted a few Latinisms for metrical reasons and
was friendly to such other foreign words as had been pretty well
established by court fashion. Marston, Hall, and Camden followed
Spenser and "E. K." in resisting any defilement of English. Puttenham assailed foreign terms in general but he admitted borrowing, if
no single English word was satisfactory. Nash preferred a racy
native English to thefts from the "Latin store-houses." Jonson put

a defense of purity into the mouth of Virgil in *The Poetaster*, and the only less scholarly Samuel Daniel expressed his wonder at the

strange presumption of some men, that dare so audaciously adventure to introduce any what soever foreign words, be they never so strange, and of themselves, as it were, without a Parliament, without any consent or allowance, establish them as free-denizens in our language.[26]

The high tide of classicism brought in no new ideas, but the French influence on English culture after 1660 caused the opposition to be directed against Gallicisms rather than against Latinisms. Against the French flood the great French critic Boileau could himself be cited. Wycherley, Etherege, Vanbrugh, and Dryden presented gallicizing Englishmen as butts of ridicule. Dryden was not fanatical on the subject and allowed himself more liberty in poetry than in prose, but he acted with caution and on the advice of judicious friends. Hobbes believed that the use of unfamiliar foreign words would alienate feminine readers and lessen universality of appeal. When the French wars of William and Anne increased the danger of borrowing, Addison and Fielding did their best to laugh the fad down. In *The Spectator* Addison presented a letter written in a hybrid jargon by a soldier to his parent in which such expressions as *reconnoitre, gens d'armes, corps, commandant,* and *cartel* are noted with disapproval; while Fielding relegated the right to import French words to Grub-street in the mock treaty which ended the Paper War described in *The Covent-Garden Journal.* The *Connoisseur* took much the same attitude. Both Lady Mary Wortley Montagu and George Campbell found Bolingbroke guilty of Gallicisms, and Doctor Johnson found the same fault with Greville's *Memoirs.* In *The Preface to the Dictionary* Johnson lamented the growing Gallic influence, for which he blamed translations, and tried to direct attention to the Elizabethans as "the wells of English undefiled." In the *Dictionary* he included some words recently borrowed, but "commonly only to censure them, and warn others against the folly of naturalizing useless foreigners to the injury of natives." Professional rhetoricians like Campbell and Blair were at one with Doctor Johnson.[27]

Less was said concerning coinage than foreign borrowing, but the consensus of opinion was against it. Despite the liberality of

Horace, Saintsbury was able to declare that the "horror of the *insolens*, the *inusitatum verbum*, is the very dominant note of all Latin criticism." Jonson sounded the warning which was to be re-echoed by two centuries of English classicism:

> A man coins not a new word without some peril and less fruit; for if it happen to be received, the praise is but moderate; if refus'd, the scorn is assur'd.

In the eighteenth century Theobald tried to justify Shakespeare's freedom, but from Mandeville to Blair the age opposed his opinion. Mandeville pointed to the *beau monde* as affording the standard of taste: a new word is as much a crime against the king's English as a counterfeit piece against his coin. Much later Beattie employed the same simile. Gray found coinage hazardous; Armstrong argued that it would destroy stylistic unity of tone; Campbell found it barbarous; John Scott refused to accept a coinage even on the authority of Shakespeare or Milton; and Hugh Blair thought it, in general, incongruous with purity of style. Such was the dominant note.[28]

v

Before passing to poetic form a word must be said concerning onomatopoetic qualities of diction. Pope had written in *An Essay on Criticism* that

> The sound must seem an echo to the sense;

and, in imitation of Vida and Boileau, had proceeded to illustrate his point in an artful passage into which he wove an allusion to Dryden's *Alexander's Feast*, the stock example of onomatopoetic ingenuity. Some critics remained unconvinced, but the approval of Addison marked an important victory, and the imitative qualities of words were considered not only by minor figures such as Armstrong and Harris, but incorporated into the rhetorical theories of Kames, Campbell, and Blair.[29]

Lord Kames thought that the writer should attempt to preserve resemblance between words and their meanings—words of short syllables should be used for active and hurrying passions, long and slow words for brooding passions; words of long and many syllables for languid melancholy; smooth, gliding diction for soft, calm, and sweet emotions. A line of monosyllables could represent "laborious, interrupted motion"; an Alexandrine prolonged motion; harsh, rough words could excite a "feeling similar to that which proceeds from the labour of thought of a dull writer."[30]

Campbell was more cautious than Blair. He pointed out six possibilities of onomatopœia, but he considered it at best but a minor grace and often more the creation of the reader's fancy than of the writer's deliberate intent. Blair had still less to say, but he said it with less qualification than Campbell. He believed that the relation of sound to sense must be considered as an element of sentence harmony. For the imitation of one sound by another he cited Milton; for the imitation of motion by swiftly or slowly moving lines Homer and Virgil; for the imitation of passion by sound he recurred to *Alexander's Feast*.[31]

VI

While there were many minor divergences of opinion it can be stated with reasonable accuracy that the critics of the eighteenth century wished diction, like conduct and opinion, to be brought by means of a rational control into conformity with the general practice of the best people. This basic uniformity, founded on ideals of clarity and elegance, could then be modified according to the principles of decorum so that for each specific literary purpose there would be a specific vocabulary. Careful diction was an aspect of artistic form, itself a generic term, which, like correctness (at times almost its synonym) covered a multitude of more specialized attitudes, but always implied a careful craftsmanship in the structure of a work of art with, as its final aim, the creation of a unified structural and stylistic effect, the conscientious adaptation of subject matter to literary "kind," and a scrupulous adjustment of style to subject matter.

Literary classicism was an attempt to impose form on the unfettered fancies, the dangerous fires of genius, and the individual eccentricities of the artist. Correctness of style is one of its manifestations; but metrical perfection, avoidance of the extravagances of wit, respect for the traditional literary type, and for truth to Nature as revealed by common sense were all considered as aspects of correctness. This respect for formal qualities in literary work—for elegance and precision in diction, for polish, for organic structure, for technique in general as opposed to content—was a natural corollary of the Augustan vision of an orderly universe; it was in thorough keeping with the regimented social life of the upper classes in its respect for restraint and decorum as opposed to spontaneity; it was a product of the analytical spirit which showed itself in science and ethics as well as in art. These were positive supports in the social and intellectual background, but they, as well as the formalism they fostered in literature, owed an indeterminate amount of their strength to a reaction against the enthusiasm of the Puritans and the "metaphysical extravagance" of the Cavaliers.

In England the battle over correctness never resulted in the complete subjection of the more liberal group who took their correctness with reasonable lightness. As Horace Walpole wrote in 1765:

All that Aristotle or [the French critics] have taught us, has not yet subdued us to regularity; we still prefer the extravagant beauties of Shakespeare and Milton to the cold and well-disciplined merit of Addison, and even to the sober and correct march of Pope.

Correctness and form were the goals of an ideal achievement seldom realized completely in actuality—seldom, indeed, demanded with rigid insistence and blind disregard for the significance of genius.[82]

The struggle of native English independence to resist the burdens of the Rules of the Ancients will be examined in Book II. A swift survey must be made, however, of the general attitude of the age to correctness and poetic form. To the eighteenth-century critic correctness was seldom a fetish. He reiterated the view of Cicero in the *De Oratore* that correctness might forestall ridicule, but would seldom gain admiration; or maintained the opinion of Horace concerning the insignificance of a few flaws amid more numerous beauties. The attempt to establish an English academy showed a desire for some measure of correctness, but the failure was more significant than the attempt. Dryden lamented the lack of a prosody, a dictionary, and a grammar, and regretted the incorrectness of Shakespeare and Fletcher, but he sought to excuse them by exaggerating the ignorance of their age. *The Guardian* found the same excuse for Bacon. Pope was often lacking in correctness, and he was willing to admit that

> Not to know some trifles is a praise,

though his admirers looked upon him as the apostle of correctness. As Edward Young wrote:

> Excuse no fault; though beautiful, 'twill harm;
> One fault shocks more than twenty beauties charm.
> Our age demands correctness; Addison
> And you this commendable hurt have done.
> Now writers find, as once Achilles found,
> The whole is mortal, if a part's unsound.

Young was later to retract:

. . . great subjects are above being nice; . . . dignity and spirit ever suffer from scrupulous exactness; and . . . the minuter cares effeminate a composition.

Both Addison and Pope—bugbears of correctness to Walpole—had more respect for genius than for form. Addison wrote:

. . . the productions of a great genius, with many lapses and inadvertencies, are infinitely preferable to the works of an inferior kind of author, which are scrupulously exact, and conformable to all the rules of correct writing;

and Pope of Shakespeare:

. . . with all his faults and all the irregularity of his drama, one may look upon his works, in comparison of those that are more finish'd and regular, as upon an ancient majestick piece of Gothic architecture, compar'd with a neat modern building: the latter is more elegant and glaring, but the former is more strong and more solemn. It must be allow'd that in one of these there are materials enough to make many of the other. It has much the greater variety, and much the nobler apartments; tho' we are often conducted to them by dark, odd, and uncouth passages. Nor does the whole fail to strike us with a greater reverence, tho' many of the parts are childish, ill-plac'd, and unequal to its grandeur.

In the Age of Anne the influence of Longinus helped to disparage correct mediocrity: "the greatest natures are least immaculate; Perfect precision runs the risk of triviality"; Uninspired correctness cannot be compared to "grandeur with a few flaws."[33]

Longinus helped to modify the strictness of a correct standard; he could not stop the search for a reasonable degree of grammatical, prosodic, and artistic conformity. Chesterfield held up Dryden, Atterbury, Swift, and Bolingbroke as correct models, made lists of vulgar expressions, and recommended translation of the classics as a form of stylistic drill. He himself took pride in the correctness of his diction, and regarded style as important for the writer as dress for a gentleman. Hume felt that proper stylists were very rare and bemoaned the neglect of "elegance and propriety." Akenside pretended "chiefly to the merit of endeavoring to be correct, and of carefully attending to the best models." Johnson proposed in *The Rambler* "to refine our language to grammatical purity, and to clear it from colloquial barbarisms, licentious idioms, and irregular combinations." Goldsmith supported Johnson, while Doctor Blair was of the opinion that "the public ear is now so accustomed to a correct and ornamental style that no writer can, with safety, neglect the study of it," though, like Campbell, he knew that more was necessary than mere correctness and refused to damn a writer for occasional negligence.[34]

Such was the conservative attitude, and it was by no means blind to the limitations of correctness nor to the power of beauties to overbalance faults. A still more liberal group believed that the struggle for correctness fettered genius. Rowe struck this note in speaking of Shakespeare:

Whether his ignorance of the ancients were a disadvantage to him or no, may admit of a dispute: for though the knowledge of them might have made him more correct, yet it is not improbable but that the regularity and deference for them, which would have attended that correctness, might have restrain'd some of that fire, impetuosity, and even beautiful extravagance which we admire in Shakespeare: and I believe we are better pleas'd with those thoughts, altogether new and uncommon, which his own imagination supply'd him so abundantly with, than if he had given us the most beautiful passages out of the Greek and Latin poets.

Warburton, like Rowe, believed warmth of imagination to be incompatible with complete correctness. Robert Lloyd found that dread of incorrectness led to timidity and ridiculous precision. Even Doctor Johnson was of the liberal school:

The work of a correct and regular writer is a garden accurately formed and diligently planted, varied with shades, and scented with flowers; the composition of Shakespeare is a forest . . . filling the eye with awful pomp, and gratifying the mind with endless diversity.

With Gerard and Duff we are in the midst of the new school of spontaneous genius, whose members saw little virtue in "languid mediocrity," and "faultless insipidity" in comparison with "that noble boldness of genius," and "those most essential excellencies, . . . *fiction* and *fire*." But had not Pope already dismissed with contempt

> Such lays as neither ebb, nor flow,
> Correctly cold, and regularly low,
> That shunning faults, one quiet tenour keep?

The classicists were unwilling to abandon judgment for fancy. They were desirous of aiding genius with knowledge. The times gave them respect for the wishes of the social group whose spokesmen they were, but they were not hidebound by the Rules, not unthinking devotees at the altars of correctness, not slaves in the prison-house of form.[35]

NOTES TO CHAPTER IX

1. Horace, *Ars Poetica*, line 23; Quintilian, *Institutes of Oratory*, VIII. Preface, 19–23; Ascham, *Scholemaster*, in Gregory Smith, *op. cit.*, I, 6; Nash, *ibid.*, I, 307–309; Drayton, Epistle to Henry Reynolds, in Spingarn, *Critical Essays of the Seventeenth Century*, I, 137; Bacon, *ibid.*, I, 2; Jones, "Science and English Prose Style," *P. M. L. A.*, XLV, 978–979, 988, 996, 998–1001; Wycherley, in Pope, *Works*, I, 23; Steele, Dedication of the first volume of the *Tatler* to Arthur Mainwaring; Allan Ramsay, Preface to *The Evergreen*; Lord Kames, *Elements*, I, 165; Joseph Warton, *World*, No. 26, and "On Not Being Able to Write Verses to Delia"; Thomas Warton, *History of English Poetry*, p. 911, and Preface to *Five Pastoral Eclogues*, in Chalmers, *op. cit.*, XVIII, 136; Goldsmith, *Citizen of the World*, Letter XXXIII, and *Works*, ed. Gibbs, IV, 455–459; Cowper, *Expostulation*, lines 135–138; Aaron Hill, in Richardson, *Correspondence*, I, 129; Armstrong, *Miscellanies*, II, 140–141.

2. Swift, *Correspondence*, I, 142; Addison, *Spectator*, No. 62; John Brown, *Essays on the Characteristicks*, pp. 375–377.

3. Spingarn, *Critical Essays*, I, xxxiv, II, 22; Temple, *ibid.*, III, 100; Pope, *Works*, VI, 51, and *Essays on Criticism*, lines 289–296; Addison, *Spectator*, Nos. 62, 163; Chesterfield, *Letters*, I, 53–54; II, 32–33, 94–95, 96, 313, 341; Goldsmith, *Miscellaneous Works*, p. 441.

4. Spingarn, *Critical Essays*, I, lviii, lxxvii; Percy H. Houston, *Doctor Johnson. A Study in Eighteenth-Century Humanism*, Cambridge (Mass.), 1923, pp. 125–126; Dryden, *Essays*, I, 14, 172; Hobbes, *Leviathan*, pp. 41–44; Davenant, Preface

to *Gondibert*, in Spingarn, *op. cit.*, II, 23; Dryden, *Essays*, I, 270; Mulgrave, in Spingarn, *op. cit.*, II, 294; Locke, *Essay*, p. 102; Pope, *Works*, II, 25; Addison, *Spectator*, Nos. 62, 253; Johnson, *Lives of the Poets*, ed. Waugh, I, 28.

5. Welsted, in Durham, *op. cit.*, p. 392; Theobald, in Nicoll Smith, *op. cit.*, pp. 84–85; Thomson, *Winter*, in Chalmers, *op. cit.*, XII, 450; Kames, *Elements*, I, 28; Duff, *Essay on Genius*, pp. 47–49; Campbell, *Philosophy of Rhetoric*, pp. 22–23; Beattie, *Dissertations*, I, 188.

6. Roscommon, in Spingarn, *op. cit.*, II, 303.

7. Pope, *Works*, II, 38; VI, 51, 190; Warton, *Essay on Pope*, II, 174.

8. Addison, *Spectator*, Nos. 63, 415, and *Works*, I, 489; Shaftesbury, *Life, Letters, and Philosophical Regimen*, p. 247; Hume, *Essays*, I, 241; Thomson, *Liberty*, in Chalmers, *op. cit.*, XII, 476; Gerard, *Essay on Taste*, p. 37; Whitehead, *World*, No. 12; Joseph Warton, *World*, No. 26, and *Adventurer*, No. 127. The growing taste for Gothic will be traced in a later chapter.

9. *Tatler*, No. 159; Brown, *Essays on the Characteristicks*, p. 381; Joseph Warton, *World*, No. 26; Blair, *Rhetoric*, II, 36–37.

10. Boileau, *Œuvres*, pp. 363–365; Richardson, *Correspondence*, VI, 243; Goldsmith, *Bee*, No. VII; Blair, *Rhetoric*, I, 330–331.

11. Spingarn, *Critical Essays*, I, xxxix–xliv; Marjorie Nicholson, "The Early Stage of Cartesianism in England," *Studies in Philology*, XXVI, 373; M. W. Croll, " 'Attic Prose' in the Seventeenth Century," *Studies in Philology*, XVIII, 79–128; Clark, *Boileau in England*, p. 381; Jones, *Science and English Prose Style, in toto*.

12. John Hughes, *Of Style*, in Durham, *op. cit.*, pp. 80–82.

13. Spingarn, *Literary Criticism of the Renaissance*, pp. 231–238; Vial et Denise, *op. cit.*, pp. 70, 72–78; Emma F. Pope, "Renaissance Criticism and the Diction of the *Faerie Queene*," *P. M. L. A.*, XLI, 595–596; Deimier, in Vial et Denise, *op. cit.*, p. 71. Balzac, Ogier, Vaugelas, and Vavasseur are cited also by Vial et Denise, pp. 84, 96, 56, 58. Expressions of opposition may be found in Dryden, Hughes, and Dennis, who all refuse to censure Milton. See Dryden, Preface to *Don Sebastian*; Hughes, in Durham, *op. cit.*, pp. 80–82; and Dennis, *ibid.*, p. 233. Edward Phillips refused to admit that genius need admit control in the choice of words according to Hamelius, *op. cit.*, p. 60.

14. Quoted by Blair, *Rhetoric*, II, 236.

15. Decorum was associated with delicacy by Arthur Murphy, *Essay on Fielding*, p. 37, and by Joseph Warton, *Adventurer*, No. 105.

16. I shall revert briefly to Miltonic diction in Chap. XIV, "The Survival of Elizabethan Romanticism." Addison gave Miltonic diction a clean bill of health, because of the principle of decorum. *Cf.* Johnson, *Rambler*, No. 40.

17. Aristotle, *Poetics*, III, ii, 2; III, vii, 11; III, xii, 1; Cicero, *De Oratore*, III, 52; Puttenham, in Gregory Smith, *op. cit.*, II, 155–158; Kames, *Elements*, II, 19; Pope, *Works*, VIII, 218, and *Preface to the Iliad*.

18. Aristotle, *Poetics*, XXII; Quintilian, I, viii, 13–14; Saintsbury, *History of Criticism*, I, 436, II, 118; Emma F. Pope, *op. cit.*, 590–591; Ronsard, in Vial et Denise, *op. cit.*, p. 9; Spingarn, *Literary Criticism of the Renaissance*, p. 217; Puttenham, in Gregory Smith, *op. cit.*, II, 142–143; Addison, *Works*, I, 158, 393, and *Spectator*, No. 285; Gray, *Letters*, I, 98; Joseph Warton, quoted by R. D. Havens, *Influence of Milton*, p. 142; Johnson, *Idler*, No. 77, and *Lives of the Poets*, II, 215. *Cf.* Blair, *Rhetoric*, I, 205, and Coleridge, *Biographia Literaria*, pp. 12, 209, note 1, 226.

19. Boswell, *Life of Johnson*, III, 275, 281; Boileau, *Œuvres*, pp. 87, 178, 190, 200, 213, 466; Vial et Denise, *op. cit.*, pp. 47, 49, 52, 89; Saintsbury, *History of Criticism*, II, 251–252.

20. Thomas Warton, *Observations on the Faerie Queene*, I, 69; Beattie, *Dissertations*, II, 245, 311, 416–421; Johnson, *Rambler*, No. 168; Addison, *Works*, I, 158; Swift, *Gulliver*, etc., p. 379; Blair, *Rhetoric*, II, 26–27.

21. Du Bellay and Estienne are quoted in Vial et Denise, *op. cit.*, p. 19. Ronsard is quoted by Ker, Introduction to Dryden's *Essays*, I, xxxiii. Spingarn, *Literary Criticism of the Renaissance*, pp. 215–216; Dryden, *Essays*, I, 13, II, 236; Hobbes, in Spingarn, *Critical Essays of the Seventeenth Century*, II, 68; Dennis, *ibid.*, II, 333; Pope, *Works*, VI, 107, X, 389; Addison, *Spectator*, No. 297; Gray, *Letters*, I, 318, III, 310; Campbell, *Philosophy of Rhetoric*, pp. 286–287; Johnson, *Lives of the Poets*, I, 198, II, 229, VI, 189.

22. Cicero, *De Oratore*, III, 10 and III, 43; Horace, *Ars Poetica*, lines 70–71; Quintilian, I, vi, 39–40; VIII, ii, 12–13; VIII, iii, 24; Du Bellay, in Vial et Denise, *op. cit.*, p. 18; D'Aubigné, *ibid.*, p. 24; "E. K.," in Gregory Smith, *op. cit.*, I, 128.

23. Gascoigne, in Gregory Smith, I, 52–53; Sidney, *ibid.*, I, 196; Puttenham, *ibid.*, II, 150; Nash, *ibid.*, II, 243; Bolton, in Springarn, *Critical Essays*, I, 109; Jonson, *ibid.*, I, 34, 38; Davenant, *ibid.*, II, 6; Dryden, *Essays*, II, 28–29; Armstrong, *Miscellanies*, II, 149; Boswell, *Life of Johnson*, III, 180, note 3; Robert Lloyd, "Of Rhyme"; Prior is quoted by E. P. Morton, "The Spenserian Stanza in the Eighteenth Century," *Modern Philology*, X, 371.

24. Dryden, *Essays*, II, 28–29; R. S. Crane, "Imitation of Spenser and Milton in the Early Eighteenth Century: A New Document," *Studies in Philology*, XV, 204 and note 40; Gray, *Letters*, I, 98; Johnson, *Preface to the Dictionary*; Hurd is cited by Clark, *Boileau in England*, p. 294.

25. Spingarn, *Literary Criticism of the Renaissance*, pp. 182, 216–217; Vial et Denise, *op cit.*, p. 16; E. E. Hale, "Ideas on Rhetoric in the Sixteenth Century," *P. M. L. A.*, XVIII, 426–431; Carew and Chapman in Gregory Smith, *op. cit.*, 290, 305; Glanvill, in Spingarn, *Critical Essays*, II, 273–274; Pope, *Works*, III, 386; Welsted, in Durham, *op. cit.*, p. 359. Hannah More (*Letters*, pp. 124, 126–127), Thomas Warton (*History of English Poetry*, p. 348), and Gray (Gosse, *Gray*, p. 52), were at least not hostile to enrichment of vocabulary by borrowing.

26. E. E. Hale, *op. cit.*, pp. 432 ff.; Cheke, in Gregory Smith, I, 357–358; Saintsbury, *History of Criticism*, II, 155; "E. K.," in Gregory Smith, I, 130; Emma F. Pope, *op. cit.*, p. 605; Thomas Warton, *Observations on the Faerie Queene*, I, 127–132; Puttenham, in Gregory Smith, *op. cit.*, II, 151-152; Nash, *ibid.*, I, 309; Jonson, *Poetaster*, Act V, scene III; Daniel, in Gregory Smith, *op. cit.*, II. 384.

27. Boileau, *Œuvres*, pp. 191, 299; Wycherley, *Gentleman Dancing-Master*, Act I, scene I; Etherege, *Man of Mode*, Act III, scene II; Dryden, *Marriage à la Mode*, Act III, scene I; Vanbrugh, *Provok'd Wife*, Act I, scene II; Dryden, Dedication of the *Rival Ladies*, and *Essays*, I, 5, 17, 82, 170, II, 234; Hobbes, in Spingarn, *Critical Essays*, II, 68; Addison, *Spectator*, No. 165; Fielding, *Covent-Garden Journal*, No. 5; *Connoisseur*, Nos. 42, 71; Lady Mary Wortley Montagu, *Letters*, I, 61; Johnson, *Letters*, I, 61; Campbell, *Philosophy of Rhetoric*, p. 251; Blair, *Rhetoric*, I, 223; W. F. Bryan, "A Late Eighteenth Century Purist," *Studies in Philology*, XXIII, 365–366.

28. Horace, *Ars Poetica*, lines 46–72; Quintilian, VIII, iii, 30–36; Saintsbury, *History of Criticism*, I, 300; Vial et Denise, *op. cit.*, pp. 10, 20–23, 98; Spingarn, *Literary Criticism of the Renaissance*, p. 221; Jonson, *Timber*, in Spingarn, *Critical*

Essays, I, 37; Theobald, in Nicoll Smith, *op. cit.*, p. 86; Mandeville, *Fable of the Bees*, II, 292–293; Beattie, in Gray, *Letters*, III, 310; Armstrong, *Miscellanies*, II, 147–149; W. F. Bryan, *op. cit.*, pp. 365–366; John Scott, *Critical Essays*, p. 62, note; Blair, *Rhetoric*, I, 222–223.

29. Pope, *Essay on Criticism*, lines 365 ff. and *Preface to the Iliad*, in Durham, p. 346; Addison, *Spectator*, No. 253; Armstrong, *Miscellanies*, II, 164; Harris, *Three Treatises*, p. 72. Opposition was expressed by the *Connoisseur*, by Daniel Webb, by John Scott, and by Johnson. See the *Connoisseur*, No. 83; Scott's *Critical Essays*, p. 120, Johnson's *Lives of the Poets*, I, 77, and the *Idler*, No. 60, and the article of Eric Partridge previously cited in *Studies in Philology*, XXV, 34.

30. Lord Kames, *Elements*, I, 393–394, II, 71–75.

31. Campbell, *Philosophy of Rhetoric*, pp. 397–415; Blair, *Rhetoric*, I, 295–299, 317–320.

32. Walpole, *Letters*, ed. Mrs. Paget Toynbee, VI, 201.

33. Cicero, *De Oratore*, III, 14; Horace, *Ars Poetica*, lines 347–360; Quintilian, I, vi, 20; Dryden, *Essays*, I, 165, II, 110; *Guardian*, No. 25; Pope, *Essay on Criticism*, lines 235–236, 261–262, and *Works*, II, 28; Young, *Poetical Works*, II, 352, 165; Addison, *Spectator*, No. 291; Pope, *Preface to Shakespeare*, in Nicoll Smith, *op. cit.*, p. 62; Longinus, *On the Sublime*, XXXIII, 1–5; Spingarn, *Critical Essays*, III, 300.

34. Chesterfield, *Letters*, I, 52, 271, 371, 399–401, 409, II, 109, 344, and *Works*, V, 299–301, 306–307; Hume, *Essays*, I, 159; Akenside, *Poetical Works*, p. 45; Johnson, *Rambler*, No. 208, *Plan of an English Dictionary* and *Preface to the Dictionary*; Goldsmith, *Bee*, No. VIII; Blair, *Rhetoric*, II, 56, 162–163; Campbell, *Philosophy of Rhetoric*, p. 244.

35. Rowe, *Preface to Shakespeare*, in Nicoll Smith, *op. cit.*, p. 2; Warburton, in Pope, *Works*, II, 106; Lloyd, *Connoisseur*, No. 120; Johnson, *Preface to Shakespeare*, in Nicoll Smith, *op. cit.*, p. 135; Gerard, *Essay on Taste*, p. 155; Duff, *Essay on Genius*, p. 99.

BOOK TWO

THE WEIGHT OF THE RULES

CHAPTER X

AUTHORITY AND THE RULES

I

THE FUNDAMENTAL principles which all masterpieces of eighteenth-century classicism display—common sense, nature, universality, morality, and social reference—were largely the products of the rational and practical spirit of the Enlightenment. Respect for the Rules, the practice of imitation, and the doctrine of literary "kinds" often seemed of equal importance to contemporaries, but from a perspective of two centuries it is evident that these direct debts to the Ancients had comparatively little effect on the independent spirit of the major classicists, for the "neoclassical" Rules were often questioned, frequently modified, and, in general, respected only when it could be shown that Reason and the Rules were the same. To represent them as having won acceptance because of the *ipse dixit* of the Ancients will appear absurd to any one who studies even the Rymers and Gildons of the period with an open mind. Admiration for antiquity was linked with regard for Nature. In its simplest form the argument ran: Nature is adherence to general truth; general truth is universally pleasing; the Ancients followed Nature; by observation of the methods of the Ancients, the Modern can most readily learn how best to imitate Nature; the Rules are a summary of the practices of the Ancients, or in Pope's decisive phrase, "nature methodized." An examination of authority, imitation, and the literary "kinds" will clarify the connection between rationalism and the Rules.[1]

Submission to Ancient authority is contingent upon familiarity and respect, which in turn are dependent upon the possibility of adjusting the verdicts of authority to contemporary ideology. Familiarity was a product of the academic study of Greek and Latin; the degree of admiration for the Ancients is revealed in the Battle of the Books; the modification of the Rules by the light of Nature reveals the necessity of remolding precedent by the spirit of the times.

The supremacy of the classics in eighteenth-century education is well known. Latin authors were used as models in composition, and the method of instruction was one of imitation so close that it necessitated an intimate knowledge of Horace and Virgil, Cicero and Ovid. Cheke and Ascham had initiated the vogue of imitative composition in the mid-sixteenth century. In the middle of the seventeenth century imitation still held an important place in the educational theories of Charles Hoole, who proposed in *A New Discovery of the Old Art of Teaching School* (1660) contests in the imitation of Latin poets and orators as a means of stimulating interest in the students. Near the end of the eighteenth century another educational theorist, Vicesimus Knox, outlined in *Liberal Education* (1781) a distribution of the young scholar's time which he considered satisfactory: Monday, Latin theme; Tuesday, Latin verse; Wednesday, English or Latin letters; Thursday, English verse; Friday, Latin verse or Latin composition; for the weekend a Latin or English theme. Knox advised the master to place "the best models of composition before the eyes of the student at all times, but more particularly while he is engaged in the work of imitation." The mixture of Latin and English in the program of Knox indicated a waning of the more exclusively classical discipline, for Knox was writing near the end of the classical dispensation.[2]

From the beginning to the end of the classical period one may gather testimony as to the importance of the educational system in developing the poets, but particularly the lesser poets, of the age. Only men of the strongest individuality could completely resist the impact of the classics through so many of their formative years. Saint-Évremond testified that the Latin poets which Rochester studied at Burford and Oxford made such a deep impression on him that "he never lost a true taste of any sovereign beauty of those great authors." A century later the situation was essentially unchanged. The testimony is that of William Boscawen in 1793:

> In the commencement of our juvenile studies, we drudge through other writers with reluctance; in him [Horace] we immediately find amusement and delight: when led at an early age from classical literature by our various

pursuits, we adhere to this our first favorite, and often cherish him alone, as our associate in our pleasures, our solace in the toils, and our refuge from the inquietudes of life.

To show in each case the effect that the study of the classics in the schools and universities had on the poets between 1660 and 1800 would involve a biographical study of each poet; to argue that the influence was in general extensive would be to waste words.[3]

It is less well known that this preoccupation with the classics was the subject of frequent attack. In 1776 Beattie, in 1781 Knox, in 1784 Joseph Cornish sought to stem the growing opposition to an exclusively classical education. The attack was opened a century earlier in *Academiarum Examen*, which proposed English as a vehicle for instruction in mathematics, physics, and chemistry. Webster's early plea for a scientific curriculum was ineffective, but in 1693 Locke struck a much more significant blow at the complete dominance of the classics in the popular *Thoughts Concerning Education*, to be followed a few years later by Richard Steele who began to apply the standards of common sense to the educational system in a series of essays in *The Tatler*, *Spectator*, and *Guardian*. Neither Steele nor his coadjutor Budgell doubted the value of the classics for a gentleman, but they wished to secure a more reasonable and practical education, with the emphasis on English rather than on Latin, for the children of the commercial classes. They achieved little and the opposition was negligible until the middle of the century.[4]

Lord Chesterfield recognized that justice, simplicity, patriotism, contempt of riches, and the ideal of noble friendship could be taught by means of the classics, but he wrote to his daughter-in-law a vigorous attack on the reigning system of education:

I am not of the opinion generally entertained in this country, that man lives by Greek and Latin alone; that is, by knowing a great many words of two dead languages, which nobody living knows perfectly, and which are of no use in the common intercourse of life. Useful knowledge, in my opinion, consists of modern languages, history, and geography; some Latin may be thrown into the bargain, in compliance with custom, and for closet amusement.

In 1752 the assault on the educational system was noticed for the first time in the critical reviews, when *The Monthly* called attention to *An Essay on Education* as a premature attempt to break the hold that the custom of teaching dead languages had gained in the course of two centuries. Thomas Sheridan's *British Education* in 1756 was another effort in the same direction. In 1762 *The Defects of University Education* carried on the attack. Within a few years Buchanan's *Plan of an English Grammar School Education* (1770) called for a study of English rather than of Latin and Greek.[5]

Doctor Johnson, humanist to the finger-tips in many respects, was no bigot on the subject of education. He was quite willing to admit that learning could be obtained in English, and, guided by his keen common sense, pointed out that classical mythology could be overdone in English poetry. In *The Fool of Quality* Henry Brooke told the story of Mr. Clement to illustrate the futility of classical learning in a modern commercial world. Doctor Farmer quoted Bishop Hurd to the effect that

> Shakespeare owed the felicity of freedom from the bondage of classical superstition to the *want* of what is called the *advantage* of a *learned* education;

while in *Hermes* (1751) James Harris maintained the thesis that a solid general culture could be obtained without the dead languages; and Cowper, whose *Tirocinium* revealed many defects in the educational system, did not hesitate to admit:

> Small skill in Latin, and still less in Greek,
> Is more than adequate to all I seek.[6]

Despite this steady stream of protest the classics remained rooted in the heart of English education. It is not surprising, therefore, to find that the eighteenth century was fond of making parallels between the ancient world and modern England, appealing to the glorious past of Greece and Rome for precedents for present action, or for warning against contemporary degeneracy. The *Connoisseur* pointed out in 1755 that

> there is not one fashionable frailty, but has some stubborn antiquated virtue set in opposition to it; and our unhappy metropolis is every day threatened with destruction, for its degeneracy from the rigid maxims of Rome or Sparta.

The Age of Anne was called the Augustan Age. The virtues and the vices of Romans were found in Englishmen. Pope not only imitated Horace, but wished to believe that he resembled him in personality. Both before and after Pope, the satires of Horace and Juvenal were adapted to modern circumstance. In politics, especially, parallels were sought. *The Free Briton* for July 22, 1731, noted among the means of political scandal, the "historical, or that of drawing parallels, a practice much in vogue." This method of veiled political argument, dependent on a keen appreciation of the similarity of the ancient and the modern world, was employed by Swift in *The Contest of the Nobles and Commons in Athens and Rome,* and was of frequent recurrence in the political journals of the century. In 1756 appeared *The Parallel; or the Conduct and Fate of Great-Britain in Regard to our Present Contest with France, exemplified from the Histories of Macedon and Athens.* Almost simultaneously *A New System of Patriot Policy* was advertised as containing the "genuine recantation of the British Cicero." In June, 1757, *The Gentleman's Magazine* contained a parallel between the Punic War and the war with France then in progress. In 1759 appeared F. W. Montagu's *Reflections on the Rise and Fall of the Antient Republics. Adapted to the Present State of Great Britain.* The fear that England was corrupt and decadent gave added point to Gibbon's *Decline and Fall of the Roman Empire.* In political controversy, as well as in criticism and poetry, pseudonyms were drawn from the familiar ancient world.[7]

II

In view of this predominant emphasis on the classics it is surprising to discover how few of the critics trained in the public schools and universities made systematic appeals to the principle of authority. Aristotle typified authority *par excellence,* but though he was called by Shaftesbury "a mighty genius and judge of art," by Blair an "amazing and comprehensive genius," by Joseph Warton the Euclid of criticism, it was judged proper to support him by reason and to test him by experience. The *Poetics* was first published in modern Europe in 1536. By 1561 Scaliger had apparently established Aristotle as perpetual dictator of all the arts. In France the critics of the seventeenth century were inclined to accept his *fiat*, but even in France D'Aubigné, Corneille, Molière, La Fontaine, Boileau, Bossu, and Rapin were glad to be able to identify Aristotle and reason. After 1700 reason became sole ruler. Meanwhile the Continental translations were known in Renaissance England, but 1674 is the important date for English Aristotelianism, for in that year Thomas Rymer, "the doughtiest of all English Aristotelians," published Rapin's *Reflections* on Aristotle's treatise. Rapin and Rymer secured general respect for the views of Aristotle, but this respect fell decidedly short of reverence, and there was at no time in England any important group of neo-Aristotelians similar to the disciples of the religion of Aristotle in Italy and France.[8]

The revolt against authority began in the English Renaissance before Bacon wrote *The Advancement of Learning*, for Giordano Bruno attacked Aristotle at Oxford in 1583 and Puttenham had excluded authority as a foundation for his *Arte of English Poetry*, which he preferred to base on reason and experience. Gabriel Harvey, too, had relied on "clear and pure reason" in his criticism. These men, however, were merely advance couriers of the rebellion, which really began with Bacon's proclamation of the inductive method in thought and with the later principle of "provisional skepticism" promulgated by Descartes. The Puritan appeal to individual judgment undoubtedly aided the purely scientific arguments of Bacon and Descartes, but until that influence has been adequately studied the New Science, as it was called, must be regarded as the battering ram which demolished the strongholds of authority. To the scientific thinker submission to the past was "the mortallest enemy to knowledge."[9] Dryden asked, "Why should there be any *ipse dixit* in our poetry, any more than there is in our philosophy?" Farquhar took pride in discovering the function of comedy "without one quotation of Aristotle." Blackmore believed that Aristotle was a "great genius and a person of more than common erudition," but declared that he would

no more submit to him as a lawgiver of the poets than of the philosophers. I shall always pay respect and deference to his judgment and opinions, though not acquiesce in them as infallible and decisive decrees. And if men, from a generous principle of liberty, would renounce the unjust, though prevailing, power of authority, and claim their natural right of entering into the reason of things and judging for themselves, it is highly probable that the art of poetry might be carried on to greater degrees of perfection, and be improved, as philosophy has been.

Dennis only occasionally argued from authority, and Pope referred disparagingly to it as "at all times, with critics, equal, if not superior, to reason." To Hume authority was a "tyrannical usurper over human reason"; Chesterfield ridiculed pedantry and regarded authority as inferior to reason; Joseph Warton considered the citation of authority as a sign of mental timidity; Gerard regarded it as the refuge of those who "have not vigour of taste enough, to determine the merit of the object, by its intrinsic characters"; Lord Kames thought that only "rude ages exhibit the triumph of authority over reason"; and in 1764 John Brown could boldly proclaim that "the days are past, when it was held a point of honour to *swear* to the *opinions* of a *master*." By 1785 it was possible for Pinkerton to write:

Aristotle's work on poetry is a crude and indigested performance, written by the author in his silly vanity of dictating in every science then known to man.

The extent of this revolt against authority will be more fully revealed in the pages which follow.[10]

III

Respect for authority varied in direct relation to the degree of supremacy conceded to Greek and Roman literature over the achievement of contemporaries. At no time did the pride of Englishmen permit an unqualified recognition of such a supremacy. The Battle of the Books began in Elizabethan England, and occupied the attention of thoughtful men both there and in France for a century and a half. The controversy in literature was only a phase of a comprehensive struggle which revolved around the conflict between Reason and Authority and indeed over the general acceptance of the idea of progress. In science, first, and, then, in the arts authority was routed.

The lines of the literary battle were directly drawn in France in

1657 when Saint-Sorlin defended his Christian epic, *Clovis*, by attacking classical poetry. Boileau demonstrated the dangers of a poetic handling of Christian doctrines, just as Milton was composing *Paradise Lost* in England. After numerous minor maneuvers the Moderns launched a series of brilliant attacks with Charles Perrault's *Siècle de Louis le Grand*, an exaltation of modern French literature read before the French Academy. Perrault expanded the attack in his *Paralleles des Anciens et Modernes* which was supported by Fontenelle in his *Digression sur les Anciens et les Modernes*. La Fontaine and La Bruyère were unable to turn the tide of victory back to the Ancients, who were deserted at last even by Boileau. In the French eighteenth century Reason and the Moderns won the field.[11]

In England the early meetings of the Royal Society witnessed discussions of the respective merits of the Ancients and the Moderns, but science rather than literature was the field of battle. In 1668 Dryden analyzed the merits of the Ancients, the French, and the English in *An Essay of Dramatic Poetry* and gave the palm to the English, but after Dryden the controversy ceased in England until Sir William Temple published his *Essay on Ancient and Modern Learning* (1692), a complete vindication of the Ancients. Two years later William Wotton published his almost apologetic *Reflections on Ancient and Modern Learning* in which he conceded the supremacy of the classics in the arts but contended for modern progress in the sciences. How Boyle, Wotton, Bentley, and Swift became engaged in a controversy during which the science of philology was born, and how the Ancients were defended by one of the greatest of the Moderns while the Moderns were befriended by one of the finest classical scholars may be found in the biographies of the men engaged. The forms the quarrel took, the arguments it produced, and the role of fighters on the contending sides must concern us here.[12]

It was argued that the Ancients had discovered all the forms of art, which the Moderns could only imitate; the Ancients had stood the test of time and only the best had survived, while among the Moderns there could be no certainty of universal appeal; the Ancient languages were intrinsically superior; the Ancients followed nature more closely; the Ancients wrote under exceptionally favorable historical circumstance. At times no argument was used. The supremacy of Homer and Virgil, of Aristotle and Horace, was so clear that no argument seemed necessary.

The worship of the Ancients began in Rome with the reverence of Latin writers for the masterpieces of Greece. When Du Bellay enjoined the young poet to study by night and by day the works of antiquity he was merely paraphrasing the *Ars Poetica* (lines 268–269), as Pope was to paraphrase them after him:

> Be Homer's works your study and delight,
> Re. hem by day, and meditate by night.

In *The Temple of Fame* (1715) Pope praised the Ancients alone, and in 1717 he wrote disparagingly of modern art:

All that is left us is to recommend our productions by the imitation of the ancients; and it will be found true, ·h.t in every age, the highest character for sense and learning has been obtain d by those who have been most indebted to them.

Here Pope was almost echoing Wil. Wotton, who had written in 1694 that the best moderns "hav° re..J the Ancients with greatest care and endeavoured to imitate th ` with the greatest accuracy." Joseph Warton presented the Ancien, as the best masters to teach the rules and aims of poetry, for they had had the advantage of climate, of an harmonious language, of public encouragement, of freedom from commerce, and trom the expenditure of energy needed in learning dead languages. But by the time of Warton this was an old story; long ago Ascham had proclaimed that all that was good in modern literature was learned, borrowed, or stolen from the Greeks; and Englishmen had planned their educational system with such a conviction in their hearts.[18]

The importance of the time test can be indicated by a single quotation from Boileau:

Only the approbation of posterity can establish the true merit of works. . . . The majority of men is not mistaken after the lapse of time. . . . It is no longer a question, today, whether Homer, Plato, Cicero, and Virgil are marvellous men; it is an undisputed point, since twenty centuries have agreed: the question is to recognize the basis for this admiration; and it is necessary either to find it or to renounce belles-lettres, for which you must believe yourself to have neither taste nor genius, since you do not feel what all men have felt.

It was Boswell who suggested that the dross of the Ancients had been left behind, and "only what is pure and precious has been preserved till now." Kames, Campbell, and Cowper were among those who felt that the Ancients had a tremendous advantage in the linguistic tools at their command. The hesitation of leaders like Bacon and Milton between English and Latin, and the mass of Latin verse produced by English poets to the end of the eighteenth century further attest the respect for the ancient tongues as literary vehicles.[14]

Enthusiasm for the classics was out of all proportion to the merits of the argument. In England the partisans of the Ancients comprise a distinguished company. Even the leaders of the modern cause in science, like Bacon and Glanvill, had little inclination to contest the supremacy of the Ancients in the arts. Henry Reynolds applied the theory of the decay of Nature to poetic productivity in *Mythomystes*. Mulgrave was extravagant in his praise of Homer. Shaftesbury esteemed Terence more valuable than all the moderns. Addison agreed with Boileau that one verse of Virgil was worth all the tinsel of Tasso, and declared that the Moderns fell below the Ancients in "poetry, painting, oratory, history, architecture, and all the noble arts and sciences which depend more upon genius than experience." Dennis admitted the actual supremacy of the Ancients, though he questioned the inherent necessity of such supremacy. Swift's comparison of the useless Modern spider with the Ancient bee who produced from Nature honey and wax to furnish the world with sweetness and light is famous. Pope has been cited above. Akenside wrote:

> Genius of ancient Greece! whose faithful steps
> Well pleas'd I follow through the sacred paths
> Of Nature and of Science; nurse divine
> Of all heroic deeds and fair desires!

In the mock paper war in Grub Street Fielding sides with the Ancients, and refused the name of critic to any one who had not mastered Aristotle, Horace, and Longinus in the originals. Gibbon defended the classics in his *Essai sur l'Etude de la littérature*. Campbell admitted progress in science, but considered it doubtful whether the Ancients would ever be equaled in poetry and eloquence. The sanction of time compelled Blair to admit the general superiority of the Ancients, but he was less dogmatic than Campbell, since he made significant exceptions of Milton and Shakespeare.[15]

Since the Ancients were entrenched in the schools and had unquestionably helped to fashion the taste and judgment of the Augustans, the burden of proof was on the side of the Moderns. Their arguments can be briefly stated. Many critics were content to oppose Corneille or Molière, Shakespeare or Milton to the leading geniuses of Greece and Rome without making an effort to prove their equality. The more philosophic critics argued with Cowley and Johnson that the basis of classical art was a mythology that could no longer inspire conviction, or that genius had been equally distributed, that human nature was the same, and that the Moderns had the advantage of experience. Some critics admitted the supremacy of Ancient genius, but still contended for the supremacy of the Moderns on the ground that a Modern dwarf standing on the shoulders of an Ancient giant would, despite his actual inferiority, have a greater range of vision.[16]

Bacon's argument that the Moderns who lived in an older period of the world were really Ancients in the wisdom of accumulated experience has already been mentioned. The idea was well known in France even before Fontenelle adopted it in his *Digression sur les Anciens et les Modernes* in 1688. An analogy of similar tendency pictured the Modern as a dwarf perched on the shoulders of the Ancient giant and thus surpassing his bearer in vision. This idea occurs at least as early as 1621 when Burton presents it in *The Anatomy of Melancholy*.[17]

Argument and analogy were supported by the citation of the great names of modern literature. In Elizabethan England Richard Carew contended that the English could emulate any vein of classical style. He compared Ascham to Cicero, Daniel to Ovid, and Shakespeare and Marlowe to Catullus without, however, making it clear whether he was supporting the actual equality of the English.

Henry Peacham suggested hesitantly that modern England produced "as fertile wits" as Greece and Rome. Sir Robert Howard
and John Dryden preferred English to Greek drama. Gildon found
Dryden himself superior to Sophocles and Euripides, and Dennis
declared that Jonson bore away the prize in comedy from both Ancients and Moderns. Chesterfield believed Pope to be superior to
Horace, and was secretly bored with Greek tragedy. *The Connoisseur* paralleled Milton and Shakespeare to Homer and Sophocles.
John Gilbert Cooper was enthusiastic for the Moderns, for he declared Gray's *Elegy* better than anything of its kind in Ovid,
Tibullus, or Propertius; Collins' *Ode to Evening* better than any
descriptive ode of Horace, and Joseph Warton's *Ode to Fancy*
equally good. Johnson's *Vanity of Human Wishes* he found superior
to Juvenal, and Mason's *Elfrida* better than all Seneca. Goldsmith
was almost equally extravagant when he compared the Irish bard
Carolan to Pindar. Duff believed that Milton had equaled Homer.
The author of *The World*, No. 137, declared many English poems
"perhaps equal to anything in Greek and Latin," and pointed
specifically to *Paradise Lost* and *An Essay on Criticism*. An enthusiast for Pope, he preferred the *Dunciad*, the *Moral Essays*, and
the *Essay on Man* to anything in antiquity. He valued *Alexander's
Feast* more than the odes of Pindar, and considered that the dia-
logs of Addison and Berkeley rivaled those of Xenophon, Plato,
and Cicero. The Aikins preferred Molière and Congreve to Terence,
and Pinkerton thought *Alexander's Feast* worth all of Pindar, and
the modern lyric in general equal to the ancient. The correctness of
these views is of less importance than the indication they give that
quite normal and fundamentally conventional critics were not in-
timidated by the reverence for antiquity.[18]

IV

Despite the persistent questioning of the dominant position of the
dead languages in education, of the principle of authority, and of
the superiority of ancient literature it would seem that the extensive
familiarity with the ideals of ancient art, implied even by the opposition to their hold, would render the acceptance of the Rules

a comparatively easy matter. Such was not the case. The Rules won no general acceptance on the basis of authority, and even when they were supported by the arguments that they were merely Nature methodized, and that they were justified by success, it was impossible to impose them on the many liberals who countered with the argument that the Rules did not satisfy popular taste, that they fettered genius, that they failed to explain the creation of great art before the Rules were discovered, and that they were applicable only to the age that produced them. In this last argument it is permissible to see an aspect of that historical criticism which was to undermine not only the Rules but the attempt to establish a standard of taste as well.

The Rules applied either to the whole of art or to specific literary kinds. Some were regarded as obligatory, others as arbitrary. The obligatory Rules were rooted in the nature of art itself and consequently indispensable to any successful achievement, while the arbitrary Rules were the product of customary usage and could be safely modified without disaster. No hard-and-fast distinction is possible, but most critics would regard as obligatory probability, decorum, the imitation of Nature, poetic justice, perspicuity, singleness of artistic purpose, unity of action, and the moral aim in art. More arbitrary Rules called for the action of the epic to begin *in medias res*, for the five-act division in tragedy, for the avoidance of hiatus in verse, for the avoidance of similes in the first book of an epic, and the like. Each of the arbitrary Rules had its ardent defenders, but by and large they were more often attacked than the artistic principles classified here as obligatory. Unfortunately it can seldom be certain which of the less important Rules and which of the Rules of the "kinds" are included in any individual defense of the Rules.[19]

The first line of defense for the Rules was the contention that they were in conformity with reason. Any one who conscientiously analyzed the nature of art would reach the very conclusions that the Ancients had reached. This was the conviction of Puttenham, who defined art as "a certain order of rules prescribed by reason, and gathered by experience." In France D'Aubignac insisted that the Rules were founded not on authority, but on reason; they were established not by example, but by natural judgment; they were called the Rules of the Ancients because the Ancients had practised them so brilliantly after studying the Nature of the moral world and the probabilities of human actions. In England Rymer in 1674 declared the basis of the Rules as "clear as any demonstration in *mathematics*. 'Tis only needful that we understand them for our consent to the truth of them." Four years later Dryden urged the acceptance of the Rules founded upon "good sense, and sound reason, rather than on authority." Shaftesbury felt that the "skill and grace of writing is founded . . . in *knowledge* and *good sense*." Such statements connected the Rules with the scientific spirit of the age. A quotation from Chapelain, unparalleled in its fullness by any English critic, will show how respect for the Ancients was identified with respect for reason—the reason of the great ancient masters in contrast to that of the ordinary unreflecting modern:

What! that which was the fruit of so many hours of wakeful thought, of so much speculation, of the thoughts of all that antiquity could produce in the way of great men, that which was amassed piece by piece, that with which they did not swell their treasure until they had sought at leisure through the treasure-house of Nature . . . ; this light—true, sure, and produced by so much diverse controversy and so many diverse speculations, shall it be found in an ordinary man, by common sense alone joined with some knowledge of the world, with no more effort than a few moments' thought?

The answer of the classicist was a decisive no.[20]

In the second place the Rules were Nature methodized. As C. C. Green has succinctly phrased it the classicist conceived of Nature as the universal:

It is that which excludes exceptions, oddities, queernesses, the things that exist *here* and *now* and nowhere else, and for that reason cannot be generalized into, or subsumed under, a rule. The neo-classicist . . . was therefore congenitally disposed to welcome the rules, because the idea of rules agreed perfectly with his idea of the "natural."[21]

Rapin first expressed this idea clearly: "The *Poetics* is, to speak correctly, only Nature methodized, and good sense reduced to principle." Dryden quoted Rapin with approval in 1679, and Dennis used almost the same words in his *Impartial Critick* in 1693. Gildon insisted on the necessity of Rules if the world of art were to be as orderly as the external universe. Without Rules "all must be governed by *unruly fancy* and *poetry* become the land of *confusion*, which is, in reality, the kingdom of *beauty, order,* and *harmony.*" In 1759 Goldsmith was still calling attention to the famous couplet in which Pope had phrased this argument for the preservation of the Rules:

> These Rules of old discovered, not devised,
> Are Nature still, but Nature methodized.[22]

In the third place art was by definition a system of principles based on experiment. What the intuitive genius did once and found successful became a portion of the Rules of art which those who followed after could neglect only at their peril. Ben Jonson formulated the argument:

> Whatsoever Nature at any time dictated to the most happy, or long exercise to the most laborious, that the wisdom and learning of Aristotle hath brought into an art, because he understood the causes of things; and what other men did by chance or custom he doth by reason; and not only found out the way not to err, but the short way we should take not to err.

Dryden declared flatly in 1695 that the very word *art* implied Rules. Dennis stated the classical position clearly in 1704:

> In short, poetry is either an art, or whimsy and fanaticism. If it is an art, it follows that it must propose an end to it self, and afterwards lay down proper means for the attaining that end: for this is undeniable, that there are proper means for the attaining of every end, and those proper means in poetry we call the rules.

Addison regarded the Rules as the legitimate reflection of practice. Harris echoed Dryden's correlation of art and Rules in 1765, and Blair showed the persistence of this attitude by explaining one of the functions of criticism as the induction of general principles from practice in order to form "rules . . . concerning the several kinds of beauty in works of genius."[23]

In the fourth place adherence to the Rules assured success. In the France of the late seventeenth century Racine, Corneille, La Fontaine, and Molière all believed that the principal duty of the artist was to please, and that the Rules were subordinate, but generally effective, means to that end. This was in 1677 the view of Dryden, as it was to be the view of Hume and Blair. William Melmoth, however, most completely explained this position in the *Letters of Sir Thomas Fitzosborne* (1749):

By observing the peculiar construction of those compositions of genius which have always pleased, we perfect our idea of fine writing in particular. It is this united approbation, in persons of different ages and of various characters and languages, that Longinus has made the test of the true sublime. . . . Thus the deference paid to the performances of the great masters of antiquity is based upon just and solid reasons; it is not because Aristotle and Horace have given us the rules of criticism that we submit to their authority; it is because those rules are derived from works that have been distinguished by the uninterrupted admiration of all the more improved part of mankind, from their earliest appearance down to the present hour. For whatever, through a long series of ages, has been universally esteemed beautiful, cannot but be conformable to our just and natural idea of beauty.[24]

Two important pronouncements concerning the function of the Rules in the education of the artist reveal a basis of support that can scarcely be included under the four principal defenses of the Rules. In *Of Education* (1644) Milton wished to train the student through a knowledge of "those organic arts, which enable men to discourse and write perspicuously, elegantly, and according to the fitted style of lofty, mean, or lowly"; and to inculcate taste by means of that "sublime art" which in Aristotle, Horace, and the Italian critics teaches "what the laws are of a true *epic* poem, what of a *dramatic*, what of a lyric, what decorum is, which is the grand master piece to observe." More than a century later, Sir Joshua Reynolds regarded the Rules as a means of mental discipline to be implicitly obeyed by young students who should not too soon seek

To snatch a grace beyond the reach of art.

This elementary stage of perfect adherence to rule was to be followed, in Sir Joshua's system, by the imitation of different masters, and then by a period in which judgment could be used to decide which of the Rules had the support of reason. With a trained judgment and a memory stored with the great models of the past the student might at last be safely trusted, for "the mind that has been thus disciplined may be indulged in the warmest enthusiasm, and venture to play on the borders of the wildest extravagance."[25]

The opponents of the Rules were always numerous, and their numbers grew with the passage of the years. Five main lines of argument can be distinguished in their critical position—the Rules did not satisfy popular taste; they checked genius, spirit, fire, or sense; they were applicable only to the culture which produced them; they were "mechanical" and contrary to Nature; and they were clearly unnecessary since the arts had flourished before the Rules had been codified.

The Rules did not satisfy popular taste. At the very beginning of the seventeenth century it was already apparent that the irregular drama of Shakespeare and Fletcher had won its way into the hearts of the people with its swift action, its dramatic surprises, and its acute portrayal of the human heart. Jonson mocked at it in vain. In England no more than in Spain, where Lope de Vega insisted on giving the people what they wanted, was it possible to persuade the theatre-going public to take the Rules seriously. The rationalists strove futilely against popular sentiment, which they frequently recognized clearly enough, as did Gildon who confessed that

there is indeed a very formidable party among us, who are such libertines in all manner of poetry, especially in the drama, that they think all regular principles of art an imposition not to be borne.

Gildon chose to side with the few against the many, but many writers who sincerely wished to please the public took the restraint of the Rules lightly or abandoned them entirely.[26]

Jonson had assailed Shakespeare for his neglect of the Rules, but in the address *To the Readers of Sejanus* he was compelled to admit that he could not "observe the old state and splendor of dramatic poems with any preservation of popular delight." In the Prologue to *Every Man Out of His Humour* Cordatus, the "author's friend," objected to seeing the poet "tied to those strict and regular forms which the niceness of a few . . . would thrust upon us." Webster confessed the same inability to preserve at the same time pleasure and the Rules in the Preface to *The White Devil*. It was Molière who stated the liberal position most clearly: "If plays which are according to the Rules do not please, and those which please are not according to the Rules, it follows of necessity that the Rules have been poorly made." The Epilogue to *Aureng-zebe* (1676) shows the persistence of the same attitude in England:

> A pretty task! and so I told the fool,
> Who needs would undertake to please by rule:
> He thought that, if his characters were good,
> The scenes entire, and freed from noise and blood; . . .
> He thought, in hitting these, his bus'ness done. . . .
> But, after all, a poet must confess,
> His art's like physic, but a happy guess.
> Your pleasure on your fancy must depend: . . .

Farquhar admitted to his audience in the Prologue to *Sir Harry Wildair* (1701),

> You are the rules by which he writes his plays,

and returned to the matter in 1702 when he contended that only plays that have dispensed with the Rules please, and that the authority of Aristotle has been lost with all persons of "a free and unprejudiced reason." Dennis did not believe in the retention of Rules that hindered the poet, and Akenside justified Shakespeare for failing to follow "the measur'd walks of Grecian art." In general, admiration for Shakespeare implied a criticism of the Rules on the ground that they were not essential for the enduring pleasure of great art.[27]

In the second place the Rules imposed a restraint on genius. Among the popular writers of Elizabethan days there must have been many who would have agreed wholeheartedly with James VI of Scotland that the Rules were subordinate to Nature. I have retained the Scots spelling of the King:

> For gif Nature be nocht the cheif worker in the airt, reulis wilbe bot a band to Nature, and will mak yow within short space weary of the haill airt: quhair as, gif Nature be cheif, and bent to it, reulis will be ane halp and staff to Nature.

In the heart of the age of reason Sir William Temple warned against the loss of natural spirit and grace by too strict adherence to the Rules. It is more surprising to find William Walsh writing to Pope that too much attention to correctness according to mechanical Rules would result in loss of spirit, for it was Walsh who seemed to his own age a pattern of correctness. Farquhar declared that the spirit of poetry was alone the *True Art of Poetry*. Edward Young, of course, supported genius against the Rules in his declaration of poetic independence, the *Conjectures* of 1759. Duff took the same attitude in 1767, and with the clearness of intellect usual with him, unless he was talkjng for victory, Doctor Johnson saw that the Rules which codified the practice of genius could be subverted by a new writer of genius. It seemed to Johnson that many rules were the product of accident, and that there was always "an appeal open from criticism to nature." The Rules must be a tool and not a chain.[28]

In the third place it was argued that the Rules were applicable only in the culture which formulated them. This was one of the most important arguments produced by the opponents of the Rules, for it was to overthrow not only the universal applicability of principles of art, but also the universally valid standard of taste in order to establish a conception of art as the product of geographical, social, and historical forces which gave birth to a different ideal of beauty in each civilization—Græco-Roman, Oriental, Celtic, Norse, and modern English. In 1628 Ogier stated the position clearly:

> The Greeks wrote for the Greeks, and in the judgment of the best men of their time they succeeded. But we should imitate them very much better by giving heed to the tastes of our own country, and the genius of our own language, than by forcing ourselves to follow step by step both their intention and their expression.

Corneille expressed the same view four years later, but it failed to take hold in France. To the north of the Channel Hughes took this important line of defense in 1715 when he exonerated Spenser from violation of the rules of Homer and Virgil by simply denying that he was in any way bound by them. The analogy by which Hughes enforced his point was significant, for it established a separate canon for Gothic architecture. Pope's defense of Shakespeare took the same line:

> To judge therefore of Shakespeare by Aristotle's rules, is like trying a man by the laws of one country, who acted under those of another.

Later Richard Hurd employed the same argument to defend romance, and Mrs. Montagu repeated it once more in a support of the chronicle plays of Shakespeare.[29]

In the fourth place some of the Rules were discovered to be contrary to Nature. Warburton advanced this argument in his *Preface to Shakespeare*. Genius must be judged by Nature and common sense, not by the mechanical rules of Dacier, Rapin, and Bossu. Spence declared that to follow Nature and common sense was the best of Rules, and Wilkie published with the second edition of the *Epigoniad* "A Dream—in the Manner of Spenser," in which he defended Nature against the mechanical school of criticism. But these were all minor men, though it would shock Warburton to hear it, and by the major critics no distinction was made between Nature and genius in the opposition to the Rules.[30]

Little was made of the final argument that art flourished before the Rules were formulated, for the opposition was generally willing to concede the point. In his *Essay on Genius* (1774) Gerard represents sure judgment enabling the first artists to achieve an instinctive perfection from which the Rules had been deduced.[31]

Jonson, Dryden, Pope, Young, and Johnson have been cited as liberals in regard to the general validity of the Rules. Other prominent names can be added. Samuel Butler reproved those who wished to

> Reduce all tragedy by rules of art,
> Back to its antique theatre, a cart. . . .

Rowe praised Shakespeare:

> In such an age, immortal Shakespeare wrote
> By no quaint rules, nor hampering critics taught.

Fielding plied the attack on the Rules vigorously in the prefatory chapters of *Tom Jones*. Goldsmith preferred "sublimity, sentiment, and passion" to the Rules of Aristotle, which had been collected "not from Nature, but a copy of Nature." Sterne ridiculed in his inimitable manner the rule-of-thumb critics:

And what about this new book the whole world makes such a rout about? oh! 'tis out of all plumb, my Lord,—quite an irregular thing! not one of the angles at the four corners was a right angle.—I had my rule and compasses, etc., my Lord, in my pocket.—Excellent critic!—And for the epic poem your lordship bid me look at—upon taking the length, breadth, height, and depth of it, and trying them at home upon an exact scale of Bossu's—'tis out, my Lord, in every one of its dimensions.—Admirable connoisseur!

Welsted was a minor figure, but a word must be spared for one of his opinions, since it shows how the Rules could be sacrificed and yet the spirit of a classical art be preserved. In his *Dissertation on the State of Poetry* Welsted rejected the neo-classic Rules as too mechanical, but contended that there was a truth in poetry as absolute as that of algebra. This poetic truth, however, must be expressed in flexible, internal, organic laws discovered by a careful study of things as they actually are, combined with observation of the great poets to perceive the nature of their greatness. The theory of Welsted was the practice of the Addisons, Fieldings, and Johnsons of the period: it implied a careful attention to artistry, but an independence of judgment on any specific question of Rule.[32]

v

Any attempt to survey completely the extensive controversy concerning the Three Unities would necessitate a volume in place of the brief section which the actual significance of the controversy allows. Many of the supporters of authority defended the Unities by implication; most of the defenders of the Rules on more rational grounds included the Unities in their defense; most of the arguments in behalf of the Rules in general were applicable to the Unities as well. The specific defense of the Unities of Time and Place was based on the supposed authority of Aristotle, or on the doctrine of complete illusion in the theatre. If the dramatist designed to delude the audience into believing that they were "bodily present at the time and place of the supposed action" he must refrain from changing the scene and must make dramatic time conform absolutely to the time of performance. Once the intent to delude was granted, the Unities were necessary as a portion of the laws of probability, but such an intent was vigorously denied by Dryden, Farquhar, Hurd, and others, and the Unities of Time and Place were generally neglected in the English theatre, and often, especially after 1700, ignored or attacked in theory.[33]

The Unity of Action was more important. It implied a separation of the tragic and the comic and was supported by the rigid adherents of the literary "kinds" and by those critics who believed whole-heartedly in decorum. A single action was also desirable from the standpoint of order and simplicity; it was felt to be in conformity with the demands of probability which necessitated an intimate inter-linking of scene and scene; and it was in line with the tendencies of the age to emphasize clarity. The example of Shakespeare was un-fortunately on the other side, and that example was in time powerful enough to secure tolerance, if not dominance, for the double plot and for the mixed form of tragicomedy.

The opponents of the Unities of Time and Place had much the best of the argument. They could point to exceptions in the Greek and Roman theatre, to the protests of French dramatists who were restless under the restraint, to the absence of positive rule in the *Poetics*, and to the almost complete neglect of the Unities in the Elizabethan theatre. More specifically they were able to argue that the Unities of Time and Place had been justified only by the con-stant presence of the chorus on the Greek stage, that the admission of *any* discrepancy between acting time and dramatic time destroyed all logical support for the Unity of Time on the basis of complete deception, that the attempt to reduce dramatic time to two or three hours—logically imperative—led to gross violation of probability in characterization, and, finally, that the assumption that the design of the dramatist should be the complete delusion of the audience was totally unfounded. Since Dryden's day "the willing suspension of disbelief" in the presence of the imaginative power of great art has been generally accepted in England as the correct interpretation of the relation of author and audience. By the time that Johnson published *The Preface to Shakespeare* with its attack on the Unities it was only necessary to puff away the last smoke from a battlefield that had long been won by the opponents of the Rules.[34]

NOTES TO CHAPTER X

1. The best presentation is in Pope, *An Essay on Criticism*, Part I.

2. Charles Hoole, *A New Discovery of the Old Art of Teaching School*, Syracuse (New York), 1912, pp. 210, 280; Knox, *Works*, London, 1824, III, 415.

3. Rochester, *Collected Works*, ed. Heywood, London, 1926, p. xxi; William Boscawen, *The Odes, Epodes, and Carmen Seculare of Horace*, London, 1793, pp. iii–v; Christopher Wordsworth, *Scholae Academicae. University Studies in the Eighteenth Century*, London, 1908; Norwood and Hope, *The Higher Education of Boys in England*, London, 1909; John Sergeant, *Annals of Westminster School*, London, 1898. There is much interesting information in the early chapters of Masson, *Life of Milton*, Cambridge, 1859.

4. David Masson, *op. cit.*, I, 232; Locke, *Thoughts Concerning Education*, pp. 53, 81, 146; Steele, *Tatler*, May 18, 1710, *Guardian*, June 29, 1713; Budgell, *Spectator*, April 15, 1712; *Monthly Review*, LXX, 369; Alexander Dyce, *Memoir of Beattie*, in *The Poetical Works of Akenside and Beattie* (Aldine Edition), Boston, 1880.

5. Chesterfield, *Works*, IV, 489, V, 91, 388, and *World*, No. 98; *Monthly Review*, VII, 473, XIV, 81, XXVI, 234, XXVII, 135, XLIII, 154.

6. Samuel Johnson, *Idler*, No. 92, and *Lives of the Poets*, ed. Hill, II, 202; Henry Brooke, *Fool of Quality*, p. 73; Farmer, *Essay on the Learning and Genius of Shakespeare*, in Nicoll Smith, *op. cit.*, p. 187; Cowper, *Tirocinium*, lines 385–386; *Monthly Review*, LXXIII, 228.

7. *Connoisseur*, No. 74; Knox, *Works*, I, 17; Walpole, *Letters*, ed. Toynbee, VII, 380; Warburton, *Works*, ed. Hurd, London, 1811, XIII, 161; Pope, *Works*, VII, 483; *Gentleman's Magazine*, I, 297, II, 697, III, 115, 143, V, 130, VI, 403, XI, 646; *Monthly Review*, XIV, 456–457; *Gentleman's Magazine*, XXVII, 253; *Monthly Review*, XX, 419; John Nichols, *Illustrations of the Literary History of the Eighteenth Century*, London, 1817–1858, III, 255.

8. Edward Young, *Conjectures*, in Jones, *English Critical Essays*, XIV–XVIIIth Centuries, p. 325; Shaftesbury, *Characteristicks*, I, 244; Blair, *Rhetoric*, III, 22; Joseph Warton, *Essay on Pope*, I, 162; Gildon, *Art of Poetry*, in Durham, *op. cit.*, p. 45; Spingarn, *Literary Criticism of the Renaissance*, pp. 137–142; Bray, *Formation de la doctrine classique*, pp. 53, 59, 122, 124–125. Submission to authority occurs occasionally. *Cf.* Spingarn, *Critical Essays of the Seventeenth Century*, I, xv; Dryden, *Essays*, I, 271–272; Addison, *Spectator*, Nos. 70, 74, 267; W. L. Phelps, *The Beginnings of the English Romantic Movement*, p. 151; Goldsmith, *Essays*, XXII; Bolingbroke, Preface to Lansdowne's *Heroick Love*; Boswell, *Journal of a Tour to the Hebrides*, ed. Hill, p. 87, note 1; Johnson, *Lives of the Poets*, ed. Waugh, II, 218; Herrick, *Poetics of Aristotle in England*, pp. 17–18, 35, 57, 81.

9. Sir Thomas Browne, quoted by Paul Elmer More, *Shelburne Essays*, VI, 163.

10. Miller, *The Historical Point of View in English Literary Criticism*, p. 53; Gregory Smith, *Elizabethan Critical Essays*, II, 247; R. F. Jones, "Background of the Battle of the Books," pp. 118–120; Stephen, *English Thought in the Eighteenth Century*, I, 22; Nicolson, "The Early Stage of Cartesianism in England," *Studies in Philology*, XXVI, 359 and note 10; Masson, *Milton*, VI, 393; Dryden, *Essays*, I, 138; Farquhar, *Discourse upon Comedy*, in Durham, *op. cit.*, p. 272; Blackmore, quoted by Herrick, *Poetics of Aristotle in England*, p. 99; Dennis, in Durham, *op. cit.*, p. xxviii, 218; Pope, *Works*, IV, 100; Hume, *Essays*, I, 184, and *Letters*, I, 13; Chesterfield, *Letters*, I, 206–208; Joseph Warton, *Adventurer*, No. 75; Gerard, *Essay on Taste*, pp. 142–143; Kames, *Elements*, I, 20–21; Brown, *Rise and Progress of Poetry*, p. 119; Pinkerton, *Letters of Literature*, pp. 230–231.

11. Gustave Lanson, *Histoire de la littérature française*, 19ème edition, Paris, n. d., pp. 598 ff.

12. R. C. Jebb, *Bentley*, London, 1902, p. 40 ff.; Jones, "Background of the Battle of the Books," *passim*.

13. Du Bellay, in Vial et Denise, *op. cit.*, p. 6; Pope, *Essay on Criticism*, lines 124–125, and *Works*, I, 9; Wotton, in Spingarn, *Critical Essays*, III, 203; Joseph Warton, *Adventurer*, Nos. 49, 127; Miller, *Historical Point of View*, p. 44.

14. Boileau, *Réflexions critiques sur Longin*, *Œuvres*, pp. 458–460; Boswell, *Hypochondriack*, II, 126; Kames, *Elements*, II, 67; Campbell, *Philosophy of Rhetoric*, pp. 498–499; Cowper, Letter to John Unwin, June 2, 1785.

15. Jones, "Background of the Battle of the Books," pp. 102–104, 115–116, 129; Reynolds, *Mythomystes*, in Spingarn, *Critical Essays*, I, 141–144; Mulgrave, *ibid.*, II, 295; Shaftesbury, *Life, Letters, and Philosophical Regimen*, p. 412; Addison, *Spectator*, Nos. 5, 249; Parnell, in Fausset, *Minor Poets of the Eighteenth Century*, London (Everyman's Library), 1930, pp. 141, 149; Swift, *Gulliver*, p. 554; Akenside, *Pleasures of the Imagination*, Book I, lines 567–570; John Brown, *Rise and Progress of Poetry*, p. 266; *World*, No. 94; Fielding, *Covent-Garden Journal*, Nos. 1, 3; Gibbon, *Autobiography*, pp. 95 ff.; Campbell, *Philosophy of Rhetoric*, p. 5; Blair, *Rhetoric*, III, 30, 35.

16. Cowley, *Essays*, pp. 15–16; Johnson, *Lives*, ed. Waugh, II, 65–66, III, 24.

17. Bacon, *Novum Organum*, quoted Guyer, *op. cit.*, p. 259. *Cf.* Guyer, pp. 260–264; Fontenelle, in Vial et Denise, *op. cit.*, 267, 274; Burton, *Anatomy of Melancholy*, I, 23; Hobbes, *Leviathan*, p. 527.

18. Richard Carew, in Gregory Smith, *op. cit.*, II, 293; Peacham, in Spingarn, *Critical Essays*, I, 129; Sir Robert Howard, *ibid.*, II, 98; Dryden, *Essays*, I, 33, II, 6; Gildon, in Durham, *op. cit.*, pp. 14–17; Dennis, in Nicoll Smith, *op. cit.*, p. 43; Chesterfield, *Works*, II, 444–445, III, 383, IV, 31; *Connoisseur*, No. 42; Cooper, *Letters Concerning Taste*, pp. 96–97; Goldsmith, *Essays*, XX; Duff, *Essay on Genius*, p. 234; Aikin, *Miscellaneous Pieces in Prose*, p. 23; Pinkerton, *Letters of Literature*, pp. 33–34, 117, 130–131.

19. George B. Dutton, "The French Aristotelian Formalists and Thomas Rymer," *P. M. L. A.*, XXIX, 154; Herrick, *The Poetics of Aristotle in England*, pp. 5–6; James Beattie, *Dissertations*, I, 222–225; Joseph Warton, *Essay on Pope*, I, 120–122, 250, 269; Pope, *Works*, VI, 78; Blair, *Rhetoric*, II, 433.

20. Puttenham, in Gregory Smith, *op. cit.*, II, 5; D'Aubignac, in Vial et Denise, *op. cit.*, p. 117; Rymer, in Spingarn, *Critical Essays*, II, 165; Dryden, *Essays*, I, 288; Shaftesbury, *Characteristicks*, I, 193; Bray, *Formation de la doctrine classique*, p. 108.

21. Clarence C. Green, *The Neo-classic Theory of Tragedy in England During the Eighteenth Century*, Cambridge (Mass.), 1934, p. 14.

22. Rapin, quoted by Clark, *Boileau and the French Classical Critics in England*, p. 277; Dryden, *Essays*, I, 228; Dennis, in Spingarn, *Critical Essays*, III, 194; Gildon, in Durham, *op. cit.*, pp. 18, 55; Goldsmith, *Works*, ed. Gibbs, IV, 396; Pope, *Essay on Criticism*, lines 88–89.

23. Jonson, *Timber*, in Spingarn, *Critical Essays*, I, 56; Dryden, *Essays*, II, 134; Dennis, in Durham, *op. cit.*, p. 145; Addison, *Spectator*, No. 273; Harris, *Three Treatises*, pp. 16–17; Blair, *Rhetoric*, I, 43–44.

24. Bray, *op. cit.*, p. 111; Dryden, *Essays*, I, 183–184; Hume, quoted by Joseph Warton, *Essay on Pope*, I, 238; Blair, *Rhetoric*, I, 44; Melmoth, quoted by Lovejoy, "Parallel of Deism and Classicism," *Modern Philology*, XXIX, 295.

25. Milton, *Of Education*, in Spingarn, *Critical Essays*, I, 206, 208–209;

H. H. Epps, "Two Notes on English Classicism," *Studies in Philology*, XIII, 196; Reynolds, *Discourses*, pp. 4–5, 12.

26. Gildon, quoted by Durham, *op. cit.*, p. xiii; Spingarn, *Literary Criticism of the Renaissance*, pp. 233–234; P. S. Wood, "The Opposition to Neo-classicism in England between 1660 and 1700," *P. M. L. A.*, XLIII, 190–192.

27. Bray, *op. cit.*, pp. 56–57; Molière, quoted in Spingarn, *Critical Essays*, II, 336, and Molière in Vial et Denise, *op. cit.*, pp. 162, 175; Farquhar, in Durham, *op. cit.*, p. 263; Gould, quoted by Clark, *Boileau and the French Classical Critics in England*, p. 282; Dennis, quoted by Hamelius, *op. cit.*, p. 120; Akenside, "The Remonstrance of Shakespeare."

28. James VI, in Gregory Smith, *op. cit.*, I, 210; Sir William Temple, in Spingarn, *Critical Essays*, III, 83–84; William Walsh, in Pope, *Works*, VI, 54; Farquhar, in Durham, *op. cit.*, p. 271; Matthew Green, *The Spleen*, lines 519–523; Young, *Conjectures*, in Jones, *Critical Essays of the XVI-XVIIIth Centuries*, p. 327; Duff, *Essay on Genius*, pp. 281–291; Johnson, *Rambler*, Nos. 125, 152, 156, 158, and *Preface to Shakespeare*, in Nicoll Smith, *op. cit.*, p. 119.

29. Ogier, *Preface to Schelandre's Tyr et Sidon*, quoted by Spingarn, *Literary Criticism of the Renaissance*, p. 235; Bray, *op. cit.*, pp. 56–57; Hughes, in Durham, *op. cit.*, p. 106; Pope, *Preface to Shakespeare*, in Nicoll Smith, *op. cit.*, p. 50; Hurd, *Letters on Chivalry and Romance*, pp. 121–122; Mrs. Montagu, *Essay on Shakespeare*, pp. xi, xv, 33. There is an interesting quotation from *The Critical Review* of September, 1763, in Hooker, "The Reviewers and the New Criticism, 1754–1770," *Philological Quarterly*, XIII, 190.

30. Warburton, *Preface to Shakespeare*, in Nicoll Smith, *op. cit.*, p. 105; Spence, in Richardson, *Correspondence*, II, 321. For Wilkie see Phelps, *The Beginnings of the English Romantic Movement*, p. 85.

31. Gerard, *Essay on Genius*, pp. 72–73.

32. Butler, in Spingarn, *Critical Essays*, II, 278; Rowe, Prologue to *Jane Shore*; Fielding, *Tom Jones*, Book II, Chapter I, Book IV, Chapter I; Chesterfield, *Works*, III, 389; Goldsmith, *Works*, ed. Gibbs, IV, 251, and *Miscellaneous Works*, pp. 421–422; Sterne, *Tristram Shandy*, Book III, Chapter II, Book IV, Chapter X, Book VIII, Chapter II. For Welsted see Sarma, "Two Minor Critics of the Age of Pope," *Modern Language Review*, XIV, 389–390.

33. C. C. Green, *op. cit.*, pp. 40, 115; Dryden, *Essays*, I, 40 ff.

34. C. C. Green, *op. cit.*, pp. 195–206; Spingarn, *Literary Criticism of the Renaissance*, pp. 208–209; Kames, *Elements*, II, 323–327; Johnson, *Preface to Shakespeare*, in Nicoll Smith, *op. cit.*, pp. 128–131; Thomas M. Raysor, "The Downfall of the Three Unities," *Modern Language Notes*, XLII, 1.

CHAPTER XI

THE DOCTRINE OF LITERARY
IMITATION

I

THE DIRECT imitation of Greek and Roman authors is a second aspect of the respect for the Ancients. Although rational arguments were presented for imitation, it should be evident that imitation could be popular only in a culture which was thoroughly attuned to the idea of the greatness of the classics. In the struggle between Ancients and Moderns the matter of most interest to us is the degree to which the creative artists of the period acquiesced in the practice and theory of imitation. The term imitation was used to include everything—a line-by-line adaptation of a classical poem to a modern situation, the comparatively free use of a theme, a mode of approach, an arrangement of incidents. The employment of a technique or form apart from content will be noticed in the following chapter.

To Augustan critics imitation seemed to serve various needs. It was a means of preserving great works of art by eliminating dull or difficult passages and adapting a foreign style to the taste of elegant ladies and gentlemen. As editor of Juvenal in 1693 Dryden justified the use of imitation rather than translation on the ground that only in that way could he please his readers. Only occasionally were English customs and manners introduced, but Juvenal was made to "speak that kind of English which he would have spoken if he liv'd in England, and had written to this age." Pope's *Homer* is the classic example of this free and elegant translation. The more frequent method of modernization was justified by Elkanah Settle who addressed Henry Higden, an obscure imitator of Juvenal:

> You naturalize the author you translate
> And classick Roman dress in modern state.

> Sprightly and gay he makes his visit here,
> Drest al-a-mode, and speaks en cavalier.

The same arguments were employed by Rowe in 1708 for Ozell's adaptation of Boileau's *Lutrin*.[1]

In the second place it was felt that the imitation of the great writers of antiquity would mean the application of the most effective remedies to modern ills. Why should the eighteenth-century moralist break his puny weapons in the struggle against vice and crime when the arsenals of Horace and Juvenal were at hand? Unfortunately the weapons of the Roman satirists were dulled by the English reader's unfamiliarity with allusions of all sorts that had once been a part of the town-talk of Rome. In Rome Crispinus had then been as well known as Locke in England, Hannibal as Charles XII. Why not sharpen these weapons and render them as effective as they ever were by finding parallels in the English world for the men and manners of Rome? In this way Roman satire could be actually popularized, the necessity for explanatory notes obviated, and the English reader could profit to the full by the mockery of Horace, the scathing denunciation of Juvenal, or the shrewd admonitions of Ovid's *Art of Love*.[2]

A third justification was found in a measure of objectivity which the imitation of the classics gave. In the Advertisement of the *Satires* Pope declared that "The occasion of publishing these Imitations was the clamour raised on some of my Epistles. An answer from Horace was both more full, and of more dignity, than any I could have made in my own person. . . ." It was, in fact, a cover for self-laudation and vicious attack on his personal enemies.[3]

Other imitators appealed to the pleasure which an educated reader could obtain by comparing ancient and modern manners or even, by the publication of English and Latin on opposite pages, to the delighted surprise at a skillful display of ingenuity in the choice of parallels. The first of these two purposes was admitted by Richard Owen Cambridge in the Advertisement to *The Intruder* (1754):

> Those who have imitated the writings of preceding ages have, by applying ancient manners to modern times, afforded . . . scope for the mind to entertain itself by the comparison.

Steele also admitted the artistic validity of this pleasure of recognition:

> But, over and above a just painting of nature, a learned reader will find a new beauty superadded in a happy imitation of some famous ancient, as it revives in his mind the pleasure he took in his first reading such an author.

Richard Hurd and Joseph Warton recognized the satisfaction a happy parallel could afford and Doctor Johnson agreed that adaptation gave a twofold pleasure—in the intrinsic value of the sentiment, and in the skill of the parallelism—but he thought that the latter amusement was based not on reason or passion, but on memory alone.

Still other imitators regarded imitation as a stimulating form of rivalry. Bishop Hurd's essay *On Imitation* is woven about the central theme that imitation is not a sign of artistic inferiority, but a legitimate attempt to improve the work of one's predecessor. Unfortunately for Hurd's contention, Pope's *Imitations of Horace* is perhaps the only example of such successful rivalry.[4]

These rational imitators did not work alone. Poetasters and poeticasters of slight ability found in the doctrine of imitation a surcease from the pain of original composition, and they bent Horace and the other elegant Roman poets to all the various burdens imposed by the amenities of social life or by the occasional necessities of the churchman or the politician. Horace was used to extend a compliment, to issue an invitation, to celebrate a marriage, to court a pretty chambermaid, to record a great frost or a shipwreck, to lament a friend or lampoon an enemy, to plead for abolition, to give vent to college spirit, to spur on the English soldier, and to bemoan the decline of the church. These modernizations published in the magazines of the period were mostly anonymous, but the names of Yalden, Anna Seward, Thomas Marriott, Archibald Campbell, and Henry James Pye will serve to suggest the artistic caliber of such unimaginative versifiers.[5]

II

The illustrations just given of the multifarious uses to which minor writers put imitation suggest a justification for imitation which was not often mentioned by those who practised it: imitation was an easy road to reputation as a wit. The graduate of the universities, whether he were a noble lord who entered Parliament, or a poor scholar who became a curate or a literary hack, felt that a part of his equipment was the ability to rime for an occasion. The mob of gentlemen who wrote with ease included Dorset, Mulgrave, Wyndham, Lyttleton, Granville, Walpole, Chesterfield, and Lord Hervey. Verse-making clergymen throng the pages of John Nichols' *Illustrations of the Literary History of the 18th Century* and the *Literary Anecdotes of the 18th Century*. Doctor Sneyd Davies (1709–69), archdeacon of Derby, is representative. He wrote many vers de société and imitated many Latin odes and epistles. Men like Davies seldom took verse seriously. They acquired the habit of writing verse at school; they continued it later because it was the fashion. Lacking for the most part original poetic ideas and seldom feeling a genuine need for emotional expression, they were naturally imitators. The wit was obliged to establish his reputation by a well-turned copy of verses, and everything in the life of the day was seized upon as an occasion for rime. Amongst these "correct" but unimaginative verses adaptations of the classics would be received without criticism of their lack of originality provided they were clever and seasonable. Their popularity is revealed in the crowded pages of the contemporary miscellanies and magazines.[6]

Unwilling to admit a lack of creative ability, the minor eighteenth-century critic grasped at any justifications for imitation. There was the precedent of the classics to follow, as Walsh pointed out to Pope. Ascham, Webbe, Langbaine, Ozell, Tom Brown, Spence, Nathan Drake, and William Clubbe all pointed to imitation in the Roman poets. It was discovered that classical criticism lent support to classical practice. Neither Horace nor Quintilian was enthusiastic for originality, and even Longinus justified a moderate imitation of the great historians and poets of the past as one of the roads to sublimity, for through admiration of greatness one becomes inspired with some of the spirit of greatness. Longinus pointed out numerous imitators of Homer and concluded that "such borrowing is no theft; it is rather like taking an impression from fine characters as one does from moulded figures or other works of art." The support of imitation continued strong among the critics of the Italian and French Renaissance.[7]

There was also the belief that the classics had pre-empted all the natural emotions and manifestations of human life, and that any attempt to escape from them could lead only to eccentricity in choice of subject or in treatment. Roman satire especially had so thoroughly covered the mores of humanity that there was little for a classically minded age to do but to adapt the material of Roman satire to modern conditions. This conviction that the Ancients had occupied all the profitable fields of art was frequently expressed. Robert Burton frankly admitted that "We can say nothing but what hath been said. . . ." Carew spoke of the "rifled fields" where the "prime buds of invention" had been culled "many a hundred years." Walsh suggested to Pope that "the best of the modern poets in all languages are those that have the nearest copied the Ancients. Indeed, in all the common subjects of poetry, the thoughts are so obvious . . . that whoever writes last must write things like what have been said before." Addison felt that new observations were impossible: "We have little else left us, but to represent the common sense of mankind in more strong, more beautiful, or more uncommon lights." Richard Hurd and Joseph Warton agreed with Addison. Doctor Johnson quoted La Bruyère to the effect that the Moderns could only glean from the Ancients, and contended that the Ancients had been able to use fresh and natural sentiments, but had left to the Moderns nothing but servile repetitions or forced conceits. This despair of originality was favorable both to the vogue of imitation and to the emphasis on form at the expense of content.[8]

Imitation was further supported by the belief that human nature was immutable and artistic genius invariable. What had been said of love in Rome might be said of love in England. Fashions in dress might alter; there were no fashions in the human heart. Men of similar genius describing in their poetry a similar human nature would naturally enough, so proponents of imitation thought, employ the same art forms or adapt the old art forms with merely superficial alteration to a new age that differed from the old only superficially. The habit of regarding Englishmen and Romans as alike, the closely allied tendency of finding direct parallels between English events and Roman, and the belief that human nature in the Age of Augustus was identical with human nature in the Age of Anne —these things are met with on every hand.

In 1647 Stapylton quoted from Juvenal himself to show that Roman satire was useful to all ages and to all nations, for

> Posterity can no new vices frame,
> Our nephews will but wish and act the same.

In his Preface to *A Modern Essay on the Thirteenth Satyr of Juvenal* (1686) Henry Higden expressed the belief that the vices which Juvenal scourged in that satire are "amongst ourselves, though perhaps something altered in dress and fashion." Congreve wrote:

> For virtue now is neither more or less,
> And vice is only varied in the dress. . . .

The spirit of the age is revealed in Farquhar's ironic answer to those who question Aristotle's authority:

Why, by the authority of two thousand years standing, because thro' this long revolution of time the world has still continu'd the same. By the authority of their being receiv'd at Athens, a city, the very same with London in every particular; their habits the same, their humours alike, their publick transactions and private societies *alamode* France; in short, so very much the same in every circumstance, that Aristotle's criticisms may give rules to Drury Lane. . . .

Johnson was fully convinced of the identity of human nature which Farquhar ridiculed:

Writers of all ages had the same sentiments, because they have in all ages had the same objects of speculation; the interests and passions, the virtues and vices of mankind, have been diversified in different times, only by unessential and casual varieties.[9]

Still other critics argued that art was an imitation of Nature, but that the external world offered only imperfect models, from which the artist, proud of his independence, must select traits here and there to compose the ideally beautiful. The Ancients, however, had already studied the external world and created a second Nature, approved as beautiful by the judgment of two thousand years, and doubtless superior because it had eliminated the imperfections and confusions of the crude external world. The artist was advised by painters like De Piles, Du Fresnoy, and Le Brun, and by critics like Boileau, to imitate the ideal reconstruction of Nature in ancient art and to profit by the selection which the ancients had practised.[10]

III

Imitation fades into translation. The defense of the numerous free translations by which many talented writers won a more certain livelihood than was possible by original composition followed the same line of argument. A more interesting phenomenon is the adaptation of both foreign and native authors to suit contemporary taste. Dryden and Pope were the high priests in the cult of adaptation. Dryden, eager to justify his judgment that Chaucer was superior to Ovid, decided that "by turning some of the *Canterbury Tales* into our language as it is now refined" he would set Chaucer and Ovid "in the same light, and dressed in the same English habit" so that "a certain judgment may be made betwixt them by the reader." Some further remarks will show how similar any defense of this practice was to the excuses offered by the imitators of ancient satire:

I have not tied myself to a literal translation; but have often omitted what I judged unnecessary, or not of dignity enough to appear in the company of better thoughts. I have presumed further, in some places, and added somewhat of my own where I thought my author was deficient, and had not given his thoughts their true lustre, for want of words in the beginning of our language.[11]

Lesser writers were as sure of their ability to improve the old poets as were the literary giants of the age. In 1703 Oldmixon modernized Drayton's *Heroical Epistles,* which he found "rude and unharmonious" in meter, and "obsolete" in diction. His method of revision affords another revelation of the attitude of the period:

I have in many places, preserv'd his thoughts, where they were natural, and not poor, tho' in this whole four and twenty epistles, he has not furnish'd me with one couplet, and the world will, I hope, not lose by the exchange.

As late as 1795, William Lipscomb, motivated not by a desire to popularize Chaucer by making the few changes necessary to insure ease in reading, but, like Dryden and Pope, impelled by a desire to make the old poet "correct," published a revised Chaucer in which he added his own adaptations to those of Pope, Dryden, Ogle, Boyse, and Betterton.[12]

The element of timeliness played some part in these adaptations as it did in the modernizations of the classics. Suckling's *Sessions of the Poets* was modernized, probably by Rochester, to apply to the poets of his day. In the edition of Boileau's complete works, published under the editorship of Ozell, not only is an adaptation of French references to England the rule in the satires, epistles, *L'Art Poétique*, and in portions of *Le Lutrin*, but in successive editions outworn applications were brought up to date.[13]

In modernizing Donne Pope brought the allusions as well as the style into conformity with current events and current tastes, a practice almost identical with that of the *Imitations of Horace*. Indeed Pope might be called the "adapter-general" of the age. If, in imitating Horace, he was motivated principally by the desire to turn an effective battery of satire on his contemporaries, he was influenced also by ethical, linguistic, and metrical considerations in the imitations of Chaucer. As was the fashion with the adaptations from the Latin the relevant passages from Chaucer were printed at the foot of Pope's revision in the 1736 edition. Pope nearly extended his modernizations of early English satire to Hall, but he resisted that impulse as well as the suggestion of Atterbury that he revise *Samson Agonistes*, a project that would probably have resulted in a work comparable to Dryden's rime-tagged *Paradise Lost*.[14]

Modernizations of the classics were much more frequent than such revisions of earlier English poems. The ever-popular Horace was modernized by innumerable poets. Pope, Swift, Prior, Rowe, Boyse, Duke, Tom Brown, Christopher Pitt, Fenton, Hughes, Jenyns, and William King all engaged in the pastime. In *The Gentleman's Magazine* alone there were seventy-five adaptations of Horace between 1730 and 1800. In *The European Magazine* eleven were published between 1790 and 1800. *The Odes and Satyrs of Horace* published in 1717 by Tonson contained many adaptations. In Duncombe's *Horace* (1757–59) adaptations of twenty-eight odes, sixteen epistles, and three satires were added to the more closely translated version. The second edition ten years later included adaptations of nearly every poem and some of the favorites were represented twice. The names of the contributors no longer glimmer even faintly in the *Life of Johnson* or in the *Correspondence* of Samuel Richardson. Between 1671 and 1800 there were at least sixty modernizations of Roman satire in England by Flatman, Rochester, Oldham, Higden, Dryden, Tom Brown, Swift, Pope, William Guthrie, George Ogle, Loveling, William King, Johnson, Smart, Cambridge, Duncombe, Nevile, Fielding, Canning, Burnaby Greene, Murphy, and Gifford.[15]

The use of "echo" passages was designed to recall the verses of some older poet and to add the pleasures of memory to the other joys of poetry. Echo passages were particularly popular in mock-heroic verse, where they merge into parody, but they formed a recognized aspect of the technique of the more serious work of Milton, Dryden, and Pope. These passages were not plagiarisms, for if the borrowed line was not recognized the artistic purpose of the poet was foiled. A single passage from Dryden's description of Shimei must serve to illustrate this form of imitation, which won the critical approval of Addison and Joseph Warton and the tolerance of Doctor Johnson:

> For Shimei, tho' not prodigal of pelf,
> Yet loved his wicked neighbor as himself.
> When two or three were gather'd to declaim
> Against the monarch of Jerusalem,
> Shimei was always in the midst of them.[16]

IV

Taine has explained what he considers the lack of orginality in English literature of the classical period by the absorption of the best energies and mental powers of the age in the struggles of clique and sect and party—in the controversies between Cavalier and Puritan, Anglican and Dissenter, Whig and Tory, Jacobite and Hanoverian; or in literature between Ancient and Modern, between Dryden and Shadwell, between Pope and the Dunces. The subject matter of literature was often petty, continued Taine, and the writers were notable rather for the competent treatment of trivialities than for bold originality. "In this sterility, art was soon reduced to reclothing borrowed thoughts and the writer became an antiquary or a translator." Taine's remarks are applicable only to the period ending in 1715, and they are much too sweeping even for that period. The imitations and translations of Dryden and Pope bulk large, but Dryden was often a resolutely independent critic and satirist, and Pope was not always a borrower. Nor can the age which produced *Hudibras* and *The Tale of a Tub*, *Moll Flanders* and *The Careless Husband*, *Absalom and Achitophel* and the Sir Roger de Coverly papers be said to be lacking in originality and inventiveness.[17]

It is true that the social consciousness of the Age of Reason, so apparent in the satire and comedy of the period, led some men of letters to regard originality and eccentricity (the terms were so often thought of as synonyms) with questioning eye. This was as true of life as of art. In religion, in morals, in art one must be a gentleman, and a gentleman must conform to the standard of common sense. *The Tatler*, for instance, expected men of real merit to "avoid anything particular in their dress, gait, or behaviour." Addison declared in *The Spectator:* "Odd and uncommon characters are the game that I look for. . . ." Gay's fable, "The Goat without a Beard," enforced conformity in the couplet:

> Coxcombs, distinguish'd from the rest,
> To all but coxcombs are a jest.

Chesterfield thought that one should eschew "every singularity that may give a handle to ridicule." Fielding was of the same opinion, and blamed the educational system of the day for failing to stamp out humorous individuals. Matthew Green found it better to go

> To Mecca with the caravan.

That ideal gentleman, Sir Charles Grandison, declared that "singularity is usually the indication of something wrong in judgment." Doctor Johnson, blind to his own failings, believed singularity to be "universally and invariably displeasing." A quotation from Reynolds must be allowed to complete the picture:

A man who thinks he is guarding himself against prejudices by resisting the authority of others, leaves open every avenue to singularity, vanity, self-conceit, obstinacy, and many other vices, all tending to warp the judgment, and prevent the natural operation of his faculties. This submission to others is a deference which we owe, and indeed, are forced involuntarily to pay. In fact, we never are satisfied with our opinions . . . till they are ratified and confirmed by the suffrages of the rest of mankind.[18]

Despite this desire for social conformity, originality in art made steady inroads on the imitative attitude. Not every one was willing to agree with Boileau and Pope that true wit was "what oft was thought but ne'er so well expressed," or with Doctor Johnson, who damned *Tristram Shandy* because nothing odd will do long.[19] The disciples of Longinus mark a transition from imitation of the classics to emulation of them. Addison believed that a modern author could strengthen his powers by asking himself how Homer or Plato would have written. Milton had doubtless, so Addison thought, "very much raised and ennobled his conceptions by such an imitation as that which Longinus has recommended." Gilbert Cooper, William Mason, Thomas Warton, and Joshua Reynolds were patently followers of Longinus in advocating emulation, not close imitation, as a means of achieving the sublime. A quotation from Sir Joshua will make this clear:

The habit of contemplating and brooding over the ideas of great geniuses, till you find yourself warmed by the contact, is the true method of forming an artist-like mind; it is impossible, in the presence of those great men, to think, or invent in a mean manner; a state of mind is acquired that receives those ideas only which relish of grandeur and simplicity.[20]

Preference for emulation indicates a distrust of the value of imitation. Direct attacks on imitation and specific appeals for originality grew in frequency between 1650 and 1800. In the Preface to *Gondibert* (1650) Davenant argued:

. . . whilst we imitate others, we can no more excel them, than he that sailes by others maps can make a new discovery.

Cowley agreed that no copy could exceed the original. Dryden presented Eugenius arguing in *An Essay of Dramatic Poesy* that imitation not only prevented the acquisition of any new perfection, but was likely to entail the loss of some of the old. Dennis lamented the imitative nature of modern poetry. Shaftesbury argued against the imitation of a single model no matter how perfect, and was apparently skeptical even of drawing from various models, for he concluded that "nothing is agreeable or natural, but what is original." Addison declared that, "An imitation of the best authors is not to compare with a good original." Steele believed that the imitator neglected the "just, proper, and natural" to copy the affectations of his model. Joseph Trapp, the Oxford professor of poetry, objected to imitation in his *Praelectiones Poeticae*. Gay made his attitude plain in the Invocation to *Trivia* and in "An Epistle to a Lady":

> One common fate all imitators share,
> To save mince-pies, and cap the grocer's ware.

Welsted found imitation the bane of writing. Gray was suspicious of it. *The Gentleman's Magazine* reprinted an article from *The Daily Gazeteer* of September 25, 1741, in which the anonymous author pleaded against treading circumspectly in the old paths of literature. In 1755 Robert Lloyd struck a vigorous blow against

> dull imitators,
> Those younger brothers of translators.

He urged the poet:

> Write from your own imagination,
> Nor curb your muse by imitation;
> For copies show, howe'er exprest,
> A barren genius at the best.[21]

After 1750 the chorus of protest against imitation rose to its climax in Young's *Conjectures* of 1759. Fielding, Goldsmith, Johnson, and Armstrong reiterated: "The best imitator can at best only be second to his original"; "There is not in nature a more imitative animal than a dunce"; "No man was ever great by imitation"; "A Poet . . . that imitates closely will never excel." Young, however, wrote by far the most significant program for the opposition:

Imitators only give us a sort of duplicates of what we had, possibly much better, before; increasing the mere drug of books, while all that makes them valuable, knowledge and genius, are at a stand.

Young argued that the quality of imagination which puts us "at the writer's mercy" was present only in original composition; reading such a work "we have no home, no thought of our own; till the magician drops his pen." Recalling the arguments of the Quarrel of the Ancients and the Moderns Young insisted that the modern mind has an equal capacity with the ancient and a positive advantage over it from accumulated experience. All that was necessary was that the writer should know and reverence himself as an antidote against reverence for antiquity. More specifically Young objected to imitation because it deprived the liberal arts of the advantages which the mechanical arts enjoy by the employment of successive discoveries, because it was unnatural to imitate when Nature "brings us into the world all originals," and because imitation makes men "think little and write much." "While the true genius is crossing all public roads into fresh untrodden ground," the imitator, "up to the knees in antiquity, is treading the sacred footsteps of great examples, with the blind veneration of a bigot saluting the papal toe. . . ."[22]

Duff and Gerard battered away at servile imitation in the manner of Young. It was Cowper's "aversion." To Thomas Warton imitation seemed characteristic of early and rude periods. Blair saw its value in pedagogy, but felt that, despite Pope's success with Horace, "the servility of imitation . . . is a proof of the entire want of genius." John Pinkerton was in some respects a complete rebel, and to him imitation was anathema:

All kinds of imitation, all imitation whatever, sink into that class of poetry which we read to ladies at a tea-table. . . . Originality is co-essential with genius.

The mature opinion of Doctor Johnson must conclude this survey of the direct attacks on imitation. In the criticism of Pope Johnson sang his palinode for his own *London* and *The Vanity of Human Wishes*:

The plan was ready to his hand, and nothing was required but to accommodate as he could the sentiments of an old author to recent facts or familiar images; but what is easy is seldom excellent; such imitations cannot give pleasure to common readers. The man of learning may be sometimes surprised and delighted by an unexpected parallel; but the comparison requires knowledge of the original, which will likewise often detect strained applications. Between Roman images and English manners there will be an irreconcilable dissimilitude, and the work will be generally uncouth and party-coloured; neither original nor translated, neither ancient nor modern.[23]

If the protests against imitation were numerous, the pleas for originality and the praises of original writers were even more so. Despite the attempt to induce social conformity England remained a land of humorists and eccentrics. Both the continuous failure of social satire and comedy to establish respect for common sense and the established modes, and the continued resistance to the logical classical position in art are explainable in part by the inherent unwillingness to conform noted in Englishmen by such commentators upon English life as Misson, Sorbière, Muralt, and Gordon. The author of *Guardian*, No. 144, was in thorough agreement with these travelers. Sir Roger and Uncle Toby are only the most famous embodiments of the eighteenth-century humorist whose name is legion in the essays, comedies, and novels of the period.[24]

Literary pleas for originality occur early in the Restoration period. The authors of *The Rehearsal* show Bayes making a fool of himself:

Why, sir, when I have nothing to invent, I never trouble my head about it, as other men do; but presently turn over this book, and there I have, at one view, all that Perseus, Montaigne, Seneca's Tragedies, Horace, Juvenal, Claudian, Pliny, Plutarch's Lives, and the rest, have ever thought upon this subject; and so, in a trice, by leaving out a few words, or putting in others of my own, the business is done.

Dryden declared that invention was a mark of genius and a gift of Nature not obtainable by rules. Even if the writer's theme was not new, invention should be shown in the fashioning of the argument, the insertion of the episodes, and in the creation of the characters. Swift, in *A Tale of a Tub*, "resolved to proceed in a manner that should be altogether new, the world having been already too long nauseated with endless repetitions upon every subject," and Doctor Johnson later admitted Swift's success. Addison advocated originality in *The Spectator*, No. 160. Pope justified the pre-eminence of Homer because he excelled in invention, "which is the very foundation of poetry." For the same reason Hughes praised Spenser in 1715, and Prior Milton in 1718.[25]

In the Preface to his *Works* in 1731 Allan Ramsay disclaimed imitation. Matthew Green wrote of his own poems:

> Nothing is stolen: my Muse, though mean
> Draws from the spring she finds within;

and later in *The Spleen* he attacked the literary imitator as a plagiary. In 1733 Theobald glorified Shakespeare for his originality. Chesterfield found fiction or invention "the soul of poetry." Aaron Hill stole a march on Joseph Warton by condemning Pope because his genius was not "native nor inventive." Richardson took pride in borrowing from nobody. Fielding defined invention as "a quick and sagacious penetration into the true essence of all the objects of our contemplation," and considered it an attribute of genius. In 1756 Joseph Warton retracted his early admiration for Pope as an exalted and truly original genius and relegated him to the second rank because of his barrenness of invention.[26]

Warton's *Essay on Pope* and Young's *Conjectures* marked a new era. Imitation had been attacked before, and invention had been praised, but after 1759 there was a more confident assurance in the power of genius to choose its own path and to succeed by obeying two commandments—"Know Thyself," and "Reverence Thyself." Young's *Conjectures* was the "Self-Reliance" of the eighteenth century, a plea more in keeping with the spirit of the age than Emerson's in nineteenth-century America. Johnson was on the side of the angels on this point:

> No man ever yet became great by imitation. . . . Fame cannot spread wide or endure long that is not rooted in nature and manured by art. That which hopes to resist the blast of malignity, and stand firm against the attacks of time, must contain in itself some original principle of growth. The reputation that arises from the detail or transposition of borrowed sentiments, may spread for a while, like ivy on the rind of antiquity, but will be torn away by accident or contempt, and suffered to rot unheeded on the ground.

So also was Goldsmith, who regarded originality as "that characteristic of true genius"; and Arthur Murphy, who called invention "the first great leading talent of a poet"; and Mrs. Montagu who approved "daring incursions into unexplored regions of invention";

and *The Mirror,* and *The Lounger,* and Doctor Blair. But it was perhaps William Duff who most fully elucidated the role of originality in the composition of the genius. To him originality meant "that *native* and *radical* power which the mind possesses, of discovering something new and uncommon in every subject"; it is marked by a plastic power of the imagination to disclose new truths, present series of events never before contemplated, originate new sentiments, and find surprising and uncommon combinations of ideas.[27]

When this praise of originality is associated with the praise of genius and of imagination and with the opposition to the Rules and to Authority it should be apparent that there was even in the heyday of classicism much more reliance on one's own judgment, common sense, imagination, and constructive ability than has been allowed by critics who have been content to peer from the Romantic brink into the dark abyss of classicism rather than to journey downward to make a study from within.

NOTES TO CHAPTER XI

1. Dryden, *Essays,* II, 114; Settle, Preface to Henry Higden's *A Modern Essay on the Tenth Satyr of Juvenal,* London, 1687; Rowe, "Some Account of Boileau . . . and this Translation," prefixed to Ozell's *Le Lutrin,* London, 1708.

2. William King, in Anderson, *British Poets,* VI, 680.

3. Pope, *Works,* III, 287.

4. Richard Owen Cambridge, Advertisement to *The Intruder,* London, 1754; Steele, *Guardian,* March 25, 1713; Hurd, *Works,* London, 1811, II, 224; Joseph Warton, *Essay on Pope,* II, 266; Johnson, *Lives of the Poets,* ed. Waugh, VI, 57; Boswell, *Life of Johnson,* I, 141; Hurd, *Works,* II, 114.

5. Anderson, *British Poets,* VII, 777; *Monthly Review,* LXIII, 71, XXVIII, 400, XX, 279, XXXVI, 399; *Monthly Review,* New Series, XVII, 352, XII, 472; *Gentleman's Magazine,* IV, 622, XV, 161, XVI, 557, VIII, 656, XV, 56 and 156, XIX, 96, XXXIII, 332, VIII, 483, IX, 377, LVI–1, 426, VI, 101, LVIII–2, 823; XVI, 276, XVIII, 183, XXIII, 485, XVII, 108, XXI, 181, LXVI–2, 860, XXII, 576, LXV–1, 424, LVI–1, 249, LVIII–1, 348, XLVI, 572, XVII, 93.

6. Nichols, *Illustrations of the Literary History of the XVIIIth Century,* London, 1817–58, I, 574, 579, 605, 685, 696, 702; Yvon, *Horace Walpole as a Poet,* Paris, 1924, pp. 4 ff.

7. Pope, *Works,* VI, 53; Ascham, *The Scholemaster,* ed. Edward Arber, London, 1903, p. 119; Webbe, *Discourse of English Poetrie,* ed. Arber, London, 1870, p. 52; Dryden, *Essays,* I, 239; Langbaine, *An Account of the English Dramatick Poets,* Oxford, 1691, p. 145; Ozell, Dedication to Boileau's *Lutrin . . . rendered into*

English Verse, London, 1708; Tom Brown, *Works,* London, 1720, I, 20; Spence, Preface to *Polymetis,* London, 1755; *Monthly Review,* LXXVIII, 55; Nathan Drake, *Literary Hours,* London, 1800, II, 306; William Clubbe, *Six Satires of Horace, in a Style between Free Imitation and Literal Version,* Ipswich, 1795; J. W. Draper, "Theory of Translation in the Eighteenth Century," *Neo-philologus,* VI, 241; Walter L. Bullock, "The Precept of Plagiarism in the Cinquecento," *Modern Philology,* XXV, 293; Quintilian, *Institutes,* X, 11; Horace, *Ars Poetica,* lines 128–135, 268–269; Longinus, *On the Sublime,* XIII, 2–4 and XIV; Spingarn, *Literary Criticism of the Renaissance,* pp. 131, 178–179, 191; Vial et Denise, *op. cit.,* pp. 5–6.

8. Burton, *Anatomy of Melancholy,* I, 23; Carew, "Elegy upon the Death of Doctor Donne"; Pope, *Works,* VI, 53; Addison, *Spectator,* No. 253; Gildon, in Durham, *op. cit.,* pp. 61–67; Hurd, *Works,* II, 228; Joseph Warton, *Adventurer,* No. 63; Boswell, *Life of Johnson,* II, 410, note 3, and IV, 272; Johnson, *Rambler,* Nos. 143, 169, and *Adventurer,* No. 96; *World,* No. 44; Duff, *Essay on Genius,* p. 277; *cf.* La Bruyère, in Vial et Denise, *op. cit.,* p. 203, and the opinion of Goethe according to Eckermann, *Gespräche,* p. 239.

9. Robert Stapylton, Preface to *Juvenal's Sixteen Satyrs,* London, 1647; Henry Higden, *A Modern Essay on the Thirteenth Satyr of Juvenal,* London, 1686; Congreve, *Complete Works,* IV, 178; Farquhar, *Works,* London, 1728, I, 86; Johnson, *Works,* Oxford, 1824, IX, 77; *Monthly Review,* LXXXI, 482; *Monthly Review,* New Series, XXIV, 261; *Spectator,* April 4, 1711; *Guardian,* March 25, 1713; *Adventurer,* June 12, 1753; Nichols, *Illustrations,* II, 196.

10. Bray, *op. cit.,* p. 171; W. G. Howard, "Ut Pictura Poesis," *P. M. L. A.,* XXIV, 93, 100–101.

11. *Gentleman's Magazine,* LV–2, 817; Dryden, *Essays,* II, 265.

12. Oldmixon, *Amores Britannici,* London, 1703; *Gentleman's Magazine,* LXV–1, 495.

13. Clark, *Boileau and the French Classical Critics in England,* pp. 115, 182.

14. Pope, *Works,* IX, 49; Austen Warren, *Pope as a Critic and Humanist,* Princeton, 1929, pp. 224 ff.

15. *The Works of Horace in English Verse,* by Mr. Duncombe, Sen., J. Duncombe, and other hands, London, 1767. Further details concerning adaptation, and a list of the English adaptations of Roman satire will be found in my MS. doctoral dissertation, *English Adaptations of Roman Satire, 1660–1800,* in the University of Michigan library.

16. Dryden, *Absalom and Achitophel,* lines 599–603; Addison, *Spectator,* No. 339; Joseph Warton, *Adventurer,* No. 63 and *Essay on Pope,* I, 34, note, and I, 95, where Boileau is cited; Johnson, *Lives of the Poets,* ed. Waugh, V, 65, 224.

17. Taine, *Histoire de la littérature anglaise,* Paris, 1892, III, 240.

18. Evelyn, *Diary and Correspondence,* III, 350; *Tatler,* No. 96; Addison, *Spectator,* Nos. 108, 576; Gay, *Poetical Works,* p. 253; Chesterfield, *Works,* II, 431; Fielding, *Covent-Garden Journal,* Nos. 55–56; Green, *The Spleen,* lines 353–354; Richardson, *Writings,* XIX, 163; Johnson, *Adventurer,* No. 131; Boswell, *Life of Johnson,* I, 578, II, 85, note 2; Reynolds, *Discourses,* p. 117; *cf.* Blunt, *op. cit.,* I, 305; Pinkerton, *Letters of Literature,* p. 62; and a letter of Cowper to John Johnson of January 21, 1791.

19. Aristotle, *Poetics,* IX, 6–7; Horace, *Ars Poetica,* lines 128–132; Longinus, *On the Sublime,* V; Boileau, in Vial et Denise, *op. cit.,* p. 166; Joseph Warton,

Essay on Pope, II, 22; Johnson, *Lives of the Poets*, ed. Waugh, I, 30; Boswell, *Life of Johnson*, II, 514.

20. Gregory Smith, Introduction to *Elizabethan Critical Essays*, I, xxxviii–xxxix; Jonson, in Spingarn, *Critical Essays of the Seventeenth Century*, I, 26, 53–54; Blackmore, *ibid.*, III, 240; Addison, *Spectator*, No. 339 and *Guardian*, No. 152; *Guardian*, No. 86; John Gilbert Cooper, *Letters Concerning Taste*, p. 50; Thomas Warton, *Observations*, I, 54; Reynolds, *Discourses*, pp. 91, 97, 203; R. S. Crane, "Imitation of Spenser and Milton in the Early Eighteenth Century: A New Document," *Studies in Philology*, XV, 196–199; J. W. Draper, "Aristotelian 'Mimesis' in Eighteenth Century England," *P. M. L. A.*, XXXVI, 377.

21. King James I, in Gregory Smith, *op. cit.*, I, 220–221; Nash, *ibid.*, I, 309; *The Return from Parnassus*, Act, I, Scene II; Daniel, in Gregory Smith, *op. cit.*, II, 366–372; Davenant, in Spingarn, *Critical Essays*, II, 7; Cowley, *Essays*, pp. 19–20; Dryden, *Essays*, I, 43; Durham, Introduction to *Critical Essays*, p. xxviii; Vial et Denise, *op. cit.*, pp. 40, 252, 259, 274; Shaftesbury, *Characteristicks*, III, 259, note; Addison, *Spectator*, No. 160; Steele, *Spectator*, No. 140; Gay, *Poetical Works*, pp. 59, 148; Welsted, in Durham, *op. cit.*, p. 377; Gray, *Letters*, I, 183; *Gentleman's Magazine*, XI, 487; *Connoisseur*, Nos. 67, 125; R. D. Havens, "Romantic Aspects of the Age of Pope," *P. M. L. A.*, XXVII, 297.

22. Fielding, *Covent-Garden Journal*, No. 52; Goldsmith, *Miscellaneous Works*, p. 423; Johnson, *Rasselas*, Chap. X; Armstrong, *Miscellanies*, II, 168; Young, *Conjectures*, in E. D. Jones, *op. cit.*, pp. 319, 333, 338 *et passim*.

23. Duff, *Essay on Genius*, pp. 131–132; Gerard, *Essay on Genius*, pp. 9–12; Cowper, Letter to Unwin, Nov. 24, 1781; Thomas Warton, *History of English Poetry*, p. 226; Blair, *Rhetoric*, II, 54, 307, III, 171; Pinkerton, *Letters of Literature*, pp. 127, 234, 356–359, 361, 363; Johnson, *Lives of the Poets*, ed. Hill, III, 176, 247.

24. P. S. Wood, "The Opposition to Neo-classicism in England between 1660 and 1700," *P. M. L. A.*, XLIII, 183–185; *Guardian*, No. 144. Cf. *Mirror*, No. 61; Blair, *Rhetoric*, III, 379, and Section IV of the following chapter of this study for further notes on English humor.

25. *The Rehearsal*, Act, I, Scene I; Dryden, *Essays*, I, 47, 58–59, II, 138–139, 198–199; Congreve, Dedication of the *Double Dealer*; Swift, *Gulliver*, etc., ed. Eddy, pp. 370–371; Boswell, *Life of Johnson*, II, 365; Addison, *Spectator*, Nos. 160, 321, 476; Pope, *Preface to Homer*, in Durham, *op. cit.*, pp. 323–325; Hughes, in Durham, p. 89; Prior, in Chalmers, *op. cit.*, X, 206.

26. Allan Ramsay, quoted Phelps, *Beginnings of the English Romantic Movement*, p. 32; Green, *The Spleen*, lines 13–14, 524–532; Theobald, in Nicoll Smith, *op. cit.*, p. 64; Chesterfield, *Letters*, I, 68, 99, II, 211; Aaron Hill, in Richardson, *Correspondence*, I, 106, 110; Richardson, *ibid.*, IV, 72; Fielding, *Tom Jones*, Book IX, Chap. I; Joseph Warton, *Adventurer*, No. 63, and *Essay on Pope*, I, 9.

27. Young, *Conjectures*, in Jones, *op. cit.*, pp. 319–324, 337; Johnson, *Rasselas*, Chap. X; Goldsmith, *Bee*, No. IV; *Miscellaneous Works*, pp. 438–439, 509, and *Works*, ed. Gibbs, IV, 297, V, 63; Murphy, *Essay on Fielding*, p. 29; Mrs. Montagu, *Essay on Shakespeare*, pp. xi–xii; *Mirror*, No. 99; *Lounger*, Nos. 37, 68; Blair, *Rhetoric*, III, 276; Duff, *Essay on Genius*, pp. 86–87, 89–90, 126, 129–130.

CHAPTER XII

THE LITERARY "KINDS"

I

THE ATTEMPT to acclimatize the classical literary "kinds" in England was motivated by the desire of the Moderns to emulate each great Ancient in his own province, and thus give to England a native Homer, Sophocles, or Pindar. The apparent feasibility of pouring new wine into old bottles was supported by respect for form and technique, by the laws of decorum in style, and by the belief that the Ancients who, in general, worked within a single "kind" had explored all the possibilities of the various "kinds." Numerous essays on the form of epic, satire, or pastoral; frequent production of works which fall clearly under this or the other type; and the distaste for any mixture of "kinds" indicate the preoccupation of neo-classicists with the Rules of specific literary forms. The effort to impose the ideal of the "kinds" on English literature was even more futile than the attempt to set up authority or to establish the mode of literary imitation. Heroic tragedy, narrative satire, the social essay, and the novel either had no patterns in antiquity, or had been in antiquity neglected forms with no neatly woven code of precepts for classically minded Englishmen to follow.

The systematic classification of literary forms began early. In *The Scholemaster* Ascham had distinguished poetry, history, philosophy, and oratory, and proclaimed that each had its proper decorum necessary for perfect imitation. Sidney, leaning on Scaliger, distinguished sacred, philosophic, and "right," or creative poetry not bound to fact. "Right" poetry was then carefully subdivided. Time passed, but two generations later Boileau in France and Edward Phillips in England were still giving advice on the different poetic kinds. Phillips, in fact, thought that no new kind was possible:

. . . whoever should desire to introduce some new kind of poem, of dif-

ferent fashion from any known to the Ancients, would do no more than
he that should study to bring a new order into architecture.

Rowe questioned the validity of mock-heroic, since it was so new
and had been done so seldom. Shaftesbury was particularly hostile
to literature which could not be fitted readily into a familiar pattern.
It was Pope who suggested the difficulty in producing masterpieces
in various kinds:

> One science only will one genius fit;
> So vast is art, so narrow human wit;
> Not only bounded to peculiar arts,
> But oft in those confined to single parts.

After Pope the rigid demarcation of "kinds" became less popular,
and in such critics as Blair and Kames there is a significant uncertainty of attitude, shifting from a conventional acceptance of the
belief in types to a more liberal attitude in which they are willing
to admit that the "kinds" often shade off into each other.[1]

Elizabethan critics disliked the mixture of tragedy and comedy,
although they were unable to rein in the swift development of drama
in conformity with popular taste. Sidney was reasonable, but he
warned dramatists against "mingling kings and clowns . . . with
neither decency nor discretion." Milton, however, considered that
"mixing comic stuff with tragic sadness and gravity, or introducing
trivial and vulgar persons" was an "absurd concession" to gratify
the populace. Sir Robert Howard believed that tragic and comic
effects nullified each other. Dryden decried the mixture as "Gothic
barbarity." *The Tatler* lamented the lack of decorum in tragicomedy. Addison was unhesitating in his condemnation:

> The tragi-comedy . . . is one of the most monstrous inventions that
> ever entered into a poet's thoughts. An author might as well think of weav-
> ing the adventures of Æneas and Hudibras into one poem, as of writing
> such a motley piece of mirth and sorrow. But the absurdity of these per-
> formances is so very visible, that I shall not insist upon it.

Hume, Gray, and Mason held to this conservative attitude, but by
1715 Gay had already poked fun at the distinction of the "kinds"
which Doctor Johnson was finally to annihilate in the *Preface to
Shakespeare* (1765) by an appeal from criticism to Nature.[2]

Despite the preference of Aristotle for tragedy many of the classicists felt that a great epic would most completely crown the literary glory of a nation. From the criticism of Aristotle and the models of Homer and Virgil the definition and characteristic features of a true epic poem were formulated by Italian, French, and English critics. The ideal epic should have a noble subject—of illustrious men moving through illustrious actions—and it should extend one's ideas of human perfection by exciting admiration. In this excitation of admiration through the presentation of a perfect hero performing marvellous actions epic differed from tragedy, which was expected to show the fate of a man neither entirely good nor entirely bad in a series of probable actions that should move the audience through verisimilitude and produce a purgation of emotions. In the epic admiration was to be excited by the use of the supernatural which could be reconciled to artistic probability, so Dryden, Blackmore, and others advised, by the use of the epic "machinery" of gods, whose marvellous powers could justify events which did not occur in the actual world. The necessity for both probability and admiration made the use of "machinery" one of the most essential parts of the theory of the epic.

On other points there was more dissent, but it was generally agreed that the epic should relate one action with reasonable adherence to truth, while romance might treat several loosely connected actions of one hero with a considerable mixture of magic and miracle. The epic action should have an historical foundation to enhance probability, but idealization was permissible in the hero's character and happy destiny. The epic action should begin *in medias res* in order that the time of the action might not surpass a year— a unity of time paralleling the twenty-four-hour limitation of strict neo-classical tragedy. Early incidents could be brought in by way of episode to add variety to the present action without destroying the concentration needed in a great work of art.[3]

The ideal epic form was discussed in England long after the last successful example, *Paradise Lost,* was written. The *Prince Arthurs* and *Epigoniads* of Blackmores and Wilkies constitute no part of

England's literary glory, but Blackmore may be allowed to represent the vain hope that the lucid delimitation of a technique might fire mediocrity into genius. In 1695 Blackmore defined the epic as "a feign'd or devis'd story of an illustrious action, related in verse, in an allegorical, probable, delightful, and admirable manner, to cultivate the mind with instructions in virtue." The hero must be of noble rank and possessed of extraordinary courage, but (and here Blackmore modifies the main tradition) he need not be morally impeccable. The epic manner was created by "sublime thoughts, clear and noble expressions, purity of language, a just and due proportion, relation, and dependence between the parts, and a beautiful and regular structure and connection discernible in the whole." Blackmore elsewhere insists that there must be "one action . . . , not a series of actions happening to one person." The epic differs from all other poetry in that it attempts to please by "astonishing and amazing the reader" by means of elevated thoughts, noble episodes, and an action as wonderful and surprising as can be reconciled with probability. Two generations later Doctor Blair essentially echoed Blackmore, but was more conventional in stressing the virtue of the hero who must "excite admiration" by extending our ideas of human perfection. Blair and Blackmore together give a normal view of the epic as a neo-classical literary "kind."[4]

The chief note of dissent against the Aristotelian conception of the epic was sounded by a numerous body of writers who sought to bring to birth a Christian epic as a modern parallel to the pagan epics of Homer and Virgil. Since the epic was designed to instruct like other forms of art, to many sincere Christians it seemed absurd to attempt to derive such instruction from classical mythology or from the ethical code of a vanished paganism. The perfect epic protagonist must be a Christian hero, an Arthur or a Godfrey, rather than an Æneas or Achilles. In the achievement of the marvellous the angels and demons of Christian story could replace the pagan "machinery."[5]

Inspired by Italian critics numerous French epicasters designed vast Christian epics, and Christian tragedies as well, between 1641 and 1645. The epics were still-born, but the creative ferment produced a body of argument in favor of a Christian epic. The pagan myths were absurd and could not be rendered probable, while the Christian themes were not only superior in grandeur, but their verity ensured artistic probability. A clinching argument pointed to the fact that Greek and Roman poets had employed only native themes. If these arguments were sufficient to convince the poet and he chose a Christian theme, he should then avoid any mixture of paganism and remain faithful to sacred history, but he must still adhere to the general features of the Aristotelian epic—the Unities of action and of time, the perfect hero, the fortunate denouement, the employment of "machinery," the description of a military conflict, and the like.[6]

In England Davenant chose "such persons as profess'd Christian religion" for *Gondibert* because the principles of Christianity "conduce more to explicable virtue, to plain demonstrative justice, and even to honor . . . than any other religion." Cowley, author of the abortive and fragmentary *Davideis*, was sure that Christianity could easily match paganism in its wealth of epic themes. Dryden was a little disturbed by the difficulty of reconciling Christian humility and resignation with the extraordinary and heroic actions essential to the epic poem, as well as by the difficulty of suspense in a conflict against an omnipotent power, but he felt that the Christian epic was a possibility. Blackmore, author of a series of dismally pious epics on Arthur and Alfred, had no such doubts and looked proudly upon his own productions as proof of the feasibility of a poem, heroic yet impeccably Christian. The sad tale of the ghostly epics by the eighteenth- and nineteenth-century Miltonists has been told by Raymond D. Havens in *Milton and English Poetry*, and need not be retailed here.[7]

Some of the greatest of the classical critics failed to be convinced by the reasoning of the Christian epicasters. Boileau believed that the ornamentation of pagan mythology was essential to poetry, and that the awe-inspiring mysteries of Christian faith were not susceptible of poetic embellishment. Doctor Johnson could not agree with Boileau about the use of myths, but he found the Christian epic difficult because a modern reader could not imagine himself in a situation in which the miraculous rule of a theocracy was still visible, nor could the modern poet exalt omnipotence by poetic treatment. Johnson also felt that Christian themes were too few and too familiar to allow scope for invention, if the poet was to avoid impiety. Among lesser men Saint-Évremond, Temple, and Shaftesbury held the same views.[8]

III

Tragedy, the favorite "kind" with Aristotle, was of almost equal importance with the epic in neo-classical theory. The *Poetics* defined tragedy as

an imitation of an action that is serious, complete, and of a certain magnitude; in language embellished with each kind of artistic ornament, the several kinds being found in separate parts of the play; in the form of action, not of narration; through pity and fear effecting the proper *katharsis* or purgation of these emotions.

This definition was by no means sufficiently precise for those meticulous critics who explained and supplemented the master. Successive distinctions limited tragedy to the affairs of persons of high rank preferably with an historical foundation. Tragedy must have dignity, and consequently indecorous, cruel, improbable, and unworthy actions must be avoided. By the end of the sixteenth century Renaissance critics had formulated a series of distinctions between tragedy and comedy which remained valid until the appearance of bourgeois tragedy in the eighteenth century: (1) tragic characters must be of high rank, the characters of comedy private citizens; (2) tragic action must be great and terrible, comic familiar; (3) tragedy must begin happily and end terribly, while comedy must end joyfully; (4) the style of tragedy must be elevated, that of comedy colloquial; (5) tragedy might use an historical subject, while the comic fable must be invented; (6) tragedy should be concerned with "exile and bloodshed," comedy with "love and seduction."[9]

Comparatively few new ideas concerning tragedy were added by the French neo-classical critics, but there was some shift in emphasis. Though the French critics were anxious to preserve the sudden alteration of fortune (peripeteia) and the recognition scenes recommended by Aristotle in the interest of that surprise which was to arouse wonder, they simplified the intrigue and held rather rigidly to the single action of which only the last stages were actually to be represented on the stage. Simplification of plot provided time for a more extensive analysis of passion. Pity was emphasized more than fear or terror, and love was stressed (though not by Corneille) as best suited to the production of pity. Influenced by epic theory the French critics raised wonder or admiration to an equal plane with pity and terror as a tragic emotion capable of inculcating virtue in an audience overwhelmed by the perfect goodness of the protagonist.[10]

In England the conception of tragedy was similar to that which prevailed in Renaissance Italy and in seventeenth-century France. Tragedy was an imitation of that portion of Nature which exhibited rule, order, and harmony. Its function was to teach and delight. It must preserve probability, poetic justice, decorum, and the Unities. The characters should be of high rank, but neither entirely good nor entirely bad (though the lawless and romantic Heroic Tragedy did not conform on this point), because only the medium characters could arouse pity and fear—as Aristotle had shown—and because such characters were more "natural" representations of normal humanity. High rank was demanded because the misfortunes of the great taught acquiescence and patience to the people, and moved the audience more than the mishaps of the middle classes by the greater social implications of tragic fate and the greater impressiveness of a danger from which not even the exalted were free. Most critics wished violence to be avoided, in conformity with French practice, on the grounds that it was improbable in presentation and shocking to the feelings of the audience; but, in contrast to the French critics, admiration was almost ignored as a tragic emotion save during the heyday of Heroic Tragedy, and love was often regarded as too soft an emotion for the Tragic Muse.[11]

A special æsthetic problem was raised by the question of the pleasure produced by tragedy. Hume made a serious attempt to solve the difficulty by urging that the pleasure natural to all imitations of life combined with delight at artistic mastery to overbalance the pain of the tragic theme. A theme too atrocious or too close to the hearts of the audience would destroy the artistic illusion and result in an overbalance of painful emotion. Lord Kames differed from Hume in suggesting sympathy as the basis of a pleasure sufficiently strong to overcome pain at the distress of the characters. Kames's theory was expanded by the Aikins who suggested that not only sympathy, but self-approbation at the exercise of virtuous sympathy, was combined with curiosity in the unfolding of a series of incidents and "the pleasure constantly attached to the excitement of surprise from new and wonderful objects" to suppress the painful sensations at the sight of misery. Sympathy was produced by love for mental and moral excellence which must remain dominant over suffering if the mind of the spectator is not to be stunned and shocked by misfortunes too atrocious and horrid. The Aikins, with a love of elegance characteristic of the period, wished the mean and the disgusting to be avoided as liable to destroy "the grace and dignity of suffering" and check the rise of sympathy. George Campbell also emphasized the role of sympathy which he analyzed as a compound of commiseration (painful), benevolence (mixed pleasure and pain), and love (sufficiently pleasant to give a preponderance of pleasure to the whole). The pleasure of the audience was further increased by complacency at its own physical security, and freedom from such great vices as the tragic characters displayed. This last point seems difficult to reconcile with the proper tragic catharsis, and Campbell made no attempt to overcome the difficulty.[12]

IV

In the contrast between tragedy and comedy the essential aspects of the neo-classical conception of comedy as a dramatic form have been given. Comedy could not hope to deal with great evils, for great evils would produce pity and fear, emotional states incompatible with the comic spirit. Its province was the minor vices, its method often satiric, its character types those that were offensive to the social sense of the group. Even in dramatic satire it was difficult, in England, to impose an ideal universality on comic characters. On the stage the "characters" or types so frequent in the periodical essays and verse satires were exposed to the rivalry of a surviving comedy of humors which treated the whimsical and eccentric individual. The ingenious attempts to reconcile humor with Nature and probability were generally more specious than convincing.[13]

The humors were popularized in comedy by Ben Jonson. The mediæval basis of the humors in medicine was not always remembered, but a humor was regarded as

> the bias of the mind,
> By which, with violence, 'tis one way inclined;
> It makes our actions lean on one side still,
> And, in all changes, that way bends the will.

This definition of Shadwell seemed satisfactory to Dennis who thought that humor was the province of comedy, which must necessarily concern itself with low life, because education and the cultivation of manners tended to suppress eccentricity and humor. Chesterfield emphasized the fact that the humorous individual produces laughter only when he is unconscious of his peculiarities. Kames agreed with Chesterfield, and even tended to neglect the dominance of any peculiar trait in favor of the unintended contrast between seriousness of manner and ridiculous traits. Campbell followed Dennis in arguing that humor, which he found close kin to pathos, was the province of comedy:

A just exhibition of any ardent or durable passion, excited by some adequate cause, instantly attacheth sympathy, the common tie of human souls, and thereby communicates the passion to the breast of the hearer. But when the emotion is either not violent or not durable, and the motive not anything real but imaginary, or at least quite disproportionate to the effect; or when the passion displays itself preposterously, so as rather to obstruct than to promote its aim; in these cases a natural representation, instead of fellow-feeling, creates amusement, and universally awakens contempt.

This is the humorous, and in comedy "Humour is all."[14]

The critics of the eighteenth century did not penetrate very deeply into the causes of laughter. Hobbes found the explanation of laughter in a feeling of superiority. This was obviously unsatisfactory, and Hutcheson suggested that an unexpected opposition or incongruity lay at the root of laughter. Hutcheson's explanation was accepted by Akenside, Gerard, Campbell, and Morgann, and became familiar in Fielding's Preface to *Joseph Andrews*. Most of these critics also demanded in the laughable an absence of emotion, though Lord Kames was quick to point out that scorn was an emotion generally found in combination with the ridiculous.[15]

V

As was the case with comedy, satire, pastoral, and the Pindaric ode either received scant attention as *literary forms,* or failed to play any significant part in the literary picture. Classical satire was written in pentameter couplets; it was serious and morally righteous in tone; it was closely unified in its fierce excoriation of a single vice; it employed type characters, and for the most part it eschewed narrative or allegory. As a "kind" it reached perfection with Pope. Johnson's *Vanity of Human Wishes* and *London* linger in academic memories and university anthologies. Oldham, Churchill, and Gifford are now forgotten. Dryden diverged from the type in the direction of narration, Swift in the direction of burlesque, and Gay in the direction of the animal fable. In an age of brilliant satire it was not Horace, Juvenal, and Perseus who furnished the molds into which the majority of men of real genius poured the vials of their wrath. Comic drama, burlesque, mock-heroic, and the novel were the chief vehicles for the scornful laughter of the sensible at their erring fellow citizens. The presiding geniuses were Lucian and Aristophanes; but it was their spirit and not the literary forms they used which proved to be of high significance for eighteenth-century England.[16]

After *Lycidas* the English pastoral was effete. The poems of Namby-Pamby Philips and of young Alexander Pope were of no great moment in the current of English literature, but they exemplify the decaying "kind." The models were, of course, primarily Virgil and Spenser, who had himself imitated Virgil, Mantuan, and Marot. The pastoral was brief, its characters the ideal denizens of a Golden Age, its descriptions generalized, its themes love and death with songs of gratulation or of mourning performed for a rural prize before some rustic arbiter. Variety was obtained by the inclusion of veiled panegyric or satire. Always there was an air of *préciosité,* of artifice, and often a mood of gentle regret for the simple life which civilized man could live no more. There was no vitality, no local color, no reason, in short, for claiming the enduring interest of mankind. Doctor Johnson could have spared his invective, for even in 1750 when he approached the subject in *The Rambler* the form was dead. Johnson helped, however, to eliminate even the memory of it from the minds of men by condemning the pastoral as "easy, vulgar, and therefore disgusting"; as requiring no "acquaintance with the living world"; as "unnatural," but never novel; as monotonous in theme; and as innocent of any observation of Nature.[17]

There was little theory concerning lyric poetry, save in the field of the Pindaric, where theory was based on incomplete understanding, and imitation produced almost nothing worthy of remembrance before the time of Gray. Who treasures now the Pindarics of Cowley, or who seeks in Dryden's *Miscellany* for the harsh, extravagant, and grandiloquent efforts of the minor poetasters who are entombed there?

All in all the attempt to reproduce the classical literary "kinds" in England was a failure. Milton's *Paradise Lost* was the only epic, Pope's *Imitations of Horace* and *Moral Essays* the only satires, Dryden's *All for Love* the only tragedy approaching mastery which have survived. The whole effort to codify and to delimitate the forms of art was of doubtful validity; certainly the attempt to follow closely the art forms suitable to a vanished civilization was a mistake. Fortunately, it was a mistake which did not waste the best energies of the men of real genius. They produced in new or modified forms for which they only occasionally sought, as Fielding did. for the novel, to formulate principles, a literature that was essentially classical, not in its imitation of definite models or specific "kinds," but in its observation of normal Nature, in the balance it preserved between reason and emotion, in its respect for the *mores* of the social group, and in its conception of beauty founded on proportion and sanity.

NOTES TO CHAPTER XII

1. Ascham, in Gregory Smith, *op. cit.*, I, 23–25; Sidney, *ibid.*, I, 158–159; Spingarn, *Literary Criticism of the Renaissance*, pp. 43–44; Boileau, *Œuvres*, pp. 195–200; Phillips, in Spingarn, *Critical Essays*, II, 266; Rowe, quoted by Clark, *Boileau and the French Classical Critics in England*, p. 13; Shaftesbury, *Characteristicks*, III, 5–7, 25; Pope, *Essay on Criticism*, lines 60–63; Blair, *Rhetoric*, I, 48, III, 269, 281; Kames, *Elements*, II, 292, note.

2. George Williamson, "Sir Thomas More's View of Drama," *Modern Language Notes*, XLIII, 294; Gregory Smith, Introduction to *Elizabethan Critical*

Essays, I, xliv; Sidney, *ibid.*, I, 175, 199; Milton, Preface to *Samson Agonistes*; Howard, in Spingarn, *Critical Essays*, II, 100; Dryden, *Essays*, II, 146–147; *Tatler*, No. 45; Addison, *Spectator*, No. 40; Hume, *Treatise*, p. 379; Gray, *Letters*, II, 8, note 2; Gay, *Poetical Works*, p. 339; Johnson, *Preface to Shakespeare*, in Nicoll Smith, *op. cit.*, p. 119.

3. This brief picture of the ideal classical epic has been formulated from Spingarn, *Literary Criticism of the Renaissance*, pp. 108–113, 120–122; R. C. Williams, "Epic Unity as Discussed by Sixteenth Century Critics in Italy," *Modern Philology*, XVIII, 383–400; Bray, *Formation de la doctrine classique*, pp. 235–238; Vial et Denise, *op. cit.*, pp. 229–231, 235; Harington, in Gregory Smith, *op. cit.*, II, 216; Dryden, *Essays*, I, 11; II, 27–29, 155; Edward Phillips, in Spingarn, *Critical Essays*, II, 268; Hobbes, *ibid.*, II, 68 ff.; Rymer, *ibid.*, II, 171–172; Addison, *Spectator*, Nos. 267, 273, and the Milton papers, *passim*; Hughes, in Durham, *op. cit.*, p. 95; Thomas Warton, *Observations on the Faerie Queene*, I, 8–10; Duff, *Essay on Genius*, p. 137.

4. Blackmore, *Preface to Prince Arthur*, in Spingarn, *Critical Essays*, III, 235–239; Blair, *Rhetoric*, III, 221–238.

5. Spingarn, *Literary Criticism of the Renaissance*, p. 229, and *Critical Essays*, II, 332; Saintsbury, *History of Criticism*, II, 56.

6. Bray, *op. cit.*, pp. 290–294, 297–299; Desmarets, in Vial et Denise, *op. cit.*, p. 240.

7. Davenant, in Spingarn, *Critical Essays*, II, 9; Blackmore, *ibid.*, III, 240; Cowley, *ibid.*, II, 89–90; Dryden, *Essays*, II, 31 ff.

8. Boileau, *Œuvres*, pp. 206–207; Johnson, *Lives of the Poets*, ed. Waugh, I, 62–64, II, 62; Lessing, *Werke*, IV, 343; Shaftesbury, *Characteristicks*, I, 358; Hamelius, *Die Kritik*, p. 59; Temple, in Spingarn, *Critical Essays*, III, 99.

9. Aristotle, *Poetics*, VI, 2; Spingarn, *Literary Criticism of the Renaissance*, pp. 61–68, 76–81.

10. *Ibid.*, pp. 202–203; Bray, *op. cit.*, pp. 308–322; Herrick, *The Poetics of Aristotle in England*, pp. 74–75; Vial et Denise, *op. cit.*, pp. 123, 128, 134, 145, 180, 182–186.

11. Green, *The Neo-Classic Theory of Tragedy in England*, pp. 54–56, 150–155, 181–193; Bernbaum, *The Drama of Sensibility*, p. 57; Dryden, *Essays*, I, 208–210; Blair, *Rhetoric*, III, 332.

12. Hume, *Essays*, I, 259–264; Kames, *Elements*, I, 352, note; Aikin, *Miscellaneous Pieces in Prose*, pp. 120, 125–126, 194–198, 200; Campbell, *Philosophy of Rhetoric*, pp. 172–180.

13. Spingarn, *Literary Criticism of the Renaissance*, pp. 102–104; Bray, *op. cit.*, p. 335.

14. Shadwell, Preface to *The Humorists*; Dennis, in Durham, pp. 118–123; Chesterfield, *Works*, III, 150–151; Kames, *Elements*, I, 293; Campbell, *Philosophy of Rhetoric*, pp. 31–33.

15. Hamelius, *op. cit.*, p. 143; Akenside, *Poetical Works*, pp. 196–197; Gerard, *Essay on Taste*, pp. 66–68; Campbell, *op. cit.*, pp. 36, 51; Morgann, in Nicoll Smith, *op. cit.*, pp. 292–294; Kames, *Elements*, I, 219–220.

16. *Cf.* Dryden, *Essays*, II, 100–104.

17. Pope, *Works*, I, 258–260; Johnson, *Rambler*, No. 36, and *Lives of the Poets*, ed. Waugh, I, 10, 173, IV, 8, 83; Gay, *Poetical Works*, pp. 28–29; Blair, *Rhetoric*, III, 132–144; *Guardian*, Nos. 22, 23, 30.

CHAPTER XIII

THE CLASSICAL IDEAL OF BEAUTY

THE CLASSICAL ideal of beauty rested on ideas of regularity and utility fostered by the philosophy, the science, and the ethical preoccupations of eighteenth-century England. Beauty was a rational concept capable of explanation and analysis, though it might be perceived by an internal æsthetic sense before the admission of such analysis. Beauty was normalcy, fitness, proportion, clarity, tranquillity, and restraint. This identification rested on the concept of a regular and harmonious universe. Beauty was not a matter of individual taste, for right judgment aided by the study of past masterpieces should lead all men to the perception of the absolute beauty born of truth as easily as to the perception of truth itself. It was comparatively late in the century before a new æsthetics based largely on associational psychology introduced the idea that beauty was dependent upon a complex of memories and desires differing from individual to individual; it was only after an extended struggle that vagueness, strangeness, spontaneity, melancholy, and infinite yearning were fashioned into a new Romantic beauty. The sublime, which eighteenth-century critics developed in opposition to the beautiful, tended to disrupt the solidarity of the classical viewpoint and became in time a powerful factor in the pre-romantic movement. As a disruptive force it will be treated later.

Before examining the separate components of the classical ideal of beauty it is well to outline briefly some of the typical æsthetic doctrines between Hutcheson and Alison. In 1715 De Crousay, a Cartesian thinker, published his *Traité du Beau* in which he reached the conclusion that beauty consisted of unity in variety, the relation of all the parts of the object to the whole. This characteristically geometrical explanation was accepted by Hutcheson, the first important student of æsthetics in England, as the basis of pure or absolute beauty. For Hutcheson beauty was "a compound ratio of uniformity and variety: so that where the uniformity of bodies is equal, the beauty is as the variety; and where the variety is equal, the beauty is as the uniformity." This pure beauty was perceptible by a sixth æsthetic sense but its intuitive judgments were susceptible of rational analysis. Pure beauty lay in the object. A secondary æsthetic pleasure lay in the mind which perceived the skill of the artist in fulfilling his aim and was moved by the sentimental and moral ideas involved. These subordinate pleasures were in time to be developed into the æsthetics of sensibility.[1]

Gerard followed Hutcheson in seeking beauty in some combination of uniformity, variety, and proportion. Regular figures he esteemed superior to irregular ones, for "equality [symmetry or balance of parts] is requisite to the beauty of every piece of painting," though this equality must be enlivened with variety, lest it degenerate into "dull formality." Gerard bound proportion closely to the fitness of a structure for the end designed, for in the most perfect of Nature's works elegance of form was always found united to fitness to subserve a definite end. Gerard's classical sense of fitness and proportion naturally led him to condemn Gothic architecture.[2]

Lord Kames demanded simplicity, symmetry, and utility in the beautiful, but he distinguished absolute beauty resident in the object itself from the beauty that was relative to some good end or purpose. When Lord Kames reverted to the idea of beauty in the second volume of his *Elements* he gave a much greater significance to fulfilment of function, for he rather categorically proclaimed that "it is the perfection of every work of art, that it fulfils the purpose for which it is intended; and every other beauty, in opposition, is improper."[3]

Blair also started from regularity and variety, but he laid much the greater stress on variety, for the idea that Nature loved symmetry was giving way before closer study, and Blair was able to support his love of variety by pointing to the apparent neglect of regularity in the external world, which was undoubtedly the work of the most graceful artist—Nature. Such beauty as regularity did possess seemed to Blair to be dependent upon ideas of fitness, propriety, and use. Blair was a step in advance of Gerard and Kames in emphasizing the beauty of color, but he did not entirely neglect the beauty of proportion, which he associated with conscious design, as distinct from the variety and color of Nature, with which man had nothing to do. Architecture was the chief field for the display of the beauties of proportion.[4]

It will be necessary to return to the æsthetics of Burke in considering the cult of the sublime. Burke carefully distinguished the beautiful from the sublime, and denied that proportion or fitness lay at the root of beauty. Instead he attempted to reveal beauty as the result of certain qualities in objects which produced a sensation of pleasure, as opposed to the fear and pain that were intimately linked to the idea of sublimity. On beauty Burke may be left to speak for himself:

On the whole, the qualities of beauty, as they are merely sensible qualities, are the following. First, to be comparatively small. Secondly, to be smooth. Thirdly, to have a variety in the direction of the parts; but, fourthly, to have those parts not angular, but melted as it were into each other. Fifthly, to be of a delicate frame, without any remarkable appearance of strength. Sixthly, to have its colours clear and bright, but not very strong or glaring. Seventhly, or if it should have any glaring colour, to have it diversified with others. These are, I believe, the properties on which beauty depends; properties that operate by nature, and are less liable to be altered by caprice, or confounded by a diversity of tastes, than any other.[5]

The attempt of Reynolds to reconcile average and ideal beauty has been touched upon briefly at the close of Chapter VIII. By the time that Reynolds began to deliver the lectures before the Royal Academy æsthetic ideas concerning the sublime and the picturesque were already more popular with all save some few conservative critics than were the classical ideals of proportion, fitness, and restraint. At the same time the new æsthetics of association, hinted at by Hutcheson and clearly present to the mind of Burke, was being developed more fully by Alison. Though founded on the psychology of Locke, Hume, and Hartley—a product of the Age of Reason—associational æsthetics turned away from classicism in its subordination of design to sentiment. It was a subjective æsthetic which sought beauty in the emotions of the percipient, not in the unchanging qualities of the thing perceived. As such it was truly revolutionary.

Alison's æsthetics must be briefly sketched as an illuminating contrast to the classical ideal. Since the beautiful is dependent on the richness and variety of associations evoked by an object, the mind must be free from practical considerations and critical intention, for only then can the imagination evoke the latent associations freely. This flow of the imagination would vary according to the sentimental associations of the individual mind, and would create an impression of beauty proportionate to the wealth of feeling and memory in the percipient. The artist should seek, however, to appeal to the general feelings of mankind and thus produce a unified and emotional train of associations. Youth, according to Alison, perceived beauty more readily than age, for maturity developed logical and practical ideas hostile to the sentimental associations which give birth to beauty. In this æsthetics of sensibility judgment, the essential faculty for the classical critic, was of little use, since judgment *distinguished* but did not *associate* ideas; while design and fulfilment of function were relegated to a minor role since they were less moving, less permanent, and less universal than the permanent feelings of humanity. Alison thus rejected beauty of proportion for the very reason which had led earlier critics to accept it, the degree to which it could be considered absolute and universal; and posited for sensibility, which had been distrusted by all rationalists as hostile to any possible standard of taste, a universal validity.[6]

To the classicist sensibility seemed lawless and unaccountable; proportion was dear to his heart because it could be linked with average, normal nature. In the case of the human body "the perfection of form and beauty is contained in the sum of all men." The ideal was the average from which all individual bodies diverged. It could be discovered by painstaking measurements of living men, or by accepting the proportions of ancient sculpture, whose creators had already worked out the ideal standards. In architecture Palladio studied the system of proportions in Vitruvius and measured ancient buildings to establish the architectural proportions of Italian—and later of English—classical architecture. Among English architects Christopher Wren identified natural beauty with the geometrical beauty of proportion, and was able to conceive of Nature only in this geometrical sense.[7]

The love of proportion and symmetry is apparent throughout the classical period in England. Hume and Kames proclaimed distinctly the identity of proportion and conformity to common (average) nature, and when such an identification was not made it was usually implied. Congreve declared that "nothing can be called beautiful without proportion." Vanbrugh, to whom the mantle of Wren descended, was equally Palladian in his insistence that proportion, not ornament, made for beauty. Steele believed that the beauty of the body consisted in proportion and health (the ability to fulfil a normal function). Lady Mary Wortley Montagu disliked architecture that was lacking in regularity and proportion. Smollett agreed. In poetry proportion must be shown by what Doctor Johnson termed "poetical architecture," the proper interconnection of parts and their subordination to the total effect. Both Goldsmith and Johnson were scornful of the planless familiar essay, and Johnson laughed at the violation of Aristotelian literary architectonics in *Samson Agonistes,* which had no middle at all, since nothing happened between the beginning and the end to hasten or delay the death of the hero.[8]

By the middle of the century there was a growing restlessness against the tyranny of mathematical beauty. In 1753 Hogarth pointed out that symmetry could not be the cause of beauty, for in that case the greater the regularity the greater would be the beauty, which was obviously not true. Hawkesworth, in the same year, declared that expressiveness, not immobile proportion, explained the beauty of the human face. In 1754 John Gilbert Cooper was still willing to regard symmetry and proportion as the bases of beauty, but he was sure that "the human form . . . may receive *additional* charms from education, and steal more subtly upon the soul of the beholder from some adventitious circumstances of easy attitudes or motion, and an undefinable sweetness of countenance, which an habitual commerce with the more refined part of mankind superadds to the work of nature." Armstrong was likewise certain that "air, meaning, and expression" were superior to regularity, while at the same time mediævalists like Mason were learning to admire Gothic precisely because

No modern art
Had marred with misplaced symmetry the pile.

The escape from regularity resulted in the picturesque movement in architecture which placed irregularity in the high place of worship. Reynolds, himself, hovered at times in the outer court of the new temple, but Uvedale Price was the high priest of the cult.[9]

Closely associated with proportion, regularity, and normality was the view that the beautiful was connected with fitness, with the perfect fulfilment of function. Burke stood almost alone in his categorical denial of any relation between beauty and function, for most critics believed that in the harmonious universe

the beauty of human bodies corresponds . . . with that economy of parts which constitutes them good; and, in every circumstance of life, the same object is constantly accounted both beautiful and good, inasmuch as it answers the purposes for which it was designed.

I have quoted from Xenophon, but Englishmen agreed that the average dimensions which were at the basis of geometrical beauty must be the dimensions which Nature—or the God of Nature—had designed to insure in each case the adequate fulfilment of some function. Quintilian wrote: "The athlete whose muscles have been formed by exercise is a joy to the eye, but he is also better fitted for the contests in which he must engage. In fact true beauty and usefulness always go hand in hand." Shaftesbury agreed with him:

. . . the proportionate and regular state is the truly *prosperous* and natural state in every subject. . . . Even in the imitative or *designing* arts . . . the *truth* or *beauty* of every figure or statue is measur'd from the perfection of nature, in her just adapting of every limb and proportion to the activity, strength, dexterity, life and vigor of the particular species or animal design'd.

Thus beauty and truth are plainly join'd with the notion of *utility* and *convenience*. . . .

Hume agreed with Shaftesbury, while Akenside became almost lyrical on the theme:

> Does beauty ever deign to dwell where health
> And active use are strangers? Is her charm
> Confess'd in aught, whose most peculiar ends
> Are lame and fruitless? . . .
> . . . The generous glebe
> Whose bosom smiles with verdure, the clear tract
> Of streams delicious to the thirsty soul,

The bloom of nectar'd fruitage ripe to sense,
And every charm of animated things,
Are only pledges of a state sincere,
The integrity and order of their frame,
When all is well within, and every end
Accomplish'd. . . .
. . . For Truth and Good are one,
And Beauty dwells in them, and they in her,
With like participation.

Hogarth was unwilling to accept any preconceived mathematical scale of proportions, but he demanded that forms—of furniture, of pillars, of arches—be so applied that they seem to fulfill specific functions. Hogarth believed that Englishmen, guided by "plain good sense," had carried simplicity, convenience, and neatness, "the necessary parts of beauty, to a great degree of perfection."

On this point John Gilbert Cooper was a complete classical conformist. For him truth, beauty, and utility were inseparable. The rural scene that pleased taste instantaneously was the scene that would reveal upon analysis its fitness to produce "the necessaries, the conveniences, and emoluments of life." In architecture likewise

. . . every rule, canon, and proportion in building did not arise from the capricious invention of man, but from the unerring dictates of nature, and . . . even what are now the ornamental parts of an edifice, originally were created by necessity. . . .

The good, the useful, and the beautiful were closely linked:

Whatever . . . is proportionable and harmonious, is good; everything that is so, is *natural;* we judge of *beauty* by *nature,* consequently *good* and *beauty* are the same. Thus we form our opinion of an image. Every limb and feature ought to agree with the whole in size, age, sex, etc., and this is called *symmetry;* this symmetry is most perfect when made for the use and strength of the species, and that produces beauty.[11]

Reynolds and Beattie must conclude this survey of the importance of fitness in the classical ideal of beauty. Reynolds believed that man's idea of beauty was determined by an observation of what was typical of a certain form and hence adequate for easy functioning in a well-designed universe. By experience a man could learn to distinguish between

accidental blemishes and excrescences which are continually varying the surface of Nature's works, and the invariable general form which nature most
frequently produces, and always seems to intend in her productions.

Every species of the animal as well as the vegetable creation may be
said to have a fixed or determinate form towards which nature is continually
inclining. . . .

Beattie declared a feature out of the proportion "which is most
common, and known to be most convenient, displeases, by suggesting
painful ideas of excess, or deficiency, disease, or imperfection."[12]

A derivative from the ideals of proportion and fitness was the
belief that the parts of a work of art should be subordinated to the
total effect. Excrescence and ornament, "purple patches" and disproportionate episodic excursions should be avoided. As Beattie
phrased it, "no part is in proportion if it detracts from the whole";
or as Pope:

> In wit, as nature, what affects our hearts
> Is not th' exactness of peculiar parts;
> 'Tis not a lip, or eye, we beauty call,
> But the joint force and full result of all.
> Thus when we view some well-proportioned dome,
> (The world's just wonder, and ev'n thine, O Rome!)
> No single parts unequally surprise,
> All comes united to th' admiring eyes;
> No monstrous height, or breadth, or length, appear;
> The whole at once is bold, and regular.

Addison was willing to sacrifice the beautiful autobiographical passages in *Paradise Lost* as "unjustifiable excrescences." Hume objected to Gothic because the "minute attention to the parts" destroyed the effect of the whole, and in this opinion he was the
spokesman for many of the anti-Mediævalists. Gerard warned the
readers of the *Essay on Taste* that

in composition the most refined reflections, the most elaborate descriptions,
the warmest pathos displease; if they break the unity, if they do not promote
. . . the main design, to which all the parts should be subordinate.

Lord Kames felt that man was "framed by nature to relish order
and connection," and that each work of art must "like an organic
system" have "its parts . . . orderly arranged and mutually con-

nected, bearing each of them a relation to the whole." Blair was at one with Kames, and both of them, of course, were agreeing with Aristotle.[13]

The respect for proportion generally implied a preference for line over color, and frequently a preference for the straight line over the curve, though on the latter question a considerable controversy developed in the field of landscape gardening. To classical artists like Poussin and to critics like Du Fresnoy in France, whose standard book was translated at an early date from Latin into English, drawing or design was the essence of painting, and color only an agreeable accessory, useful in filling space and clarifying lines. This was the opinion of Shaftesbury who thought that painting

borrows help indeed from colours, and uses them, as means, to execute its designs; it has nothing, however, more wide of its real aim, or more remote from its intention, than to make a *shew* of colours, or from their mixture, to raise a separate and flattering pleasure to the *sense*.

John Brown considered that "rich and luscious" coloring detracted from "truth, simplicity, and design" in decadent periods of art. Brown's opinion was repeated almost *verbatim* by Joseph Warton in *The World*.[14]

In the seventeenth century English gardening was dominated by Le Nôtre, and this French school of symmetry and regularity was supported by the Dutch school with its emphasis on straight lines and artifice. Englishmen like Evelyn admired the streets of Dutch cities, "so exactly straight, even, and uniform, that nothing can be more pleasant," or like Gray in the early part of his life esteemed "streets all laid out by the line" among the beauties of Turin. Others must have felt like Colman and Garrick, who represent their artistically inclined citizen in *The Clandestine Marriage* as proclaiming

Ay—here's none of your strait lines here—but all taste—zigzag—crinkum-crankum—in and out—right and left—to and again—twisting and turning like a worm;

or like William Chambers, the opponent of Langley and Kent in gardening, who believed that serpentine lines and "paths twining in regular esses" would lead the visitor to a manor to curse "the line of beauty." "The line of beauty" and "the line of grace" were discovered by Hogarth to be almost the sole explanations of beauty in figure or motion, but before 1753 Kent had proclaimed that Nature abhorred a straight line. On the foundations laid by Kent and Hogarth landscape architect and critic were to erect an æsthetics based on the "natural" curve in opposition to the earlier preference for formal straight lines.[15]

Emphasis on proportion and design suggests another element in beauty—clarity. The ideal in style is to present the idea as nakedly and distinctly as possible, illuminated by a strong and pure intellectual light, in contrast to the romantic tendency to evoke auxiliary images and to transform the idea by subjecting it to the roseate glow of the imagination. In the plastic arts outlines must be clear, and the atmospheric colors, blue and green, must be avoided. Daylight was preferred to moonlight, a transparent atmosphere to one of mist and cloud. Chiaroscuro was a forerunner of the new romantic art which strove to suggest the inexpressible, and chose as its vehicles not prose, sculpture, and architecture, but poetry with its evocative figures and rhythms, painting with its soft harmonies of colors, and music which lies nearest to the mystery of emotions too deep for words. This desire for clarity of artistic intention in literature, of outline in painting, and of design in architecture paralleled the demand for precision and perspicuity in prose style, and was equally a product of the rational spirit of the Enlightenment.[16]

Poise and repose, a serenity that imparts a feeling of acquiescence and relief to the spectator, were demanded of beauty by the classical critic. Art should not raise vague, unrealizable longings, or evoke from the depths of the individual consciousness desires that had rested quiescent until their profundities were plumbed by the disturbing intensity of an emotional masterpiece. The function of art was catharsis, its final effect tranquillity, its message one of stability, of calm certainty in the enduring value of ideals and institutions, and of the permanent worth of humanity.

In the art of the eighteenth century objectivity, respect for common sense, and attention to the universal rather than to the particular aided the attainment of tranquillity. All intense expression of emotion was considered ugly. Restraint contributed to allurement. Beauty, according to Beattie, composed, while sublimity elevated the soul.

Blair made the same distinction: beauty produced an "agreeable serenity." Even Coleridge and Wordsworth preserved a regard for calmness, for self-possession, and for the veil that reflection threw between excitement and the artistic expression of emotion as it was "recollected in tranquillity." Eighteenth-century music and architecture preserved the same ideal. J. W. Draper's brief analysis of music can scarcely be improved:

> In music, symmetry was particularly apparent, not only on a minute scale in the repetitions in musical phrasing but on a larger scale in the *da capo* form of songs and arias and in the balancing themes at the opening and close of sonatas and of the first movements of symphonies. It was an "absolute" music, a music that calmed and satisfied, like the gardening of the age, with perfection of design—an arabesque of harmonies rather than a programatic representation of natural sounds or a dissonant stimulus to the emotions. It was chamber-music for the drawing room, a sort of entr'acte in polite conversation, symmetrical in form, unemotional in quality and . . . conceived as an adjunct to social intercourse.

Classical architecture was designed to give the same simplicity and repose. A building like a poem was composed of classical elements "adapted to social need, and, in its preference for horizontal and vertical lines [was] designed æsthetically to allay the emotions— for the rousing of emotion is not calculated to maintain the social *status quo*." As the years of the eighteenth century passed quietness and dignity were lost in the incipient romanticism of Piranesi, who sought to develop "soaring, irregular masses, crumbling surfaces, masses of shadow, and prodigious movement." This attempt to reproduce in architectural masses the effects of "hill and dale, foreground and distance, swelling and sinking" was a sign of the approaching victory of the picturesque, and with that victory the death of a genuinely classical architecture.[17]

Restraint in the artist corresponded to tranquillity in the effect of art. "If you mean to preserve the most perfect beauty *in its most perfect state*," Sir Joshua Reynolds wrote, "you cannot express the passions, all of which produce distortion and deformity, more or less, in the most beautiful faces." Certainly one could not express one's own intimate passions in an age during which all passion was frowned upon from the high places of authority. The quality of ideal art was the quality of social life, for here also passion and emotional display were regarded askance. Emotions were, as Herbert Read has recently expressed it, "individual, disparate, and must be disciplined in a social community." The moralists early inveighed against passion. Charron's *Of Wisdom* and Senault's *Use of the Passions*, both popular in seventeenth-century England, taught control of passion by reason. Locke considered that

the great principle and foundation of all virtue and worth is plac'd in this: that a man is able to *deny himself* his own desires, cross his own inclinations, and purely follow what reason directs as best, tho' the appetite lean the other way.

Swift believed that passion relaxed the sinews of the mind. Shaftesbury considered passion "the only poison to reason." *The Tatler*, No. 176, proclaimed self-control and equanimity "the greatest of human perfections." *The Spectator*, No. 408, declared the passions designed for subjection. Fielding, Young, Thomson, and Johnson all praise

the virtuous man
Who keeps his temper'd mind serene and pure,
And every passion aptly harmoniz'd
Amid a jarring world with vice inflam'd.

Richardson was a conservative moralist and wished sexual desire in particular to be controlled. *The World* followed *The Tatler* and *The Spectator* in proclaiming turbulent passions "the greatest enemies to happiness." Boswell wrote an essay *On Reserve* advocating discipline as a road to a human perfection that Boswell himself could not obtain. Cowper approved men whom reason led to virtue, so

That no restraint can circumscribe them more
Than they themselves by choice, for wisdom's sake;

while Burke considered that nine out of ten virtues were virtues of restraint.[18]

The well-known hostility to boisterous laughter is another aspect of this restraint. Aristotle, Plato, *Ecclesiastes*, and the "conduct books" could be quoted in opposition to loud laughter, which was considered ungentlemanly and æsthetically ugly. In 1694 Congreve ridiculed his Lord Froth for thinking laughter unbecoming a man of quality, but the ridicule would have had no comic force unless there was clearly a fashionable sentiment against laughter. *The Tatler* objected to boisterous mirth and to convulsive fits of laughter. Shaftesbury admitted the utility of laughter as a means of social pressure, but believed that the man of perfect self-command would eliminate it, as inhumane, indecorous, and "abhorrent (in every kind) to the τὸ καλόν." Addison considered *excess* of laughter as a mark of folly. *The Guardian* could approve only a smile or "a faint constrained kind of half-laugh." Neither Swift nor Pope laughed, and Lord Chesterfield's advice to his son is the *locus classicus* on the subject:

> Having mentioned laughing, I must particularly warn you against it: and I could heartily wish, that you may often be seen to smile, but never heard to laugh while you live. . . . Loud laughter is the mirth of the mob, who are only pleased with silly things; for true wit or good sense never excited a laugh, since the creation of the world.

Young could not bring himself to regard laughter as a sin, but was compelled to brand it as "half-immoral" as a vent for the spleen and a dissipation of thought. Boswell found that his hero Paoli did not laugh, and was led to reflection on the matter:

> Whether loud laughter in general society be a sign of weakness or rusticity, I cannot say, but I have remarked that real great men, and men of finished behaviour, seldom fall into it.

The Connoisseur, No. 14, and *The Mirror*, No. 12, favored laughter, as did the group recorded by Hannah More who "stood round . . . laughing in defiance of every rule of decorum and Chesterfield" at the humorous sallies of David Garrick and Doctor Johnson.[19]

Restraint, however, was the rule for the gentleman in his daily conduct. Clearly no richly emotional or distinctly personal art could be produced, until the movement of sensibility transformed the fashionable ideal, and substituted feeling for common sense as a basis for the good life. Steele was the father of this movement of emotional revolt. A distinctly emotional man himself, he sought to justify tears as compatible with decency and to overthrow insensibility as a correct social pose. In the famous Preface to *The*

Conscious Lovers he proclaimed an aptness "to give way to the impressions of humanity" as "the excellence of a right disposition and the natural working of a well-turned spirit." To Steele, to Broome, and to Richardson tears were quite compatible with reason and good sense.[20]

In literature the influence of Longinus was brought to bear against the ideal of restraint. For him ecstasy was the goal of the writer, a state of transport which, as Sir William Temple pointed out in 1690, could be effected only by raising the passions. It is curious to hear the polished man of the world venting such an opinion. It is curious, too, to hear the reasonable Addison inveigh against the "insipid serenity" of English oratory. Dennis, as a confessed disciple of Longinus, was eager to identify poetry with the excitation of passion as a means of instructing and reforming the reason which could not be influenced by passionless philosophy. Pope was not unaffected by the emotional theory of art:

> To know the poet from the man of rhymes:
> 'Tis he who gives my breast a thousand pains,
> Can make me feel each passion that he feigns;
> Enrage, compose, with more than magic art,
> With pity, and with terror, seize my heart;
> And snatch me, o'er the earth, or through the air,
> To Thebes, to Athens, when he will, and where.

As time passed the tranquil spirit of classical art was assailed by the primitivist, by the man of sensibility, and by the enthusiasts for Spenser, Shakespeare, and Milton, who displayed, according to Joseph Warton, "the sublime and the pathetic . . ., the two chief nerves of all genuine poetry." Imagination and genius were soon identified by their votaries with deep emotionality. Again it is Joseph Warton who gives the key to the new attitude: "If the imagination is lively, the passions will be strong. True genius seldom resides in a cold and phlegmatic constitution. The same temperament and sensibility that make a poet or a painter, will be apt to make a lover and a debauchee." Even Doctor Johnson came to believe that Addison had too little "ardour, vehemence, or transport"; he knew that to make men weep the poet must weep himself. A quotation from Blair will show the final victory of the passions in academic criticism:

A writer of genius conceives his subject strongly; his imagination is filled and impressed with it; and pours itself forth in that figurative language which imagination naturally speaks. He puts on no emotion which the subject does not raise in him; he speaks as he feels but his style will be beautiful, because his feelings are lively.

Passion, when in such a degree as to rouse and kindle the mind, without throwing it out of the possession of itself, is universally found to exalt all human powers. It renders the mind infinitely more enlightened, more penetrating, more vigorous and masterly, than it is in its calm moments. A man, actuated by a strong passion, becomes much greater than he is at other times. He utters greater sentiments, conceives higher designs, and executes them with a boldness and a felicity, of which, on other occasions, he could not think himself capable. . . . Almost every man, in passion, is eloquent.[21]

Blair's *Rhetoric* appeared in 1783. Classicism was dying. Burns and Blake were on the horizon. The Medieval Revival was in full swing. Sensibility was the fashion, for even the last proponents of the life of reason in the circle of Doctor Johnson were by no means free from it. Imagination, genius, and primitivism were the slogans of the hour. Laurence Sterne had already plunged across the English literary heavens with meteoric suddenness. A generation had wept for Clarissa and for George Barnwell. Taste had become a personal matter, and the Rules were regarded as the lumber of pedantry. The attempt to impose a conscious artistic ideal in England had failed for numerous reasons: (1) the masterpieces of Elizabethan romanticism had been too great to be forgotten, and so long as men read them it was impossible to impose on the public an æsthetic ideal to which the Elizabethan did not conform; (2) the attempt to impose a universal standard of taste had broken itself against English individualism and had been met by an unquenchable liking for novelty which opposed the *Bible* and the *Arabian Nights*, the strange beauty of Celtic and Norse myth, and the color and charm of Mediæval romance to the majestic calm of Virgil and Sophocles; (3) the proponents of the classical ideal had been too willing to admit the *je ne sais quoi* in beauty, the grace beyond the reach of art; and as they were consequently unable to insist on absolute conformity, they suffered the fate of all tolerant groups who are attacked by enthusiasts and dogmatists; (4) the cult of the sublime had entered early into competition with the cult of beauty, and led to the rebirth of feelings of awe, fear, and wonder incompatible with the conception of a tidily harmonious universe which men could understand and control. These attitudes were a part of the classical view of life in England. No picture of classicism is complete without a distinct realization of the degree to which they modified the opinions of the masters of the period, and yet each was a disruptive force tending to tear asunder a never-too-securely-founded rationalism in life and art. These forces must next be examined.

NOTES TO CHAPTER XIII

1. Francis Hutcheson, *Inquiry*, pp. 17, 25, 31 ff., 38, 44, 263; J. G. Robertson, *Studies in the Genesis of Romantic Theory in the Eighteenth Century*, p. 203.

2. Gerard, *Essay on Taste*, pp. 31–40.

3. Kames, *Elements*, I, 159–161, 206, II, 5, 356, 370.

4. Blair, *Rhetoric*, I, 53, 98–101, 104–106.

5. Burke, *Works*, I, 165.

6. Alison, *Essays on Taste*, pp. 23, 25, 27–28, 30, 51, 61, 76, 90–91, 255–279, 328, 448–455.

7. Chambers, *History of Taste*, pp. 64–70, 74–75, 90, 93, 129; Spengler, *Decline of the West*, I, 177.

8. Hume, *Treatise*, p. 483; Kames, *Elements*, I, 90; Congreve, *Complete Works*, IV, 85; Vanbrugh, *Works*, IV, 15; Steele, *Spectator*, No. 104; Evelyn, *Diary*, p. 53; Shaftesbury, *Philosophical Regimen*, p. 246; Pope, *Works*, IX, 408; Lady Mary Wortley Montagu, *Letters*, I, 272; Smollett, *Humphrey Clinker*, p. 217; Johnson, *Rambler*, Nos. 139, 158; Goldsmith, *Works*, ed. Gibbs, IV, 319, V, 154.

9. William Hogarth, *The Analysis of Beauty*, Pittsfield (Mass.), 1909, pp. 31–33; Hawkesworth, *Adventurer*, No. 82; Cooper, *Letters Concerning Taste*, pp. 9–11; Armstrong, *Miscellanies*, II, 176; Mason, quoted by Lovejoy, "The First Gothic Revival and the Return to Nature," *Modern Language Notes*, XLVII, 440; Hussey, *The Picturesque*, pp. 187, 192.

10. Burke, *Works*, I, 152; Xenophon, *Memorabilia*, III, 8; Quintilian, *Institutes of Oratory*, VIII, iii, 11; Shaftesbury, *Charactertisticks*, III, 180 ff.; Hume, *Treatise*, pp. 299, 576, and *Essays*, II, 177; Akenside, *Pleasures of the Imagination*, Book I, lines 350–353, 364–372, 374–376; Hogarth, *Analysis*, pp. 23, 90, 131–132, 138.

11. Cooper, *Letters Concerning Taste*, pp. 3–5, 8, and *Essays on the Characteristicks*, pp. 161–164.

12. Reynolds, *Idler*, No. 82, and *Letters*, ed. F. W. Hilles, Cambridge, 1929, pp. 90–93; Beattie, *Dissertations*, I, 165. On the idea of fitness compare Browne, *Religio Medici*, in *Works*, II, 342; Joseph Warton, *Essay on Pope*, I, 351–352; Alison, *Essay on Taste*, pp. 284–287, 393; Eckermann, *Gespräche mit Goethe*, pp. 213, 264, 491–492.

13. Beattie, *Dissertations*, I, 139; Pope, *Essay on Criticism*, lines 243–252; Addison, *Spectator*, No. 315; Hume, *Essays*, I, 241; Kames, *Elements*, I, 30–32; Blair, *Rhetoric*, I, 106; Shaftesbury, *Characteristicks*, I, 143, III, 259, note; Lessing, *Werke*, IV, 246–247, V, 15.

14. Chambers, *History of Taste*, pp. 90, 93–95; Shaftesbury, *Characteristicks*, III, 390–391; John Brown, *Essays*, p. 388; Joseph Warton, *World*, No. 26; *Adventurer*, No. 127.

15. Evelyn, *Diary*, p. 16; Gray, *Letters*, I, 43, 48; Colman and Garrick, *The Clandestine Marriage*, Act II, scene II; Manwaring, *op. cit.*, pp. 124–127, 148–149; Hogarth, *Analysis*, pp. 50 ff.; Hussey, *The Picturesque*, pp. 58, 137; Kames, *Elements*, I, 202; J. and A. L. Aikin, *Miscellaneous Pieces in Prose*, p. 84; Beattie, *Dissertations*, I, 141; Alison, *Essay on Taste*, pp. 212, 221, 202.

16. Sir Sidney Colvin, quoted by Beers, *A History of English Romanticism in the Eighteenth Century*, New York, 1926, p. 17; Spengler, *Decline of the West*, I, 243, 245, 253; Aristotle, *Rhetoric*, III. ii. 1; III. v. 6; Hume, *Letters*, I, 50; Chesterfield, *Letters*, II, 30; Goldsmith, *Works*, ed. Gibbs, IV, 243–244; Armstrong, *Miscellanies*, II, 133, 251–252; Campbell, *Philosophy of Rhetoric*, pp. 274–275, 309; Joseph Warton, *Essay on Pope*, II, 160–162; Blair, *Rhetoric*, I, 218–220; Burke, *Works*, I, 111, 114, 130.

17. A. O. Lovejoy, "Schiller and the Genesis of Romanticism," *loc. cit.*, pp. 2–3; Joseph Spence, *Crito*; Beattie, *Dissertations*, I, 140; Coleridge, *Biographia Literaria*, p. 22; O. J. Campbell and Paul Mueschke, "Wordsworth's Æsthetic Development, 1795–1802," *University of Michigan Studies in Language and Literature*, Ann Arbor, 1933, X, 43; Lewis, *Time and Western Man*, p. 34; J. W. Draper, "The Rise of English Neo-classicism," *Revue Anglo-Américaine*, Juin, 1933, p. 401; Hussey, *The Picturesque*, pp. 188–190; *Deutsche Literatur. Reihe Irrationalismus*, II, 341; Draper, *op. cit.*, p. 400.

18. Reynolds, *Discourses*, p. 59; Herbert Read, *Reason and Romanticism*, p. 15; George Williamson, "The Restoration Revolt Against Enthusiasm," *Studies in Philology*, XXX, 589; Locke, *Some Thoughts Concerning Education*, p. 28; Swift, *Gulliver*, p. 540; Shaftesbury, *Characteristicks*, I, 91, and *Philosophical Regimen*, pp. 87–88, 144–145; Fielding, *Champion*, Feb. 2, 1740; Young, *Poetical Works*, I, 251; Boswell, *Life of Johnson*, III, 62; Thomson, in Chalmers, *op. cit.*, XII, 425; Brown, *Essays*, p. 104; Richardson, *Writings*, XX, 226; *World*, No. 95; *Mirror*, No. 15; Boswell, *Hypochondriack*, I, 284–285, and *Letters*, p. 46; Cowper, *Task*, II, lines 792–793; Burke, *Selected Letters*, pp. 303–304.

19. V. B. Haltzel, "Chesterfield and the Anti-laughter Tradition," *Modern Philology*, XXVI, 73–90; Congreve, *The Double Dealer*, Act I, Scene II; *Tatler*, Nos. 45, 63; Shaftesbury, *Philosophical Regimen*, pp. 152–153, 225–226; Addison, *Spectator*, No. 598; *Guardian*, No. 29; Boswell, *Life of Johnson*, II, 434, note 1; Chesterfield, *Letters*, I, 212–213, 285; Young, *Poetical Works*, I, 237; Boswell, *Account of Corsica*, p. 223; Hannah More, *Letters*, p. 31.

20. Steele, *Spectator*, No. 520; Broome, in Pope, *Works*, VIII, 63; Richardson, *Writings*, IX, 53.

21. Sir William Temple, in Spingarn, *Critical Essays*, III, 85; Addison, *Spectator*, No. 407; Dennis, in Durham, *op. cit.*, pp. 146, 148–149, 151–152, 196; Pope, *Works*, III, 369; A. D. McKillop, "A Critic of 1741 on Early Poetry," *Studies in Philology*, XXX, 510–511; Joseph Warton, *Essay on Pope*, I, vi–vii, 102, 136, 317; Johnson, *Lives of the Poets*, ed. Waugh, III, 151, I, 48; Blair, *Rhetoric*, II, 3, 172.

BOOK THREE

SEEDS OF REVOLT

CHAPTER XIV

THE SURVIVAL OF ELIZABETHAN
ROMANTICISM

I

THE RESTORATION and eighteenth century were never completely out of touch with the glorious heritage of Elizabethan literature. Admiration for Shakespeare and Milton, and to a lesser degree for Spenser, meets one on every hand—in Dryden, in Edward Phillips, in Mulgrave, in Langbaine, in Dennis, in Addison, and after Addison in almost every poet and critic of the century. This admiration could not be stilled by an invidious comparison with the Ancients. Instinctive liking was stronger than Reason and the Rules, for the Rules were accepted uneasily or else variously modified when it was discovered that the choice lay between Aristotle, Horace, and the French critics on the one hand, and England's own literary heritage on the other. So long as men read and esteemed Shakespeare and Spenser no imported literary code could weigh too heavily upon the creative spirits of Englishmen.[1]

The editions of the Elizabethans bear witness to the steady interest of the Age of Reason. More than a hundred editions of *Paradise Lost* were required, approximately fifty of Shakespeare and ten of Spenser. Even Massinger came alive in three editions, and Dodsley esteemed it a profitable venture to publish an edition of old plays in twelve volumes. The miscellanies give the same impression. The Dryden-Tonson *Miscellany* (1716 edition) contained many Elizabethan and early seventeenth-century poems by Milton, Suckling, Marvell, Cowley, Jonson, Donne, Drayton, and Carew, an indication that the editors thought that general interest on the part of the public justified their inclusion. Pope's favorite English poets were Chaucer, Spenser, Shakespeare, Milton, and Dryden, and only the last was "intimately connected with eighteenth-century ideals of correctness and regularity." Pope's knowledge of even the lesser Renaissance poets was "far from superficial." Temple considered Sidney the "greatest poet and noblest genius" of modern times. Armstrong ranked Spenser, Shakespeare, and Milton above Pope, and so, of course, did Joseph Warton. By the mid-century the supremacy of the Elizabethans was no longer an unorthodox idea. Hurd admired their pictorial imagination, and their "pure, strong, and perspicuous" diction with its high imaginative quality that had not yet been controlled by the "prosaic genius of philosophy and logic." Thomas Warton spoke of the Elizabethan period as of a Golden Age, "the most *poetical*" in English literature. It was a

period, propitious to the operation of original and true poetry, when the coyness of fancy was not always proof against the approaches of reason, when genius was rather directed than governed by judgment, and when taste and learning had so far disciplined imagination, as to suffer its excesses to pass without censure or control, for the sake of the beauties to which they were allied.[2]

Among the Elizabethans it was Milton, the last and the least romantic, who became the most popular writer of the eighteenth century. Raymond D. Havens has brilliantly described his influence:

His life and his works furnished reading and topics of discussion as inexhaustible and as unescapable as the weather. In truth, a contemporary of Johnson or Cowper would have found it exceedingly difficult to avoid the poet whom he is charged with slighting. If he went to the theatre, he was likely to witness a production of *Comus*, or at least to pass a "busto" of the god in the lobby, and he might hear Sheridan recite from *Paradise Lost*; if he preferred music, there were several popular oratorios drawn from Milton's poems; if he fled to the "movies" of the day, Pandemonium confronted him; if he chose to wander through Vauxhall, he passed under the "temple of Comus" and encountered a statue of the blind bard as Il Penseroso. He went to church only to hear the religious epic quoted, and returned to find his children committing passages of it to memory. His son had probably caught the Miltonic madness at college; at any rate, the "Pietas et Gratulatio" volume, which the fond parent preserved in full leather binding because of his offspring's academic verses, contained little English poetry that was not Miltonic. If his friends were clergymen or lawyers, they were likely to be literary and have ideas on blank verse or be writing letters to *The Gentleman's Magazine* on *Paradise Lost*; if they were ardent republicans, they made him listen to passages from the *Areopagitica*, if dilettantes they spouted *Allegro*. If he picked up a magazine, Miltonic blank verse stared him in the face, and he would turn the page only to encounter Miltonic sonnets and octosyllabics or an essay on the indebtedness of *Paradise Lost* to the *Iliad*; the letters to the editor were likely to deal with some Miltonic controversy then raging, and the reviews discussed poems "in imitation of Milton" and editions of the poet's works. If he turned to books it was no better, even though he chose his reading carefully; for poetry, essays, biographies, volumes of letters, works on theology, language or literature, were sure to quote, imitate, or discuss "the greatest writer the world has ever seen."

If he fled London for Edinburgh, he ran into a "nest of ninnies" on the subject of Milton among both poets and critics; if he turned to Bath, there was Lady Miller's coterie prattling phrases from the minor poems, if to Lichfield, he encountered its famous Swan

> Between her white wings mantling proudly

and rowing her state with Miltonic feet. In remote Devonshire and Cornwall there were Richard Polwhele and his group of sonneteers and scribblers of blank verse, while in remoter Wales lurked Milton's follower John Dyer. No village was free from the contagion; and if he sought peace in the country, he came upon Il Penseroso alcoves, upon travellers reading *Paradise Lost* by the roadside, ploughboys with copies of it in their pockets, and shepherds, real shepherds, "poring upon it in the fields." Even among the poor and the uneducated it was the same: not only ploughboys and shepherds, but threshers, cotters, cobblers, and milkwomen read and imitated the poet who expected his audience to be "few."[8]

No one has ever dominated English literature more completely than Milton. In addition to the hundred editions of *Paradise Lost*, the century demanded more than seventy editions of the complete poems, fifty-seven editions of *Paradise Regained*, sixty-two of *Samson*, seventy-seven of *Comus*, and sixty of *Lycidas*. *L'Allegro* and *Il Penseroso* appeared 130 times between 1640 and 1801. This popularity was not limited to the Dissenting reading public. Addison took pains to extend it; Pope borrowed from Milton 190 times; the scholar made him the subject of investigation. *Paradise Lost* was the first English poem to be published in a critical edition, the first to have a variorum edition, and the first to be the subject of a separate critical study. As was the case with Shakespeare, esteem bordered on reverence. Idolaters like Cowper "danced for joy" over the discovery of *Paradise Lost,* which by others was ranked with or above the *Iliad* and the *Æneid* as "the best poem in the world," "the greatest poem ever written by man."[4]

The influence of Milton was not always antagonistic to classicism. *Paradise Lost* was an imitative epic, a product of the controversy in late Renaissance criticism concerning the classical and Christian epic as literary "kinds." Milton himself was a devoted student of the classics. His blank verse was classical in origin. His diction was formed on Latin models by classical rules. His *Samson* was the one superb example of a completely Aristotelian tragedy. These classical traits and predilections made acceptance of his greatness comparatively easy, though it was soon discovered how his verse and diction could be turned into engines of the reaction against the heroic couplet and the diction of Pope. There were, furthermore, less classical aspects of Milton which loomed larger and larger in popular consciousness as the minor poems began to rival the major works in popularity. Then it was found that Milton contained elements of religious mysticism, traces of pensive melancholy, rich concreteness in description, a mastery of varied metrical forms, a lovely lyric quality, an imaginative power refreshing to an age of wit and reason, and, finally, "the color, music, fragrance, and freedom which spell Romanticism." To quote again from Havens, who is the constant guide for the study of Milton in the eighteenth century, these Romantic qualities were accepted by readers because they were found in combination with "the exquisite finish, the restraint, the reserve, and the impersonality to which they were accustomed." Milton "possessed for them the fascination of the strange without the shock of the inelegant, the thrill of adventure without its dangers and discomforts."[5]

An important aspect of the Miltonic influence during the eighteenth century was the weight that his influence lent to the vast output of blank verse during the period, much of which was written in deliberate opposition to the closed couplet developed by Jonson, Waller, Denham, Dryden, and Pope to the point at which it was the perfect vehicle for the well-turned wit of the classical satirist and didactic poet. Balance, antithesis, medial cæsura, the arrangement of the satiric thrust on sharply stressed syllables, and the effort to complete the thought within the couplet marked with Pope the completion of a century of evolution of the verse form that has been with some justice indissolubly connected with the classical spirit in poetry. Apparently the influence of Ben Jonson and of Boileau ensured the supremacy of the closed pentameter couplet. For serious verse it had no rival for fifty years, and with its more lightly tripping companion, the Hudibrastic tetrameter couplet with doggerel rime, it occupied the attention of occasional poets, moralists, and satirists grim and gay until Miltonic blank verse shook its supremacy.[6]

Successive editions of the Dryden-Tonson *Miscellanies* show that inroads were being made on the vogue of the couplet. In the last three volumes of the mid-century *Miscellany* by Dodsley only 25 per cent of the verses are in couplet form. The rigid regularity, which frowned upon triplets, Alexandrines, and feminine rimes, of the heroic couplet led to monotony at last, though the imperative necessities of the form did save much of it from the complete inanity and verbosity of the minor blank verse.[7]

Though Milton must bear the responsibility for much of this contemptible verse, there is another side to the question. Freedom and flexibility were greatly needed. Blank verse could be justified on classical grounds as the only adequate parallel for the unrimed measures of antiquity, and might be turned against the couplet as a weapon to secure the freedom for which all but the strictest classicists yearned. Regarded in this light blank verse was a mark of a wide-spread revolt in which almost every poet of the century had his hand. Before 1750 there were 350 blank-verse poems and the output was doubled in the next half century. It was the vehicle for many once popular poems—*The Seasons, Night Thoughts, The Grave, The Pleasures of the Imagination,* and *The Task.* The name of Milton occurred in most of the critical defenses of blank verse; and though not all eighteenth-century blank verse was Miltonic, even in non-dramatic poetry, many of the hundreds of blank verse productions were Miltonic imitations or bore unmistakable stylistic signs of Miltonic influence.[8]

In the Preface to *Paradise Lost* Milton defended his choice of measure on purely classical grounds:

The measure is *English* heroic verse without rime, as that of *Homer* in *Greek,* and of *Virgil* in *Latin,*—rime being no necessary adjunct or true ornament of poem or good verse, in longer works especially, but the invention of a barbarous age, to set off wretched matter and lame meter. . . .

In so writing Milton aligned himself with the more classically minded among earlier critics, who opposed rime as Gothic. The greater freedom of the poet, and the precedent of antiquity continued to be the dominant notes in the arguments of the post-Miltonic supporters of blank verse—Edward Phillips, Roscommon, Edmund Smith, Shaftesbury, Henry Felton, and Blackmore, who all, great and small, pointed likewise to the illustrious example of Milton himself. Dryden abandoned couplets in drama during the course of the controversy and proclaimed that "he who can write well in rime may write better in blank verse" for "rime is certainly a constraint even to the best of poets."[9]

Little in the way of argument was added by later critics to the remarks of Milton and Dryden, but some indication must be cited of the extensive support given by critics to the freer form. In 1716 Atterbury urged Pope to abandon rime for blank verse. Joseph Warton found rime "a circumstance sufficient of itself alone to overwhelm and extinguish all enthusiasm, and produce endless tautologies and circumlocutions." To Young rime was a "Gothic demon . . . how unlike the deathless, divine harmony of three great names (how justly joined!) of Milton, Greece, and Rome." Daniel Webb and Mrs. Montagu were enthusiasts for blank verse. Lord Kames preferred blank verse because of the use of melodic units greater than the couplet, the additional freedom allowed to the imagination, the more easily varied pauses, and the absence of the childish jingle of the riming words. Blair chose Pope's *Homer* as an illustration of the difficulty of reaching the simplicity essential to true sublimity in the rimed couplet with its "constrained elegance," smoothness of riming sound, and tendency to demand superfluous words to complete the sense.[10]

These arguments did not silence the devotees of the couplet entirely. To Aaron Hill the yoke of riming was "beautifully necessary" as an artistic check on "luxuriant wantonness." To Johnson it seemed that the freedom of blank verse produced more loquacity than sublimity. To Goldsmith only the greatest sublimity of subject matter could make blank verse acceptable. It is interesting to note that Goldsmith explained the vogue of blank verse by "a desire of grafting the spirit of the ancient languages upon the English"—a neo-classic, not a Romantic phenomenon.[11]

The opposition of such men as Johnson and Goldsmith neither checked the production of blank verse, nor lessened the number of direct Miltonic imitations—another sign of Milton's influence. The first significant imitator of Milton was John Phillips, who in *The Splendid Shilling* displayed numerous Miltonic characteristics— elision, absence of extra syllables, absence of trisyllabic feet, run-on lines, and the use of the verse paragraph. Addison, Gay, Fenton, and Armstrong toyed with the Miltonic style before Thomson published *Winter* in 1726, the most important landmark in the history of blank verse in the eighteenth century.[12]

After the appearance of *Winter* the influence of Phillips, Thomson, and Milton is more difficult to untangle. A poem such as Mallet's *Excursion* (1728) may be quite Miltonic in diction and prosody, and yet be an obvious imitation of *The Seasons*. In another such as Somerville's *The Chace* the presence of all three of the popular masters of blank verse may be felt. Young's *Night Thoughts* contains much that is Miltonic, but it illustrates, as does Blair's *Grave*, the incorporation of a Shakespearean influence into the blank verse tradition, and itself became a powerful force for the continuation of the tradition since its popularity rivalled that of *The Seasons* and of *Paradise Lost*.[13]

Miltonic diction also had its vogue. Generally, the direct imitation of Milton meant imitation of both prosody and diction, but many of the blank verse poems were not characterized by distinctive marks of the Miltonic manner, and approval of blank verse did not always imply approval of the peculiarities of Milton's diction. As the field of eighteenth-century diction came to be divided rather equally between the followers of Milton and of Pope it is necessary to note the principal features of Miltonic diction—inverted word order, the use of adjective or adverb for the noun, unusual compounds, apposition, parenthesis, elision, latinity, enumeration of proper names, participial constructions, and archaisms. These characteristics were felt to be suitable to "the venerable antiquity and sublime grandeur" of the subject, but even Milton's admirers were unable to refrain from using his mannerisms occasionally in mock-heroic vein. Witness *The Splendid Shilling* of John Phillips:

> My galligaskins that have long withstood
> The winter's fury, and encroaching frosts,
> By time subdued, (what will not time subdue!)
> A horrid chasm disclose, with orifice
> Wide, discontinuous, at which the winds
> *Eurus* and *Auster*, and the dreadful force
> Of *Boreas*, that congeals the Cronian waves,
> Tumultuous enter with dire chilling blasts,
> Portending agues.

There was always an element of opposition to the diction of Milton. From Welsted, who found Milton's phraseology "an uncouth, unnatural jargon, . . . a second Babel, or confusion of all languages," to Goldsmith, who lamented the misguided attempts of poets since Pope and Parnell to restore English verse style to its "pristine barbarity" in the vain imagination that "the more their writings are unlike prose, the more they resemble poetry," the adherents of correctness as conformity with polite usage resisted the Miltonic invasion.[14]

Milton's influence was important also in the sonnet revival, another minor note of rebellion against the more rigid forms of classicism. The sonnet is by no means alien to the classical ideal in the control that it imposes on emotion by the rigidity of its form, but during the eighteenth century it was for a time used as a vehicle of opposition to the dominance of the couplet by writers who wished to express the melancholy, the love of Nature, and the praise of gentle love which were born of the far more significant revolt of sensibility against the rule of reason. The several thousand sonnets written between 1740 and 1800 by Thomas Edwards, Benjamin Stillingfleet, Thomas Warton, and William Mason and their peers are of slight artistic merit, though of considerable historical significance.[15]

The influence of Milton's minor poems was scarcely less profound than that of *Paradise Lost*. Professor Sherburn has shown that they were mentioned or imitated by about fifty poets before 1740. Dryden, indeed, stood almost alone in his scornful attitude. After 1740 their popularity was even more extensive, and with the group composed of Collins, Gray, Mason, and the two Wartons they were perhaps the most significant formative influence. In the work of these men Miltonic echoes occur in almost every stanza. It was the mood of pensive melancholy, however, in which Milton's influence was most important, for he ignored the customary connections of melancholy with disease, madness, and fear, and established "a new set of connotations, with saintliness, with wisdom, with beauty, with leisure, with poetry, philosophy, and music, with lovely outdoor scenes, and with a widening experience maturing with age" which gave most of their romantic charm to the odes of the group. A comparison of *Il Penseroso* with the work of Thomas Warton, who described in *The Pleasures of Melancholy* the solemn glooms, and twilight cells

> Where thoughtful melancholy loves to muse,

would immediately reveal the significance of the minor poems of Milton for the minor players on the melancholy lyre in the mid-eighteenth century. Solitude, the pensive joys, the religious music in dim cathedrals, the moon, the ivy, and the owl were all a part of that "machinery" used by the lovers of gentle melancholy to evoke the atmosphere which they found propitious to love, to religion, and to art.[16]

II

The importance of the Spenserian stanza like that of the Miltonic sonnet has been grossly overestimated as a sign of Romantic revolt. The significance of Spenser lay far more in the stimulus he gave to the imaginative conception of poetry, to the Mediæval revival, and to a richer, more sensuous diction. Spenser and Pope, as William Lyon Phelps long ago pointed out, "stand exactly in opposition; the latter all intellect, didactic and satirical; the poet of town life and of fashionable society; the former all imagination and exaggeration; the poet of dreamland, of woods and streams, of fairy and supernatural life." It is not surprising then to find that with some significant exceptions Spenser was rejected by the Augustans, who could perceive his didactic significance, but not his pictorial beauty. The imitations of Spenser in satiric vein or with humorous intent were not pre-Romantic, though they did indicate acquaintance with his works. Testimony that he was not ignored comes from other sources as well. Pope made Spenser an early favorite and continued to admire him to the end. Dennis considered Spenser a powerful genius. Prior praised him, though he made alterations in the Spenserian stanza. Hughes edited and extolled him in 1715. A new edition of the *Works* in 1750 was followed by three editions of the *Faery Queene* within the decade, and by new editions of the *Works* in 1778, 1782, and 1793.[17]

In Jacob's *Historical Account of the Lives and Writings of Our Most Considerable Poets* Spenser was given twice as much space as Dryden and spoken of as "a genius beyond any that have writ since Virgil." In Theophilus Cibber's *Account of the Lives of the Poets* (1753) Spenser was praised for his "flow of poetry, . . . elegance of sentiment, a fund of imagination, and an enchanting enthusiasm." Spenser was admired for his music, his rich descriptions, and his freedom from pointed wit, but the chief cause for esteem was the power of his imagination. Nicholls records that Gray never sat down to compose without previously reading a passage of Spenser. Thomas Warton, with the *Observations on the Faerie Queene* in 1754, and Richard Hurd, with the *Letters on Chivalry and Romance* in 1762, were chiefly responsible for elevating Spenser to the secure position he has since held among the immortals of English poetry.[18]

Spenser's archaisms raised a separate debate. Sidney and Jonson expressed their disapproval early. During the Restoration period Spenser's style was generally considered "antiquated" or "rustic." In 1706 Prior's Spenserian *Ode to the Queen* promptly produced an attack on "dull antiquated words." Even William Thompson, who imitated Spenser's manner in general, deprecated a too frequent resort to archaism. Doctor Johnson confessed that "the style of Spenser might by long labour be justly copied," but argued that life was "surely given us for higher purposes than to gather what our ancestors have thrown away, and to learn what is of no value, but because it has been forgotten." Steele, however, cited Horace in a specific approval of Spenser's diction. Such direct support was rare, but approval was often implied by critics who justified archaism in general, as well as by the group of imitators.[19]

The Spenserian stanza won its victory after a hard struggle. E. P. Morton found only five poets who used it in the seventeenth century as compared with the forty-six of the eighteenth century. There was considerable critical opposition to parallel the general neglect. Ben Jonson, William L'Isle (translator of Du Bartas), and Sir William Davenant were early opponents. Thomas Rymer found the stanza "in no wise . . . proper for our language," because of the repeated rimes. Dryden was a more formidable opponent. Edward Bysshe recorded his opposition in *The Art of English Poetry*. Even Hughes, the 1715 editor of Spenser, concluded that the stanza was defective for narrative, for the full stanzaic stop was tiresome and too often broke the sense. He might have added also that the Alexandrine slowed the current of narrative too much. So late as 1751 John Upton could still speak of the "foolish choice" of the stanza. In the same year Doctor Johnson found it "at once difficult and unpleasing; tiresome to the ear by its uniformity, and to the attention by its length." In 1754 Thomas Warton granted that it added "fullness and significancy" to many of Spenser's descriptions, but considered it faulty because it produced redundancy and repetition, the introduction of "puerile" ideas to fill out the rimes, and the frequent expansion of trifling circumlocutions to fill out the stanzas. It must be remembered that this was the viewpoint of a decided Spenserian.[20]

In addition to the actual imitators who either admired or were at least intrigued by the stanza there was some expression of critical approval. Gabriel Harvey liked the added Alexandrine on the eight-line pentameter stanza. Henry More granted its musical power. Edward Phillips preferred it to couplets or quatrains for a stately, majestic epic. Shenstone thought the meter "pretty" and the final Alexandrine majestical. James Thomson liked Spenserian stanzas for allegorical poetry. William Thompson, a minor imitator of the Spenserian style, spoke of the "sweetness and solemnity" of the stanza and of the peculiar grace of the close. With Beattie appreciation reached what Marr has called the full modern note. Writing

to Doctor Blacklock in 1766 Beattie denied any difficulty in employing the stanza which he considered

the most harmonious ever contrived. It admits of more variety of pause than
either the couplet or the alternate rhyme; and it concludes with a pomp and
majesty of sound, which, to my ear, is wonderfully delightful.[21]

The actual imitators of Spenser are easily distinguishable into two
groups which have been designated the Elizabethan and the Augustan Spenserians. The first group was most fully aware of Spenser's
romantic glow and sensuous charm, and attempted to capture his
distinctive blending of earthly loveliness with high moral meaning.
The second group imitated Spenser's epic quality and his archaic
diction in burlesque or lightly humorous vein, with a progressive
deepening of admiration as time passed. Those later poets like
Shelley or Byron who employed the Spenserian stanza for completely original artistic purposes testify to the final victory of the
stanzaic form but can hardly be regarded as imitators. A few poets,
among whom Beattie was conspicuous, marked the transition between
imitative and non-imitative users of the stanza.[22]

A few of the Spenserian imitations are famous—*The School-
mistress*, *The Castle of Indolence*, and *The Minstrel*—but the imitative movement had not waited on men of talent. Among the ghostly
early imitators Samuel Croxall should be mentioned for his *An
Original Canto of Spenser's Faery Queene* in 1713, the success of
which led him to several other imitations. Pope, Prior, Akenside,
and R. O. Cambridge penned burlesques of Spenser in the general
manner adopted by Thomson and Shenstone. These Augustan imitations were less significant of the break with classical taste than the
less inspired but more romantic work of Thompson and Mendez.
Thompson's work revealed a close study of the Elizabethans, whose
spirit and diction he caught in both the *Epithalamium* and the *Na-
tivity*, while Mendez's *Squire of Dames* was one of the best of the
imitations by the mob of gentlemen who wrote with ease. The
influence of Spenser on the effete eighteenth-century pastoral is
uncertain, but undoubtedly slight. Prior "improved" the Spenserian
stanza (ababcdcdee, with a final Alexandrine) in his *Ode to the
Queen* in 1706 and was followed by a score of feeble imitators who

may have felt some vague connection with the mighty Elizabethan who, like Shakespeare, suggested even to neo-classical improvers something of the imaginative freedom, concrete sensuousness, and independence of "kind" needed to preserve the English Augustans from too much Rule and Reason.[23]

III

The influence of Shakespeare, like that of Milton, was enormous. The name of Shakespeare was cited to support the idea of original genius, to justify "the fairy way of writing," to oppose decorum, to show the limitations of the neo-Aristotelian Rules, and the undesirability of rigid literary "kinds," but there was no easily recognizable group of Shakespeareans equivalent to the Miltonists and Spenserians since the genius of Shakespeare was "too comprehensive and universal . . . to become the peculiar badge of any literary coterie."[24] Almost every classicist respected him; many ranked him with the best that "insolent Greece or haughty Rome" could show; many others idolized him. The significance of Shakespeare as a lever with which to roll aside the stones blocking egress to artistic freedom has been assessed in each of the chapters treating aspects of rational and authoritarian classicism. There the names of Rowe, Pope, Theobald, Johnson, Farmer, Mrs. Montagu, and Morgann have appeared. The fifty editions of Shakespeare bespeak an enduring popularity which Rymer had been powerless to check—a popularity which far outweighs the misguided efforts of some of Shakespeare's admirers to "improve" his work by adapting it to what they deemed the changing taste of an age of elegance.

The history of taste in the eighteenth century is, indeed, in one of its phases the history of the progressive recognition of Shakespeare as the artist who "possessed, in the highest degree of perfection, all the most excellent talents of all the writers ever known." This tribute of Martin Sherlock in 1786 is typical of the closing decades of the century. Not only was Shakespeare exalted as the poet of Nature, the great original genius who could defy the Rules, but in time judgment and art were claimed for him also; he came to be regarded as a moral philosopher; and he was found to illustrate the psychology of the passions and the laws of mental associations as expounded by Locke, Hume, Burke, and Hartley.[25]

The interest in Shakespeare was both scholarly and popular. The scholarly interest was shown in the fifty editions, in the attempt to establish the canon of Shakespeare's text, in the collection of illustrations, in the preparation of glossaries and concordances, and in the investigation of biographical data. The Ireland forgeries were in themselves a proof of this growing interest in documentary evidence concerning Shakespeare the man. On the moot points of criticism scholars defended Shakespeare for violating the Unities on the ground that Nature was greater than the Rules, that the rules of one age could not apply to another, and that Aristotle himself did not support the Unities. He was defended for violations of decorum on the ground that in real life grandeur was mixed with buffoonery, and on the plea (an aspect of historical criticism) that he was compelled to please the audience of his age. The extensive controversy among scholars concerning the degree of Shakespeare's learning is of interest to criticism in general principally as an aspect of the controversy concerning nature and art in poetic creation. On this point Farmer's *Essay* was generally acknowledged to have secured the dramatist as an ally of the proponents of Nature.

The criticism of Shakespeare in the eighteenth century offers a striking proof of the growing popularity of historical criticism. In freeing Shakespeare from each charge of the conservative classicist the historical point of view was brought to bear to a certain extent. More specifically it may be noted that his language was studied in connection with the language of his age by Richard Warner, Joseph Ritson, J. M. Mason, and William Whiter; that his plays were studied with reference to the audience for which he wrote by Mrs. Montagu, Mrs. Griffith, Hugh Blair, Tom Davies, and others; that the sources of his plays were studied and a collection of six source plays published by J. Nichols in 1779; that his dramas were interpreted in the light of contemporary themes and dramatic types; and that the history of the stage was examined in an effort to clarify points of production. Before the end of the century the mass of this historical criticism was truly imposing.

The popular interest flowed in many channels. The magazines

were filled with poetic tributes. Messages in the Letter-from-the-Dead-to-the-Living tradition were composed from Shakespeare in heaven. There were sequels to some of his plays; forty-two operas were composed on Shakespearean subjects between 1673 and 1800; and there was a succession of new productions in Shakespeare's general manner which included Rowe's *Jane Shore,* Young's *The Revenge,* Lillo's *Marina,* and Cibber's *Papal Tyranny in the Reign of King John.* In more playful mood magazine writers applied Shakespeare's descriptions of characters to contemporary figures in order to illustrate the permanent truth of Shakespeare's portrayal of human nature; for the young the "beauties" of Shakespeare were collected and commented upon by William Dodd and others; for the nation at large the jubilee at Stratford in 1769 was the occasion for great enthusiasm, and became in turn the theme for three dramatic productions.

The tremendous extent of this Shakespearean vogue has been traced not only by Babcock (*The Genesis of Shakespeare Idolatry in the Eighteenth Century*), but by Nichol Smith (*Eighteenth Century Essays on Shakespeare*), by H. S. Robinson (*English Shakespearean Criticism in the Eighteenth Century*), and by G. C. D. Odell (*Shakespeare from Betterton to Irving*). This brief recapitulation will show that Shakespeare took his place beside Milton and Spenser as one of the obstacles in the way of the rationalist who sought to impose on art the conclusions of common sense. The defense and final enthusiastic approval of Shakespeare by the critics of the century is so indissolubly interwoven with the artistic outlook of the age that it has seemed best to include the diverse aspects of the attitude to Shakespeare in the sections that analyze the classical attitude and the revolt against it.

NOTES TO CHAPTER XIV

1. R. F. Jones, *The Background of the Battle of the Books,* p. 135; Marr, *History of Modern English Romanticism,* pp. 19–20; Hamelius, *Die Kritik,* pp. 47 ff.

2. Marr, *op. cit.,* pp. 19–20; Clara F. McIntyre, "Were the 'Gothic Novels' Really Gothic?" *P.M.L.A.,* XXXVI, 646–647; R. D. Havens, "Changing Taste in the Eighteenth Century," *P.M.L.A.,* XLIV, 506–508; Armstrong, *Miscellanies,* II, 161–162; Temple, in Spingarn, *Critical Essays,* III, 91; Hurd, *Dialogues Moral and Political,* in *Letters on Chivalry and Romance,* pp. 70–72; S. W. Stevenson,

" 'Romantic' Tendencies in Pope," *ELH*, I, 126; Thomas Warton, *History of English Poetry*, pp. 944, 951.

3. R. D. Havens, *Influence of Milton*, pp. 70–71.

4. Havens, *op. cit.*, pp. 4–9, 22, 71, 114; Marr, *op. cit.*, p. 26; Dennis, in Durham, *op. cit.*, p. 172.

5. Havens, *op. cit.*, pp. 433, 437; Marr, *op. cit.*, pp. 177, 227; Phelps, *The Beginnings of the English Romantic Movement*, p. 87.

6. Johnson, *Lives of the Poets*, ed. Waugh, V, 227; Ben Jonson, in Spingarn, *op. cit.*, I, 210; Felix Schelling, "Ben Jonson and the Classical School," *P.M.L.A.*, XIII, 235; Clark, *Boileau and the French Classical Critics in England*, pp. 411–417.

7. R. D. Havens, *Changing Taste in the Eighteenth Century*, *loc. cit.*, pp. 504–505, 523–524; S. W. Stevenson, *op. cit.*, p. 155; Addison, *Spectator*, No. 60; Swift, *Correspondence*, V, 162; Johnson, *Lives of the Poets*, ed. Waugh, II, 262; Scott, *Critical Essays*, p. 106; Armstrong, *Miscellanies*, II, 158–159; Joseph Warton, *Essay on Pope*, I, 143.

8. Havens, *Influence of Milton*, pp. 46–47; Marr, *op. cit.*, pp. 161–163.

9. Milton, in Spingarn, *Critical Essays*, I, 206–207; Gregory Smith, Introduction to *Elizabethan Critical Essays*, I, xlix; Ascham, Webbe, and Campion, in Gregory Smith, *op. cit.*, I, 29–32, 240, II, 329; Phillips and Roscommon in Spingarn, *op. cit.*, II, 266, 308–309; Edmund Smith, quoted by Marr, *op. cit.*, pp. 114–115; Shaftesbury, *Characteristicks*, I, 217; R. D. Havens, "Romantic Aspects of the Age of Pope," *P.M.L.A.*, XXVII, 299, note 1, 321–322; R. S. Crane, "Imitation of Spenser and Milton in the Early Eighteenth Century: A New Document," *Studies in Philology*, XV, 204–205; Dryden, *Essays*, II, 220–221.

10. Pope, *Works*, IX, 7; Joseph Warton, *Essay on Pope*, I, 277; Young, *Conjectures*, *loc. cit.*, p. 340; Kames, *Elements*, II, 108, 127–130; Eric Partridge, "The 1762 Efflorescence of Poetics," *Studies in Philology*, XXV, 34; Mrs. Montagu, *Essay on Shakespeare*, p. 190; Blair, *Rhetoric*, I, 80.

11. Aaron Hill, in Richardson, *Correspondence*, I, 103, Johnson, *Lives of the Poets*, ed. Waugh, II, 102–103, VI, 148, 172, *Hurd-Mason Letters*, p. 150; Goldsmith, *Miscellaneous Works*, p. 439.

12. Marr, *op. cit.*, pp. 114–115, 167–169.

13. *Ibid.*, pp. 118–120, 217.

14. *Ibid.*, pp. 96–97, 128–131, 137; Gildon, in Spingarn, *Critical Essays*, III, 198; Goldsmith, *Miscellaneous Works*, p. 483.

15. The whole sonnet movement has been treated in detail by R. D. Havens in *The Influence of Milton on English Poetry*. See also Marr, *op. cit.*, pp. 197–198; Phelps, *op. cit.*, pp. 45–46; Gosse, *Gray*, pp. 59–60.

16. George Sherburn, "The Early Popularity of Milton's Minor Poems," *Modern Philology*, XVII, 259 ff., 515 ff.; Havens, *Influence of Milton*; Marr, *op. cit.*, pp. 178–180; Reed, *Background of Gray's Elegy*, pp. 19–20; Thomas Warton, in Chalmers, *British Poets*, XVIII, 95–97, 102, 105 ff.

17. R. D. Havens, "Changing Taste in the Eighteenth Century," *loc. cit.*, p. 525; Phelps, *op. cit.*, p. 47; H. E. Cory, "Spenser, Thomson, and Romanticism," *P.M.L.A.*, XXVI, 51–91; Marr, *op. cit.*, pp. 21–24, 94; Pope, *Works*, X, 120; Dennis, quoted by Hamelius, *op. cit.*, p. 112; Prior, in Chalmers, *British Poets*, X, 178; E. P. Morton, "The Spenserian Stanza in the Eighteenth Century," *Modern Philology*, X, 371.

18. Marr, *op. cit.*, pp. 24–25; Morton, *op. cit.*, p. 376; Goldsmith, *Works*, ed. Gibbs, IV, 334–335; Gray, *Letters*, II, 279.

19. Marr, *op. cit.*, pp. 47–50, 52, 54; Phelps, *op. cit.*, p. 51; Morton, *op. cit.*, p. 376; Johnson, *Rambler*, May 14, 1751; Steele, *Spectator*, No. 541; Goldsmith, *Works*, V, 155–157, 159.

20. Morton, *op. cit.*, p. 365; Marr, *op. cit.*, pp. 32–33, 35–37; Davenant, in Spingarn, *Critical Essays*, II, 6; Rymer, *ibid.*, II, 168; Johnson, *Rambler*, May 14, 1751; Thomas Warton, *Observations*, I, 114–115.

21. Marr, *op cit.*, pp. 32–34, 38, 43; Phillips, in Spingarn, *Critical Essays*, II, 265.

22. Marr, *op. cit.*, pp. 59, 90, and Appendix III; Morton; *op. cit.*, p. 365.

23. Marr, *op. cit.*, pp. 60, 63, 65–85, 91–94, 102–107; Phelps, *op. cit.*, pp. 61, 73, 78–79; Addison, *Guardian*, No. 152; Morton, *op. cit.*, p. 371.

24. Marr, *op. cit.*, p. 191.

25. In this brief section I am following R. W. Babcock's *The Genesis of Shakespeare Idolatry, 1766–1799*—perhaps the most thorough presentation of Shakespeare's great popularity—and H. S. Robinson's *English Shakesperian Criticism in the Eighteenth Century*, New York, 1932.

CHAPTER XV

THE STANDARD OF TASTE

I

THE SURVIVAL of Elizabethan romanticism offered one difficulty to the classicists intent on establishing a universal standard of taste; for the beauty of Shakespeare, Spenser, and Milton could not always be justified by the criteria deduced from Nature by Reason. There were even greater difficulties, however, in the way of setting up a standard. The proponents of a universal rational standard could not find a common basis of agreement: some were forced to admit that the acquisition of taste was difficult; others disagreed as to the amount of knowledge needed; a few, like Hume, admitted that taste was incomprehensible in actuality while they still clung to the theoretical desirability of a standard. This disagreement among the rationalists afforded a foothold for those who preferred to regard taste as a question of sensibility, or as dependent upon the apperceptive background of the individual mind. There were even men, in other respects classicists, who admitted the *je-ne-sais-quoi*, the incommunicable quality of beauty; men who believed that there must always be an unexplainable residue, a grace beyond the reach of art; men who admitted the validity of an historical point of view in criticism; men who stoutly maintained that *de gustibus non est disputandum*. The opposition to a standard of taste was always vigorous in England, but during the eighteenth century the consciousness of a divergent, yet fascinating, Elizabethan mode of beauty was strengthened by a deepening knowledge and growing appreciation of the Charms of Oriental, Norse, Celtic, and Mediæval art, as well as by the concept of sublimity which came to be recognized as antithetical to, but equally important with, the concept of beauty.

To the pure classicist taste was rational; to his opponent it was often a product of sensibility—a feeling, an intuition. The metaphorical use of the word *taste* had been popularized in Spain by Gracian, and was originally used for an awareness of literary merits which the Rules could neither create nor explain. The process of Rationalization soon checked such early æsthetic anarchy. The right of individual taste was denied, or reason was substituted for sentiment as the basis of taste. A slight residue of the earlier freedom remained, however, for the "school of taste" preferred to note the beauties and to tolerate the faults (violations of correctness) in a work of art, and was generally willing to grant that some portion of beauty must remain unexplainable. Moreover, each rational explanation of taste was a personal explanation which found few followers, and, though based on reason, it seldom went further than vague generalizations concerning simplicity, order, harmony, the necessity of universal appeal as a sign of actual reliance on the common light of Nature, and the identification of defective taste with defective knowledge. The attempt to be more definite set prominent thinkers like Shaftesbury, Hume, Burke, and Reynolds at variance, much to the satisfaction of satirists like Robert Lloyd who ridiculed the furor concerning taste in *The Connoisseur:*

> Blest age! when all men may procure
> The title of a connoisseur;
> When noble and ignoble herd
> Are govern'd by a single word;
> Though, like the royal German dames,
> It bears an hundred Christian names;
> As genius, fancy, judgment, gout,
> Whim, caprice, je-ne-sais-quoi, vertu;
> Which appellations all describe
> *Taste,* and the modern tasteful tribe.

Other critics—Fielding, Goldsmith, Morgann, and Boswell among them—were led by the disagreement in the camp of the universalists to suggest that taste must be a decidedly esoteric, difficult, incommunicable, and uncertain quality since its true nature was so obscure.[1]

The most serious attempts to find a foundation for universal taste were directed to common sense, the Cartesian belief in an undifferentiated reason common to all mankind which would enable all men to agree on a concept of beauty and to mark those who disagreed as deficient in taste because of some lack of knowledge or of effort to understand. This attitude dominated the French seventeenth century. Balzac wrote, "Reason is a citizen of all countries"; La Mesnardière, "Reason is a citizen of all ages"; Chapelain, "Reason is not subject to alteration"; Chapelain again referred to "this universal beauty which ought to please every one"; Racine declared that

good sense and reason are the same in all ages. The taste of Paris has been found like that of Athens; my spectators have been moved by the same things that once brought tears to the learned people of Greece.[2]

In England one finds the standard of taste based on the view of uniform mentality as early as Carew's "To the Reader of Master William Davenant's Play" (before 1639). To Carew it seemed that

> Things are distinct and must the same appear
> To every piercing eye or well-tun'd ear,

and that disagreement could only be a sign of defective senses or of some limitation in knowledge. It was 1700, however, before the rational basis for a uniformity of taste became a prominent feature of æsthetic thought. In 1725 Hutcheson insisted on the universality of taste, though he felt that the perception of beauty depended on an inner sense which operated without the aid of knowledge. By granting the existence of a lesser beauty based on sentimental associations he hoped to reconcile the reality of an absolute intellectual beauty with the anarchy that was apparent in the writings of his contemporaries. Disagreement in taste was caused by the difficulty of eliminating moral preoccupations and personal reactions from the æsthetic experience. Above and beyond such minor divergences there was the real beauty which would appeal to men everywhere, in every age. Swift, writing in French to the Abbé des Fontaines, was equally sure of the validity of a universal taste to which the artist must appeal:

Mais nous sommes portes a croire, que le bon goût est le même par tout, ou il y a des gens d'esprit, de jugement et de scavoir. . . . L'auteur, que n'escrit que pour une ville, une province, un royaume, ou même un siecle, merite si peu d'être traduit, qu'il ne merite pas d'etre lû.

Hume founded taste on sound sense as the only principle of unity possible in the complex analysis of works of genius: as all men share the passions and sentiments of their fellows they may be aroused by the same stimuli which it is the business of this sound judgment or sound sense to detect.[3]

In his *Inquiry into the Sublime and Beautiful* Burke declared it probable "that the standard both of reason and taste is the same for all human creatures." Even ordinary intercourse would be impossible without some common principles, and in criticism and æsthetics especially there could be only futility, "if ideas of beauty are whims and fancies dependent on caprice." Taste was founded on the senses, the imagination, and the judgment. According to Burke men for the most part perceive objects in the same way, and even the imagination can only vary these given sense impressions and must consequently produce a similar effect. A secondary pleasure of the imagination was derived from the comparison of the artistic object with the original, but here, too, the pleasure could only be dependent on knowledge and the judgment founded on experience and observation which detects the resemblance. Taste must therefore be the same, and any difference in degree was simply a difference arising from defect of knowledge or of natural sensibility. "The cause of a wrong taste," Burke decided, "is a defect of judgment."[4]

Gerard found taste to be a composite of certain mental powers such as the sense of novelty, sublimity, beauty, imitation, harmony, ridicule, and virtue. Despite this range of ideas in his concept of taste Gerard was insistent on the possibility of obtaining uniformity through proper cultivation of the imagination and judgment, for

there are qualities in things, determinate and stable, independent of humour or caprice, that are fit to operate on mental principles, common to all men, and, by operating on them, are naturally productive of the sentiments of taste. . . .

While sensibility was in Gerard's view highly desirable in a man of taste, judgment and good sense were essential in the comparison of things with Nature and with each other to see if truth and justice, "the foundation of every beauty," had been preserved.[5]

Lord Kames considered that æsthetics was, like morals, a rational science "rooted in human nature, and governed by principles common to all men"; and that taste was neither transient nor local, though it might be partially vitiated by "fashion, temper, and education." Mrs. Carter discovered that the appeal of Nature "equally and universally through every revolution of time" afforded a standard for the beautiful and the sublime. Hannah More was a perfect rationalist when she wrote as late as 1789: "Taste is of all ages, and truth is eternal; and there is a truth in taste almost as demonstrable as any mathematical proposition." Even Thomas Warton felt compelled in late life to surrender the dream of mediæval romantic art before the concept of a universal beauty and truth in

> The just proportion and the genuine line.

He admitted that Sir Joshua Reynolds had brought him back

> To truth, by no peculiar taste confin'd
> Whose universal pattern strikes mankind
> To truth, whose bold and unresisted aim
> Checks frail caprice, and fashion's fickle claim. . . .[6]

For the æsthetician who believed that taste was founded on universal reason the test of time was the test of greatness. This was the same test that was used by the stricter classicists in support of the Rules. As the Greeks and Romans had been approved by reasonable men everywhere, they became a test of taste and the study of their masterpieces a means of improving a defective taste to the point of enjoyment of those works which had been uniformly found beautiful. Addison admitted that some measure of taste must be born with one, but he argued that such inborn taste could be cultivated by reading, by conversation with intelligent men, and by the study of criticism; and he was quite firm in his contention that the man who failed to like what had stood the test of time or won the sanction of "the politer part of our contemporaries" should conclude that he wanted taste. Chesterfield and Joseph Warton also looked to the Ancients as means of forming true taste.[7]

Failure to perceive true beauty was caused by faulty knowledge. Sir Joshua Reynolds was a typical figure:

It is the very same taste which relishes a demonstration in geometry, that is pleased with the resemblance of a picture to an original and touched with the harmony of music.

All these have unalterable and fixed foundations in nature, and are therefore equally investigated by reason, and known by study; some with more, some with less clearness, but all exactly in the same way. A picture that is unlike is false. Disproportionate ordonnance of parts is not right; because it cannot be true, until it ceases to be a contradiction to assert, that the parts have no relation to the whole. Colouring is true, when it is naturally adapted to the eye, from brightness, from softness, from harmony, from resemblance; because these agree with their object, *Nature,* and therefore are true; as true as mathematical demonstration; but known to be true only to those who study these things.

But besides real, there is also apparent truth, or opinion, or prejudice. With regard to real truth, when it is known, the taste which conforms to it is, and must be uniform.

To Reynolds taste rested on the knowledge of what is truly Nature— the general forms of external nature, and the general laws of the human mind. Knowledge was needed before the individual could perceive this truth, this point of perfection; taste was not the possession of the multitude, but the prized possession of the gentleman, scholar, and critic who could improve his judgment by exercise and study.[8]

In 1661 Glanvill had elevated knowledge to an important position in matters of taste:

The most artful melody receives but little tribute of honour from the grazing beasts; it requires skill to relish it. . . . A gay puppet pleases children more, than the exactest piece of unaffected art: it requires some degree of perfection, to admire what is truly perfect. . . . Indeed the unobservant multitude may have some general confus'd apprehensions of a kind of beauty, that gilds the outside frame of the universe; but they are nature's coarser wares, that lie on the stall, expos'd to the transient view of every common eye; her choicer riches are lock't up only for the sight of them, that will buy at the expense of sweat and oil.

Dennis believed that taste degenerated in ages of commerce or of political agitation because inadequate education and application disqualified the mind for correct judgment. Shaftesbury was equally insistent that "use, practice, and culture" must precede the understanding, for "a legitimate and just taste can neither be begotten,

made, conceiv'd, or produced without the antecedent labour and
pains of criticism." Addison, Joseph Warton, and *The Mirror*
stressed training as a road to taste. Cowper believed that taste was
superior in an older man. Doctor Johnson declared that difference
of taste rested on difference of skill. In the midst of the Romantic
movement Coleridge accepted this general position.[9]

I I

Opposed to the exponents of an ideal standard of taste founded
on reason was a group of critics who represented taste either as an
attribute of sensibility or as a product of mental associations differing among individuals. A still more radical group boldly accepted
the idea of *de gustibus* and refused to admit even the possibility
of uniformity. A third group of historical critics, not content with
the bare denial of a standard, turned to a consideration of divergent
cultures as an explanation for divergent but equally legitimate
modes of art.

Though critics like Shaftesbury and Hutcheson clung to a standard of taste in theory, they paved the way for the school of sensibility in taste by their admission of an inner sense capable of perceiving beauty before the judgment could analyze the basis for such
appreciation. It was not until the middle of the eighteenth century,
however, that this conception of taste as sensibility became popular.
In 1762 the author of *An Art of Poetry on a New Plan* (probably
John Newbery) spoke of "that power of feeling or sensibility resulting from nature and accurate observation, which we call *good
taste*." In 1767 William Duff defined taste as that

internal sense, which, by its own exquisitely nice sensibility, without the assistance of the reasoning faculty, distinguishes and determines the various
qualities of the objects submitted to its cognisance; pronouncing, by its own
arbitrary verdict, that they are grand or mean, beautiful or ugly, decent
or ridiculous.

Duff subordinated judgment to taste, and allowed no appeal from
the decisions of taste. Gerard's position was a compromise, for he
found sensibility essential to the perfection of taste, and judgment

necessary to eliminate nonessentials, to control an irregular imagination, and to attain unity of atmosphere. With Blair taste as sensibility was fundamental, but reason could assist and enlarge its powers. Sensibility was particularly important in aspects of art where human nature was involved, for in such cases delicacy and tenderness of heart were essential to a "thorough feeling . . . of beauty." Blair attempted to distinguish delicacy of taste—"the perfection of that natural sensibility on which taste is founded"—from correctness of taste based on reason and acquired culture. Blair could not entirely reconcile himself to the absence of a standard of taste, though he again straddled by admitting that there were different kinds of beauty, and that there were limitations to a standard. His effort to establish this vague standard in the accepted manner on universal agreement and the test of time fails to remove the impression that the impact of the movement of sensibility had led to the disintegration of the standard of taste even in the hands of the Scotch rationalists.[10]

The psychology of association related beauty to the apperceptive background of the individual mind. Since each man had a sentimental education peculiar to himself, he would respond in an individual manner when brought face to face with beauty, the response being conditioned by the train of ideas set up by the object of contemplation. Such a theory of æsthetics was irreconcilable with any absolute standard of taste, and though sentimental beauty was at first carefully subordinated to absolute beauty, the situation was reversed between Hutcheson and Alison when sentimental associations became of prime importance in calling forth a feeling of beauty dependent on the personal experience of the man of taste.

In 1710 *The Tatler* had suggested that one's way of life and one's imagination must condition the taste of an author. While this statement falls short of a clear recognition of the significance of the personal element in the experience of beauty, it showed a willingness to excuse divergences of taste as the natural result of divergent personalities. In 1719 the influential French critic, Du Bos, not only elevated pleasure in art above instruction, but based pleasure on taste as a rule to itself, dependent not on reason but on "our organization, our present inclination, and the situation of our spirit."

Akenside, a disciple of Shaftesbury and Hutcheson, went further than they in the recognition of individual difference:

> Different minds
> Incline to different objects: one pursues
> The vast alone, the wonderful, the wild;
> Another sighs for harmony and grace,
> And gentlest beauty.

According to Akenside each race perceives a partial beauty and fails to grasp the "infinite consummate form" which cannot be grasped by mortal man, though it has existed from eternity in the mind of God. Goldsmith recognized the relativity of taste in his *Inquiry into the Present State of Polite Learning* in 1759, and Boswell looked to associational psychology to explain the differences of taste which he admitted could not be eliminated.[11]

Just as Blair found difficulty in reconciling sensibility and reason, Beattie was at a loss to explain the comparative roles of the universal and the individual in taste. He declared for a general taste, but granted in the next breath that each individual might form peculiar ideas of beauty from early association with certain colors, forms, attitudes, and sensations; and that divergent faculties of perception would introduce further limitation to the actual attainment of uniformity. The perfection of taste was thus purely imaginary, for all men had limitations of sense organs, of imagination, of sensibility, of sympathy, or of judgment—all qualities which must cooperate to form a true taste. Beattie thus surrendered the standard and recognized the role of sentimental associations, but he betrayed his rational leanings by emphasizing the part played by judgment and learning as well as by his apparent regard for the absolute beauty in which he no longer had any real faith. The way was paved for Alison's complete repudiation of everything except sentimental beauty.[12]

Exponents of a standard of taste founded it on reason; their more thoughtful opponents based the idea of beauty on sensibility and the psychology of association. Still other writers merely called taste a God-given gift, and associated it with genius and inspiration as an inborn ability which man could never hope to explain, or else fell

back on the simple assertion that there could be no argument concerning taste. Pope was able to recognize the rarity of agreement
in taste, and felt compelled to regard it as an innate ability:

> In poets as true genius is but rare,
> True taste as seldom is the critics' share;
> Both must from heav'n derive their light
> These born to judge, as well as those to write.

A decade later Tamworth Reresby confessed even more explicitly
the impossibility of explaining taste:

> When we have a *fine taste by Nature,* instructions, or comments . . .
> seem superfluous. What we dignify with this title, is a *natural sentiment,*
> *inherent in the Soul,* and altogether independent of the *sciences. A good*
> *taste is . . . a sort of instinct of right reason, which directs us better than*
> *all Rules and Arguments whatsoever.*

Welsted was of the same opinion:

> Many of the graces in poetry may, I grant, be talk'd of in very intelli-
> gible language, but intelligible only to those who have a natural *taste* for
> it, or who are born with the talent of judging: to have what we call *Taste,*
> is having, one may say, a new sense or faculty superadded to the ordinary
> ones of the soul, the prerogative of fine spirits!

Hume's acute powers of analysis did not enable him to define taste
further than "a sensation of pleasure from true wit, and of uneasiness from false, without our being able to tell the reasons of that
pleasure or uneasiness."[18]

The complete individuality of taste was admitted in 1575 by
Gascoigne who disclaimed any final validity for his views on poetry
with the words, "*Quot homines, tot sententiae,* especially in poetry."
In the Elizabethan period Webbe and Daniel, in mid-seventeenth
century Hobbes and Sir Robert Howard, followed Gascoigne's lead.
In 1693 Dryden admitted the indisputable nature of individual
taste. By this time the School of Taste—Méré, Bouhours, Saint-
Évremond—was exerting its influence in France on behalf of the
liberty of the individual to like what he pleased, and in any discussion of *de gustibus* in the English eighteenth century this French
influence must be reckoned with despite the slender stream of lib-
eralism in England extending unbroken from Gascoigne to Lord

Chesterfield who declared "taste in everything . . . undetermined and personal"; to Brown who despaired of making taste general even by assiduous culture; and to Armstrong who wrote in lighter vein:

> Judge for yourself; and as you find, report
> Of wit, as freely as of beef or port.

The enormous extent of this liberality can be realized only by connecting the opposition to a standard of taste revealed here with other signs of artistic freedom—the function assigned to Nature in artistic creation, the admission of imagination to a role equal or superior to that of judgment, the unwillingness to insist dogmatically on correctness, and the reluctance to accept Authority, the supremacy of the classics, or the validity of the Rules—for each of these movements implied at least a vague sense that no universal agreement was possible in the regions of beauty.[14]

III

The development of historical criticism, resulting from a gradually widening knowledge of the cultural history of mankind, was of more significance than the movement of sensibility or the development of associational psychology in breaking down the conception of a universally valid standard of taste. The recognition of the relationship between literature and its cultural background was the most important mark of historical criticism, for when this is admitted the critic, whose views are conditioned by diverse geographical, racial, and social factors, must admit the impossibility of an absolute judgment of value. The art of the pagoda must be admitted to be legitimate for the Oriental, that of the mosque for the Turk, that of the Gothic cathedral for the Christian of the Middle Ages, and that of the Parthenon for the Greek alone.

There were other signs of a dawning historical consciousness in criticism less plain, but scarcely less important, than this deterministic theory of art. The admission of divergent ideals of beauty, all equally legitimate, could precede historical knowledge as well as follow it, but would almost inevitably lead a curious mind to seek some explanation for such wide divergences in taste. The rejection of the neo-Aristotelian Rules because of a vague feeling that Englishmen should be judged by English laws might also lead to the appreciation of different cultures. The awakening interest in epochs of art other than the Græco-Roman will be traced later, but a swift glance must be given here to the development of the deterministic theory of literary history, the growing recognition of divergences of taste between different ages, and the gradually deepening awareness that there was not a single set of Rules, but two or three or many by which the provinces of the *respublica* of art were governed.[15]

There was some awareness of the fundamental differences between cultures during the Italian Renaissance. Cinthio and Guarini explained the differences between ancient and modern literature by historical conditions, and Il Lasca defended a new kind of comedy by arguments drawn from the existence of new manners and a new religion. In Elizabethan England Stanyhurst objected to the universal authority of the Rules on the ground that each country "hath his peculiar law" and "every language . . . his particular lore." James VI, in his brief treatment of poetics, recognized the validity of standards varying from age to age, from country to country. Jonson pointed to the effect of manners and fashions in a "sick State" on the language and literature, while Bacon "insisted on an exposition of the causal relation between learning—of which literature is a part—and the forces that determine its development—racial, physical, religious, political, and social." In France even such occasional intuitions of the historical point of view were delayed. Bray has suggested that the entering wedge was the consideration of the degree to which the classics must be modified to suit French taste. Ogier and others soon perceived the difference between Greeks, Romans, and Frenchmen and advised imitation only of those things which could be assimilated by French taste. The comparison of Ajax to an ass, and the barbarous subject matter of *Oedipus Rex* were the stock examples of this necessity for adaptation. In 1577 Bodin had already borrowed the idea of the general influence of climate from Aristotle, but Godeau seems to have been the first Frenchman to explain difference of taste by climatic differences. At the close of the seventeenth century Fontenelle and Saint-Évremond developed the idea of climatic determinism, and in 1670 Spinoza laid down the principle that a book could be understood only when its purpose and authorship were studied historically.[16]

In Restoration England the theory that literary modes differed according to age, climate, and social background afforded a small but persistent undercurrent of opposition to the classical desire for uniformity. Cowley, Sprat, and Howard touched upon the idea. Dryden was employing this historical viewpoint when he admitted that the English and Athenian stages had a different perfection; when he wished to be tried "by the laws of his own country"; when he admitted that Greek drama was too restricted a model for English; when he wrote

> They, who have best succeeded on the stage,
> Have still conform'd their genius to their age;

when he confessed that the excellencies of Greek drama would not satisfy an English audience; and when he explained the structure of the *Æneid*, not by rational criteria, but by the relationship between Virgil and Augustus. Temple in 1690 and Dennis in 1693 drove home the significance of historical considerations. Temple justified the greater variety and humor of the English stage by the greater variety of English life which "may proceed from the native plenty of our soil, the unequalness of our climate, as well as the ease of our government, and the liberty of professing opinions and factions." Dennis opposed Rymer's desire for an exact imitation of Greek drama with a clear statement of the relation between taste and historical circumstance:

> For to set up the *Grecian* method amongst us with success, it is absolutely necessary to restore not only their Religion and their Polity, but to transport us to the same climate in which Sophocles and Euripides writ; or else, by reason of those different circumstances, several things which were graceful and decent with them must seem ridiculous and absurd to us, as several things which would have appear'd highly extravagant to them must look proper and becoming with us.

Meanwhile the exiled Saint-Évremond was attacking the universal validity of the Rules on deterministic grounds and contending that

the Greeks would have adapted their art to the age if they had lived
in the seventeenth century.[17]

In 1699 William Nichols pointed out that eastern eloquence employed a different, but equally valid, standard of excellence from
Greek or Roman eloquence. In the *Discourse on Ancient and
Modern Learning* Addison applied historical criticism in a consideration of the effects of a literary work on different ages. Steele
explained the difference between Horace and Juvenal by differences
of social and moral background. Pope recognized the significance of
interpretation in the light of conditions that gave birth to works
of art:

> Know well each ancient's proper character;
> His fable, subject, scope in ev'ry page;
> Religion, country, genius of his age:
> Without all these at once before your eyes,
> Cavil you may, but never criticise.

In 1731 John Husbands in the Preface to his *Miscellany* reiterated
the difference between Greek and Oriental taste, and admitted the
relative nature of beauty. Not Husbands, however, but Thomas
Blackwell was the significant figure of this period, for in his *Enquiry
Into the Life and Writings of Homer* (1735) he made a serious
attempt to explain the genius of Homer by the climate, the natural
customs, the boldness of speech, the richness of religious myth, and
the heroic fullness of life in the Golden Age of Greece.[18]

The next generation saw a farther extension of the historical
idea. Influence from France was important. In 1719 Du Bos had
devoted two hundred pages of his *Reflexions Critiques* to an analysis
of the deterministic theory of genius. Du Bos was influenced by
Locke, Addison, and Wotton, but he in turn was widely read in
England where his particular attention to the arts gave him an
importance in the field of literary criticism comparable with that
of Montesquieu whose *L'Esprit des Lois* (1748) was more concerned with the influence of climate on social and political institutions. In England Thomas Warton applied the method of Blackwell
to the explanation and justification of Spenser in 1754 in an effort
to rescue him from the crime of violating the Aristotelian Rules
of the epic:

In reading the works of a poet who lived in a remote age, it is necessary that we should look back upon the customs and manners which prevailed in that age. We should endeavour to place ourselves in the writer's situation and circumstances.

Spenser's genius was influenced by tournaments and romances, pageants and tapestries and masques. The literary "kind" which he produced, allegorical romance, had its own rules and could be criticised justly by no others. Doctor Johnson congratulated Warton for his felicitous use of the historical method. Indeed, as early as 1745, Johnson had himself tentatively applied it to the criticism of *Macbeth*. In 1755 Paul Mallet applied the historical method to Scandinavian literature in his *Introduction a l'Histoire de Danemark*, a work of extreme importance for writers like Gray and Percy who sought to extend the bounds of taste in England. In 1756 Joseph Warton agreed with his brother—and with Pope—that proper æsthetic appreciation was dependent on knowledge of a writer's "climate, his country, and his age." Goldsmith adopted the historical point of view in his *Inquiry* in 1759; John Brown made a brave early effort at comparative literary anthropology in *The Rise and Progress of Poetry* (1764), an attempt to explain the rise of Greek poetry by analogy with the "savage" poetry of the Iroquois, the Norsemen, the Peruvians, the Chinese, and the early Hebrews; and in 1769 Robert Wood's *Essay on Homer* retraced Blackwell's ground in an effort to "carry the reader to the poet's age and country, before he forms a judgment of him." With the acceptance of the historical viewpoint by popular rhetoricians like Blair one reaches the close of a period, for no longer would the young be learning of the universality of taste and the absolute nature of beauty, but of the necessity for a catholic appreciation of divergent beauties formed in divergent cultures—Chinese and Celtic and Norse; Ancient, Medieval, and Modern. The progress of this extension of taste will be examined in a later chapter.[19]

NOTES TO CHAPTER XV

1. Spingarn, *Critical Essays*, I, xcii; E. N. Hooker, "The Discussion of Taste, from 1750 to 1770, and the New Trends in Literary Criticism," *P.M.L.A.*, XLIX, 583–584; Lloyd, *Connoisseur*, No. 135; Fielding, *Covent-Garden Journal*, No. 4;

Goldsmith, *Works*, ed. Gibbs, IV, 331; Morgann, in Nicoll Smith, *op. cit.*, p. 248; Boswell, *Life of Johnson*, III, 171–172.

2. Robertson, *Genesis of Romantic Theory in the Eighteenth Century*, p. 7; Bray, *op. cit.*, pp. 126–127; Racine, "Preface d'Iphegenie à Aulis," in Vial et Denise, *op. cit.*, p. 167.

3. Hutcheson, *Inquiry*, pp. 8–11, 80, 83, 87; Swift, *Correspondence*, III, 407; Hume, *Essays*, I, 93, 172.

4. Burke, *Works*, I, 65–82.

5. Gerard, *Essay on Taste*, pp. 77–78, 104–105.

6. Kames, *Elements*, I, 14–15; Mrs. Carter, *Reflections Suggested by the Sight of Ruins*, Aug. *1767*, quoted by Reed, *Background of Gray's Elegy*, p. 223; Hannah More, *Letters*, p. 125; Thomas Warton, in Chalmers, *op. cit.*, XVIII, 94.

7. Addison, *Spectator*, No. 409; Chesterfield, *Letters*, I, 70; Joseph Warton, *Essay on Pope*, I, 198.

8. La Bruyère, quoted by Spingarn, *op. cit.*, I, xcviii; Mandeville, *Fable of the Bees*, I, 326; Reynolds, *Discourses*, pp. 102–105, 107.

9. Glanvill, *Vanity of Dogmatizing*, pp. 246–247; Dennis, in Durham, *op. cit.*, p. 137; Shaftesbury, *Characteristicks*, III, 164–165; Addison, *Spectator*, No. 409; Joseph Warton, *Essay on Pope*, I, 198; *The Mirror*, No. 48; Cowper, Letter to Unwin, July 3, 1784; Boswell, *Life of Johnson*, I, 219, note 1, and II, 219; Coleridge, *Biographia Literaria*, pp. 209, note 1, and 245; Chambers, *History of Taste*, pp. 72–73; Shaftesbury, *Characteristicks*, II, 414–415; Marriott, *World*, No. 117.

10. John Newbery (?), quoted by Partridge, "The 1762 Efflorescence of Poetics," *loc. cit.*, p. 32; Duff, *Essay on Genius*, pp. 11–12; Gerard, *Essay on Genius*, pp. 392, 398–399, 406; *Mirror*, No. 2; Blair, *Rhetoric*, I, 20–26, 28, 30, 32–39, 42.

11. *Tatler*, No. 173; Chambers, *History of Taste*, p. 120; Hutcheson, *Inquiry*, p. 83; Akenside, *Pleasures of the Imagination*, Book III, lines 546–550; Boswell, *Hypochondriack*, I, 116, 321, II, 155; Miller, *The Historical Point of View in English Criticism*, pp. 133–134.

12. Beattie, *Dissertations*, I, 168–171, 177–178, 202, 212, 233; Hussey, *The Picturesque*, p. 15.

13. Pope, *Essay on Criticism*, lines 11–14, and *Imitations of Horace*, Book II, Epistle II, lines 268–269; Reresby, quoted by Green, *Neo-classical Theory of Tragedy*, p. 124; Welsted, in Durham, *op. cit.*, p. 366; Hume, *Treatise*, p. 297.

14. Gascoigne, in Gregory Smith, *op. cit.*, I, 46–47; Webbe, *ibid.*, I, 243; Daniel, *ibid.*, II, 383; Hobbes, in Spingarn, *Critical Essays*, I, xcvii; Howard, *ibid.*, II, 106–107; Dryden, *Essays*, II, 84; Chesterfield, *Works*, V, 197; John Brown, *Essays*, p. 189; Armstrong, "Of Taste."

15. Miller, *Historical Point of View*, pp. 35–36.

16. Spingarn, *Literary Criticism of the Renaissance*, p. 163, and *Critical Essays*, I, ci–cii; Miller, *op. cit.*, pp. 49, 51, 71; Jonson, in Spingarn, *Critical Essays*, I, 28; Bray, *op. cit.*, pp. 174–175; Preserved Smith, *History of Modern Culture*, I, 285.

17. P. S. Wood, "The Opposition to Neo-classicism in England Between 1660 and 1700," *P.M.L.A.*, XLIII, 195 ff.; Miller, *op. cit.*, pp. 20–21, 98–99; Green, *Neo-Classical Theory of Tragedy*, p. 21; Temple, in Spingarn, *Critical Essays*, III, 104; Dennis, *ibid.*, III, 148.

18. Steele, *Tatler*, No. 242; Pope, *Essay on Criticism*, lines 119–123, 233–234;

R. S. Crane, "An Early Eighteenth-century Enthusiast for Primitive Poetry: John Husbands," *Modern Language Notes*, XXXVII, 33–34; Lois Whitney, "Thomas Blackwell, a Disciple of Shaftesbury," *Philological Quarterly*, V, 198; Miller, *op. cit.*, p. 122.

19. Lois Whitney, "English Primitivistic Theories of Epic Origins," *Modern Philology*, XXI, 348–351; Miller, *op. cit.*, pp. 22–23; Thomas Warton, *Observations*, II, 87–89; Van Tiegham, *Préromantisme*, p. 112; Joseph Warton, *Essay on Pope*, I, 5; Boswell, *Life of Johnson*, I, 314; Johnson, *Miscellaneous Observations on the Tragedy of Macbeth*; Goldsmith, *Miscellaneous Works*, p. 420; John Brown, *The History of the Rise and Progress of Poetry*, *passim*; Robert Wood, *An Essay on Homer*, pp. 114, 181; Blair, *Rhetoric*, II, 177–178, III, 196 ff.

CHAPTER XVI

THE GRACE BEYOND THE REACH OF ART

I

FEW CLASSICISTS of major rank were willing to dogmatize concerning art. The hostile camps that faced each other on every point of literary theory—judgment, taste, correctness, authority, the Rules—bear witness to the critical ferment that is so seldom given adequate recognition by critics who prefer generalities concerning the "classical" period to the more difficult task of tracing the conflicting currents of opinion. Disagreement was as rife before 1800 as after that date, and in face of such disagreement it was difficult for a thoughtful man to preserve an absolute certainty concerning any rational position. The uncertainty was shown by the use of the phrase *je-ne-sais-quoi* with reference to the various aspects of human affairs which seemed to escape definition; by the admission, more especially in æsthetics, that there was a grace beyond the reach of art; and by the feeling that man as a creative artist was subject to limitations which would make it forever impossible for him to rival the skillful hand of God in external nature.

The phrase *je-ne-sais-quoi* was the French equivalent for the Latin *nescio quid,* and it was in its French form that it became popular in England. By 1557 it was used in Italy to indicate an indescribable charm. Montaigne, and later the Precièuses, employed it. In his discussion of taste the influential Bouhours devoted a chapter to "Le Je Ne Sais Quoi." In England Shaftesbury seems to have been first in applying it directly to æsthetics.[1]

Already Congreve, Farquhar, and Vanbrugh were employing the *je ne sais quoi* for an indefinable quality of personal charm. Gay noted the popularity of the phrase. Prior admitted that a picture might be

> Exact to rule, exempt from fault:
> Yet, if the colouring be not there,
> The Titian stroke, the Guido air;
> To nicest judgment show the piece,
> At best 'twill only not displease:
>
> .　　.　　.　　.　　.　　.　　.
>
> Thus, in the picture of our mind
> The action may be well designed;
> Guided by law, and bound by duty;
> Yet want this *je ne scai quoi* of beauty: . . .

In 1718 Gildon ridiculed La Mode's pleasure in "a je ne scai quoyish beauty" found in an old piece of needlework "without order, beauty, or harmony of parts." Hutcheson applied the phrase to certain graces that formed a part of the subordinate beauties of sentiment in the human countenance. Chesterfield employed the expression for the indefinable qualities of good breeding on occasion after occasion. Hume referred the perception of "a certain je ne scai quoi of agreeable and handsome" to "a certain sense, which acts without reflection," and Burke applied the term particularly to the complicated qualities of ease, roundness, and delicacy of attitude and motion that comprise grace. After 1760 the term was seldom used, for the hold of Reason on æsthetics had by that time been weakened.[2]

II

The actual words of Pope concerning the grace beyond the reach of art cannot be traced back to the Renaissance, but the idea was behind Bacon's denial of the supreme beauty of geometrical proportion. The painter who wishes to create a beautiful face must do it "by a kind of felicity (as a musician . . . maketh an excellent air in music), and not by rule." The influence of Bacon's "Of Beauty" has not been traced, but the idea of a grace superior to art was familiar to Méré, Bouhours, Saint-Évremond, and La Bruyère, as well as to the more influential Boileau, who spoke of La Fontaine's naïveté of language as in effect that *molle* and *facetum* which Horace attributed to Virgil and which Apollo gives only to his favorites. This beauty is the kind one does not prove. It is the *je ne sais quoi* that charms us, and without which beauty itself would have neither grace nor beauty.

Not only *agrément* and *sel* but sublimity too was incapable of proof or demonstration, according to Boileau, who preceded Pope in the admission that it was one of the mysteries of art that the occasional violation of the Rules was in itself a rule.[3]

The classic expression of the indefinable grace is Pope's

> Some beauties yet no precepts can declare,
> For there's a happiness as well as care.
> Music resembles poetry; in each
> Are nameless graces which no methods teach,
> And which a master hand alone can reach.
> If, where the rules not far enough extend,
>
> .   .   .   .
>
> Some lucky license answer to the full
> Th' intent proposed, that license is a rule.
>
> .   .   .   .
>
> Great wits sometimes may gloriously offend
> And rise to faults true critics dare not mend;
> From vulgar bounds with brave disorder part,
> And snatch a grace beyond the reach of art, . . .

Pope's caution that such deviation from the Rules must be rare and in accord with some classical precedent was less in tune with the languid support of the Rules among major writers than the beautifully phrased passage just quoted. Pope himself was capable of other references to Pindar's irregular greatness and to Horace's brave neglect, and his admiration for Shakespeare's illegitimate beauties has already been mentioned. Addison considered the Rules important, but he also knew that grace might lie beyond the reach of art, for he admired that "something that elevates and astonishes the fancy, and gives a greatness of mind to the reader, which few of the critics besides Longinus have considered," and confessed that a rule may be disregarded when the result is "a much higher beauty than the observation of such a rule would have been." Welsted was aware of beauties which are "rather to be felt, than describ'd." Hume also admitted the presence of a "something mysterious and inexplicable" in beauty—"a *MANNER*, a grace, an ease, a genteelness, an I-know-not-what." This kind of attractiveness "must be trusted to the blind, but sure testimony of taste and sentiment." Hogarth was running counter to the general feeling that grace was an inexplicable quality when in 1753 he attempted to formulate its secret in a certain serpentine line ("the line of grace") and exemplify it in sculpture, acting, and dancing.[4]

III

The place of nature poetry in the outlook of English classicism is one of the most difficult problems that the student of the period has to face. Earlier critics, looking primarily for straws that would indicate the direction of the wind towards the personal and pantheistic nature worship of the Romanticists, have overemphasized the importance of Thomson and Lady Winchelsea, Dyer, and Armstrong—writers who were in most respects typical Augustans in their love for quiet and leisure, for the Horatian ideal of life. English classicism was social in spirit. In so far as the love of Nature was an escape from the companionship of man it can be considered as a direct movement of revolt. English classicism was imbued with the sense of form. In so far as the admiration of Nature indicated a desire to escape from the artistry of man to the artlessness of Nature it was unclassical. English classicism was humanistic. In so far as the cult of sublimity elevated external forces, terrible and uncontrollable, and humbled the awed and fearful human being before them, it was a breakdown in man's feeling of power based on the conception of an orderly universe. English classicism was objective. In so far as Nature served as a stimulus for peronal lyricism nature poetry was romantic in embryo at least. But much of the so-called nature poetry of the century was thoroughly classical in its general tone. To abstract single "significant" passages is to falsify the whole picture. To regard the nature poetry of the eighteenth century as an illustration of any *primary* Romantic trend is to be false again to the spirit of the age. Man's thoughts were led back to Nature by sensibility which brought into action keenness of observation, a more specific vocabulary, and an emotionalism which found satisfaction in Nature when it was alienated by man's inhumanity to man; by sentimentality with its exaltation of natural goodness and the noble savage brought up beyond the contaminating influence of the complex and corrupt city; and in a lesser measure by the dream of an early age of simple virtue in Celtic, Norse, or Mediæval wonderlands where the dreamer joined hands with the sentimentalist in a vain regret for the idyllic or heroic years beyond recall.

An attempt to distinguish the basic classical attitude towards Nature from the various strands of revolt, and then to distinguish these distinct movements as sublime, or picturesque, as evidences of sensibility or of sentimentality or of the dream would be disconcerting to any one who prefers simplicity to honesty; but to deal with the "return to nature" as a single *primary* movement rather than as the complex *result* of several trends of thought which led deviously back to Nature would mean the continuance of an error of organization which has already caused much confusion in the analysis of English classicism. Sublimity deserves a separate treatment, but an examination into the "return to nature" as an aspect of the search for grace beyond the reach of art is here in order.

The revolution in landscape architecture which introduced the "natural" garden was the most important single movement away from artistry, regularity, and form. But this movement in gardening was itself an aspect of a larger movement towards the recognition that the beauty of Nature was inimitable by the hand of man. This new appreciation of the natural in the external world—essentially a revolt from form and from the philosophic concept of an orderly universe—is discoverable in articles and books on landscaping, in private letters, and in miscellaneous verse and prose as well as in that group of nature poets whose work represents the shift from an attention to Nature determined by considerations of science and natural religion to the more æsthetic, sentimental, or picturesque attitudes held by nature lovers of the late eighteenth century. In this section I shall examine briefly the approach to freedom, taken frequently with stumbling steps, as revealed in three channels— landscape gardening, the love of wild nature, and landscape poetry.

The Augustans were not blind to the song of the birds in spring nor to the delicate green of April trees, though they sometimes loved the social life of London even more. As a group they were not hostile to rural retirement, but they sought in the country companionship with men and books, the pleasures of the chase, or the satisfactions of the gentleman farmer in his stud, his cattle, and his fields of corn. Professor Myra Reynolds has studied most completely what might be called the ultra-classical attitude, of which the main features were a dislike for the grand and the terrible (mountains, storms, winter scenes), an equal dislike for the mysterious and the remote, a decided friendliness for gently idyllic pastoral regions, a desire for formal gardens and parks, and a lack of close observations which resulted in generalized, conventional, and imitative description in poetry. It must be remembered, however, that such generalizations are subject to numerous exceptions, and that during the course of the century taste was in a rapid process of change.[5]

Some instances of the extreme classical attitude will illuminate generalities. John Evelyn could appreciate a sweet morning with bushes filled with nightingales, but he was more often entranced by the elegance of gardens and manorial estates, parterres of flowers, softly gliding rivers, sweet downs and valleys, good pastures, and verdant plains dotted with sheep. Another representative conservative is Gay, who in *Rural Sports* (1720) praised the country for its sports, its wholesome air, its opportunities for reveries and reading, its beauty of sea and sky, and for the stimulus it could give to the contemplation of God in his works. Addison was less of a sportsman than Gay, but otherwise his attitude was not dissimilar. The infinity of Nature led him to conventional religious speculation; the detail of Nature he glossed over in the classical manner without any effort to rival a painter with his word pictures. Chesterfield advised his son in 1746 to visit Switzerland to study the constitution, the military organization and the like, but forgot to mention the scenery. Among extreme classicists artificiality accompanied indifference to the sheer beauty of the world. The pastoral poem was an inherited portion of rural affectation which led ladies and gentlemen to be painted as shepherds and shepherdesses amid idyllic scenery, induced women of sufficiently high rank to organize country fêtes of the type described by Frances Brooke in *Lady Julia Mandeville*, and influenced statesmen with cultural interests like Bolingbroke to paint rakes and spades in their country halls so that they could call their manor houses farms. Walks and arches, seats and entrances to grottoes were arranged to frame views of picturesque character, and Nature was assisted by the hand of the artist who planned temples and pagodas, ruins and statues, to bring sentimental associations to the aid of ideas of beauty evoked by Nature's naked loveliness. In some extreme cases temples and grottoes were designed to give moral instruction, so that a manor might contain, as did Aaron Hill's, grottoes of Power, Riches, and Learning, a cave of Content and a vault of Despair. Yet not all was artifice. Pope could on occasion prefer the pleasures of the advancing spring to poetry; Swift could seek out fine prospects and appreciate the budding willows and cherry trees; Johnson could lament the existence of men insensible to the delights of May.[6]

Landscape architecture is an art, and as such has always implied the interference of the artist working by some sort of rule or theory with the natural beauties of the terrain. In gardening the escape from formality could never be as complete as the lover of wild, untrammeled Nature desired, but though progress was limited and stumbling it began early and is significant as one of the forces leading to the breakdown of rational classicism.

The English garden of the seventeenth century had been dominated by the formalist, Le Nôtre. Walls separated the comparatively small garden plot from the "wild," untrimmed meadows and hillsides beyond the garden pale. Water toys, artificial perspectives on painted canvas, and topiary work were used. Walks were straight. Seats were accommodated to "elegant" views. In the eighteenth century Bridgman, Langley, and Kent tried to reduce this artificial formalism. Bridgman retained straight walks for the main divisions of his gardens, but developed the "wilderness" in each of the divided parts and invented the ha-ha or sunken hedge as a means of eliminating the hitherto clearly drawn distinction between the garden and the other grounds. In 1728 Langley declared the "stiff, regular" garden shocking, but his tolerance for canvas ruins to terminate a prospect shows that he could not escape from artificiality.

Kent's ruling principle was that Nature abhorred a straight line, but despite his study of Salvator Rosa and Poussin, or rather because of such study, he "imitated" Nature so completely as to insert dead trees into his landscape and he continued to frame artificial picturesque prospects. Temples and statues also won Kent's approval as means of centering scenes and ending walks. Shenstone developed the idea of making pictures in landscape and focusing attention on them by means of skillfully located seats and summer houses. To some literary men this artifice was appealing. Sir William Temple, an early figure of course, discussed the irregular garden only to reject it in favor of the beauty of "some certain proportions, symmetries, or uniformities." Thomson enjoyed the "regulated wild" and genius when "tam'd by cool judicious art." *The Lounger*, as late as 1785, went so far as to suggest that "the romantic scenes of nature might be much aided and improved by the skilful hand of art," and William Cowper could write

> But elegance, chief grace the garden shows,
> And most attractive, is the fair result
> Of thought, the creature of a polish'd mind.[7]

These passages extend more than a century beyond Milton's description of the flowers of Eden,

> which not nice art
> In beds and curious knots, but nature boon
> Poured forth profuse, on hill, and dale, and plain;

and reveal the painful slowness with which a taste developed for the majesty and grace of the inimitable Divine Workman whose effects no artist or gardener could hope to emulate. Yet the progress towards freedom was a logical accompaniment of the growing preference for natural talents or genius in the artist, for the primitive as opposed to the sophisticated in art, and for the increasing dissatisfaction with the Rules and with the beauty founded on regularity and proportion. The movement was begun by classicists who felt the insufficiency of rule to explain or duplicate the beauty of the world.[8]

Addison was the first important literary artist to prefer Fontainebleau's rude stones and its "river winding through woods and meadows" to the statues and whimsical fountains of Versailles. In

The Spectator Addison had laughed at the trimming of greenery into cones, globes, and pyramids. Shaftesbury's view of the harmonious universe led him to praise the glories of Nature in the person of Philocles in *The Moralists* who determined to

no longer resist the passion growing in me for things of a *natural* kind; where neither *art,* nor the *conceit* or *caprice* of man has spoil'd their *genuine order,* by breaking in upon that *primitive state.* Even the rude *rocks,* the mossy *caverns,* the irregular unwrought *grotto's,* and broken *falls* of waters, with all the horrid graces of the *wilderness* itself, as representing NATURE more, will be the more engaging, and appear with a magnificence beyond the formal mockery of princely gardens.

Pope was in the movement for more of Nature and less of art. He was intimate with Bridgman and Kent, and his own opinion was regarded as authoritative on small gardens. In 1722 he admired the irregular gardens of Sherburne with wilderness and winding walk and ruinous bridge—views "more romantic than imagination can form them." In the *Moral Essays* he urged that "improvements" should be suited to "the genius of the place":

> To build, to plant, whatever you intend
> To rear the Column, or the Arch to bend,
> To swell the Terrace, or to sink the Grot;
> In all let Nature never be forgot.
>
> .   .   .   .
>
> Consult the Genius of the Place in all;
> That tells the Waters or to rise, or fall;
> Or helps th' ambitious Hill the heavens to scale,
> Or scoops in circling theatres the Vale;
> Calls in the Country, catches op'ning glades,
> Joins willing woods, and varies shades from shades;
> Now breaks, or now directs, th' intending Lines;
> Paints as you plant, and, as you work, designs.

The same *Essay* contains a satiric picture of the formal garden:

> On every side you look, behold the Wall!
> No pleasing Intricacies intervene,
> No artful wildness to perplex the scene;
> Grove nods at grove, each Alley has a brother,
> And half the platform just reflects the other.

> The suff'ring eye inverted Nature sees,
> Trees cut to Statues, Statues thick as trees; . . .

Pope was not alone among the more significant classicists in his preference for the natural. Lady Mary Wortley Montagu had already written:

> Give me, great God! said I, a little farm . . .
> Where a clear Spring gives birth to murm'ring brooks,
> By nature gliding down the mossy rocks;
> Not artfully by leaden pipes convey'd,
> Or greatly falling in a forc'd cascade. . . .

Hume objected to the "clipt evergreens which they call a garden" in Holland. Fielding described Squire Allworthy's park as seeking to owe less to art than to Nature. R. O. Cambridge pointed to Book IV of *Paradise Lost* as "containing all the views, objects, and ambition of modern designing in gardening." Gilbert West attacked artificial landscape gardening in his dull Spenserian imitation, *Education*.[9]

Meanwhile Gray had followed Addison's lead and had branded Versailles as "a huge heap of littleness" in his private correspondence, and he and Walpole had been moved by the Alps. Joseph Warton in *The Enthusiast* had pleaded with the "green-rob'd Dryads" to lead him "from gardens deck'd with art's vain pomps." He too scorned Versailles, but he scorned Kent as well:

> Can Kent design like Nature? . . .
>
> .   .   .   .
>
> Though he, by rules unfetter'd boldly scorns
> Formality and method, round and square
> Disdaining, plans irregularly great.

Horace Walpole was perhaps more influential in persuading the readers of *The World* that the taste for "clipped hedges, regular platforms, [and] straight canals" was exploded.[10]

After 1750 illustrations of the feeling for the beauty beyond art in landscape are numerous. From the obscure Lady Echlin, who refused to use artificial shellwork because "what nature affords, growing on my rocks, . . . appears more beautiful in my eye, than the formal delicacy of laboured art," to the famous Edmund Burke, who disbelieved in the beauty of proportion and favored an escape from the geometrical garden, the approval of Nature *au naturel* meets one on all hands. Hogarth felt the "infinite variety of nature" superior to the "limited and insufficient" forms of art. Amory found Nature more delightful than "art has been able to form in the finest gardens of the world." Goldsmith approved the revolution in taste. Lord Kames found that Nature best fulfilled the need for uniformity and variety which was at the root of man's feeling for beauty. Armstrong believed English taste to be better in landscape than in any other field, though he found that there were still too many "temples, ruins, pyramids, obelisks, statues, and . . . other contemptible whims." Fanny Burney's Evelina considered Vauxhall gardens too formal. Cowper preferred "the performance of a God" (in contradiction to other of his statements) to

> Th' inferior wonders of an artist's hand!
> Lovely indeed the mimic work of art;
> But nature's work far lovelier.

Among landscape gardeners of the mid-century and beyond Capacity Brown with his passion for the serpentine reflected most completely perhaps the new conception of the universe—no longer an ordered universe but a profuse creation of infinite differentiation where regularity was unknown.[11]

These typical quotations just given indicate either a direct preference for the natural over the artistic or contain implications to that effect so clear that there can be no doubt of the writers' views. In a consideration of the appreciation of wild landscape the purely æsthetic attitude—the awareness of natural beauty beyond the power of art to reproduce—is much more difficult to disentangle from the feeling for sublimity. When the eighteenth-century nature lover did *not* share in the cult of the sublime his attitude was frequently religious, moral, or merely antisocial, and consequently of small importance in the development of the concept of a grace beyond the reach of art. Most frequently his attitude was the picturesque, for he attempted to find in Nature an imitation of the famous pictures of Salvator, Lorrain, and Poussin. This picturesque movement was highly important in eighteenth-century æsthetics, but it was a hindrance, not a help, in the quest for the natural as opposed to the

artistic. So long as poets looked for the great rock masses and precipices, the torrents, ruins, and caves, the "trees dense of growth," the
"blasted trunks and shattered boughs" of Salvator Rosa; or for
rolling plains or wide valleys with framing hills adorned with
groves, villas, Palladian bridges, castles, or antique temples familiar
to the students of Claude Lorrain, there was no possibility of an
escape from art or of any realization that art with its rules was impotent to match the profuse hand of the Creator. The picturesque
attitude developed side by side with the purer appreciation of Nature
and lent its aid whenever the amateur of Nature forgot what might
have been a necessary stimulus to observation in a delight for cloud
and stream and hill quite independent of any real or fancied resemblance to the continental masters of landscape.[12]

The appreciation of Nature apart from religious, moral, agricul-
tural or other considerations was for many reasons late in coming
to birth. The Greeks had tended to personify natural forces in their
mythology, and the early Christian church had converted the ancient
gods of stream and forest into fearful evil spirits. The slow growth of
civil institutions and of material civilization, particularly of highways
and of safe modes of travel in regions unimportant for agriculture
or commerce, made it difficult and even dangerous to visit regions of
wild beauty. The early patrons of the Renaissance artists had been
churchmen or great nobles who had demanded historical and religious
canvases to adorn their cathedrals or portraits to adorn their castles,
and landscape could at first be no more than a background for the
all-important story of Christian martyrdom or heroic valor. Even
when Nature was noticed for her own sake the classical theories of the
general and the ideal led painters to strive for the superior beauty
which the forms of the material world were struggling to achieve
rather than for any reproduction of the actual lines and colors before
their eyes. The awakening came with the removal of some of these
conditions. Most important was the increasing safety of travel beyond the political and commercial centers. The Grand Tour became
more and more popular with wealthy young Englishmen and it
meant the passage of the Alps and the possibility of studying Italian
landscape painting or even of purchasing pictures and prints for
English galleries. The result of the Grand Tour was not always

the picturesque attitude, but occasionally the development of genuine observation of the beauty of the lakes and glens of England. Keenness of observation was increased at the same time by the movement of sensibility, and even the movement of sentimentality may have led some few individuals through an exaltation of the primitive to an artistic awareness of the grander aspects of the external world.[13]

Some few instances of æsthetic appreciation of wild Nature occur at early dates. John Evelyn was capable of it when in no physical danger. He found the "horrid" (*cf.* Latin *horridus*, rugged) Alps pleasant, and the Apennines in 1644 "one of the most pleasant, new, and altogether surprising objects that I had ever beheld." The passage of John Dennis across the Alps in 1688 must be treated in connection with the Cult of the Sublime. It was not until the beginning of the new century that appreciation of Nature's wonders became fairly general. Addison was aware of such beauty before 1705. He got the "noblest summer-prospect in the world" when he saw from Berne a huge range of mountains buried in snow; and he enjoyed traveling along the river Inn where on either side there was "a vast extent of naked rocks and mountains, broken into a thousand irregular steeps and precipices." In *The Spectator*, however, he was more concerned with sublimity. In 1712 James Haywood wrote that "the beautiful wildness of nature opens to me a more agreeable scene, than the most studi'd elegancies of art." In 1716 the anonymous "On Solitude" in Dryden's *Miscellany* revealed admiration for mountains and ocean. Even the social luminary, Lady Mary Wortley Montagu, would have enjoyed the Alps in 1718 but for the cold and the rain. Later she was to enjoy such scenes. Bishop Berkeley liked the "romantic confusion" of hills and vales and barren mountains at Inarime. In 1729 Edmund Law justified mountains in a note to King's *De Origine Male* as not only useful for their vines and minerals and wholesomeness of air but likewise for "most pleasant prospects." Mallet found Tenby in Wales delightful for its cliffs and rock formations in 1734 and in the next year he admired the scenery around Lake Leman.[14]

In the development of appreciation for landscape Gray was an important figure. He had felt the pleasure of the "little chaos of

mountains and precipices" near Burnham in 1737. In 1739 he
gloried in the romantic beauty of the Alps. In 1769 he made one
of the first tours of the Lake region and sent his impressions (published by Mason in 1775) to his friend Wharton in journal form.
In accurate and fresh observation Gray was in advance of his contemporaries, though even he carried with him his perspective glass to
accentuate the picturesque beauty of Nature. Gray's enthusiasm for
the Alps and for the Lakes is too well known to justify quotation.
It will be more profitable to show that many of Gray's contemporaries had similar feelings.[15]

Joseph Warton's *Enthusiast* has already been quoted. Meanwhile
Thomson had had occasional Pisgah views of the loveliness of Nature
apart from the conventional thoughts of the sublimity of the harmonious Shaftesburean universe. Pope sometimes enjoyed wild
landscape. Hume found "wild agreeable prospects" in Stiria. John
Whaley admired the cliffs and brooks near Tintern Abbey in 1745.
Thomas Amory went into ecstasies over the Lake Country, though
it must be confessed that his descriptions in *John Buncle* are often
suspiciously similar to the conventional canvases of Salvator Rosa.
In 1766 Mrs. Montagu was enthusiastic over the Scotch highlands.
In 1770 Smollett followed suit. Hannah More, Fanny Burney,
James Boswell, and Richard Graves all expressed a love for Nature
that was sometimes free from attitudinizing about the picturesque.
And in the meanwhile Gray's account of the Lakes had been followed
by the excursions, guides, and surveys of Hutchinson (1776),
Thomas West (1778), and James Clarke (1787). The tours of
Gilpin were numerous, and his influence was great, but he was a
high priest in the worship of the picturesque.[16]

The nature poets of the eighteenth century will be disappointing
to any one who expects to find a sincere and unpretentious love for
the beautiful. There is much scientific and religious speculation on
Nature as the revelation of God the divine workman; there is a joy
in the open for its invigorating effects; there is a pleasure in rural
sports; there is some conscious imitation of Latin nature poetry;
there is an agrarian interest in the well-kept landed estate; there is
the poetry of the specific locality—the progeny of *Cooper's Hill*—
filled with almost everything except actual observation; there is the

picturesque; and there is the growing interest in the sublime; but there is little indication of an escape from formality and rule sufficiently important to justify the attention bestowed on poetry which —before the period of Gray and Collins—was artistically poor, and in substance conventionally classical, the product of rational country gentlemen who failed to feel the spirit deeply interfused and would not permit their hearts to leap at rainbows in the sky.[17]

There was, it must be confessed, some slow progress in the direction of a spontaneous lyricism at the beauty of Nature, but the love of quietude and leisure, the Horatian convention of rural retirement, and the scientific preoccupations which led to the study of the orderly structure of the best of all possible worlds explain most of the early nature poetry—and these attitudes were all in keeping with rational classicism. G. G. Williams has shown how science led to a new observation of Nature through the actual investigations of the members of the Royal Society, through Locke's insistence on sense experience, through Berkeley's emphasis on perception and vision, through Addison's consequent insistence on visual images in the *Pleasures of the Imagination* papers, and through Newton's conception of the world of "perfect order and universal goodness" ruled by a God of law. Deism was important in eliminating the Calvinist conception that the imperfections of Nature were the result of original sin. Thomas Burnet's *Telluris Theoria Sacra* (1681–89) had developed this theory and given rise to a considerable controversy in the course of which attempts were made to show the utility and sometimes the beauty of mountains and waste places in order to justify the goodness and wisdom of the universal God. It was difficult to submerge these rational, scientific, and conventionally "classical" attitudes in a new appreciation for the beauty of scenery untouched by the hand of man.[18]

During the Restoration period there was practically no intimate nature poetry based on actual æsthetic experience. Such nature passages as do occur are in imitative elegies and pastorals; in tragedies where they match in unreality the honor, courage, and love of Aurengzebes and Almanzors; or in the panegyrical, moral, and historical "hill poems." Even Milton, whose Eden was to be pointed out as a model in the eighteenth century, looked on Nature largely through books and seems to have preferred an impossible Arcady to the "real features of a simple English scene."[19]

It was the Age of Pope which produced the first genuine nature poetry—a few lyrics such as "To the Nightingale" and "Nocturnal Reverie" by the otherwise conventional Lady Winchelsea; a passage or two in Croxall's Spenserian "Vision"; a touch in Allan Ramsay, who stooped too often from direct observation of Nature to moralize his song; the trio of winter poems by Armstrong, Riccaltoun, and Thomson in 1726; and the fairly direct description of the view from Grongar Hill by Dyer. Armstrong's blank verse poem *Winter* was a description of a Scotch winter remarkably free from the twin curses of reflection and generalized description. Robert Riccaltoun's *A Winter's Day* was a product of early eighteenth-century melancholy in which the poet revealed a delight in darkness and storm which suited his gloomy mood. Thomson was essentially scientific and objective. Only in the exactness of his observation—itself in his case a product of scientific interest—and in his appreciation of the sublimity of the wild frozen north does he point forward to nineteenth-century Romanticism. Not this early group of writers, but the mid-century Miltonists—Gray, Collins, Mason, and the Wartons —carried the day for the love of wild Nature. Dodsley's *Miscellany* contained many of their poems and stands as an interesting landmark of the changing taste of the eighteenth century, for altogether it contained almost fifty poems which revealed real observation or genuine love of Nature.[20]

NOTES TO CHAPTER XVI

1. W. G. Howard, "Ut Pictura Poesis," *P.M.L.A.*, XXIV, 86; Chambers, *History of Taste*, p. 318; Clark, *Boileau and the French Classical Critics in England*, p. 263 ff.; Spingarn, *Critical Essays*, I, c.

2. Congreve, *Double-Dealer*, Act II, scene I; Vanbrugh, *Provok'd Wife*, Act II, scene II and Act IV, scene II; *Æsop*, Act V, and *The False Friend*, Act II; Farquhar, *Beaux-Stratagem*, Act II, scene II; Shaftesbury, *Characteristicks*, I, 137; Gay, *Poetical Works*, p. 320; Prior, in Chalmers, *op. cit.*, X, 155; Gildon, in Durham, *op. cit.*, p. 40; Hutcheson, *Inquiry*, p. 250; Fielding, *The Miser*, Act III, scene IV; Chesterfield, *Letters*, I, 212, 372, 385, II, 74, 89, 153, 206, 225 and *Works*, V, 347–352; Hume, *Treatise*, p. 612; Burke, *Works*, I, 167; Mrs. Montagu, in Blunt, *op. cit.*, I, 153, II, 6; Fanny Burney, *Early Diary*, I, 24.

3. Spingarn, *Critical Essays*, I, xciii–xcvii; Boileau, *Œuvres*, pp. 304–305, 21, 262–263, 477; Locke, *Essay*, p. 102.

4. Pope, *Essay on Criticism*, lines 141–146, 148–149, 152–155, 163–166, and *Temple of Fame*, in *Works*, I, 215–216; Addison, *Spectator*, Nos. 409, 592; Welsted, in Durham, *op. cit.*, p. 364; Hume, *Essays*, II, 244; Hogarth, *Analysis*, p. 75.

5. Myra Reynolds, *The Treatment of Nature in English Poetry between Pope and Wordsworth*, Chicago, 1909, p. 57.

6. Evelyn, *Diary*, pp. 163, 167, 281–282, 315, 447; Gay, *Poetical Works*, pp. 108–109; Chesterfield, *Letters*, I, 149; W. J. Courthope, *Addison*, pp. 45, 50; Pope, *Works*, VI, 338, VIII, 12; Manwaring, *Italian Landscape*, pp. 128, 172; Goldsmith, *Miscellaneous Works*, p. 464; Frances Brooke, *Lady Julia Mandeville*, pp. 47–48, 60; Swift, *Correspondence*, III, 173, note 1, and *Journal to Stella*, March 19, 1710–11, March 26, April 6, April 20, May 1, May 19, August 27, 1711, January 25, 1711–12, July 1, July 18, 1712.

7. Manwaring, *op. cit.*, pp. 122–127, 129–133, 135; Temple, *Upon the Gardens of Epicurus*; Thomson, *Autumn*, in Chalmers, *op. cit.*, XII, 443; *Lounger*, No. 9; Cowper, *Task*, Book III, lines 638–640.

8. Milton, *Paradise Lost*, Book IV, lines 241–243.

9. Addison, *Works*, IV, 326, I, 412; *Guardian*, No. 101; *Spectator*, Nos. 414, 477; Shaftesbury, *Characteristicks*, II, 393–394; George Sherburn, *The Early Career of Alexander Pope*, pp. 281–287; Pope, *Works*, IX, 300–303, III, 175–176; *Guardian*, No. 173; Warton, *Essay on Pope*, II, 176–178; Lady Mary Wortley Montagu, *Letters*, II, 464; Hume, *Letters*, I, 117; Fielding, *Tom Jones*, Book I, Chapter IV; R. O. Cambridge, *World*, No. 118; Phelps, *op. cit.*, p. 64.

10. Gray, *Letters*, I, 27; Joseph Warton, in Chalmers, *op. cit.*, XVIII, 159–160; Walpole, *World*, No. 6.

11. Lady Echlin, in Richardson, *Correspondence*, V, 69; Burke, *Works*, I, 148; Hogarth, *Analysis*, pp. 209–210; Amory, *John Buncle*, p. 192; Goldsmith, *Citizen of the World*, Letter XXXI; Kames, *Elements*, I, 264, II, 349, 353; Armstrong, *Miscellanies*, II, 239; Burney, *Evelina*, p. 238; Hussey, *The Picturesque*, p. 137.

12. Manwaring, *op. cit.*, pp. 95, 115.

13. Hussey, *op. cit.*, pp. 6–8, 12; Manwaring, *op. cit.*, pp. 7–12.

14. Evelyn, *Diary*, pp. 88, 224, 226; R. S. Crane, Review of Claire-Elsame Engel's "La Littérature alpestre en France et en Angleterre au XVIIIe et XIXe siècles," *Philological Quarterly*, XI, 175; Addison, *Works*, I, 511, 518, 537; James Haywood, quoted by Havens, "Romantic Aspects of the Age of Pope," *loc. cit.*, p. 304; R. D. Havens, "Changing Taste in the Eighteenth Century," *loc. cit.*, p. 514; Lady Mary Wortley Montagu, *Letters*, I, 265, II, 160; Berkeley, in Pope, *Works*, IX, 4; Edmund Law, quoted by C. A. Moore, "The Return to Nature in English Poetry of the Eighteenth Century," *Studies in Philology*, XIV, 243.

15. Gray, *Letters*, I, 7, 38, 44, 48, 235, 302, II, 265, III, 35, 93, 152, 288; Gosse, *Gray*, pp. 16, 185 ff.; Phelps, *op. cit.*, pp. 169 ff.; Manwaring, *op. cit.*, p. 53.

16. Thomson, in Chalmers, *op. cit.*, XII, 425; Pope, *Works*, VIII, 513, IX, 312; Hume, *Letters*, I, 130; Amory, *John Buncle*, pp. 87 ff.; Whaley, quoted Manwaring, *op. cit.*, p. 110; Smollett, *Humphrey Clinker*, p. 305; Hannah More, *Letters*, p. 98; Burney, *Early Diary*, I, 252, 261; Graves, *Spiritual Quixote*, II, 180, 218; Boswell, *Account of Corsica*, p. 65.

17. Marr, *Modern English Romanticism*, p. 228; Hussey, *The Picturesque*, pp. 20–24.

18. G. G. Williams, "The Beginning of Nature Poetry in the Eighteenth Century," *loc. cit.*, pp. 583–608; C. A. Moore, *op. cit.*, pp. 250–255.

19. Amy Reed, *op. cit.*, pp. 142–144; V. P. Squires, "Milton's Treatment of Nature," *Modern Language Notes*, IX, 454 ff.

20. Phelps, *op. cit.*, pp. 28–31; Reed, *op. cit.*, pp. 146–147, 149, 152; Marr, *op. cit.*, pp. 184–185; G. G. Williams, *op. cit.*, *passim*; C. A. Moore, *op. cit.*, *passim*; Herbert Drennon, "James Thomson's Contact with Newtonianism and His Interest in Natural Philosophy," *P.M.L.A.*, XLIX, 71 ff., and "Scientific Rationalism and James Thomson's Poetic Art," *loc. cit.*, pp. 460–471.

CHAPTER XVII

THE EXTENSION OF THE BOUNDS
OF TASTE

I

THE DIFFICULTY of finding a tenable basis for the standard of taste was accentuated by the growing interest in cultures which diverged from the classical ideal. Oriental, Norse, Celtic, and Mediæval influences deepened the doubts of an absolute beauty which the persistent interest in the Elizabethans had initiated. Chaos in taste was sometimes the result. A proud connoisseur could assure his guest that it was "but a little way from the Palladian portico to the Gothic tower; from the Lapland to the Chinese house, or from the temple of Venus to the hermitage." Amid these various modes of beauty the ideal of uniformity in taste was lost.[1]

The study of the Bible as literature opened the door to an insight into the beauty of the Orient. Milton found models for the literary kinds in Scripture as valid as those of Greece and Rome: for instance, *Job* was a model for the brief epic, the *Song of Solomon* for the pastoral drama. Cowley agreed. Addison often praised the Bible for its magnificent and sublime style and found the *Psalms* superior to Horace or Pindar in imaginative power and in freedom from "absurdity and confusion of style." John Husbands exalted Hebrew poetry far above the classics, for the sublimity of the psalmists and the prophets permitted the mind of man to delight in what was great and unbounded and gave it room to exert all its faculties. To Husbands the poetry of the Hebrews was the poetry of a primitive people—strong, energetic, and sublime—with a notable boldness in personification, allegory, metaphor, and rhythmic repetition.[2]

It was not until the middle of the century that the most important contribution to the literary study of the Bible appeared in Bishop Lowth's *Praelectiones Academicae de Sacra Poesi Hebraeorum* (1753). This Latin work was not translated into English until 1787, but by that time it had brought to Lowth a European reputation as an interpreter of the poetic form of Hebrew verse and as a champion of an Oriental style of beauty equally valid with that produced by the rational spirit of the Enlightenment on a Græco-Roman foundation. Lowth was influenced by Longinus, but his interest in Scripture as literature was neither entirely derivative nor exclusively academic. He was moved to genuine enthusiasm by the sublimity of *Isaiah* and *Job*, and was able to impart some of his own feeling to men like Warburton, Hurd, Joseph Warton, and Blair, who defended his cause and developed the idea adumbrated by Lowth that poetic imagery drew its color and strength from the background of experience which differed for each folk. In this way the praise of the Bible was merged with the deterministic theory of literary productivity.[3]

The *Arabian Nights*, at first in French translation (1704–17), rivalled the Bible in influence. Progress was slow, however, and there was much ignorance and half knowledge. Purely antiquarian interest has little to do with literary modes; and the use of Oriental apologues for didactic purpose, and of the "Oriental traveller" for satiric ends must be received with due caution. Chesterfield, for instance, wrote an Oriental allegory, but objected to "the Oriental ravings and extravagances of the *Arabian Nights*." The orientalism of Addison, Goldsmith, Johnson, and Collins was most superficial. Joseph Warton's objection was just: "The Turks, the Persians, and Americans, of our poets, are, in reality, distinguished from Englishmen only by their turbans and feathers; and think and act, as if they were born within the bills of mortality." Whitehead and Cambridge found little genuine knowledge at the base of the Oriental fad. John Gilbert Cooper regarded the "Chinese madness" as a "deviation from truth and nature." John Brown sided with Cooper, and Goldsmith delighted in showing off the ignorance of Oriental faddists who collected all their "knowledge of Eastern manners from fictions every day propagated here, under the titles of Eastern tales and Oriental histories. At the end of the century Beattie was still hostile.[4]

Despite the opposition, interest in the Orient spread. A full account of its development in fiction has been given by Martha Conant in *The Oriental Tale in England in the Eighteenth Century.* Addison's early attitude of patronizing amusement gave way to some appreciation of exotic charm in *The Guardian,* No. 167. Pope and his friends ridiculed the *Arabian Nights* in *Martinus Scriblerus,* but Pope recommended them to Atterbury—who found them nonsense— and admitted that he might find material in them for "the wild and exotic" fairy tale or vision which he occasionally longed to write. Ambrose Philips translated Persian tales. There were slight traces of orientalism in Thomson's *Seasons,* in Somerville's *Chace,* and in Collin's *Persian Eclogues* in 1739. In 1735 Lyttelton published his *Persian Letters* in imitation of Montesquieu. Gibbon and Burke were fascinated by the Orient as young men, and in maturity they found opportunity to renew their early curiosity—Gibbon in the peripheral chapters of *The Decline and Fall,* and Burke in his Indian interests. Hawkesworth gave several Oriental tales in the *Adventurer* where at times he revealed a pleasure at the violations of rational probability permitted by the "machinery" of the genii. *The Connoisseur* was hostile to orientalism, but its persistent attacks show the growth of the fad.[5]

The work of William Chambers was important in the field of architecture and gardening. In 1757 he published his *Design for Chinese Buildings* in which he described the pleasing, "horrid," and romantic impressions made by Chinese gardens. In 1772 the *Dissertation on Oriental Gardening* stressed the symbolic meaning of the Chinese garden. In 1761 Bishop Percy translated from the Portuguese a four-volume Chinese novel, *Han Kiou Chooan,* and in 1763 he published in two volumes, *Miscellaneous Pieces Relating to the Chinese.* In 1783 Blair wrote enthusiastically of Oriental literature as a revelation of the sublimity of the primitive imagination in exotic surroundings. In the same decade Sir William Jones published the first fruits of his Persian studies. Save for Lowth and his friends in Biblical fields, Chambers, Percy, and Jones were the chief Orientalists in the arts. In history the original work of Orme on India and the translation of Du Halde's *History of China* provided food for public curiosity and exerted a certain but unassessed influence on the taste for Oriental art. Save for the new appreciation of the Bible the æsthetic influence of the Orient was slight. Only in alliance with other forces does it take on significance.[6]

II

Scholarly interest in Norse antiquities began before 1700, but the influence of this curiosity on literature was for a long time slight. Sir William Temple published two Latin translations of the song of Regner Lodbrog in his essay *Of Heroic Virtue,* and in 1703 the first translation of a complete Norse poem, "The Incantation of Hervor," appeared in Hicke's *Linguarum Veterum Septentriona-lium Thesauras.* The "Incantation" gradually became known and was put into verse at intervals throughout the century. In *The Spectator* Steele versified two Lapland odes with "improvements" which converted them into gallant love poems. "The Waking of Angantyr" was included in the 1716 edition of the Dryden-Tonson *Miscellany.* At some undetermined date the elder Thomas Warton translated into English the two Runic odes from Temple's essay. In 1741 two Danish odes idealizing Viking life as productive of enthusiastic and moving poetry appeared in *Polite Correspondence,* possibly the work of John Campbell and William Oldys. In *The Rambler* Johnson told the moral tale of Anningait and Ajut in a Greenland setting, and Wharton contributed the story of King Hacho of Lapland to *The Idler,* No. 96.[7]

The work of P. H. Mallet on Danish antiquities between 1755 and 1777 gave impetus to what had been hitherto a very minor interest in the history of taste. Mallet, by birth a Swiss, became professor of belles-lettres at Copenhagen in 1752, and there within three years he prepared his *Introduction a L'Histoire de Dannemark* on the laws, customs, and religion of his adopted country. In 1756 he published *Monuments de la Mythologie et de la Poesie des Celtes, et particulierement des anciens Scandinaves.* Mallet's confusion of Norseman and Celt was unfortunate, but despite his mistakes and his generally apologetic attitude his work became the chief resource for the poet and student curious concerning Northern Antiquities. Thomas Gray was reading it carefully by 1758, and in 1770 Bishop Percy, an amateur in all unfamiliar modes of beauty, published an English translation under the title of *Northern Antiquities*.[8]

The translation of Mallet was not the only service Bishop Percy rendered to the Norse movement. Though he could not read Norse he prepared five translations from the Latin in 1761, which were issued as *Five Pieces of Runic Poetry* in 1763. The prose translations were accompanied by the Norse originals. While Percy toiled, Gray toiled also, for it was in 1761 that he paraphrased "The Fatal Sisters" and "The Descent of Odin," though they were not published until 1768. The Norse interest was carried on by a number of minor figures—Steevens, Mathias, Williams, Sayers, Jerningham, and Anna Seward—but Mallet was the prime mover, and despite their slender productivity, Gray and Percy were the most important literary figures. To the eighteenth-century gentleman the enthusiasm for the Norsemen was incomprehensible. Walpole wrote: "Who can care through what horrors a Runic savage arrived at all the joys and glories they could conceive,—the supreme felicity of boozing ale out of the skull of an enemy in Odin's Hall?"[9]

Despite Walpole the interest in Norse awoke response from the lovers of liberty who, like Joseph Warton, regarded Scandinavia as "the source of liberty of Europe"; from those who longed, like the insignificant Jerningham, for a new poetic world to parallel the shopworn gods and goddesses of Greece and Rome; from the primitivists who found in the Norse poets examples of the advantages of early culture to the imagination of the artist, and in the Norse heroes illustrations of the hardy virtues of semibarbaric life in contact with Nature; from the passionate devotees of sublimity who found the need for awe and terror satisfied by the terrible legends of Scandinavia; and from dreamers who sought in the Norse tradition escape from the contemporary world in which they felt ill at ease.[10]

III

Some of these same aspirations of the eighteenth-century mind help to explain the Celtic revival. The strangeness of the Celtic fairyland provided a convenient focus for the revolt against effete Greek myth; in the primitive Welsh and Irish life there was an imaginative relief from sophistication; in Wales there was a plethora of wild mountain scenery dear to the adherents both of the picturesque and of the sublime; in the resistance of the Welsh and Irish to their English conquerors there was a satisfaction for the doctrinaire lovers of liberty, the Wilkites and Jacobins of the period; in Macpherson at least there was melancholy; and in the varied measures of the Welsh and Irish bards there was an interest for those who were weary of couplet or blank verse.[11]

The Celtic movement produced poems on Druidism and Celtic myth, actual translations from Irish, Welsh, and Gaelic, pretended translations and imitations, and poems on Celtic heroes, historical and legendary. The Celtic revival attracted the interest of Gray, Johnson, Percy, Mason, and Macpherson in addition to a host of lesser men. An important book on Celtic mythology was published almost every year between 1760 and 1800, and in almost every year some poet produced a translation, imitation, or original composition in the Celtic field. A group of Celtomaniacs revived the cult of the Welsh bards and made an attempt to read various Christian doctrines into their works. Three Welsh societies were founded in London—the Cymmrodorion in 1751, the Grand Lodge of the Order of the Druids in 1781, and the more strictly literary Cymreigyddion in 1795. Such widespread interest speaks plainly of the generally felt need for novel forms of beauty and for new sources of poetic inspiration.[12]

The Celtic poet Taliesin was noticed in *Polite Correspondence* in 1741 where a portion of one of his odes was cited and approved by the criteria of Nature and the classics. The anonymous authors were enthusiasts for lyric poetry which they felt might be improved by a study of Celtic and Norse poets. Llewlyn Dhy (Lewis Morris) was the moving spirit behind the Celtic revival, however. Himself an important Welsh poet he became an authority on Welsh meters, took part in the Cymmrodorion organized to study the language and literature of Wales, and corresponded extensively with English antiquarians. In 1755 Gray began *The Bard*, the material for which he found in the *History of England* by Carte, who was deeply indebted to Lewis Morris. Gray's *Bard* became the most significant popular landmark of the Celtic revival and was imitated by poetasters like Polwhele, Lovibond, and Penrose, while the massacre of the bards was being dramatized by Boaden and by Sotheby. Gray was interested in Celtic scholarship, though it is doubtful whether or not he ever learned Welsh, and he, as well as Percy, corresponded with Morris and Evan Evans, aided Mason in the composition of *Caractacus*, and translated four brief pieces from the Welsh. In a different portion of the Celtic field Gray continued to admire the work of Macpherson long after he began to distrust his professions of originality.[13]

Mason's *Caractacus* marked another important victory in the Celtic advance. The subject and setting were Celtic, and the use of the Druidical superstition popularized an atmosphere of "strange, wild beauty." The drama appeared in 1759. Six editions were sold by 1777. It was acted in 1776 and 1778, and translated into Greek, Latin, French, and Italian. Before 1811 it had been included in eleven editions of Mason's poems.[14]

In the year following the appearance of *Caractacus* Macpherson issued *Fragments of Ancient Poetry Collected in the Highlands of Scotland,* one of the most influential publications of the century. Macpherson had been preceded and perhaps influenced by Jerome Stone's translations from the Erse in *The Scots Magazine* (1755–1756) which were accompanied by remarks on the qualities of sublimity, spontaneity, and heart-moving tenderness, which seemed in the eyes of the writer to make a revival of Gaelic literature desirable. John Home, Alexander Carlyle, and Hugh Blair encouraged Macpherson to publish the *Fragments* which aroused sufficient interest to insure funds for the farther researches which led to the publication of *Fingal* in 1762 and *Tamora* in 1763.[15]

The poetic style of Macpherson is so far alien to modern taste that it is not only difficult to appreciate the tremendous significance of his work or to realize its extensive popularity, but even to read it. A quotation from Goethe will explain part of its now vanished appeal:

Ossian enticed us to Ultima Thule where we wander on a gray, endless heath amidst mossy gravestones that everywhere meet the eye; a heath with grass moved by a shivering wind around us; above us a heavily overclouded sky. Only by moonlight does this Caledonian night become day; dead heroes and wan maidens sweep near us, until at last we think we see the frightful ghost of Loda before us.

Paul Van Tieghem gives an even fuller analysis of the atmosphere of Ossian:

a green or sombre sea, lakes, desert lands, mountains, nude heaths, oaks and saplins, all covered with gray, low clouds scarcely penetrable by a melancholy sun or drowned in an eternal fog; sometimes a goat escaping or listening without movement; a huntsman pensive and solitary, with his dogs; everywhere broken trees, nameless tombs, ruined walls, remains of forgotten cities. It was a region in which one could sense the tragic end of romances, the nothingness of hopes and dreams, the melancholy fact of human destiny, the emotion of remembrance of things past, the poetry of ruins, the infinite vanity of all things.[16]

This new landscape was sublime. The impassioned lyricism, the moving plaints, the melancholy reflections on life and death awoke instant echo in the same sensitive hearts that had responded to the misfortunes of Clarissa. This general appeal to men of feeling was increased by the skill with which Macpherson gave voice to many currents of eighteenth-century thought. In Ossian one could find a picture of primitive man not yet depraved by civilization; a document for Nordic superiority; a new dignity for the poet in the picture of the last Gaelic bard; an illustration of the poet of nature ignorant of mechanical rule producing by force of sheer genius a work as beautiful and sublime, contemporaries thought, as those of Homer and Shakespeare; an example of the futility of literary "kinds"; a striking illustration of romantic love, "pure, tender, and chivalrous . . . fashioned of pity and protectiveness"; a surrender to the vague expansiveness of emotion; an apotheosis of melancholy over the instability of human life, the inevitable decay of glory, and the transiency of man's happiness on earth. When these things are borne in mind it ceases to be a matter for wonder that there were before 1800 five editions of the *Fragments*, three of *Fingal*, two of *Tamora*, and seventeen of Macpherson's *Collected Poems*, in addition to excerpts and imitations and transpositions into heroic couplets, as well as a huge body of controversial articles as to the authenticity and real rank of the work of the Scotch schoolmaster.[17]

The next significant contribution to the movement was made by Evan Evans, a scholarly Welsh curate, who was encouraged by Morris as well as by English scholars to publish *Some Specimens of Poetry of the Antient Welsh Bards* (1764) which contained ten poems with translations into English prose and a Latin treatise on the bards. Many of these poems were later put into English verse, and imitations were numerous.[18]

With Macpherson, Gray, Mason, and Evans the Celtic movement reached its artistic peak, but its popularity continued to spread. Goldsmith wrote on the Irish bard Carolan. Doctor Johnson encouraged Evans and was pleased with the *Specimens*. Beyond Goldsmith and Johnson the muster role of the Anglo-Celts is one of petty names. David Erskine Baker and Alexander Dow dramatized Ossian. Ogilvie produced *Rona* in 1777 and *The Fame of the Druids* in 1787. Henry Brooke wrote his *Cymbeline* in 1778. John Smith translated fourteen Gaelic poems and constituted himself the continuator of Macpherson; Mathias embraced both Norse and Celtic pieces in his *Runic Odes* (1781). Edward Jones produced an important work on Welsh poetry and music in 1784. J. C. Walker wrote a similar work on Irish poets in 1786. Charlotte Brooke compiled the *Reliques of Irish Poetry* (1789) which contained both translations and originals of heroic poems, elegies, and songs. There were lesser men than these, but a sufficient roll has been called to suggest that with the continued popularity of Gray, Mason, and Macpherson the Celtic movement was more extensive than either the Oriental or the Norse and consequently more effective in destroying the universal standard of taste.[19]

IV

The Oriental, the Norse, and the Celtic movements encountered little opposition. Until Macpherson stormed Europe the new interests were limited to comparatively small coteries of amateurs and seemed sufficiently unimportant to obviate the necessity of a formal opposition. Nor had these literatures during the formative period of classicism helped to mold the classical spirit by the contrast they afforded to it. With the Mediæval Revival it was different. The

Renaissance classicists were in conscious opposition to the literature
and spirit of the Middle Ages, and this opposition continued to be
widespread during the eighteenth century. *Romantic* and *Gothic*
were terms originally associated with the romances of the Middle
Ages which were looked upon with disfavor for both moral and
æsthetic reasons. The "whole pleasure" of the *Morte D'Arthur*,
according to Ascham, "lay in open manslaughter and bold bawdry."
The romances were felt to be, as Gregory Smith has phrased it, "the
disordered product of a disordered literary age. They had no decency
in proportions, no coherence of episodes." Puttenham relegated the
romances to the mob; Nashe objected to their complete unreality;
Meres presented a long list of those worthy of censure; and Ben
Jonson attacked them in *Every Man Out of His Humour*. In a
later generation Thomas Rymer dismissed the romances as obsolete;
Shaftesbury rejoiced that Cervantes had destroyed the spirit of
Gothic chivalry; Addison considered the Middle Ages as a time
of "monkish ignorance"; Mandeville was irked by the impractical,
idealistic spirit of romance literature; Swift recorded how the three
sons in *A Tale of a Tub* "travelled through several countries, encountered a reasonable quantity of giants, and slew certain dragons";
Thomson thought of Chaucer as shining through a "Gothic cloud";
Johnson laughed at collectors of ballads and books in black letter
and considered "Chevy Chase" a specimen of "chill and lifeless
imbecility"; and Cowper spoke of the "tedious years of Gothic darkness" between the great age of Rome and the Renaissance. Even
Thomas Warton, who devoted so much scholarly attention to the
period, at last sang his palinode in the "Verses on Sir Joshua
Reynolds' Painted Window" where he admitted that the truth of
Reynolds' art had at last destroyed

> The fond illusions of my wayward mind
> For long enamour'd of a barbarous age,
> A faithless truant to the classic page . . .

It is only fair to present from the same poem the poet's admission
of the fascination that he had felt at times:

> Long have I lov'd to catch the simple chime
> To view the festive rites, the knightly play,

That deck'd heroic Albion's elder day;
To mark the mouldering halls of barons bold,
And the rough castle, cast in giant mould,
With Gothic manners Gothic arts explore
And muse on the magnificence of yore.

An investigation of Warton's famous *History of English Poetry* confirms the verdict of R. D. Havens that Warton was primarily a classicist with an antiquarian interest which was for the most part satisfied to find in "the representation of ancient manners . . . that chief source of entertainment which we seek in ancient poetry."[20]

This widespread scorn for the era of Gothic darkness was not universal by any means, but it was sufficiently extensive to justify the view that the æsthetic appreciation of the romance, the ballad, and the Gothic architecture of the mediæval period marked a genuine revolution in English taste. Until the rise of the Gothic Novel late in the century the choice of mediæval subject matter for prose or poetry was rare, and the Gothic novel was pseudomediæval at best. Pope's *Eloisa to Abelard* in 1717, Mason's *Elfrida* in 1752, and various poems of Thomas Warton were the most important original works concerned with the non-Celtic Middle Ages. However, Gray, Walpole, Percy, Hurd, Leland, and Thomas Warton all took a scholarly interest in the period, and Hurd became its first great spokesman. Chatterton's forgeries intensified interest in the poetry of the Middle Ages. In time the Mediævalists attracted the attention of those who preferred nature and spontaneity to art and rule in poetic creation. The Middle Ages served as well as the land of the Bards, of the Skalds, or of the Oriental poet as a means of imaginative escape from the present, for the age of faith and sensibility, of idealism and chivalry was felt to offer an almost diametric contrast to the logic and formality, the skepticism and commercial emphasis of the reign of George III. Much of this has been touched upon elsewhere. Here it is necessary to trace as briefly as possible the revival of interest in chivalry and romance, in the ballad, and in the architecture of the Middle Ages.

Interest in the romances during the later Renaissance was slight. There was an admission by Sidney that romances might move one to "courtesy, liberality, and especially courage," an opinion of Ben

Jonson that King Arthur was the best subject for an heroic poem, and at the end of the period the interest of the young Milton in "those lofty fables and romances, which recount in solemn cantos the deeds of knighthood founded by our victorious kings." In the Restoration period Evelyn read romances but found that they had too little contact with life's realities; Rymer was familiar with old French and Provençal literature; Dryden wrote an opera, *King Arthur*, and, like Milton, contemplated an epic on the same subject. According to Joseph Warton, John Locke was fond of romances. Edmund Smith read them diligently. *The Tatler* quoted *Don Belianis*. Fielding was acquainted with the chapbook versions of *Guy of Warwick*, *The Seven Champions of Christendom* and other romances. The boy Goldsmith devoured them. Collins collected them. In 1752 Hawkesworth found the romance with its constant surprises more generally pleasing than the novel, for "fancy is still captivated with variety, and passion has scarce leisure to reflect that she is agitated with the fate of imaginary beings, and interested in events that never happened." "Moral probability" could be preserved by the use of sufficient supernatural "machinery," and the reader's first concession would be "abundantly rewarded" by new scenes and unbounded prospects.[21]

After 1752 interest in romance increased. Thomas Amory, Laurence Sterne, and David Garrick shared in it. Thomas Warton began to write a series of poems inspired by the pageant of chivalry, and his justification of Spenser in 1754 did much to throw light on the mediæval background of the poet, and to establish romance as a "kind" equally legitimate with the Virgilian epic. In 1759 Hurd began his defense of romances in *Dialogues Moral and Political* by pointing to the improvement wrought by gallantry in morals and courage, and by suggesting the historical truth of much in them that seemed false and fantastic. In 1762 his *Letters on Chivalry and Romance* gave more attention to the æsthetic approach, though Hurd was, in a measure, pleading a cause in which he did not believe wholeheartedly, for he found most of the romances barbarous and would not read them. The significance of his contribution was nevertheless great, for he argued that in romance there might be something "peculiarly suited to the views of a genius, and to the ends of poetry"; he explained the improbabilities of romance historically; he pointed to similar extravagances—the Laestrigons, Cyclops, the adventures of Hercules or of Theseus—in Greek literature; he traced the influence of feudal society on prowess, generosity, gallantry, and religion; and finally he suggested parallels between Gothic and primitive Grecian society and gave the palm to the Middle Ages because of the improved position of women and the "superior solemnity of the superstitions," and to the romances because they were "more sublime, more terrible, more alarming." In short, Hurd made it impossible for any one after him to dismiss romance with scorn as unworthy of serious consideration.[22]

To trace the interest in romance beyond Hurd would be futile, for the literary generation in which he worked with the Wartons and Gray saw not only the first extensive use of mediæval themes in poetry, but also the first modern chivalrous romance, Leland's *Longsword* (1762), and the first Gothic novel, Walpole's *Castle of Otranto* (1764).[23]

Interest in folklore scarcely survived Herrick. Dryden and Addison conceded the legitimacy of the "fairy kind of writing," and Rowe joined them in his awareness of Shakespeare's genius in treating the invisible world. Pope was tempted by fairy lore, and the machinery of *The Rape of the Lock*, mock-heroic as it is, remains the most imaginative evocation of airy beings during the century. Unimportant passages on the fairies occur in the work of Croxall, Tickell, Addison, Parnell, Sarah Fielding, and Lady Mary Wortley Montagu. Thomson mentioned the "fairy people" who throng in revelry "at fall of eve" in *Summer*, and in *The Castle of Indolence* he wrote a stanza which is famous for its evocation of the spirit world:

> As when a shepherd of the Hebrid isles,
> Plac'd far amid the melancholy main,
> (Whether it be lone fancy him beguiles;
> Or that aerial beings sometimes deign
> To stand embodied, to our senses plain)
> Sees on the naked hill, or valley low,
> The whilst in ocean Phœbus dips his wain,
> A vast assembly moving to and fro:
> Then all at once in air dissolves the wondrous show.

Collins's "Ode on the Popular Superstitions of the Highlands" was composed by 1750 but remained unpublished until 1788.[24]

The critical work of the two Wartons marked an epoch in the appreciation of "the terrible graces of magic and enchantment." The *Observations on the Fairie Queen* (1754) showed considerable interest in folklore and contained a justification of marvellous fiction and fablings that "rouse and invigorate all the powers of imagination" and store the fancy with those sublime and alarming images which true poetry delights to display. In 1756 Joseph Warton declared roundly in the *Essay on Pope* that poetry had suffered by becoming too rational to venture into fairy regions and by "totally laying aside the descriptions of magic and enchantment."[25]

Further reference to minor writers would not change the picture. There was a slight though steady interest in folkways throughout the century but it at no time assumed the dimensions of a movement. Strong-minded classicists like Fielding and Johnson had nothing but scorn for the "mummery" of elves and fairies, but for the most part the interest in folklore (except as a part of the Celtic and Norse movements) was too slight to draw fire from critics who had much more serious battles to fight in their war against unreason.

The interest in ballads, on the other hand, developed into a well-defined movement supported not only by the antiquary but by the æsthetic critic who sought here as in the work of Homer, Ossian, and Shakespeare, for evidences of the superiority of primitive art. Ever since Sidney's heart had been "moved more than with a trumpet" by the old song of Percy and Douglas there had been a few ballad enthusiasts among whom Pepys, Dorset, and Dryden must be included. Bolingbroke quoted "Chevy Chase" in 1702, and it was praised by the *Muse's Mercury* in 1707. Addison defended the ballad, but Wagstaffe and Dennis ridiculed it. Addison's *Spectator* papers, Nos. 70 and 74, containing the comparison of "Chevy Chase" to the *Aeneid* in order to win for it the sanction of neoclassical formalists, are well known. Gay permitted his shepherds in *The Shepherd's Week* to sing both "Chevy Chase" and "The Children in the Wood." Prior can scarcely be counted among the genuine enthusiasts for the ballad, though his elegant *Henry and Emma* brought the "Nut Browne Mayde" into prominence. Before 1725

Tickell had composed "Colin and Lucy," Lady Wardlaw had written "Hardyknute," and Hamilton had produced "The Braes o' Yarrow." The ballad imitations were beginning.[26]

Meanwhile ballads were being collected and published. James Watson issued *A Choice Collection of Comic and Serious Scots Poems, both Ancient and Modern* in 1706, 1709, and 1711. Primarily a song miscellany, these poems in Scotch dialect did much to revive interest in native Scotch poetry and seem to have been particularly influential on Allan Ramsay who published *The Evergreen* in 1724, a collection of old and new poems containing a defiant introduction which attacked the heroic couplet and compared the rude strength of the old with the insipid elegance of the new poetry. Unfortunately Ramsay was not a scrupulous editor. Like the later Chatterton he palmed off new songs, including his own "Vision," as old ballads, and in reprinting old poems he made additions and omissions, modernized the versification, and paid little heed to spelling. Even these attempts at compromise failed to win success for a venture which did not go into a second edition until 1761. Meanwhile to the south there were ballad additions to the Dryden-Tonson *Miscellany* in 1716, but despite the presence of "Chevy Chase," "Johnnie Armstrong," and one of the Robin Hood ballads, the majority of the additions were street-songs, broadside ballads, and artificial pastoral songs. The three-volume *Collection of Old Ballads*, 1723–1725, probably edited by Ambrose Phillips, was more important, for its historical introduction helped to spread knowledge of the ballads, and though the attitude of the editor was apologetic, he attempted a comparison between English ballad makers and Homer, Pindar, and Anacreon. Many modern songs helped to float a fairly comprehensive selection of genuine ballads. It was, indeed, the first significant effort at a revival.[27]

After 1725 interest again languished until mid-century. In 1760 Capell's *Prolusions; or Select Pieces of Antient English Poetry* contained a single ballad, "The Nut-browne Mayde," among other Tudor poems, but the advance in accuracy of editing was important. Gray and Goldsmith both expressed interest in balladry, but it was their friend Percy who did most to popularize the type, despite his apologetic attitude and his various "improvements." In the Preface to the famous *Reliques* (1765) Percy made it clear that his purpose in publishing such "a strange collection of trash" was not æsthetic but historical. He found in some of the ballads "a pleasing simplicity, and many other graces" capable of interesting the heart, but he considered them important primarily as illustrations of the history of language, of popular opinion, and of manners. Scarcely a poem, however, was published without alteration and expansion to render it elegant, smooth, and sentimental; and modern lyrics helped to give variety to the three-volume work. The "improvements," it is true, insured success. The accompanying *Essay on the Ancient Minstrels* inspired Beattie's poem, and the collection as a whole apparently encouraged Chatterton in his Rowley forgeries.[28]

Chatterton ranks with Percy and Macpherson as a force in the revival of mediæval poetry. His career is well known. Stirred by Bristol Cathedral where his uncle was sexton he began at an early age to people the past of the cathedral with a host of imaginary figures centering around Master William Canynge, a merchant, mayor, and cathedral patron. Rowley was presented as a parish priest who collected manuscripts for Canynge and composed poems often in ballad form. The means by which the "marvellous boy" disseminated his forgeries must be sought in the biographies. In a period of considerable philological ignorance many people believed them genuine, though Tyrwhitt's edition in 1777 should have effectually put an end to the controversy. To the modern philologist the jumble of archaic words from different dialects and periods seems terribly inept, and to the modern critic it is apparent that the poetic merit was grossly exaggerated by sentimentalists who deplored the tragic suicide of the young poet whom they regarded as a striking example of the native genius fashioning his high poetic compositions without the aid of formal education and neoclassic rules. The modern reader may discover a quaint attractiveness in the Rowley disguise, but he will find it difficult to admire much except "An Excellent Balade of Charitie" and the brilliant "Bristowe Tragedy."[29]

Chatterton and Percy made England safe for the ballad, if it was properly sugar-coated for consumption in an age still too fond of elegance to enjoy the direct, crude, and primitive spirit of the actual border minstrelsy. To the improvers—Ramsay, Percy, Evans, and later to Walter Scott—the age lent its ear, but it largely ignored the more serious work of David Herd, the most scrupulous of the ballad editors before Ritson. Herd's *Ancient and Modern Scottish Songs* was issued in 1769. The old and the new were grouped haphazardly without editorial comment, but the texts were handled in a much more scholarly fashion than was then the rule. Between 1783 and 1795 Ritson edited four volumes of ancient songs and ballads—*A Collection of English Songs* (1783), *Ancient Songs from Henry III to the Revolution* (1790), *A Collection of Scottish Songs* (1794), and *A Collection of all the Ancient Poems . . . relating to Robin Hood* (1795). Ritson's irascible temper led to frequent quarrels with other antiquaries, among them Thomas Warton and Bishop Percy, but these very quarrels, like the controversies concerning Rowley and Ossian, were beneficial in sharpening critical perception, stimulating collections, and maintaining public interest in forms of art outside the Græco-Roman pale.[30]

Gothic architecture evoked the scorn of many early classicists. *The Tatler* and *Spectator* disparaged it. Shaftesbury thought it outside the æsthetic pale. Thomson described Gothic buildings as "heavy monuments of shame." Hume and Gerard declared that multiplicity of ornament destroyed totality of effect. Whitehead objected to the tricks, conceits, and violations of proportion in Gothic. Joseph Warton was typical in his opinion of it:

A multiplicity of minute ornaments; a vast variety of angles and cavities; clusters of little columns, and a crowd of windows, are what distinguish meanness of manner in building from greatness; that is, the Gothic from the Grecian; in which every decoration arises from necessity and use, and every pillar has something to support.

In *The Adventurer* Warton asserted that classical architecture

has never once been called in question. . . . This art . . . has never been improved in later ages in one single instance; but every just and legitimate edifice is still formed according to the five old established orders, to which human wit has never been able to add a sixth of equal symmetry and strength.

Thomas Warton also preferred Grecian to Gothic.[31]

These conventional classical opinions reveal the revolution in taste necessary to restore Gothic architecture to favor. Several forces co-operated in bringing about the change. The antiquarian interest in the past could develop from an enthusiastic hobby to a genuine æsthetic love. The Gothic could appeal to the developing appreciation for melancholy and gloom. Its broken lines of ruined castles could attract the devotee of picturesque beauty. The growing conviction that Nature was complex and its patterns irregular lessened the demand for simplicity and proportion in the architectural mass.[32]

In 1725 Pope had concluded his *Preface to Shakespeare* with a comparison of the poet to an "ancient majestic piece of Gothic architecture" deficient in elegance but superior in strength and solemnity. In the previous year William Stukely had shown "the most hearty appreciation" of Gothic in his *Itinerarium Curiosum.* Expressions of admiration for the cathedrals of the continent occur in Gray's letters as early as 1739, and about the year 1754 he composed a treatise on Norman architecture which was finally published in 1814 as *Architectura Gothica.* In the opinion of Gosse the work entitles Gray to an important place among historians of architecture, though in its unpublished state it remained without influence on the Gothic revival. It was Batty Langley who was the prime mover in the Gothic renascence with his *Ancient Architecture Restored* in 1742 and the *Gothick Architecture Improved by Rules and Proportions* in 1747. Langley was enthusiastic for the "magnificence and beauty" of the best Gothic buildings and found them superior to "all that have been done by both Greeks and Romans." The Gothic doll's house of Walpole at Strawberry Hill was a sign of the new fad, not in itself an important step in the development. Fielding respected the Gothic style and was interested in the renovations that his friend Sanderson Miller was making at Radway. Akenside and Hogarth were also receptive to the fascination of the gloomy Gothic style.[33]

In 1762 Hurd defended Gothic architecture on the same basis that had led him to approve the *Faerie Queene:*

When an architect examines a Gothic structure by Grecian rules, he finds nothing but deformity. But the Gothic architecture has its own rules, by which when it comes to be examined, it is seen to have its merit, as well as the Grecian. The question is not, which of the two is best conducted in the simplest or truest taste; but, whether there be not sense and design in both, when scrutinized by the laws on which each is projected.

After Langley's books on practical architecture, Hurd's justification on principle, and Walpole's dilettante experiment with his miniature castle, expressions of approval became frequent enough. Kames preferred Grecian building, but admitted the grandeur of Gothic; Thomas Warton's position was hesitant, but occasional passages in his poetry (in the words of Professor Amy Reed) showed a "genuine and sincere appreciation of the mystical beauty of Gothic art." Duff declared that "those stupendous Gothic structures, that appear so magnificent in their ruins" were the work of great originals, ignorant of classic architecture, working at the "insuppressible impulse of genius." Blair connected the Gothic style with sublimity. Pinkerton followed Hurd in defending Gothic as a legitimate mode of beauty. His view will serve to show the complete rejection of the standard of taste by the last decades of the century: ". . . every art admits of infinite modes of beauty; and . . . to confine it to one of these modes is the reverse of an attempt to enlarge human knowledge and enjoyment."[34]

The name of almost every prominent classicist has been cited among the enthusiasts for some nonclassical mode of beauty—Oriental, Norse, Celtic, or Mediæval. Complete conformity to the classical ideal of beauty was exceptional. The classicist would not fix his eyes on the road laid down for him by rational rule and precedent; he permitted them to stray in quest of exotic loveliness; he was restless, ill at ease in following a chart, which somehow, he knew not how, had been left incomplete. As time passed he came to see that beauty could be found by other paths than his, and though he often continued on his premeditated course he no longer thought that it was the only course to the artistic goal. He had become too tolerant to insist that beauty was better than sublimity, or that the beauty of proportion was superior to the irregularity of the picturesque. In his uncertainty he allowed his path to become deserted, while the humble by-paths were broadened into the highroads to romanticism.

NOTES TO CHAPTER XVII

1. Cambridge, *World*, No. 76.

2. G. M. Miller, *Historical Point of View*, pp. 78–81; Addison, *Spectator*, Nos. 160, 177, 333, 399, 405, 441, 453, 489, 571; *Tatler*, No. 233; R. S. Crane, "An Early Eighteenth Century Enthusiast for Primitive Poetry," *loc. cit.*, pp. 27–33.

3. Oliver Elton, *A Survey of English Literature, 1730–80*, New York, 1928, II, 124–126; Hamelius, *op. cit.*, pp. 164–166; Joseph Warton, *Adventurer*, Nos. 51, 57, and *Essay on Pope*, I, 10, 17; Blair, *Rhetoric*, I, 70–73, 77.

4. Evelyn, *Diary*, pp. 501, 732; Chesterfield, *Letters*, II, 27, and *Works*, V, 144; J. Warton, *Essay on Pope*, I, 272; Whitehead, *World*, No. 12; Cambridge, *World*, No. 70; *World*, Nos. 59, 88, 205; Cooper, *Letters Concerning Taste*, pp. 58, 64, and *Essays on the Characteristicks*, pp. 170, 192, 213; John Brown, *Estimate*, p. 32; Goldsmith, *Citizen of the World*, Letters XIV, XXXIII, CX, and *Vicar of Wakefield*, Chap. XX; Beattie, *Dissertations*, II, 240; Conant, *op. cit.*, *passim*; W. F. Gallaway, "Goldsmith as a Sentimentalist," *loc. cit.*, *passim*. There is an interesting quotation from John Shebbeare, in *Johnson's England*, ed. Turberville, II, 36–37.

5. Pope, *Works*, III, 255, IX, 431, X, 294; Swift, *Journal to Stella*, April 28, 1711; Gibbon, *Autobiography*, p. 27; Burke, *Selected Letters*, p. 4; Hawkesworth, *Adventurer*, Nos. 20, 32, 38, 72–73, 76, 103, 114, 132; *Connoisseur*, No. 94; Marr, *op. cit.*, p. 119.

6. Manwaring, *op. cit.*, pp. 145, 149; Phelps, *op. cit.*, p. 129; Blair, *Rhetoric*, I, 401, III, 112, 189 ff.

7. F. E. Farley, *Scandinavian Influences on the English Romantic Movement*, Boston, 1903; Van Tieghem, *op. cit.*, I, 78 ff.; Tucker Brooke, "The Renascence of Germanic Studies in England, 1559–1669," *P. M. L. A.*, XXIX, 144–150; Phelps, *op. cit.*, pp. 141–142; Bernbaum, *Anthology and Guide to Romanticism*, II, 432; Steele, *Spectator*, Nos. 306, 406; Havens, "Changing Taste in the Eighteenth Century," *loc. cit.*, p. 511; McKillop, "A Critic of 1741 on Early Poetry," *loc. cit.*, pp. 513 ff.; Johnson, *Rambler*, Nos. 186–187.

8. Phelps, *op. cit.*, pp. 139–141; Caroline Tupper, "Goldsmith and the 'Gentleman who signs D,'" *Modern Language Notes*, XLV, 71–77.

9. Phelps, *op. cit.*, pp. 142–144; Van Tieghem, *op. cit.*, I, 138–139; Goldsmith, *New Essays*, ed. Crane, p. xxxii; Gosse, *Gray*, pp. 160–164.

10. Joseph Warton, *Essay on Pope*, I, 358; Van Tieghem, *op. cit.*, I, 171–172.

11. E. D. Snyder, *The Celtic Revival in English Literature, 1760–1800*, Cambridge (Mass.), 1923, p. 7.

12. *Ibid.*, pp. 12–15, 157, 184.

13. McKillop, "A Critic of 1741 on Early Poetry," *loc. cit.*, pp. 504–511; Snyder, *op. cit.*, pp. 17–25, 34–68; Gosse, *Gray*, pp. 123–131, 160–164.

14. Snyder, *op. cit.*, pp. 53–55.

15. Phelps, *op. cit.*, pp. 137, 146 ff.; Snyder, *op. cit.*, pp. 71–73; Van Tieghem, *op. cit.*, I, 36–37.

16. Goethe, *Dichtung und Wahrheit*, *Werke*, XIII, 148–149; Van Tieghem, *op. cit.*, I, 203.

17. *Ibid.*, pp. 233–234, 262–283; Snyder, *op. cit.*, pp. 76–78, 106, 108, 112.

18. *Ibid.*, pp. 25–33; Phelps, *op. cit.*, pp. 144–146; Gosse, *op. cit.*, p. 164.

19. R. S. Crane, "Johnson and Evan Evans," *Modern Language Notes*, XLV, 32; J. J. Parry, "Doctor Johnson's Interest in Welsh," *Modern Language Notes*, XXXVI, 374–375; Snyder, *op. cit.*, pp. 113–115, 130, 136, 141, 150; Van Tieghem, *op. cit.*, I, 201, 242, 251.

20. Ascham, in Gregory Smith, *op. cit.*, I, 4; Gregory Smith, Introduction to *Elizabethan Critical Essays*, I, xxxvi; Puttenham, *ibid.*, II, 87; Nashe, *ibid.*, I, 323; Meres, *ibid.*, II, 308; Jonson, *Every Man Out of His Humour*, Act II, scene I; Rymer, in Spingarn, *Critical Essays*, II, 251; Shaftesbury, *Characteristicks*, III, 253, Addison, *Spectator*, No. 60; Mandeville, *Fable of the Bees*, I, 218; Swift, *Gulliver*, etc., p. 423; Johnson, *Lives of the Poets*, ed. Waugh, III, 177, and *Rambler*, No. 177; Thomson, in Chalmers, *op. cit.*, XII, 434; Cowper, *Table Talk*, line 564; Thomas Warton, in Chalmers, *op. cit.*, XVIII, 94, 101, and *History of English Poetry*, p. 495; R. D. Havens, "Thomas Warton and the Eighteenth Century Dilemma," *Studies in Philology*, XXV, 36–50.

21. Montague Summers, Introduction to Dryden's *Dramatic Works*, I, cxxiv; J. Q. Adams, *A Life of William Shakespeare*, New York, 1923, pp. 338–339; Sidney, *Apology*, in Gregory Smith, *op. cit.*, I, 173; Jonson, in Spingarn, *Critical Essays*, I, 213; Milton, *ibid.*, I, 203; Evelyn, *Diary and Correspondence*, III, 123; G. B. Dutton, "The French Aristotelian Formalists and Thomas Rymer," *loc. cit.*, p. 165; Dryden, *Essays*, II, 38; Joseph Warton, *Essay on Pope*, II, 125; Johnson, *Lives of the Poets*, ed. Waugh, III, 28; *Tatler*, No. 128; Cross, *Fielding*, I, 47; A. L. Sells, *Les Sources Françaises de Goldsmith*, Paris, 1924, p. 1; Leah Dennis, "The Text of the Percy-Warton Letters," *P. M. L. A.*, XLVI, 1176; Hawkesworth, *Adventurer*, No. 4. With this interest in romance the general respect for realism as developed in Chap. VI should be compared.

22. Amory, *John Buncle*, p. 15; Sterne, *Tristram Shandy*, Book II, Chap. 19, Book VII, Chap. 29; Thomas Warton, *History of English Poetry*, p. 434, and "The Crusade," "The Grave of King Arthur," "Ode XVIII," and "Ode XX"; Hurd, *Letters on Chivalry and Romance*, pp. 54–58, 81–114.

23. Phelps, *op. cit.*, p. 109.

24. Dryden, *Essays*, I, 153–154, and *Dramatic Works*, ed. Summers, VI, 242; Congreve, *Complete Works*, IV, 42; Pope, *Works*, I, 140–141; Swift, *Journal to Stella*, Jan. 29, 1711–12; Parnell, in Fausset, *Minor Poets*, p. 135; Joseph Warton, in Chalmers, *op. cit.*, XVIII, 161; Lady Mary Wortley Montagu, *Letters*, II, 432–434; Thomson, in Chalmers, *op. cit.*, XII, 457; Hawkesworth, *Adventurer*, No. 103; Marr, *op. cit.*, p. 195; R. D. Havens, "Romantic Aspects of the Age of Pope," *loc. cit.*, pp. 316–317; Cross, *Fielding*, II, 46–47.

25. Thomas Warton, *Observations*, I, 120, II, 268; Joseph Warton, *Essay on Pope*, I, 348; Gray, *Letters*, III, 94, and note 2; Mrs. Montagu, *Essay on Shakespeare*, pp. 115–119, 145, 155; Beattie, *Minstrel*, Book I, xxxii–xxxiii, xliv–xlv; Johnson, *Lives of the Poets*, ed. Waugh, IV, 115, and *Miscellaneous Observations on the Tragedy of Macbeth*; Fielding, *Tom Jones*, Book VIII, Chap. I.

26. Sidney, *Apology*, in Gregory Smith, *op. cit.*, I, 178; Pepys, *Diary*, Jan. 2, 1665–66, and Feb. 12, 1666–67; Addison, *Spectator*, No. 85; Bolingbroke, quoted by G. M. Trevelyan, *England under Queen Anne*, London, 1930–34, I, 155; Hamelius, *op. cit.*, pp. 100–101; Shaftesbury, *Characteristicks*, I, 258; Gay, *Poetical Works*, p. 53; Phelps, *op. cit.*, pp. 33–34.

27. R. D. Havens, "Changing Taste in the Eighteenth Century," *loc. cit.*, pp. 510–511; Phelps, *op. cit.*, pp. 119, 126.

28. Gray, *Letters*, I, 183, 335; Goldsmith, *Vicar of Wakefield*, Chap. VIII, and *Bee*, No. II, Percy, *Reliques of Ancient English Poetry*, ed. H. B. Wheatley, London, 1910, I, 7–9; Grace Trenery, "Ballad Collections of the Eighteenth Century," *Modern Language Review*, X, 288, 295; Phelps, *op. cit.*, pp. 127–136.

29. H. A. Beers, *A History of English Romanticism in the Eighteenth Century*, Chap. X. The best biography of Chatterton is by E. H. W. Meyerstein, 1930.

30. Grace Trenery, *op. cit.*, *passim.*

31. *Tatler*, No. 177; *Spectator*, Nos. 63, 415; Addison, *Works*, I, 367, 489; Shaftesbury, *Philosophical Regimen*, p. 247; Gildon, in Durham, *op. cit.*, pp. 42, 53; Thomson, in Chalmers, *op. cit.*, XII, 476; Hume, *Essays*, I, 241; Whitehead, *World*, No. 12; Joseph Warton, *World*, No. 26; *Adventurer*, No. 127; Gerard, *Essay on Taste*, pp. 7, 37; Thomas Warton, in Chalmers, *op. cit.*, XVIII, 94, and *History of English Poetry*, p. 728.

32. Hussey, *op. cit.*, p. 194; Lovejoy, "The First Gothic Revival," *loc. cit.*, pp. 426–440.

33. R. D. Havens, "Romantic Aspects of the Age of Pope," *loc. cit.*, p. 319; Gray, *Letters*, I, 17–18, 30, 58, 248, 250; II, 61, 245; III, 6, 35, and note 3 on page 35; Lovejoy, "The First Gothic Revival," *loc. cit.*, p. 432; Cross, *Fielding*, II, 164; Hogarth, *Analysis*, p. 92; Dyce, *Memoir of Akenside*, in Akenside, *Poetical Works*, p. 83.

34. Hurd, *Letters on Chivalry and Romance*, p. 118; Kames, *Elements*, I, 174, II, 381; Amy Reed, *op. cit.*, p. 186; Duff, *Essay on Genius*, p. 257; Blair, *Rhetoric*, I, 62; Pinkerton, *Letters on Literature*, p. 423.

CHAPTER XVIII

SUBLIMITY

THE CULT of sublimity with its exaltation of intensity of feeling in the presence of powerful and terrible phenomena was the greatest single force in the disintegration of the classical outlook, and yet, supported as it was by many major classicists, it must be regarded as an integral part of that outlook. The vehemence of emotion produced by the sublime was sufficient to justify irregularity and the neglect of the Rules. Since great ideas were necessary to justify great emotion, the substance of sublime art was God and God's world in its grandest and most terrible aspects. Longinus himself had emphasized grandeur of thought and vehement emotion capable of inspiring words "as it were with the breath of madness" as the fundamental sources of the sublime. When one is moved by the fervor of the writer or overwhelmed by the greatness of the theme one does not stop to analyze the formal qualities of art, magniloquence becomes magnificence and the tricks of the rhetorician are lost in the passion of the orator or poet. Boileau effectively popularized Longinus in modern Europe with his *Reflexions Critiques* which accompanied his French version. He identified sublimity with "the extraordinary, the surprising, and . . . the marvellous," with an overwhelming sense of vastness and power which ravished the soul. From Longinus and his disciple Boileau was developed the new æsthetic concept that came to be opposed to the idea of pleasing and tranquil beauty—the appreciation of nature as the field where the power of God was most manifest in the towering precipice and mighty mountain, the vast ocean and the awe-inspiring storm.[1]

In England John Dennis won the nickname of Sir Longinus because of his doughty championship of sublimity in *The Grounds of Criticism in Poetry* which he published in 1704. Dennis was seconded by the rhapsodies of Shaftesbury concerning nature, which indirectly but powerfully assisted the cause of sublimity despite Shaftesbury's own scorn for any emotion rooted in what for him was childish amazement.[2]

Dennis had felt the sublimity of nature before he treated the sublime in art. He described a passage of the Alps in 1688:

> The impending rock that hung over us, the dreadful depth of the precipice, and the torrent that roar'd at the bottom gave us such a view as was altogether new and amazing. . . . In the meantime we walk'd upon the very brink, in a literal sense, of destruction. . . . The sense of all this produc'd different motives in me, viz. a delightful horrour, a terrible joy, and at the same time that I was infinitely pleas'd I trembled.

The Alps gave him the "transporting pleasure" that Longinus demanded of the sublime in art. Intense feeling was produced by the magnitude and the terror of the scene:

> Ruins upon ruins, in monstrous heaps, and heaven and earth confounded. The uncouth rocks that were above us, rocks that were void of all form, but what they had received from ruin: the frightful view of the precipices, and the foaming waters that threw themselves headlong down them, made all such a comfort [*sic*] for the eye, as that sort of music does for the ear, in which horrour can be joyn'd with harmony.[8]

Upon the cult of sublimity in art Dennis exerted his greatest influence. Poetry must be deeply emotional and religious to belong to the first rank, for sublimity was associated in the mind of Dennis with the divine. Basing his opinions on those of Hermogenes, Dennis showed that the sublime was produced by ideas of God, of the works of God (Nature), and by noble passions and overwhelming human ideas that might be considered divine, such as justice, temperance, fortitude, number, power, and might. More specifically Dennis showed that angels and demons, prophecies and visions, miracles and prodigies, produced admiration, wonder, and fear at the mysterious power of God. Even the phenomena of Nature and the Godlike virtues of men were less likely than religion to produce the awe, the exaltation, the thoughts soaring beyond the power of words to express, the irresistible impressions essential to the sublime. In still another passage Dennis listed the ideas productive of enthusiastic terror. It is notable that it is only in the violent and forceful manifestations of the animate and inanimate world of Nature that he finds sublime material. The list was as follows:

Gods, deamons, Hell, spirits, and souls of men, miracles, prodigies, enchantments, witchcrafts, thunder, tempests, raging seas, inundations, torrents, earthquakes, volcanos, monsters, serpents, lions, tigers, fire, war, pestilence, famine, etc.

Dennis made the generalizations of Longinus and Boileau specific; he directed attention to the effect of sublime objects on the mind; he wrote vigorously and with a pen that could not be denied in behalf of an emotional art and a view of Nature alien to the common-sense outlook of the Augustans. The sublime was from henceforth a rival of the beautiful: it could be kept separate, perhaps, but it could not be ignored by the classicists who followed Dennis.[4]

Addison was influenced by Longinus, Boileau, and Dennis. He found three qualities pleasing to the imagination—greatness, beauty, and strangeness. Greatness was to be found in Homer and in Nature, beauty in Virgil, strangeness in Ovid. Of all objects the ocean affected the imagination most, but deserts, mountains, high rocks, and precipices yield a "rude kind of magnificence" which produces that greatness (sublimity) in which the imagination delights. Thomson urged Mallet to study the awful aspects of Nature—earthquakes, tempests, and abysses, and in his own poetry he wrote extensively of the devastating force of tempests, storms, and famines, according to the formula of Dennis, with an astonishing disregard of the fact that he was contradicting his own views of the harmony of the universe. Walpole as well as Gray could appreciate the sublimity of the Alps. Amory exaggerated the horrors of the Peak and Lake regions to make them seem more sublime. Joseph Warton wrote of extension as one of the ideas productive of sublimity. And then in 1757 came Burke's *On the Sublime and Beautiful*.[5]

Even more clearly than Dennis, Burke exalted sublimity at the expense of beauty, and associated it with the terror produced by ideas of pain and danger. Sublimity was for Burke the strongest emotion of which the heart was capable, for it implied a degree of astonishment in which all the motions of the soul are suspended with fear. To produce the sublime, ideas of infinity, power, darkness, and vastness must be invoked—ideas antithetical to those of proportion, regularity, design, and clarity so important in the classical idea of beauty. Obscurity seemed to Burke to be particularly desirable, since it permitted the mind to expand into the region of indefinable forces productive of an awe that could not possibly be aroused by any force with recognizable limits.[6]

In the *Essay on Taste* in 1759 Gerard repeated Dennis and Burke with small addition. He found that the most sublime ideas were those associated with God. Terror was sublime because it implies "astonishment, occupies the whole soul, and suspends all motion." Mental qualities that excite wonder and astonishment are also sublime. Gerard laid particular stress on amplitude, quantity, and simplicity, and declared that sublimity was present in the universal principles and general theorems of science as well as in human virtues, because of the extensive sphere in which such principles displayed themselves.[7]

In his *Lectures on Rhetoric* Lord Kames based sublimity on greatness. Regularity, proportion, order, and color, which are the usual elements of beauty, become less important, Kames discovered, as size increases. When the emotion of grandeur is powerful

the spectator is conscious of an enthusiasm, which cannot bear confinement, nor the strictness of regularity and order: he loves to range at large, and is so enchanted with magnificent objects, as to overlook slight beauties or deformities.[8]

In his Essay on Genius, 1767, William Duff announced that the sublime was "the proper walk of a great genius." The elegances of art were capable of pleasing, but the "rude magnificence" of Nature

throws the soul into a divine transport of admiration and amazement, which occupies and fills the mind, and at the same time inspires that solemn dread, that religious awe, which naturally results from the contemplation of the vast and wonderful. By dwelling on such subjects, the soul is elevated to a sense of its own dignity and greatness.[9]

Between Duff and Blair one finds traces of the feeling for sublimity in Doctor Johnson who admired the "terrific grandeur" of

Wales, and described the horror and "turbulent pleasure" of the precipices at Hawkestone:

He that mounts the precipices at Hawkestone, wonders how he came thither, and doubts how he shall return. His walk is an adventure, and his departure an escape. He has not the tranquillity, but the horror of solitude; a kind of turbulent pleasure, between fright and admiration.

In the journey to Scotland Johnson recorded that the Fall of Foyers struck the mind "with all the gloom and grandeur of Siberian solitude." Gray termed the mountains of Scotland "ecstatic":

None but these monstrous children of God know how to join so much beauty to so much horror. A fig for your poets, painters, gardeners and clergymen, that have not been among them; their imagination can be made up of nothing but bowling-greens, flowering shrubs, horse-ponds, Fleet-ditches, shell-grottoes, and Chinese rails.

Arthur Young found pleasure in "the terrible sublime." Reynolds declared the perspectives of the Dutch landscape and the perseverance of the Dutch people in fighting the sea, sublime. Even the mild Cowper, whose taste was more often for the "garden aspects" of Nature, was led by religious feeling to some appreciation of the ocean which

exhibits, fathomless and broad,
Much of the power and majesty of God.[10]

Near the end of the century Hugh Blair and James Beattie wrote at length on the sublime, and Alison found occasion in his *Essays on Taste* to associate sublimity with ideas of danger, power, and strong emotion. Blair had touched upon the subject briefly in the *Critical Dissertation on Ossian* in 1763, but it was only in the *Rhetoric* (1783) that he analyzed the subject fully. To Blair grandeur and sublimity were almost synonymous. The sublime creates

a kind of admiration and expansion of the mind; it raises the mind much above its ordinary state; and fills it with a degree of wonder and astonishment, which it cannot well express. The emotion is certainly delightful; but it is altogether of the serious kind: a degree of awfulness and solemnity, even approaching to severity, commonly attends it when at its height.

Sublimity in its simplest form was to be found in the vast and boundless prospects of Nature. The infinite or the extensive in space, numbers, or time was also sublime. Power and force, the solemn and the awful, darkness, solitude, silence, woods, and torrents, obscurity and disorder; in short, the external world of the Romantic creates sublimity. Ideas of God were sublime; in character, magnanimity and high virtue. Of particular interest was Blair's insistence on the contrast between the disorderliness of objects which create sublimity and the regularity of things productive of beauty:

As obscurity, so disorder too, is very frequently compatible with grandeur; nay frequently heightens it. Few things that are strictly regular, and methodical, appear sublime. We see the limits on every side; we feel ourselves confined; there is no room for the mind's exerting any great effort. Exact proportion of parts, though it enters into the beautiful, is much disregarded in the sublime.

Blair believed that ideas of power were more important than ideas of terror and pain in arousing sublime emotions. To Blair it seemed that the Scriptures afforded the highest instances of the sublime in literature, an opinion which was in conformity with his belief in the superiority of primitive art—of Homer, Ossian, Isaiah, and Job.[11]

Beattie also looked for the sublime in Nature. In his essay *Of Memory and Imagination* he showed a partiality for wild Nature, which was present also in *The Minstrel:*

The daily contemplation of the grand phenomena of nature, in a mountainous country, elevates, and continually exercises, the imagination of the solitary inhabitants; one effect of which is, to give those sensibilities to the nervous system, which render the mind in a peculiar degree susceptible of wild thoughts, and warm emotions.

Magnitude in the physical or moral realm creates a pleasing astonishment, an expansion of man's faculties as if one were exerting his whole capacity to comprehend the vastness of whatever thus commands his attention. Beattie insisted on the absence of actual pain or danger in the composition of this pleasing astonishment: either a sense of physical safety in actual contact with sublimity must underlie the feeling of horror at the forces of Nature, or the sublime must be imaginary as in a poem or play. Beattie knew that Nature was more sublime than art, but he pointed out the means of obtaining sublimity in art. Poetry was sublime if it elevated the mind, if it created horror, if it aroused a great affection such as piety or patriotism, if it gave a vivid idea of the grand in Nature or in man, or if it showed noble passions in operation. Sublimity could be destroyed by minuteness of description, by overamplification and hyperbole, or by "low" diction. A common object, however, might be rendered sublime by association with grand objects. Clarity was less important than suggestiveness in creating sublimity, for hints of things too dread to mention or too intense for utterance would oppose no check to that delightful activity of the mind, to that expansiveness of emotion which to Beattie was the result of the contact with sublimity.[12]

The extensive popularity of the sublime with its emphasis on infinities of space and power was the most significant single factor in the collapse of the classical concept of beauty, though other non-classical preferences emerged out of the battle over the nature and universality of taste. In place of clarity, proportion, and fitness, vagueness, picturesqueness, strangeness, and transiency became popular catchwords. Beauty was to be no longer a thing of objective geometrical measurement but a product of sentiment, of the melancholy regret for things beyond recall, of the unappeasable yearning for things more perfect than this world of mingled light and shadow could provide; of the sad awareness of the fleeting quality of fragile joy in a world of constant change.

These new preferences were never merged into a coherent, consciously held romantic ideal of beauty, but there was in what seemed distinct æsthetic attitudes an underlying unity which escaped contemporary criticism. From the clear and the finite, taste moved on to the inexplicable and the infinite. Form implied limitation: form must be sacrificed to the expansive emotionality of the artist. Couplet and stanza lost ground before the run-on line and the verse paragraph. Vagueness in expression allowed the mind to roam through infinite fields of suggestion. Incompleteness and melancholy were important aspects of the picturesque attitude. The novel and the strange gave the reins to wonder. Analytic thought became less important than an intuitive perceptive power which was admittedly beyond the reach of rational explanation. The new beauty of Romanticism was not to be founded on common sense, but on man's sentimental experiences and on his limitless expansiveness of soul. The change from classicism to romanticism in æsthetics was a change from geometrical beauty to an infinite calculus of the never-to-be-sounded mysteries of time and space, of matter, and of man's mind questing eternally for the Blue Flower that fades into the distance endlessly.

NOTES TO CHAPTER XVIII

1. The best treatment of sublimity is Samuel H. Monk's *The Sublime: A Study of Critical Theories in XVIII-Century England*, New York, 1935. It should be consulted by every student of the period. Longinus, *On the Sublime*, VIII, 1, 4; XV, 2; XXXVIII, 5; Boileau, in Vial et Denise, *op. cit.*, p. 199, and in *Œuvres*, pp. 201, 292–293.

2. Clark, *Boileau and the French Classical Critics in England*, pp. 364–369; Shaftesbury, *Characteristicks*, I, 242–243.

3. Dennis, in Manwaring, *op. cit.*, pp. 5–6.

4. Dennis, in Durham, *op. cit.*, pp. 155–194.

5. Addison, *Spectator*, Nos. 412, 417, 489; Hussey, *op. cit.*, p. 46; J. Warton, *Essay on Pope*, I, 391.

6. Burke, *Works*, I, 91 ff.

7. Gerard, *Essay on Taste*, pp. 17–27.

8. Kames, *Elements*, I, 171–174.

9. Duff, *Essay on Genius*, pp. 152–153.

10. Boswell, *Life of Johnson*, V, 494–495; Johnson, *Journey to the Western Islands of Scotland*, p. 46; Gosse, *Gray*, p. 172; Manwaring, *op. cit.*, pp. 180–181; Reynolds, *Letters*, p. 85; Cowper, *Retirement*, lines 525 ff.

11. Alison, *Essays on Taste*, p. 123; Blair, *Critical Dissertation*, p. 172, and *Rhetoric*, I, 55–66, 70–72.

12. Beattie, *Dissertations*, I, 107; II, 360–422.

CHAPTER XIX

CONCLUSION

WITHIN its own soil English classicism nourished the seeds of its own dissolution. Unable to forget the Elizabethan past, unable to focus its attention completely on Greece and Rome, unable to establish a standard of taste, unable to convince itself that the Rules were sufficient to explain all the graces of literature, and unable to close its eyes to the significance of sublimity, it was consequently unable to present a solid front to the rising emotionalism that was the prelude to the Romantic Movement proper. The study of the development of sensibility, sentimentality, and the dream escape into "faery lands" evoked by the creative poetic imagination lies within the province of the historian of Romanticism. The student of classicism has fulfilled his task when he has fully portrayed the normal classical attitude toward life and art as revealed by the undisputed masters of English classicism. It is true that sensibility, sentimentality, and the dream were deeply rooted in the eighteenth century, but they were rooted in an emotionalism that classicism found abhorrent though it could not conquer; they were things contemporaneous with but apart from classicism, and as time passed they became more and more clearly opposed to it in their offer of roads of escape from the intellectual acceptance of the mingled good and evil in man and in man's environment which the classical realist attempted to rationalize and control by the use of common sense—that "light of nature" which was the contribution of the founders of the Enlightenment to the interpretation of man's psychology. The significant men of letters in England conformed to this rational ideal to a greater or less degree. No one, except perhaps Thomas Rymer, was an unqualified and consistent rationalist. No one, except perhaps William Blake, broke completely with the Age

of Reason to throw himself into the dark abyss of intuition and
emotionality into which no rays of common sense could penetrate.
Classicism, in other words, had no blind devotees. The Queen Anne's
men were unwilling to ride relentlessly toward the four-square walls
of the City of Common Sense. The byways of desire were pleasant,
and the bridle paths of emotion afforded many a delightful canter to
rationalists who knew much of wandering by the way. For a single
Rymer there were a dozen Drydens who would have felt ill at ease
in a Zion constructed with the plumb line of reason. The student of
the eighteenth century cannot separate the elect from the damned
with the finality of a critical Rhadamanthus. He can do no more than
present the classical viewpoint as it was founded on the investigation
of Nature in the light of common sense, and indicate to what extent
each of the great Augustans accepted the corollaries that were deduced inevitably from the conception of a regular universe and of a
light of reason shared by men everywhere in every age. Some writers
were more complete rationalists than others, but as men of conspicuous ability are seldom doctrinaires, one finds in the leaders of
eighteenth-century criticism a notable tolerance for "Romantic"
tendencies in art. There were, of course, no "Classicists" or "Romanticists" in the eighteenth century; there were writers and critics
striving to find a satisfying code of morality and of art in divers
directions that have been labelled "Classical" or "Romantic" by later
investigators of a period as confusing and as complex as any in
English literary history.

There were no classicists and no Romantics, but the struggle over
the separate sectors of the battlefield was much more consciously
fought than has been generally admitted. The "Romantic" attitude
was readily detected by the classical realist who fought it as impractical, ideal, untrue, fantastic, and absurd. The embodiment of the Romantic spirit in novel and romance was sternly resisted by convinced
realists. Common sense was opposed to intuition, rational morality
to the instinctive moral sense, intellect in religion to the inner light.
Judgment based on experience with men and books was opposed to
the inspired imagination of the untrained genius. Tradition was
opposed to originality, Ancient to Modern, correctness in taste to
the peculiar predilections of the erratic individualist. Divergent

ideals of life aroused conflict as intense as divergent ideals of art. The will of the social group was enforced with the weapons of ridicule against the will of the irresponsible rebel. The realistic acceptance of human nature was opposed to the doctrine of man's natural goodness. The restraint of emotion was opposed to emotional indulgence as a means to happiness. The gains of civilization were defended against the primitivist; the present was defended against those who idealized the past; a calm contentment in a reasonably satisfactory world was defended against the restless longing for a Never-Never Land of dreams. In this ceaseless struggle between Reason and Romanticism neutrality was impossible: partisanship was implied by one's very mode of life, by one's religion, moral code, and critical taste.

These struggles were fought, however, only among a small and essentially aristocratic minority. A moderate classicism was the prized possession of a small group of civilized men who had accepted a view of Nature on which they strove to erect a coherent attitude toward life and art. This view of Nature was born of an age of science with Descartes and Newton. Its essential feature was regularity, submission to scientific law. The true was the normal as revealed by common sense. Classical realism was a scientific realism, with a scientific preoccupation with normality, probability, and decorum. The validity of its postulates as well as the validity of the art produced according to its postulates was to be tested by universal acceptance. The Rules codified the practices which, as time had shown, produced general satisfaction. The literature of Greece and Rome was esteemed because it had stood this test of time. Reason was fundamental; respect for authority the remote deduction in a chain of reasoning. Reason demanded the discovery of a standard of taste to which all sensible men could conform, and Reason sought such a standard in the unemotional realm of mathematical proportion, in the scientific realm of the average form, or in the empirical realm of fitness of function. Classical beauty was the beauty of the well-proportioned, the normal, the fit. It could be no other and be consistent with the image of the universe in the minds of men during the period of the Enlightenment.

The universe was not only regular; it was fundamentally good, the creation of an all-wise and beneficent God which the Age of Reason complacently created in its own image, a God whose attributes were those of an enlightened despot glibly deduced from questionable, but generally unquestioned, postulates. This God had created the best of all possible worlds. In His universe virtue normally triumphed, and the artist was expected to reveal that victory by adhering to the rule of Poetic Justice. He must as a socially responsible individual in a socially-minded age uphold the life of reason and reveal the disastrous consequences of divergence from the social norm. The art of the Enlightenment was a profoundly moral art because the artist who adhered as a scientific realist to the law of probability believed sincerely that here or hereafter vice would bring its own punishment. The moral note was uppermost. Pleasure was the end of art only because pleasure was essential to the success of instruction. Satire and comedy, the social essay, the didactic poem, and the realistic novel were the characteristic vehicles of this moral emphasis. It was in these art forms that the vices of society were scourged.

Familiarity with the Greek and Roman classics modified, but did not profoundly alter, the artistic outlook of English classicism. The influence of the Ancients was most conspicuous in the defense of authority, literary imitation, and the Rules of the literary "kinds." But reason was considered superior to Aristotle, and the Rules were defended on a rational basis. Imitation won no universal support, and it also was defended by rational deductions drawn from the uniformity of human experience and the universal success of classical models. The Græco-Roman literary "kinds" were discovered to be effete. No new wine could be poured into the old bottles of the Homeric epic, the Aristotelian tragedy, and the Virgilian eclogue. It was largely in new literary forms, or in forms considerably modified from the models of antiquity—in social essay, informal satire, comedy of manners, and prose fiction—that the writers of the eighteenth century created their masterpieces. The English Augustans found affinities between themselves and the contemporaries of Maecenas in a realistic, ethical bias towards life, in an urbane wit, and in an ideal of restraint in art, but these qualities were the product of the rational and scientific milieu in which the English Augustans lived; they were strengthened but not produced by contacts with an ancient world whose literary masterpieces might conceivably have remained buried in the dusty libraries of the monks without their loss effecting any decided change in the principal masterpieces of English literature between 1660 and 1800.

The urbane common sense which was the dominant note of English classicism failed to establish an enduring hold even among the small minority which created the cultural life of the nation, because of suspicion of reason on the part of classicists themselves, because of the inability of the classicists to convince themselves of the sufficiency of their own standards, and because of the failure to secure general adherence to a standard of taste.

The men of the Age of Anne desired to live the life of reason, but they could not blind themselves to the limitations upon reason as a guide to life. Philosophic skepticism suggested the general inadequacy of reason in the discovery of final truths. In a more practical sphere it was apparent that men's actions were often motivated by a dominant humor or ruling passion, or by a consideration of resultant pleasure or pain which constituted in the eyes of some thinkers a wise selfishness, and in the eyes of others a system of mechanistic reactions which reduced reason to impotence. The sure instinct of animals was also disconcerting to men who wished to be proud of their intellects. Soon the apparently happy lives of the unreflecting peasant or savage suggested new reasons for distrust. Examination of the mechanism of mind by more philosophic thinkers like Hume resulted in the analysis of reason into imagination and belief, of common sense into intuition. The basis of classical art was shattered by these blows from men who grew increasingly uncertain of the power of reason, and uncertainty paved the way for the emphasis on emotion as the most important factor in life and art.

The classicist was furthermore unable to convince himself that Nature and the Rules founded on Nature interpreted by common sense, the light of Nature, furnished a sufficient explanation of beauty. Nature as the foundation of the Rules was variously interpreted to suit the convenience of the artist. The Rules could be violated, if

widespread delight could be gained, for there was no justification
for the Rules other than the pragmatic justification of success. In
any case there was a *je ne sais quoi*, an unexplainable element in
beauty, a grace beyond the reach of art, a felicity obtainable only
by the intuitive, inspired genius of the poet. Uncertain of the complete validity of his own standards, the classicist battled half-
heartedly—and lost.

The attempt to set up a standard of taste resulted in a third
defeat. The universal light of reason should have enabled all men to
unite on an ideal of beauty, since they participated in the sense common to every one who did not allow it to be submerged by pedantry
and prejudice. The test of beauty should be universal approbation.
Whatever appealed to one generation only, to one race only, was not
in conformity with ideal taste. As the literature of Greece and Rome
came nearest to satisfying the test of universal approbation it was
established as the standard of taste. Unfortunately the three great
masters of Renaissance literature in England—Shakespeare, Milton,
and Spenser—remained popular despite their manifold divergences
from the strict classical standard. They were popular with the critics
themselves. Dryden, Addison, and Pope felt their fascination in full
measure and were compelled to sacrifice rigidly rational critical
principles to justify their instinctive admiration. To the survival of
Elizabethan Romanticism as a disconcerting memento of divergence
in taste, the Oriental, Norse, Celtic, and Mediæval movements soon
added their strength to turn the question of a standard into a certainty that no standard could control the likes and dislikes of a nation
always conspicuous for its individualism. *De gustibus non est disputandum.* By 1750 classicists were readily admitting the chaos in
taste. One man constructed a Chinese pagoda, another masked an
icehouse in a Gothic ruin; one man inclined to the sublime, another
to the beautiful, a third to the picturesque; some found in regularity
the key to æsthetic appeal, others acclaimed the curved line of beauty
or the serpentine line of grace. Soon all ideals of beauty were confessed by some to be equally legitimate, since beauty was dependent
on an individual association of ideas. Beauty, like so much else amid
the ruins of classicism, became a matter of sentiment: the beautiful

was whatever was found to be satisfactory to the apperceptive background of the individual.

Unprepared to support reason without considerable reservation, unwilling to follow consistently the corollaries necessarily deduced from the postulates of reason, unable to establish uniformity of taste, the English classicist was forced to sacrifice common sense, general truth, and the universal appeal of art to the idols of an emotional cult—sensibility, sentimentality, and the dream. The literature of the nineteenth century evolved towards a greater accuracy in the reflection of truth as it appeared to the individual temperament of the artist, towards a surface realism of the single historic event in contrast to the scientific truth of the probable event, towards an increased attention to the spontaneous, unconscious life of the human mechanism freed from rational control. The result was romanticism, realism, naturalism. Romanticism was born of the emotion of the individual when it sought to evolve a world-view satisfactory to the yearning heart. Nineteenth-century realism was at times, as with George Eliot and Trollope, close to the ideals of eighteenth-century classicism— a swing of the pendulum away from the extravagances of romanticism—, but it too often reported the exceptional case, sacrificing average truth to an accurate report of the anomalous instance. Naturalism, scientific in its initial postulates, led rapidly to the observation of desire uncontrolled by reason, because the reactions of the human beast could best be observed in those abnormal cases in which the checks *normally* operative among civilized men (and hence closer to the abiding truths of human nature) were in temporary or permanent abeyance. Naturalism eventually led to the psychoanalytic account of the irrational subconscious mind, to the study of the instincts of child, peasant, and savage. Impressionism was an attempt to catch the appearance of the moment in the external world, the mood of the moment in the individual, without any intervention of rationalization. Expressionism was an attempt to return to significant truth, but it was largely to truth as it seemed significant to an individual, to a racial or a social group, and in extreme cases to the truth of the dream or the fantasy which brought it into alliance with the wish-fulfilment of psychoanalysis. Only the classical realist attempts to see life steadily and see it whole, to enforce the ideal of artistic probability, to impress a sense of social responsibility upon the artist, and to defend the life of reason against the forces of an irrational world-view created by Rousseau, Nietzsche, Freud, Vaihinger, Bergson, and Marcel Proust.

BIBLIOGRAPHY

The bibliography is a selected list of those books and articles of a specifically critical nature most useful to the advanced student or general reader who wishes to undertake a serious investigation of classicism. The much more numerous creative writers whose opinions have been cited in the text will be found listed in the notes to the respective chapters.

Aikin, J. and A. L., *Miscellaneous Pieces in Prose*, London, 1773.

Alison, Archibald, *Essays on the Nature and Principles of Taste*, New York, 1844.

Armstrong, John, *Miscellanies*, London, 1770.

Babbitt, Irving, *Rousseau and Romanticism*, Boston, 1919.

Babcock, R. W., *The Genesis of Shakespeare Idolatry, 1766–1799*, Chapel Hill, 1931.

Barbauld, Laetitia, ed., *The British Novelists*, London, 1810.

Beattie, James, *Dissertations Moral and Critical*, Dublin, 1783.

Beers, H. A., *A History of English Romanticism in the Eighteenth Century*, New York, 1926.

Bernbaum, Ernest, *The Drama of Sensibility*, Cambridge (Mass.), 1925.

Blair, Hugh, *Critical Dissertation on the Poems of Ossian*, in *The Poems of Ossian*, Boston, 1866.

 Lectures on Rhetoric and Belles Lettres, Dublin, 1783.

Boswell, James, *The Life of Johnson*, ed. Birkbeck Hill, New York, n. d.

Bray, René, *La Formation de la Doctrine Classique en France*, Paris, 1927.

Bredvold, L. I., *The Intellectual Milieu of John Dryden*, Ann Arbor, 1934.

Brown, John, *Essays on the Characteristics*, London, 1751.

 An Estimate of the Manners and Principles of the Times, Dublin, 1757.

Brown, John, *The History of the Rise and Progress of Poetry*, Newcastle, 1764.

Burke, Edmund, *Works*, ed. William Willis and F. W. Raffety, Oxford (World's Classics), 1925.

Bury, J. B., *The Idea of Progress*, London, 1921.

Campbell, George, *Philosophy of Rhetoric*, Baltimore and Boston, n. d.

Chambers, F. P., *A History of Taste*, New York, 1932.

Clark, A. F. B., *Boileau and the French Classical Critics in England (1660–1830)*, Paris, 1925.

Cobban, Alfred, *Edmund Burke and the Revolt Against the Eighteenth Century*, London, 1929.

Collins, A. S., *Authorship in the Days of Johnson*, London, 1927.

Conant, Martha, *The Oriental Tale in England in the Eighteenth Century*, New York, 1908.

Cooper, John Gilbert, *Letters Concerning Taste and Essays on Similar and Other Subjects*, London, 1757.

Courthope, W. J., *A History of English Poetry*, London, 1897.

Damon, S. F., *William Blake, His Philosophy and Symbols*, New York, 1924.

Drake, Nathan, *Literary Hours*, London, 1800.

Draper, J. W., *The Funeral Elegy and the Rise of English Romanticism*, New York, 1929.

Dryden, John, *Essays*, ed. W. P. Ker, Oxford, 1926.

Duff, William, *An Essay on Original Genius*, London, 1767.

Durham, W. H., ed., *Critical Essays of the Eighteenth Century, 1700–1725*, New Haven, 1915.

Eddy, W. A., *Gulliver's Travels. A Critical Study*, Princeton, 1923.

Elton, Oliver, *A Survey of English Literature, 1730–1780*, New York, 1928.

Fairchild, H. N., *The Noble Savage. A Study in Romantic Naturalism*, New York, 1928.
The Romantic Quest, New York, 1931.

Foster, John, *Essays in a Series of Letters*, London, 1833.

Gerard, Alexander, *An Essay on Genius*, London, 1774.
An Essay on Taste, London, 1759.

Green, C. C., *The Neo-classic Theory of Tragedy in England During the Eighteenth Century*, Cambridge (Mass.), 1934.

Green, F. C., *Minuet*, New York, 1935.

Grierson, H. J. C., *The Background of English Literature and Other Collected Essays and Addresses*, London, 1925.

Hamelius, Paul, *Die Kritik in der englischen Literatur des 17. und 18. Jahrhundert*, Leipzig, 1897.

Harris, James, *Three Treatises*, London, 1772.

Havens, R. D., *The Influence of Milton on English Poetry*, Cambridge (Mass.), 1922.

Henn, T. R., *Longinus and English Criticism*, Cambridge, 1934.

Herrick, M. T., *The Poetics of Aristotle in England*, New Haven, 1930.

Hogarth, William, *The Analysis of Beauty*, Pittsfield, 1909.

Houston, P. H., *Doctor Johnson. A Study in Eighteenth Century Humanism*, Cambridge (Mass.), 1923.

Hume, David, *Essays Moral, Political, and Literary*, ed. T. H. Green and T. H. Grose, London, 1907.

Hurd, Richard, *Letters on Chivalry and Romance, with the Third Elizabethan Dialogue*, ed. Edith Morley, Oxford, 1911.
Works, London, 1811.

Hussey, Christopher, *The Picturesque. Studies in a Point of View*, London, 1927.

Hutcheson, Francis, *An Inquiry into the Original of our Ideas of Beauty and Virtue*, London, 1726.

Jones, R. F., "The Background of the Battle of the Books," *Washington University Studies*, vol. VII, 1920.

Kames, Henry Home, Lord, *Elements of Criticism*, Boston, 1796.

Knox, Vicessimus, *Works*, London, 1824.

Langbaine, Gerard, *An Account of the English Dramatick Poets*, Oxford, 1691.

Manwaring, Elizabeth, *Italian Landscape in Eighteenth Century England*, New York, 1925.

Marr, H. G. de, *A History of Modern English Romanticism*, Oxford, 1924.

Miller, G. M., *The Historical Point of View in English Criticism from 1570–1770*, Heidelberg, 1913.

Montagu, Elizabeth, *An Essay on the Writings and Genius of Shakespeare*, London, 1810.

Percy, Thomas, *Reliques of Ancient English Poetry*, ed. H. B. Wheatley, London, 1910.

Phelps, W. L., *The Beginnings of the English Romantic Movement*, New York, 1893.

Pinkerton, John (pseudonym, Robert Heron), *Letters of Literature*, London, 1785.

Praz, Mario, *The Romantic Agony*, Oxford, 1933.

Randall, H. R., *The Making of the Modern Mind*, New York, 1926.

Read, Herbert, *Reason and Romanticism*, London, 1926.

Reed, Amy, *The Background of Gray's Elegy. A Study in the Taste for Melancholy Poetry, 1700–1751*, New York, 1924.

Reynolds, Sir Joshua, *Discourses*, ed. Helen Zimmern, London, 1887.

Reynolds, Myra, *The Treatment of Nature in English Poetry between Pope and Wordsworth*, Chicago, 1909.

Robertson, J. G., *Studies in the Genesis of Romantic Theory in the Eighteenth Century*, Cambridge, 1923.

Routh, James, *The Rise of Classical English Criticism*, New Orleans, 1915.

Saintsbury, George, *A History of Criticism and Literary Taste in Europe*, New York, 1908.

Scott, John, *Critical Essays on Some of the Poems of Several English Poets*, London, 1785.

Shaftesbury, Anthony Ashley Cooper, Earl of, *Characteristicks of Men, Manners, Opinions, Times*, London, 1723.
Life, Unpublished Letters, and Philosophical Regimen, ed. Benjamin Rand, New York, 1900.

Smith, D. Nichol, ed., *Eighteenth Century Essays on Shakespeare*, Glasgow, 1903.

Smith, Gregory, ed. *Elizabethan Critical Essays*, Oxford, 1904.

Smith, Preserved, *A History of Modern Culture,* New York, 1930–1934.
Snyder, E. D., *The Celtic Revival in English Literature,* Cambridge (Mass.), 1923.
Spence, Joseph, *Polymetis,* London, 1755.
Spengler, Oswald, *The Decline of the West,* New York, 1926.
Spingarn, J. E., ed., *Critical Essays of the Seventeenth Century,* Oxford, 1908–1909.
A History of Literary Criticism in the Renaissance, New York, 1925.
Stephen, Leslie, *A History of English Thought in the Eighteenth Century,* New York, 1927.
English Literature and Society in the Eighteenth Century, London, 1907.
Tinker, C. B., *Nature's Simple Plan. A Phase of Radical Thought in the Mid-eighteenth Century,* Princeton, 1922.
Turberville, A. S., ed., *Johnson's England. An Account of the Life and Manners of the Age,* Oxford, 1933.
Van Tieghem, Paul, *Le Préromantisme. Études d'Histoire Littéraire Europeenne,* Paris, 1924–1930.
Vial, Francisque et Denise, Louis, *Idées et Doctrines Littéraire du XVIIe Siècle,* Paris, 1925.
Warren, Austin, *Pope as a Critic and Humanist,* Princeton, 1929.
Warton, Joseph, *An Essay on the Genius and Writings of Pope,* London, 1806.
Warton, Thomas, *The History of English Poetry,* London, n. d.
Observations on the Fairy Queen of Spenser, London, 1762.
Whitehead, A. N., *Science and the Modern World,* New York, 1926.
Whitney, Lois, *Primitivism and Progress in English Popular Literature of the Eighteenth Century,* Baltimore, 1934.

ARTICLES

Alderman, W. E., "Shaftesbury and the Doctrine of Moral Sense in the Eighteenth Century," *P. M. L. A.,* XLVI, 1087.
"The Significance of Shaftesbury in English Speculation," *P. M. L. A.,* XXXVIII, 175.
Allen, B. S., "William Godwin as a Sentimentalist," *P. M. L. A.,* XXXIII, 1.
Allen, E. S., "Chesterfield's Objection to Laughter," *Modern Language Notes,* XXXVIII, 279.
Babbitt, Irving, "Schiller and Romanticism," *Modern Language Notes,* XXXVII, 257.
Bliss, Isabel, "Young's *Night Thoughts* in Relation to Contemporary Christian Apologetics," *P. M. L. A.,* XLIX, 37.
Bohn, W. E., "The Development of John Dryden's Literary Criticism," *P. M. L. A.,* XXII, 56.

Bredvold, L. I., "Dryden, Hobbes, and the Royal Society," *Modern Philology*, XXV, 417.
"The Tendency toward Platonism in Neo-classic Esthetics," *ELH.*, I, 91.

Broadus, E. K., "Addison's Discourse on Ancient and Modern Learning," *Modern Language Notes*, XXII, 1.

Brooke, C. F. T., "The Renascence of Germanic Studies in England, 1559–1689," *P. M. L. A.*, XXIX, 135.

Bundy, M. W., "Bacon's True Opinion of Poetry," *Studies in Philology*, XXVII, 244.

Campbell, O. J. and Mueschke, Paul, " 'Guilt and Sorrow': A Study in the Genesis of Wordsworth's Æsthetic," *Modern Philology*, XXIII, 293.
"Wordsworth's Æsthetic Development, 1795–1802," *University of Michigan Studies. Language and Literature*, vol. X, Ann Arbor, 1933.

Canby, H. S., "Congreve as a Romanticist," *P. M. L. A.*, XXXI, 1.

Chew, S. C., "An English Precursor of Rousseau," *Modern Language Notes*, XXXII, 321.

Clark, H. H., "A Study of Melancholy in Edward Young," *Modern Language Notes*, XXXIX, 129, 193.

Cory, H. E., "Spenser, Thomson, and Romanticism," *P. M. L. A.*, XXVI, 51.

Crane, R. S., "An Early Eighteenth-Century Enthusiast for Primitive Poetry: John Husbands," *Modern Language Notes*, XXXVII, 27.
"A Neglected Mid-Eighteenth Century Plea for Originality and Its Author," *Philological Quarterly*, XIII, 21.
"Anglican Apologetics and the Idea of Progress," *Modern Philology*, XXI, 273, 349.
"Imitation of Spenser and Milton in the Early Eighteenth Century: A New Document," *Studies in Philology*, XV, 195.
"Johnson and Evan Evans," *Modern Language Notes*, XLV, 31.

Crofts, J. E. V., "Enthusiasm," *Eighteenth Century Literature. An Oxford Miscellany*, Oxford, 1909.

Draper, J. W., "The Rise of English Neo-classicism," *Revue Anglo-Américaine*, Juin, 1933.
"Aristotelian 'Mimesis' in Eighteenth Century England," *P. M. L. A.*, XXXVI, 372.
"The Theory of Translation in the Eighteenth Century," *Neo-Philologus*, VI, 241.

Drennon, Herbert, "James Thomson's Contact with Newtonianism and His Interest in Natural Philosophy," *P. M. L. A.*, XLIX, 71.
"Henry Needler and Shaftesbury," *P. M. L. A.*, XLVI, 1095.
"Scientific Rationalism and James Thomson's Poetic Art," *Studies in Philology*, XXI, 453.

Duncan, C. S., "The Scientist as a Comic Type," *Modern Philology*, XIV, 281.

Dutton, G. B., "The French Aristotelian Formalists and Thomas Rymer," *P. M. L. A.*, XXIX, 152.

Freeman, Edmund, "A Proposal for an English Academy in 1660," *Modern Language Review*, XIX, 291.

Gallaway, W. F., "Goldsmith as a Sentimentalist," *P. M. L. A.*, XLVIII, 1167.

Greenlaw, Edwin, "Modern English Romanticism," *Studies in Philology*, XXII, 538.

Griffin, N. E., "The Definition of Romance," *P. M. L. A.*, XXXVIII, 50.

Guyer, F. E., "C'est nous qui sommes les Anciens," *Modern Language Notes*, XXXVI, 257.

Havens, G. R., "Rousseau's Doctrine of Goodness According to Nature," *P. M. L. A.*, XLIV, 1239.

"The Nature Doctrine of Voltaire," *P. M. L. A.*, XL, 852.

"The Theory of 'Natural Goodness' in Rousseau's *Nouvelle Éloise*," *Modern Language Notes*, XXXVI, 385.

Havens, R. D., "Changing Taste in the Eighteenth Century. A Study of Dryden's and Dodsley's Miscellanies," *P. M. L. A.*, XLIV, 501.

"Primitivism and the Idea of Progress in Thomson," *Studies in Philology*, XXIX, 41.

"Romantic Aspects of the Age of Pope," *P. M. L. A.*, XXVII, 297.

"Thomas Warton and the Eighteenth Century Dilemma," *Studies in Philology*, XXV, 36.

Heltzel, V. B., "Chesterfield and the Anti-laughter Tradition," *Modern Philology*, XXVI, 73.

Hooker, E. H., "The Discussion of Taste, from 1750 to 1770, and the New Trends in Literary Criticism," *P. M. L. A.*, XLIX, 577.

"The Reviewers and the New Criticism, 1754–1770," *Philological Quarterly*, XIII, 189.

Howard, W. G., *"Ut Pictura Poesis,"* *P. M. L. A.*, XXIV, 40.

Jones, R. F., "Science and English Prose Style, 1650–1675," *P. M. L. A.*, XLV, 977.

Kaufman, Paul, "Defining Romanticism: A Survey and a Program," *Modern Language Notes*, XL, 193.

"John Foster's Pioneer Interpretation of the Romantic," *Modern Language Notes*, XXXVIII, 1.

"Heralds of Original Genius," *Essays in Memory of Barrett Wendell by his Assistants*, Cambridge (Mass.), 1926.

Krutch, J. W., "Governmental Attempts to Regulate the Stage After the Jeremy Collier Controversy," *P. M. L. A.*, XXXVIII, 153.

Lloyd, Claude, "Shadwell and the Virtuosi," *P. M. L. A.*, XLIV, 472.

Longueil, A. E., "The Word 'Gothic' in Eighteenth Century Criticism," *Modern Language Notes*, XXXVIII, 453.

Lovejoy, A. O., "Monboddo and Rousseau," *Modern Philology*, XXX, 275.

"On the Discriminations of Romanticism," *P. M. L. A.*, XXXIX, 229.

"On the Meaning of 'Romantic' in Early German Romanticism," *Modern Language Notes*, XXI, 385; XXXII, 65.

"Optimism and Romanticism," *P. M. L. A.*, XLII, 921.

"Schiller and the Genesis of Romanticism," *Modern Language Notes*, XXXV, 1, 136.

"Reply to Professor Babbitt," *Modern Language Notes*, XXXVII, 268.

"The First Gothic Revival and the Return to Nature," *Modern Language Notes*, XLVII, 419.

"The Parallel of Deism and Classicism," *Modern Philology*, XXIX, 281.

Lynch, Kathleen, "Thomas D'Urfey's Contribution to Sentimental Comedy," *Philological Quarterly*, IX, 249.

MacIntire, Elizabeth, "French, Influence on the Beginnings of English Classicism," *P. M. L. A.*, XXVI, 496.

McIntyre, Clara, "Were the 'Gothic Novels' Really Gothic?" *P. M. L. A.*, XXXVI, 644.

McKillop, A. D., "A Critic of 1741 on Early Poetry," *Studies in Philology*, XXX, 504.

"Richardson, Young, and the *Conjectures*," *Modern Philology*, XXII, 391.

"Some Details of the Sonnet Revival," *Modern Language Notes*, XXXIX, 438.

"The Romanticism of William Collins," *Studies in Philology*, XX, 1.

Moore, C. A., "Shaftesbury and the Ethical Poets in England, 1700–1760," *P. M. L. A.*, XXXI, 264.

"The Return to Nature in English Poetry of the Eighteenth Century," *Studies in Philology*, XIV, 243.

"Whig Panegyric Verse, 1700–1760. A Phase of Sentimentalism," *P. M. L. A.*, XLI, 362.

Morley, Edith, "Joseph Warton's Criticism of Pope," *Modern Language Notes*, XXXVI, 276.

Morton, E. P., "The Spenserian Stanza in the Eighteenth Century," *Modern Philology*, X, 365.

Nicolson, Marjorie, "The Early Stage of Cartesianism in England," *Studies in Philology*, XXVI, 356.

Parry, J. J., "Doctor Johnson's Interest in Welsh," *Modern Language Notes*, XXXVI, 374.

Partridge, Eric, "The 1762 Efflorescence of Poetics," *Studies in Philology*, XXV, 27.

Raysor, T. M., "The Downfall of the Three Unities," *Modern Language Notes*, XLII, 1.

Rinaker, Clara, "Thomas Edwards and the Sonnet Revival," *Modern Language Notes*, XXXIV, 272.

"Thomas Warton and the Historical Method in Literary Criticism," *P. M. L. A.*, XXX, 79.

Rogers, W. H., "The Reaction Against Melodramatic Sentimentality in the English Novel, 1796–1830," *P. M. L. A.*, XLIX, 98.

Routh, James, "The Purpose of Art as Conceived in English Literary Criticism of the Sixteenth and Seventeenth Century," *Englische Studien*, XLVIII, 124.

Sarma, D. S., "Two Minor Critics of the Age of Pope," *Modern Language Review*, XIV, 386.

Schelling, F. E., "Ben Jonson and the Classical School," *P. M. L. A.*, XIII, 221.

Scheurer, C. M., "An Early Sentimental Comedy," *Anglia*, XXXVII, 125.

Sherburn, George, "The Early Popularity of Milton's Minor Poems," *Modern Philology*, XVII, 259, 515.

Squires, V. P., "Milton's Treatment of Nature," *Modern Language Notes*, IX, 454.

Stevenson, Lionel, "Brooke's *Universal Beauty* and Modern Thought," *P. M. L. A.*, XLIII, 198.

Stevenson, S. W., "Romantic Tendencies in Pope," *ELH.*, I, 126.

Thompson, E. H. S., "The Discourses of Sir Joshua Reynolds," *P. M. L. A.*, XXXII, 339.

Tiffany, Esther, "Shaftesbury as a Stoic," *P. M. L. A.*, XXXVIII, 642.

Trenery, Grace, "Ballad Collections of the Eighteenth Century," *Modern Language Review*, X, 283.

Waterhouse, F. A., "Romantic Originality," *Sewanee Review*, XXXIV, 40.

Wedel, T. O., "On the Philosophical Background of *Gulliver's Travels*," *Studies in Philology*, XXIII, 434.

Whitney, Lois, "English Primitivistic Theories of Epic Origins," *Modern Philology*, XXI, 337.

"Thomas Blackwell, a Disciple of Shaftesbury," *Philological Quarterly*, V, 196.

Williams, G. G., "The Beginnings of Nature Poetry in the Eighteenth Century," *Studies in Philology*, XXVII, 583.

Williams, R. C., "Epic Unity as Discussed by Sixteenth Century Critics in Italy," *Modern Philology*, XVIII, 383.

"Two Studies in Epic Theory," *Modern Philology*, XXII, 133.

Williamson, George, "The Restoration Revolt Against Enthusiasm," *Studies in Philology*, XXX, 571.

Wood, P. S., "Native Elements in English Neo-Classicism," *Modern Philology*, XXIV, 201.

"The Opposition to Neo-Classicism in England between 1660 and 1700," *P. M. L. A.*, XLIII, 182.

INDEX

INDEX

This index is intended to be complete for persons and ideas. Literary works are indexed under the authors.